FIELDING'S
FREEWHEELIN'
USA

Fielding Titles

FIELDING'S FREEWHEELIN' USA

Everything You Need To Plan Your Next Open Road Adventure

by
Shirley Slater
Harry Basch

Fielding Worldwide, Inc.
308 South Catalina Avenue
Redondo Beach, California 90277 U.S.A.

Fielding's Freewheelin' USA

Published by Fielding Worldwide, Inc.

Text Copyright ©1995 Shirley Slater & Harry Basch

Icons & Illustrations Copyright ©1995 FWI

Photo Copyrights ©1995 to Individual Photographers

FIELDING WORLDWIDE INC.

PUBLISHER AND CEO **Robert Young Pelton**
PUBLISHING DIRECTOR **Paul T. Snapp**
ELECTRONIC PUBLISHING DIRECTOR **Larry E. Hart**
PUBLIC RELATIONS DIRECTOR **Beverly Riess**
ACCOUNT SERVICES MANAGER **Christy Harp**

EDITORS

Linda Charlton   **Kathy Knoles**

PRODUCTION

Gini Martin   **Chris Snyder**
Craig South   **Janice Whitby**

COVER DESIGNED BY **Digital Artists, Inc.**
COVER PHOTOGRAPHERS — Front Cover **John Warden/Tony Stone Images**
Back Cover **Rick Rusing/Tony Stone Images**
INSIDE PHOTOS **Shirley Slater & Harry Basch, David Woodworth Collection (Archival Period)**
AUTHORS' PHOTO **Donna Carrol**

Inquiries should be addressed to: Fielding Worldwide, Inc., 308 South Catalina Ave., Redondo Beach, California 90277 U.S.A., ☎ *(310) 372-4474*, Facsimile *(310) 376-8064*, 8:30 a.m.–5:30 p.m. Pacific Standard Time.

ISBN 1-56952-067-4

Library of Congress Catalog Card Number

94-068???

Printed in the United States of America

Dedication

To Marcia, who first proposed the idea,
and Sheila, who helped make it happen.

Letter from the Publisher

In 1946, Temple Fielding began the first of what would be a remarkable new series of well-written, highly personalized guidebooks for independent travelers. Temple's opinionated, witty, and oft-imitated books have now guided travelers for almost a half-century. More important to some was Fielding's humorous and direct method of steering travelers away from the dull and the insipid. Today, Fielding Travel Guides are still written by experienced travelers for experienced travelers. Our authors carry on Fielding's reputation for creating travel experiences that deliver insight with a sense of discovery and style.

Authors Harry Basch and Shirley Slater have written the most in-depth and entertaining guide to RV adventures. You'll learn everything you ever wanted to know about RVs and the freewheeling life-style. The husband/wife writing team have logged more than 50,000 miles on their 27-ft., three-year old motorhome and test driven RVs of every size and description. The award-winning travel writers have covered 156 countries over the last 20 years. Now they share their best tips for touring the U.S.A., Canada and Mexico by RV.

Today, the concept of independent travel has never been bigger. Our policy of *brutal honesty* and a highly personal point of view has never changed; it just seems the travel world has caught up with us.

Enjoy your freewheelin' adventure with Harry and Shirley.

R. YP

Robert Young Pelton
Publisher and CEO
Fielding Worldwide, Inc.

Fielding Rating Icons

The Fielding Rating Icons are highly personal and awarded to help the besieged traveler choose from among the dizzying array of activities, attractions, hotels, restaurants and sights. The awarding of an icon denotes unusual or exceptional qualities in the relevant category.

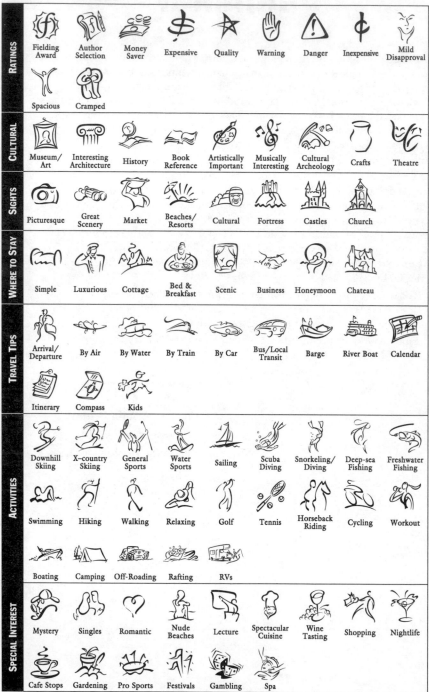

ABOUT THE AUTHORS

Authors in their RV

Shirley Slater and Harry Basch are an award winning husband-and-wife team of travel writers whose books, articles and photographs have been published internationally for the past 20 years. Former stage, film and television actors, they have written their syndicated column "CruiseViews" for the *Los Angeles Times* and other major newspapers for more than 12 years, and their *North American Ski Guide* is in its fourth annual edition for Prodigy Computer Services™.

In 1990 at the 60th World Travel Congress in Hamburg, Germany, the authors were only the third writers (and the first freelancers) ever to receive the prestigious Melva C. Pederson Award from the American Society of Travel Agents for "extraordinary journalistic achievement in the field of travel."

On assignment for publications as diverse as *Bon Appétit* and *Travel Weekly,* they have covered 156 countries on foot, by Nile barge, elephant back, Amazon dugout, hot-air balloon, cross-country skis, paddlewheel steamer and supersonic aircraft.

But their current favorite method of transportation is their two-year-old, 27-foot motor home, on which they have logged more than 50,000 miles of freewheeling adventures all over the United States, Canada and Mexico.

INTRODUCTION

The dictionary tells us that a freewheeler is, (1) a motor vehicle that has a device in the transmission that automatically disengages the drive shaft whenever it begins to turn more rapidly than the engine, (2) a person who works or lives in an independent, often daring, way, and (3) a person who is primarily concerned with having a good time.

This book is for those of us in (2) and (3) who are looking to (1), disengage the drive shaft when it starts turning faster than the engine. In other words, to get out of the rat race, kick over the traces, even if it's only for the weekend.

There's something quintessentially American about hitting the road. You can almost hum along as the wheels eat up the highway—"King of the Road"; "Hit the Road, Jack"; "On the Road Again"; "I've traveled each and every highway ...I did it my way."

You're free of airports, schedules, reservations, shuttles and public transport. Freewheelers can go anywhere without any advance reservations or preparations and always have a good time discovering something else new, interesting or weird about the world around us.

"On the road" is shorthand for freedom, independence, discovery, self-reliance. But only if you avoid routes that are off the beaten track, with an occasional jaunt over to a freeway to speed through less interesting terrain.

As TV's "On the Road" guru Charles Kuralt once warned, "Thanks to the Interstate Highway System, it is now possible to travel from coast to coast without seeing anything."

Leave the freeways to the truckers, the information highway to the computers and virtual reality to the almost-alive. With a folding camping trailer, van, travel trailer, truck camper or motorhome, a freewheeler can explore firsthand the famous, infamous and off-the-wall attractions all over North America, from the legendary Alaska Highway to the challenging run down the Baja Peninsula.

This easy-to-read guide picks and chooses overnight oases from luxurious private RV parks with heated swimming pools and golf courses to quiet, forested campgrounds in a state or national park, offbeat places to eat or pick up tasty treats to go, and things to do from mountain-biking to picking your own farm-fresh fruits and vegetables. Insider Tips offer helpful and practical suggestions about each region.

Big cities and world-famous commercial attractions are not part of the free-wheeler's travel style; anyone can find them. Instead, the freewheeler may opt to retrace the route of the Klondike Gold Rush, trying a hand at gold-panning; select a live lobster from a community lobster pound in Boothbay Harbor, Maine or go mountain biking on the famous Slickrock Trail outside Moab, Utah.

Freewheelers may drop by the California desert museum dedicated to the art of striptease, shuffle off to see the buffalo in Custer State Park (where Calvin Coolidge once slept), fiddle around with Japanese country/western violinist Shoji Tabuchi in Branson, Missouri, or place a bet at Diamond Tooth Gertie's Casino in the Yukon's Dawson City.

In winter, freewheelers can learn rock climbing in Joshua Tree National Monument or take in the sizzling Terlingua Chili Cook-Off in West Texas, set out in springtime to catch the dogwood in bloom in the Blue Ridge Mountains or the grey whales migrating along the Baja California coast.

Late summer is the time to watch an Alaskan grizzly bear as he fishes for spawning salmon, ride an amphibious Duck or angle for bass in the lakes of the Ozarks, or go river-rafting on the Colorado. Freewheelers can hang around New Hampshire to catch autumn "on Golden Pond" or head south in time for stone crab season in the Florida Keys.

For some of us, discovering America may happen only after we've had a chance to explore Europe, Asia, Africa or South America, and that makes the discoveries even richer.

The important thing, as Robert Louis Stevenson said, is "to travel for travel's sake. The great affair is to move."

Somebody else said, "Life is what happens while you're making other plans."

TABLE OF CONTENTS

LIST OF MAPS

THE TIN CAN
TOURISTS

"Tin Can Tourist" at Mammoth, 1920

They called themselves Tin Can Tourists. They braved the dust and mud to drive their tin lizzies across the United States before transcontinental roads were paved, camping by the side of the road, heating tin cans of food on a gasoline stove and bathing in cold water.

They dressed in their Sunday clothes in the days before jogging suits and running shoes. A photograph of one 1920s camping club shows owners gathered in front of their Weidman Camp Body vehicles, the men in fedoras, suits and ties, and the women in dresses, cloche hats, stockings and high heeled shoes.

Early Camping Club

It took ingenuity to travel across the country in those days before the first motel, which opened in 1925 in California. In 1921, for instance, Lee Scoles of Fort Wayne, Indiana, converted his 1916 Federal truck to "a house on wheels" and drove it on an eight-month, round-trip journey to San Francisco with 11 relatives aboard. Such additions as solid rubber tires, a canvas awning, cots, a cookstove and washtubs added to their comfort, according to his granddaughter Alice Worman, herself a motorhome owner, who chronicled the story in *Lifestyles*, a magazine for Monaco motorhome owners, one of many such publications dedicated to RVing.

The family of Charles Ulrich, according to a story in *RV West* magazine, set out for California in 1929 in a General Motors truck body mounted on a Ford chassis, with built-in bunks, overhead wardrobe storage and a dining table with six folding chairs. The interiors were polished mahogany and on the rear was a caboose-type open platform with iron railings. After their "once-in-a-lifetime" trip, which continued on to Hawaii aboard a Matson Line cruise ship, the Ulrichs stored the camper until the 1960s when it was purchased by a group of hunters to serve as a forest base camp.

A fire-engine red 1929 Ford Model A converted to a mini-motorhome camper complete with pop-up top still carries the Ray Glenn family on trips around the Seattle area, according to *MotorHome* magazine.

Originally, auto camping was regarded as a rich man's hobby. The way had been paved by the well-publicized outings of auto manufacturer Henry Ford, inventor Thomas Edison, naturalist John Burroughs and tire manufacturer Harvey Firestone, who called themselves "the four vagabonds" as they camped in America's parks. Interestingly, it was the affordability and popularity of Henry Ford's Model T, which made its debut in 1909, that helped bring auto camping to the average American.

Nobody knows more about the early history of recreation vehicles than David Woodworth of Tehachapi, California, who owns the largest collection of antique camping equipment, photography and literature known to exist.

Much of his material appeared in the 1986 Smithsonian Institution's show "At Home on the Road," which he helped produce.

Alaska-born Woodworth attributes his fascination with RVs to his childhood memories, when his family traveled around the country in a Detroit travel trailer following his carpenter father from job to job.

RV historian David Woodworth with his 1937 Hunt House Car.

At the Los Angeles RV Show in the fall of 1994, he was exhibiting his art deco-style 1937 Hunt House Car, designed and manufactured by a Hollywood cinematographer and inventor named J. Roy Hunt. (Among Hunt's many screen credits was the classic 1929 film *The Virginian* starring Gary Cooper.)

The sleek, 19-foot, teardrop-shaped motorhome, crafted on a Ford truck chassis and powered by a Ford flathead V-8 engine, includes a bathroom with hand-pumped shower, lavatory and toilet (which has to be manually removed to empty), a stove with two burners, an icebox, a sofa and a dinette, both of which convert to beds, and even a kitchen sink.

Woodworth proudly claims membership in the Tin Can Tourists, whose last surviving affiliates have appointed him "Grand Can Opener."

Among the 30 or so antique camping vehicles in Woodworth's collection are 1928 and 1931 Covered Wagon Travel Trailers, manufactured in Detroit; a 1935 York Rambler built in York, Pennsylvania; a Hays from Grand Rapids, Michigan; and a Harley Bowless, created by the builder who oversaw the construction of Charles Lindbergh's historic transatlantic aircraft, the *Spirit of St Louis*. Airstream later used the Harley Bowless as an inspiration for its famous aerodynamic travel trailer back in 1936, Woodworth says.

He can also spout nonstop historic information about auto camping and the early campers. Some of his revelations:

The first campgrounds were free, built and maintained by cities and towns hoping to attract affluent travelers who would spend money while they were in town. In the days before World War I, only the affluent had the time and money to go auto camping.

When Ford's Model T made auto camping affordable for every-one, campgrounds started charging fees to discourage some of the overflow crowds.

One early pair of auto campers was a couple who were fearful their new travel trailer might pull the rear end off their car, so the husband drove the car and the wife sat in the trailer for the entire journey intently watching the car's rear end to make sure nothing happened to it.

Highways were notoriously bad in the early days. Woodworth quotes from the memoirs of some 1924 auto campers who termed themselves "Modern Gypsies" and wrote about a local resident tell-ing them, "That's a good road; somebody just made it through there yesterday." Later, he says, the travelers commented, "When we left New York for Chicago, we were motorists. When we left Chicago for California, we were pioneers."

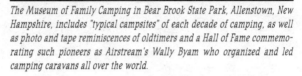

INSIDER TIP:

The Museum of Family Camping in Bear Brook State Park, Allenstown, New Hampshire, includes "typical campsites" of each decade of camping, as well as photo and tape reminiscences of oldtimers and a Hall of Fame commemo-rating such pioneers as Airstream's Wally Byam who organized and led camping caravans all over the world.

13 NOTABLE DATES IN RV HISTORY

c. 1901

The first motorhomes are built as special-order units by auto body builders.

1907

Henry Ford introduces the first mass-produced Model T Fords, automobiles with a 2.9 liter, four-cylinder engine that make auto camping affordable for most Ameri-cans for the first time.

1910–1915

The first manufactured, mass-produced RVs, folding camping trailers, start coming off the line from Los Angeles Trailer Works, Auto-Kamp Trailers in Saginaw, Mich-igan and other pioneers.

1917

The first fifth-wheel trailer is built by airplane manufacturer Curtiss-Wright; its name probably originated from the trailer hitch, which is located in the center of the towing truck's bed and could be considered a "fifth" wheel after the four on the trailer unit bottom.

1919

The Tin Can Tourists gather for their first rally, in a Florida campground near Tampa called DeSoto Park, with 20 members present, most of them Model T own-ers; by the mid-1930s, the club numbers 150,000.

1922

Fifteen million auto campers hit the road, according to *The New York Times*, most of them sleeping on cots, in tents or in "newfangled houses on wheels."

1923

There are 7000 free campgrounds in the United States, including Denver's Overland Park, with 800 campsites, piped water, a repairs garage, restaurant, beauty shop, billiards hall, soda fountain and eight electric washing machines.

1926

Fords equipped with a Weidman Camp Body are first produced in Tonawanda, New York; the 1929 model sells for $1900.

1929 Ford with Weidman Camp Body

1962

John Steinbeck publishes *Travels with Charley* about his RV journey around America with his elderly poodle.

1966

Winnebago becomes the first mass-production motorhome assembly line, turning out its early "eyebrow" models in lengths of 17, 19 and 22 feet.

1966

David Garvin begins selling RV parts and camping accessories at his family's campground in Bowling Green, Kentucky; by 1993, his chain of Camping World stores which he calls "Toys R Us for grownups" has become the world's largest retailer of camping supplies with 22 stores, 10 million mail order catalogs distributed annually and a sales base of $150 million.

1967

Charles Kuralt rents a Dodge motorhome to begin broadcasting "On the Road," his famous series of CBS-TV news features that brought small-town Americans and their stories into the living rooms of people everywhere. During his 27 years on the road, Kuralt uses six different motorhomes; the last, a 29-foot FMC motor coach, is installed at the Henry Ford Museum near Detroit.

"I think the vehicle is one of those important icons in popular culture."

**Judith Endelman, head of historical resources,
Henry Ford Museum**

1976

Winnebago Industries introduces the Heli-Home, a helicopter camper for off-road exploration that could sleep six; we note it's no longer included in their published brochures.

Authors' Observation

We have come fairly recently to the wonderful world of RVs, and because we enjoy our freewheeling life on the road so much, we shudder at every false stereotype that some uninformed person perpetuates. We find it particularly hard to take when the person is a fellow travel writer who should know his nomenclature.

SIX COMMON MISCONCEPTIONS ABOUT RVs AND OWNERS

"When you call me that, smile!"

Gary Cooper as *The Virginian*, 1929

1. A writer in a popular national travel magazine writing about driving in Utah said Arches National Park "makes even the most remote rock formations visible to wheezing geezers willing to take a short walk from motorhome to overlook." (The same writer spent much of his story bragging about how much speed his $40,000 Nissan Infiniti made on the empty highways and complaining about the dearth of gas stations and fast-food outlets in southern Utah.)

    REALITY: Puh-leeze, wheeze us no geezers! The average RV owner is 48 years old, married with children, owns his own home and has a household income of around $40,000 a year, according to a 1994 University of Michigan study. During the next decade, the highest RV ownership category by age will be college-educated baby boomers just reaching the age of 45.

2. Another writer, describing a lonely highway he drove, says he met "only a few Winnebagos" along the way.

    REALITY: While he might have met a series of RVs that were produced by the same manufacturer, Iowa-based Winnebago Industries, he probably used the term "Winnebago" to mean "recreation vehicles." While all Winnebagos are RVs, not all RVs are Winnebagos. Out of today's 64 million campers, nearly half use a recreation vehicle. When Death Valley tabulated its overnight campground stays in 1988, a total of 61,743 overnights were made in tents, 249,726 in recreation vehicles.

3. A real estate developer friend inquiring politely about our latest passion asked about our "mobile home" and was startled to be so instantly and vehemently corrected.

    REALITY: Our motorhome is not a "mobile home." The latter is not a recreation vehicle but manufactured residential housing that is infrequently moved after initially being set in place.

4. Well-meaning greenies like to say that unlike backpacking and tent camping, RVing pollutes the environment and guzzles gas and water resources.

    REALITY: Having graduated from the ranks of backpackers and tent campers, we're acutely aware of this "purist" attitude toward RVing. A recent RVIA (Recreation Vehicle Industry Association) poll shows that 98 percent of all RVers practice one or more forms of "green" RVing. In our case, our low-water toilet and quick showers use much less water than park public facilities. We put all waste water into holding tanks, which are then properly disposed of at dump stations, rather than pouring anything on the ground or into streams; we never build a campfire which leaves layers of pollution hanging in the atmosphere; never dig up the ground or tie anything to trees and bushes; and always recycle everything possible.

5. According to the University of Michigan study, some 14 percent of all potential RVers believe their state requires a special license to drive an RV.
    REALITY: No state requires a special license of any kind to operate an RV; your normal driver's license is all you need. At present, one out of every 10 motor vehicle-owning families in the United States has an RV.

6. When city officials of the former naval base town of Port Hueneme in southern California proposed to bolster the town's sagging economy by building an oceanside luxury RV resort, the proposal passed, despite a vociferous handful of residents at a town meeting that claimed "typical" RVers are "homeless, jobless, use drugs, commit crimes, belong to gangs and desecrate any area they happen to park," according to a journalist on the scene.
    Wow!—and we thought our neighbors in the next campsite were just toasting marshmallows!

THE RV LIFE: YOU SET THE LIFE-STYLE

Our introduction to RVs was during our many years as actors in film and television programs shot in Hollywood and on location, where the self-contained vehicles are used as dressing rooms. So when we leased a Winnebago motorhome in 1992 to research an on-line ski guide we were producing for Prodigy Services Company™, it was the first time we had been in an RV that actually moved, let alone under our own nervous control.

But what made us even more nervous than operating the machine itself was what we had always heard termed "the RV life-style." The suggestion was that by acquiring a recreation vehicle you bought into a life-style—we pictured communal campfire visits, campground pancake breakfasts and tours of each other's "rigs," culminating in an annual group caravan tour to some scenic area.

Instead, we quickly learned that while you could participate in group and club activities if you were so inclined, you could also use your recreation vehicle to continue whatever life-style you already practiced.

Because of our intense, high pressure work as travel writers and performers, constantly on the move and in social situations, when on vacation we prefer what we call the Garbo Gourmet Life-style. We "want to be alone" with the best food and wine and scenery, to read, go bird-watching or hiking or listen to music. This doesn't mean we don't enjoy exchanging views with fellow RVers, only that we don't want to feel we have to.

It came as a tremendous relief to learn that we were free to do as we pleased. In our first RV journey, six weeks on the road all across the United States, nobody came over to urge us to join a club or otherwise identify with some larger group. We did, however, meet some very hospitable individuals, from a campground manager in Independence, Missouri, who taught us, with a flashlight after dark, how to dump the holding tanks we'd been trying to ignore for three days, to an exuberant group of hockey fans who shared a keg of beer with us at a campground in LaCrosse, Wisconsin.

The truth of the matter is, there's not one RV life-style, there are as many life-styles as there are people who travel in RVs.

Here are only a few.

12 PERSONALTIES IDEAL FOR RVS

1. Garbo Gourmets

They like to be alone together luxuriating in the best that life can offer. They dislike tiptoeing through creaky B&Bs or suffering second-rate food and service at expensive five-star hotels and resorts, preferring to carry their own wines and food, sleep in their own beds and select their own surroundings by serendipity.

2. Sportsmen

Skiers, fishermen, surfers, golfers and mountain bikers want to be in the heart of the action with all the comforts of home, including heating, air conditioning and hot showers after a hard workout, and plenty of storage space to carry fishing rods, skis, golf clubs, bikes.

3. Weekenders

The stressed-out want to get out of the rat race and into the countryside to download the pressures of the work week. Birdsong replaces Muzak, and a campfire flickers in place of a screen saver. Their RV is always packed for a quick getaway, with only a shopping stop to load up on perishables on the way out of town. TGIF!

4. Families on vacation

They offset that visit to a pricey amusement park with their own budget hotel and restaurant at hand with self-service around the clock. A comfortable journey for the kids means no more "Are we there yet?" "I have to go potty!" "I'm hungry!" Everything they need is in the vehicle. They'll even sit still for an educational journey.

5. Eco-tourists

Go back to nature the easy way, with dawn bird-watching, twilight wildlife-spotting, photography and hiking, laying less burden on Mother Earth than heavy hotel and resort infrastructures.

6. The ultimate shoppers

Hit all the antique shops, estate sales and the world's biggest swap meets in comfort and style, with room to take all their treasures back home.

7. Relatives, retirees and empty nesters

An RV is ideal for family visits, because you bring your own bedroom and bath along with you and can even entertain your hosts in your own home on wheels. Conversely, when parked at home, the RV doubles nicely as a guest room and bath.

8. Pet-lovers

Take Fifi and Fido along for the ride, enjoy their company, and avoid facing rebellious and destructive pets after a spell of boarding them out. Many (but not all) campgrounds welcome pets.

9. Disabled travelers

If they get impatient with the well-meaning but often bungled accommodations in hotels, from hanging shelves too high to reach, to bathroom doors too narrow to navigate, a customized RV can open up the world with familiar and accessible surroundings.

10. Special events attendees

Day or overnight trips to jazz festivals, weekend art shows, outdoor dramas, garlic festivals, football game tailgate parties, jumping frog jubilees and re-creations of Civil War battles let you sidestep overbooked hotels and restaurants. RVers can take off, even on the spur of the moment, and have bed, bathroom, breakfast and lunch facilities on the spot.

11. Snowbirds

Escaping from minus 10 in Minnesota to the balmy Rio Grande Valley of Texas or heading for the high country to get out of summer's heat, an RV makes you a man for all seasons.

12. Full-timers

Whether quitting the rat race for a season or forever, chasing a dream or discovering America, an RV is the only way to go.

Of course, for these dozen life-style types there are a hundred more that are also perfectly accommodated by one or another of the various types of RVs available. We've heard about RVers who follow a clothing-optional campground itinerary (yes, Virginia, there are nudist campers, although we've personally never seen any), travel newsletter editors who use their RVs as a combination home, office and research vehicle, spa goers who toodle from one hot spring to another, singles of both sexes who opt for the wandering life of a loner without a single look back, leaf peepers who live from one fall foliage tour to the next.

The vehicle adjusts to you and becomes an extension of your own life and travel style. It is simply a means to an end, a very well-designed and comfortable way to access the wilderness, nature, sightseeing, going to the sun, heading for the beach, the mountains, the woods—whatever will make you happy and enhance your life. It's your dream—you call the shots.

Because cruise travel is one of our major specialties as travel writers, we find a strong correlation between cruise ships and RVs, from the adjustments to smaller-than-normal accommodations to the ever-changing views outside the windows. We get a great deal of pleasure out of unpacking in ship cabins, finding a place to put things out of the way and trying to figure out what that odd corner or nook was intended to store. The same thing is true of RVs.

Another similarity between the two forms of travel is the option of keeping absolutely to yourself or mingling with other people in a relaxed, undemanding milieu. A common interest in the shared type of travel creates a strong, slender link, should you wish to use it, with other people.

Just as it's easy to call up and book a cruise and its attendant shore excursions for a hassle-free trip with a guide or leader, RV group caravans and tours can take you overland on journeys to Alaska, Baja California and many parts of the U.S. and Canada. You can even combine a cruise with an overland group journey by RV, or book your own Alaska RV/cruise package (see "Driving the Alaska Highway").

Campers have always found a sense of accomplishment in day-to-day survival, cooking food over an open fire, finding a comfortable place to sleep amid rocks and hard ground, protecting yourself from the sun, rain, heat or cold.

With RVs, everything is much less work-intensive, without taking away the sense of self-reliance, of having everything you need for survival along with you.

Celebrities from Loretta Lynn to Danny DeVito, Michael Douglas to Pat Boone, John Madden to Bruce Willis are RV owners who use their vehicles for both business and pleasure. More than one film megastar has had a contract sweetened with the perk of a big-bucks motorhome, used for a private location dressing room during the shoot and given as a gift at the end of filming.

Our own favorite RV celebrity is senior golf champion Larry Laoretti, who was interviewed in his motorhome on ABC television during the U.S. Senior Open. After winning the tournament, sportscaster Brent Musberger asked him if now that he'd won $130,000 at the tournament, he would give up his motorhome to "travel first class." Laoretti retorted that in his opinion, traveling by motorhome is going first class and a six-figure payday isn't going to change that. We heartily concur.

But much as we love RVing, something we had never really anticipated before we tried it, we also will admit that perhaps not everyone is an ideal candidate for freewheeling. If your idea of the perfect vacation is to check into a luxury resort and phone for room service, you may not be ready for an RV— that is, unless you have a mate who loves to wait on you.

Here's a quick do-it-yourself quiz to test your RVC (Recreational Vehicle Compatibility).

1. Do you ever sing along with "My Way," "On the Road Again," or "King of the Road"?

2. Have you ever considered getting a second vacation home but can't decide between the mountains or the seashore?

3. Do you like to putter around the house or spend an entire Saturday morning browsing the shelves of a hardware store?

4. Did you ever envy Jack Kerouac, William Least Heat Moon or Charles Kuralt, even a little bit?

5. Do you dislike timetables and schedules, the hurry-up-and-wait routine of catching a flight, a bumper-to-bumper commute?

6. Are you tired of dress codes in chichi restaurants that want men to wear a jacket and tie and women to wear a skirt, or vice versa?

7. Do you dislike using public toilets and showers, or wonder who slept in that motel bed just ahead of you?

8. Could you find paradise with "a loaf of bread, a jug of wine and thou/ Beside me in the wilderness"?

9. Does the smoky smell of a campfire, a charred hot dog or a burned marshmallow turn you on?

10. Are you susceptible to serendipity, doing things on a whim, like turning down a side road that seems to call to you, buying something offbeat that instantly becomes a favorite possession, or striking up a conversation with an interesting-looking stranger who turns out to be a friend forever after?

If you answered "yes" to any one of the 10 questions, you might consider trying out an RV by rental. See "Renting or Buying?" for details.

If you answered "yes" to five or more of the 10 questions, check "The ABCs of RVs."

If you answered "yes" to all 10 questions, what are you waiting for? JUMP to "RV Manufacturers: Who Makes What" for a look at the wide varieties of RVs that are out there for sale.

If you answered "no" to all 10 questions, you still haven't wasted your money. Thumb over to the second part of this book, grab your car keys and a lodging guide or settle down in an easy chair, and set out on one of our freewheeling RV adventures for a fast and funny look at weird, wonderful America.

THE ABCs OF RVs

"Look, Dad, it's got a TV and everything so the driver can watch television!"

Child's comment on seeing
a van camper at the LA RV Show

At the beginning, we took solemn oaths not to refer to our motorhome as a "rig" (although we're not above calling her "Winnie" for Winnebago—but only in private). We also swore we'd never (a) wear visored caps (although they are handy to keep sun out of the driver's eyes), (b) display a carved wooden nameplate saying, "Hi, we're Harry and Shirley from LA" (and we don't), and (c) never refer to ourselves as "pilot" and "co-pilot," terms we considered unbelievably coy the first time we heard them. (We still don't use them in real life, but you'll encounter them in this text from time to time for clarity.)

Just as we had to learn certain technical terms to work as film actors, then pick up a new set of terms as professional travelers, so we've had to adopt certain accepted terms from the RV world in order to correctly describe aspects of the vehicles. Here are a few you'll need to know to get through the next couple of chapters. More glossary words will turn up from time to time in future chapters as they become necessary. Don't worry about memorizing them yet. All will be revealed, a helpful phrase we say to each other when we're stuck five hours in the Beijing airport or the ship we're waiting for in Ibiza never arrives or we're questioned by the Tunisian police who suspect we're spies because we're carrying cameras.

In the section following the glossary are full definitions and descriptions of the major varieties of RVs: type A motorhomes, type B van campers, type C mini-motorhomes, (previously termed Class A, B and C), truck campers, folding camping trailers, travel trailers and fifth-wheel travel trailers.

LEARNING THE LINGO:
A GLOSSARY OF COMMON RV TERMS

Airbag

in RV terms, a sort of shock absorber positioned at the forward and rear axles of a motorhome

Arctic Pack

also spelled Arctic Pac and Arctic Pak, an optional kit to insulate RVs for winter camping

Auxiliary battery

extra battery to run 12-volt equipment

Basement model

an RV that incorporates large storage areas underneath a raised chassis

Bunkhouse

an RV area containing bunk beds instead of regular beds

Cabover

the part of a type C mini-motorhome that overlaps the top of the vehicle's cab, usually containing a sleeping or storage unit

Camper shell

removable unit to go over the bed of a pickup truck

Cassette toilet

toilet with a small holding tank that can be removed from outside the vehicle in order to empty

Cockpit

the front of a motorized RV where the pilot (driver) and co-pilot (navigator) sit

Crosswise

a piece of furniture arranged across the RV from side to side rather than front to rear

Curbside

the side of the RV that would be at the curb when parked

Diesel pusher

a motorhome with a rear diesel engine

Drink holders

fitted wood or plastic devices attached to the dashboard area designed to hold cups or cans steady while the RV is moving

Entry level

a price deemed attractive for first-time RV buyers

Garden tub

a bathtub angled into the space so plants can be put on the wide edges against the wall

Gaucho

sofa/dinette bench that converts into a sleeping unit; a term less-used now than formerly

Generator

small engine fueled by gasoline or propane that produces 110-volt electricity, built into many RVs but also available as a portable option

Gooseneck
a colloquial name for fifth-wheel travel trailers

Hard-sided
RV walls made of aluminum or other hard surface

High profile
a fifth-wheel trailer with a higher-than normal front to allow more than six feet of standing room inside the raised area

Holding tanks
tanks that retain waste water when RV unit is not connected to a sewer

Inverter
a unit that changes 12-volt direct current to 110-volt alternating current to allow operation of computers, TV sets and such when an RV is not hooked up to electricity

Island queen
not Hawaii's Queen Liliuokalani, but a queen-sized bed with walking space on both sides

Leveling
positioning the RV in camp so it will be level, using ramps placed under the wheels, built-in scissors jacks or power leveling jacks

Pop-up
foldout or raised additions to an RV that add height for standing room

Porta-Potti
brand name for a portable plastic toilet frequently used in folding camping trailers without facilities

Self-contained
an RV that needs no external connections in order to provide short-term cooking, bathing and heating functions and could park overnight anywhere

Slideout
a unit that slides open when the RV is parked to expand the living area

Soft-sides
telescoping side panels on an RV that can be raised or lowered, usually constructed of canvas or vinyl and mesh netting

Solar panels
battery chargers that convert sunlight to direct current electricity

Streetside
the part of the vehicle on the street side when parked

Telescoping
compacting from front to back and/or top to bottom to make the living unit smaller for towing and storage

Three-way refrigerators
appliances that can operate on a 12-volt battery, propane or 110-volt electrical power

Turning radius
the distance across the diameter of an arc in which a vehicle can turn

Widebody
designs that stretch RVs from the traditional 96-inch width to 100 or 102 inches

Winterize

  prepare the RV for winter use or storage

There are two basic types of recreation vehicle based on locomotion—towable vehicles and motorized vehicles. Towables such as folding camping trailers, travel trailers and fifth-wheel travel trailers are living units which can stand alone in camp but are hitched to motor vehicles to travel. Truck campers, compact living units designed to travel atop the bed and cab of a pickup truck, are also part of the towable team.

Motorized vehicles include motorhomes and van campers, both of which are self-contained units built on a truck or van chassis with living, sleeping, cooking and bathroom facilities accessible from the driver's seat without leaving the vehicle. More and more, the dividing line is blurred between van camper and mini-motorhome as more compact units fitted with all the necessities for self-contained camping appear on the market. At the present time, however, the type A motorhome, the type B van camper and the type C mini-motorhome are still considered three different vehicle categories.

In most models and all price ranges, the buyer can specify interior colors and fabrics selected from a sample display board if the models on the lot are not to his liking.

The average prices given for RV types are approximate figures based on 1994 retail sales provided by RVIA (Recreation Vehicle Industry Association).

TOWABLE RVs

FOLDING CAMPING TRAILERS

Think of it as a modern-day covered wagon, with your own team of oxen or horses already in your garage.

Affordable, open and airy, easy to store and tow, these lightweight units are the closest thing to tent camping, will fit into a carport or garage and can usually be towed even by compact cars. From a traveling configuration that resembles a small U-Haul trailer, the RV unfolds to standing-room height with collapsible side walls to form two screened, covered wings, each containing a double bed area.

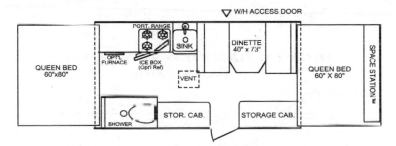

Sample Floor Plan, Folding Camping Trailer, Starcraft RV, Inc., Starmaster XL 1224

The center section has a solid floor that supports cooking, dining and lounging areas, some converting to provide even more sleeping space, as well as optional toilet and shower facilities. Some models are equipped with heating and air conditioning options, and most have a gas cookstove that can be used inside the unit or plugged into outside connections.

Generally the least expensive of the RVs, folding camping trailers are priced from $2000 to $15,000, and may sleep as many as eight. The average price is around $4500. Whereas the original units had canvas and/or screen sides, newer models also offer the choice of vinyl or even lightweight aluminum hard siding.

Budget-minded young families with small children, tent campers who seek a bit more luxury without giving up the canvas-and-campfire ambiance, and even veteran RVers seeking a simpler travel life-style enjoy these vehicles.

Folding camping trailer, Starcraft 1224, on display at the Louisville RV Show

In a study commissioned by the Go Camping America Committee during the summer of 1994, the vacation costs for a family of four, traveling in their personal automobile towing a folding camping trailer, staying at campgrounds and preparing the majority of their meals in the RV, came to $149 for two nights, $483 for seven nights and $889 for 14 nights.

FOLDING CAMPING TRAILERS: THE PLUS SIDE

1. Ease of towing—even a compact car can handle most—with good gas mileage, lower wind resistance. They can go anywhere the family car can go, and can be left behind in camp while the family sets out to explore the area by car.

2. Economical both to purchase and operate, these units offer many options found in more expensive RVs, choices such as air conditioning, heating, bathroom facilities, three-way refrigerators, awnings and roof racks that can carry boats or bicycles atop the folded unit. Naturally, the more options added, the more expensive the unit will be.

INSIDER TIP:

Features that are optional on one brand of folding camping trailer may be included on another. Consider the overall price in terms of features you get without paying extra rather than the simple base price.

3. Garage or carport storage capability of these small units eliminates the potential problems larger RVs create. Folded, they measure from 5 to 19 feet long and are usually less than 60 inches high.

4. The canvas or vinyl walls and screen sides make campers feel like they're really sleeping outdoors, but instead of the hard cold ground, they're snuggled onto a comfortable mattress.

FOLDING CAMPING TRAILERS:
THE MINUS SIDE

1. Most folding camping trailers use a hand-cranked system for raising and lowering, simple enough when the operator is fit and the weather nice, but not always pleasant in the rain when you're trying to keep the wing mattresses dry.

2. The unit is not usable when underway unless you crank it open at rest stops. Some models have front storage units that are accessible even when the unit is folded if you want to get to picnic items, toys or bicycles. Access to kitchen and toilet facilities is available only when the rig is fully set up.

INSIDER TIP:

Some families like these units for longer campground stays but find it tedious to pack and unpack, raise and lower them on one-night stands.

3. If a canvas unit is closed when wet it has to be unfolded at home and dried out completely before storing or it can mildew. Vinyl units can simply be wiped dry.

4. Some models do not contain toilet or shower facilities or offer them only as an option. Most contain a storage area for a portable toilet that has to be removed and emptied manually. So long as you're camping in areas that have public toilets and showers it won't be a problem, but self-contained camping is not feasible.

TRUCK CAMPERS

For people who already own a pickup truck, the easiest and least expensive RV addition might be a truck camper, a unit which slides onto the bed of a pickup, sometimes overhanging the cab or the rear of the vehicle. Most models sleep two to six people and cost between $2500 and $16,000, with the average price around $9803. Since the unit is slid on and off, the truck continues to be useful as a hauling and transportation vehicle without the camper.

Sportsmen particularly like the rugged outdoorsy capability of truck campers because they can remove the camper and set it up in camp, then use the truck to go to and from the ski area, fishing hole or trail head. It is also possible to tow a boat, snowmobile, horse trailer or jet skis behind a truck camper, something not permitted with other towables.

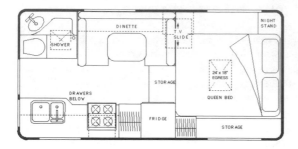
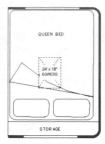

Sample Floor Plan Truck Camper

Low-profile pop-up models are available, as well as units that have optional electrical systems to load and unload the camper from the truck bed. They are often equipped with bathroom and kitchen.

Units range from seven to 18 feet long, with a cabover bed extending over the pickup's cab. Sofa or dinette built-ins may convert to form a second sleeping area, but these are usually fairly short beds. A step leads from the lower floor area up to the cabover bed.

Buyers of truck campers should plan to spend extra time matching camper to pickup. Some dealers may not be conversant with the precise details that make the combination work, so it is essential to be sure the camper's weight is compatible with the truck that will be carrying it. If an additional vehicle is being towed, the Gross Combined Weight Rating (GCWR) must also be considered.

Truck camper, Alpenlite by Western Recreational Vehicles

On a cost comparison survey made during the summer of 1994, a family of four traveling with a light-duty truck and truck camper, staying in campgrounds and preparing most of their meals at campsites, spent $152 for two nights, $492 for seven nights and $916 for 14 nights.

TRUCK CAMPERS: THE PLUS SIDE

1. **Economy**—cheaper to buy, maintain and operate than most other towables, with better gas mileage.

2. **Versatility**—the camper unit can be removed and stored at home, or set in place at the campground, and the truck used for utility. With a self-contained camper and a four-wheel-drive truck, you can go almost anywhere.

3. **Durability**—most models are made to endure tougher road conditions than other towables.

4. **Passenger convenience**—In most states, except New Mexico, North Carolina, North Dakota, Pennsylvania and Wisconsin, passengers are permitted to ride inside a truck camper. California permits passengers to ride inside only if there is communication possible with the driver and if the door can be opened from both inside and outside.

TRUCK CAMPERS: THE MINUS SIDE

1. Floor space is limited inside, with inadequate room for two adults to move around freely at the same time.

2. Weight distribution and higher center of gravity often mean more difficulty in handling these units on the road.

TRAVEL TRAILERS

These soft- or hard-sided RVs can be towed by vans, autos or pickup trucks, depending on the weight of the unit. They sleep from two to eight people and usually contain full bath and kitchen facilities. They range in length from 10 feet to 40 feet.

Models come in traditional box shape, an aerodynamic or teardrop shape and a hard-sided telescoping travel trailer that can be lowered for towing and storage and raised for campground living. Prices range from $4500 to $60,000, with an average cost of around $12,034.

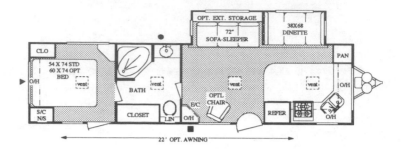

Sample Floor Plan Travel Trailer, Challenger By Damon

"Slideouts" that are expanded at the campsite to add more walking-around room have greatly enhanced the comfort of travel trailers and fifth-wheels. Some models may have as many as three slideouts. There are, however, some campgrounds that prohibit RVs using slideouts.

Travel trailers often have two doors. In the model floor plan, note the sofa and dinette slideout area, which could be made into a second sleeping area. The bath is split into two sides, and both linoleum and carpet are used on the floors, the former in the kitchen and bath, the latter in the bedroom and living room.

Interior, travel trailer, Award Classic 30-foot from ABI

During the summer of 1994, a family of four traveling in their personal car or light truck towing a travel trailer and staying in campgrounds, where they prepared most of their meals, spent an average of $158 for two nights, $504 for seven nights and $924 for 14 nights.

INSIDER TIP:

Before selecting a travel trailer to be towed with a vehicle you already own, be sure to consider how much weight you'll be adding for traveling—food, water, clothing, books, sports gear—and be sure your tow vehicle is capable of handling it.

TRAVEL TRAILERS: THE PLUS SIDE

1. Travel trailers can be unhitched at the campsite, releasing the tow vehicle for local errands and touring.

2. Travel trailer interiors come in a wide variety of floor plans, with homelike furniture, full kitchens and baths. Many models have two doors, and some offer a forward bedroom and rear bunkhouse design to sleep the whole family without converting other furniture into beds.

3. Today's travel trailers take a greater variety of tow package options, including 4 x 4s, light trucks, full and midsize cars, station wagons and minivans.

TRAVEL TRAILERS: THE MINUS SIDE

1. Some drivers find handling a travel trailer, especially when backing up, takes extra skill at the beginning.

2. Wind resistance is greater with travel trailers, and hitching or unhitching can be a nuisance in bad weather.

3. For both travel trailers and fifth-wheels, road tolls based on axles will be higher.

FIFTH-WHEEL TRAVEL TRAILERS

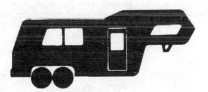

These are the most luxurious of the towables, particularly popular with full-timers who cite the ease of maneuvering and towing, the generous storage areas, large living space and homelike design. The raised forward section that fits over the truck bed allows a split-level design. This area is usually allotted to bedroom and bath, but sometimes used as a living room or kitchen/dining area instead. By the time basement storage and slideouts are added, a fifth-wheel is comparable in comfort to a home in the suburbs.

The floor plan illustration shows numerous bedroom options as well as living, dining and bath choices in a 36- foot fifth-wheel. The slideout contains sofa and dining furniture, while a second optional slideout in the bedroom area can add more room there as well. Note the space for a washer/dryer, bedroom TV, entertainment center and large sitting area.

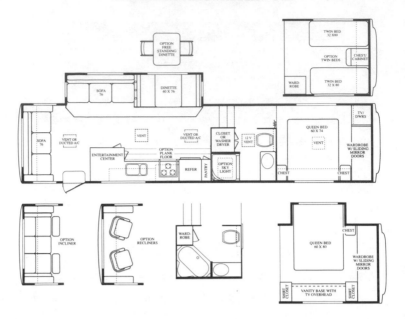

Sample Floor Plan Fifth-Wheel, Holiday Rambler Aluma-Lite

Fifth-wheels sell from $9000 to $75,000 and up, with an average cost of around $19,420. They are from 22 to 40 feet long.

For average expenditures on vacations, see "Travel Trailers."

Interior, fifth-wheel travel trailer, Royals International from Carriage

FIFTH-WHEELS: THE PLUS SIDE

1. Maneuverability and towability are major assets; it's easier to handle than a travel trailer because the hitch is in the bed of the truck with less vehicle trailing behind. This also creates a shorter turning radius.

2. Like the other towables, the fifth-wheel can be unhitched and left at the campsite while the truck is available for touring or shopping in the area.

3. The truck bed can still be used for storage with the addition of a pickup bed cover.

FIFTH-WHEELS: THE MINUS SIDE

1. Because a truck is the obligatory tow vehicle and passengers are not permitted to ride in the fifth-wheel in some 30 states, large families may find them inconvenient for long trips.

2. In many forward bedroom models, except those labeled "high profile," there is not quite enough headroom for anyone over six feet tall to stand up straight.

3. As with all towables, you have to exit the towing vehicle and go outdoors in order to enter the RV, an inconvenience in bad weather.

MOTORIZED RVs

TYPE B VAN CAMPERS

Also called type B motorhomes, these conversions are built within the framework of a van but with raised roofs or lowered floor sections to allow passengers to stand upright, at least in the center of the vehicle. Galleys, fresh-water hookups, sleeping and dining areas that convert to beds, even toilets and showers, are readily available in these versatile vehicles.

Ranging from 18 to 22 feet in length, van campers sell from $15,000 to $65,000, on the upper end comparable in price to an entry level motorhome, with an average cost of around $40,000. Most sleep two to four people, but also can carry four to six adults as a weekday commuter vehicle. The floor plan illustrated sleeps four people, two in the overhead bunk and two on the convertible sofa. A drop-in table fits in front of the sofa for dining.

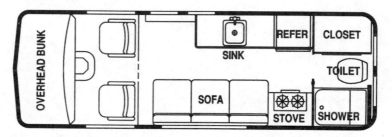

Sample Floor Plan Van Camper, Airstream 190 From Thor

One enterprising man we met at the Los Angeles RV show was buying a camper van with four swivel passenger seats to use on weekend family trips, but hoped to pay for it by carrying weekday commuters who appreciate having a toilet, microwave and TV set on the daily run.

Custom van conversions are also readily available from a number of manufacturers at an average price of around $25,500. For a complete list of manufacturers who make van conversions, contact *RVIA, PO Box 2999, Reston, VA 22090.*

During a study made in the summer of 1994, a family of four using their own van camper or van conversion, staying in campgrounds and preparing most of their meals in camp, spent at average of $155 for two nights, $501 for seven nights and $924 for 14 nights.

Van camper in a model campsite from the Los Angeles RV Show

VAN CAMPERS: THE PLUS SIDE

1. **These RVs double as a second car** to use around the house or carpooling.

2. **Easy to drive and park**, with good gas mileage, van campers can go anywhere a passenger car can, including areas in national parks where larger RVs may be restricted.

3. Self-contained van campers mean there's **no need to leave the vehicle** to use any of the facilities.

4. Unlike other motorized or towable RVs, the camping van **can fit into almost any spot** left in a campground, so it's good for TGIF getaways and late arrivals.

VAN CAMPERS: THE MINUS SIDE

1. While most van campers can sleep four people, they'd have to be very good friends, or, more likely, a couple with one or two small children. The living area is extremely compact for a family spending a rainy day inside.

2. Because it doubles as a second car, the greater mileage accrued by selling time may make it harder to sell or trade than a larger motorhome.

3. Making up some of the optional beds in these vans could knock your back out— even before you lie down.

4. Limited storage space means you carry fewer clothes and supplies than in other RVs, meaning more frequent laundry and grocery stops.

TYPE C MINI-MOTORHOMES

Familiar, convenient and affordable, the type C (think cabover bed) motorhome packs a lot of living in a compact space. Also called mini-motorhomes, the units are built on a truck or van chassis, and usually range in length from 19 to 31 feet long. Widebody designs up to 102 inches across and diesel engine options are available, as well as low-profile models that can be telescoped for travel and storage to under eight feet high. Type Cs are priced from $26,000 to $75,000 or more, with the average price around $40,603.

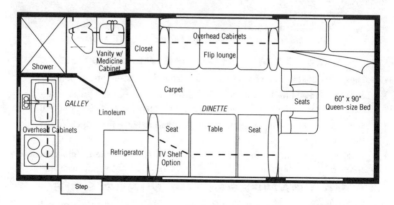

Sample Floor Plan, Scotty by Serro, Type C Mini-motorhome 23-foot on a Dodge Ram Hilander Chassis

On the illustrated floor plan, the cabover bed is above the driver's seat, while a sofa provides additional sleeping area. A dinette, rear galley and bathroom complete the interior. In other models, the cabover may be turned into an entertainment center with a double bed in back and dining on a drop-in table by the sofa.

During the summer of 1994, a family of four traveling in their own personal motorhome, staying in campgrounds and preparing most of their meals in camp, spent an average of $188 for two nights, $590 for seven nights and $1059 for 14 nights. Compare this to a family traveling in their personal car and staying at motels or hotels and eating most of their meals in restaurants, and you find the latter spent an average of $339 for two nights, $1169 for seven nights and $2257 for 14 nights.

Interior, type C mini-motorhome, Passport by Cobra looking from the kitchen toward the driver's seat

MINI-MOTORHOMES: THE PLUS SIDE

1. Type Cs are more maneuverable for beginning RV drivers than most type A motorhomes.

2. Mini-motorhomes contain all the livability of larger motorhomes but take up less parking and campground space.

MINI-MOTORHOMES: THE MINUS SIDE

1. The cabover bed is not appealing for claustrophobic adults, but kids love it. In general terms, the sleeping accommodations, except where there is a rear bedroom, are less private than in the type A motorhomes when more than two are traveling together.

2. Because of the overhang from the "cabover" bed, visibility is limited to a normal-sized windshield, while most type A motorhomes provide large, panoramic windshields.

INSIDER TIP:

Despite its generally smaller size, in our experience the type C gets no better gas mileage than a small type A, except in the Lite models.

TYPE A MOTORHOMES

A self-propelled motor vehicle chassis with a living unit built on it, the type A motorhome ranges from small, fully equipped entry-level vehicles to enormous, widebody bus-like coaches with slideouts, icemakers, washer/dryers, richly appointed furnishings and marble bathrooms that may be priced as high as $725,000.

Here is perhaps the widest range of choices in the entire RV fleet, size-wise, style-wise and price-wise, from 22 to 45 feet, priced from $30,000 to the afore-mentioned $725,000. The average is around $67,216.

Decor can vary from the casual-but-handsome Route 66 denim-and-chambray limited edition fabrics for Winnebago's Itasca label, to Bluebird Wanderlodge's cushy white leather furniture, brass trim, wood parquet floors and sculpted area rugs.

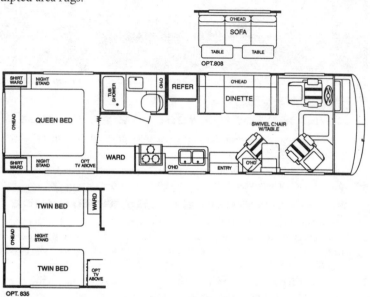

Sample floor plan, Type A motorhome, 28-foot Bounder by Fleetwood

The floor plan illustrates a fairly standard entry-level 28-foot model with cockpit seats that swivel; a choice of a sofa with drop-in tables or a dinette, either of which can be made into a bed; a side bath and rear island queen bed with an option of twin beds.

For a cost comparison of traveling in a motorhome and staying and cooking in campgrounds versus traveling in the family automobile, staying in hotels and eating in restaurants, see "Type C Mini-Motorhomes."

Interior, type A motorhome, Coachmen Intrigue 40-foot widebody model

TYPE A MOTORHOMES: THE PLUS SIDE

1. Always accessible from the driver's seat without going outside, the type A motor-home lets you pull over to fix lunch, use the bathroom or take a quick nap by the side of the road or in a parking lot.

2. Bigger windshield and windows than the type C allow greater visibility when travel-ing and better vantage points for photographs.

3. A big open sense of space and luxury makes the type A the most livable of the motorized RVs for most people.

4. In most type As, all the living areas are set up and ready for two people, not requir-ing any additional conversion on site. For sleeping more than two people, however, a sofa or dinette usually has to be made up.

TYPE A MOTORHOMES: THE MINUS SIDE

1. Unless you're towing a car, a type A requires that the motorhome has to be unplugged and moved anytime you need to go out shopping or sight-seeing away from the campground.

2. The larger type A motorhomes can offer maneuvering problems in narrow city streets with heavy traffic, as well as parking problems almost everywhere except mall parking lots. Height and width limitations prohibit entering most parking garages, clearing low overhanging roofs and narrow tunnels or bridges.

3. Gas mileage is quite low, usually under 10 miles to the gallon.

4. Choosing a size to match your travel style is critical in this category, since larger units cannot be accommodated in some rustic campgrounds and are not permitted to enter certain narrow or winding roadways in national parks such as Glacier, Big Bend and Zion.

INSIDER TIP

Vehicles or combinations longer than 20 feet are not permitted to travel across Going-to-the-Sun Highway in Montana's Glacier National Park.

10 QUESTIONS TO ASK YOURSELF

1. How often will I use the vehicle?

Some RV owners in cold climates have to winterize and store the RV. Others, either people who go south for the winter, people who go skiing or winter camping and people who live in or near mild climates, use it year-round. If you think you may use it only once a year for a two-week family vacation, it might be cheaper to rent rather than buy. (See "Chapter 5, Renting or Buying.")

2. Where will I store the vehicle?

City-dwellers like us have to rent storage space elsewhere because there's nowhere to store our motorhome on our property. But even suburbanites may face parking regulations that preclude keeping an RV in the driveway or on the street in front of the house. Owners with a large garage might consider folding camping trailers, truck campers or telescoping travel trailers which are compact enough to store inside. Some travelers who like to visit the same park or campground year after year may wish to store the vehicle permanently at the vacation location.

3. Do I already have part of an RV unit?

If you have a pickup, for example, depending on its size, you're already capable of handling a towable such as a travel trailer, truck camper or fifth-wheel. Most family cars can pull a small travel trailer or folding camping trailer.

4. How much money can I spend?

Budgeters and young families starting out often begin by buying an entry-level RV in whichever type category they want. With sticker shock a strong factor these days, more and more manufacturers are offering lower-priced models in all categories. Previous RV owners often, but not always, look to buying a larger, newer, more expensive model. A few choose instead to downgrade for a simpler travel life-style. In many cases, interest paid on your loan to purchase an RV is tax deductible as a second home. (See "Chapter 5, Insider Tip.")

5. How many people does the RV need to accommodate on a routine trip?

There's a big difference between a salesman's estimate of how many people a vehicle can sleep and the reality of the number of adults and children it can comfortably and conveniently accommodate. Some people dislike the idea of making a bed out of a sofa or dinette night after night during a holiday. Others don't want someone climbing over them in the middle of the night to go to the bathroom. A major consideration is how many seat belts are in the vehicle if it's a motorized RV. Many states now require that all passengers in the moving vehicle be secured by seat belts, and will not authorize more passengers inside than there are seat belts provided.

6. How will I be using the vehicle?

People who like to stay in one place, say a country-club-type private campground with swimming pools and putting greens, will want a more luxurious vehicle than campers who want to go out in the woods in a national park or forest, build a campfire and cook outdoors. Travelers who want to stop at a different campground every night while touring a large region need to give priority to ease of setting up camp and fuel efficiency, while snowbirds who want to stay cheaply all winter on BLM desert lands (see "Chapter 13, The California Desert") or other self-contained camping should look for vehicles with greater capacity in water storage and holding tanks.

7. Which is more important, generous living space in the vehicle or more flexible handling, parking and roadway options?

In making a decision on vehicle size, one foot in length or four inches in width can make a tremendous difference. Spend a lot of time mentally moving around in the floor plan, or even physically moving around in the vehicle at the dealer's or RV show, to assess its livability. Know your size requirements before setting out to look at vehicles, especially if you are considering a motorhome; you'll save a lot of time on the lot.

8. How important is personal privacy?

Some types of RVs offer more solid door privacy areas than others. In particular, the shower and toilet facilities in folding camping trailers or camping vans, when they are provided at all, may offer minimum privacy, while travel trailers, fifth-wheels, motorhomes and some truck campers provide facilities in a completely closed off area. Sleeping facilities as well may be open or shielded with curtains rather than doors, as in many folding camping trailers, truck campers and even type C mini-motorhomes.

9. What kind of fuel do I want the vehicle to burn, gasoline or diesel?

The general consensus is that diesel engines cost more on initial purchase but less in the long run to operate. One disgruntled RVer, however, has gone on record complaining about the high cost of oil and filters for diesel engines.

10. Will I be happy with a standard "off-the-rack" model RV or do I want some special features and options?

The next chapter discusses new trends, choices and options in RVs, and gives a rundown on the leading North American RV manufacturers and the various types of RVs they produce.

RV MANUFACTURERS: WHO MAKES WHAT

Now that you've learned the basic ABCs in the last chapter, get ready for still more ABCs and primary numbers. Most, but not all, RV manufacturers use as model numbers an abbreviated code that can give you basic information about the vehicle—28 RQ, for instance, will often mean a 28-foot vehicle with a rear queen bed, and 34 D may mean a 34-foot diesel pusher.

Two of the nation's biggest recreation vehicle shows introducing the next year's models take place late in the preview year—the trade and public show in Los Angeles in late October, and the trade-only show for dealers in Louisville in late November. With literally hundreds of models on display at each, it's easy to spot the trends in new RVs.

10 MAJOR RV TRENDS

1. More affordable entry-level vehicles in all major RV types to appeal to the baby boomer buyers just beginning to enter the market.

2. More "Lites," lightweight models designed to be pulled by sport utility vehicles, 4 x 4s, minivans and larger cars.

3. Tougher, lightweight construction from skeleton to skin promises longer unit life with less damage from environmental hazards, with most manufacturers phasing out wood in favor of steel and aluminum, and many favoring rubber roofing for its easy repairability, strength and resistance to ozone and ultraviolet exposure.

4. Widebody designs stretch the traditional 96-inch width to 100 or 102 inches, allowing for variations in furniture arrangements, from L-shaped or full-sized sofas placed across the living room area rather than along one wall, to queen-sized beds installed from side-to-side rather than front-to-back. Most states already allow 102 inch vehicles on all highways, but a few states restrict them to main roads. They are legal on all federal highways, however.

5. Slideouts in type A motorhomes, travel trailers and fifth-wheels seem to almost double the living space inside the vehicle. The slideout unit, with the furniture built on it, slides open when the RV is settled and leveling jacks activated, then slides back into traveling position at the push of a button when it's time to go. Most slideouts have alternate back-up systems.

6. Basement models add a huge amount of storage underneath a raised chassis for people who live seasonally or full time in their RVs or just like to travel with more gear, such as several sets of golf clubs or skis. Some very large basement models are capable of carrying a tiny electric auto, a sort of golf cart for tooling around the campsite or going to the grocery store without having to unhook the motorhome. (See "Nuts and Bolts, Seven Great Gizmos and Gadgets.")

7. Diesel pushers, so called because the diesel engine is in the rear of the vehicle, are growing in number, although still well behind gas engine sales. The perception is that despite extra initial cost, the diesel engine creates a savings in the long run because upkeep, repairs and fuel costs are lower. The rear engine diesel also increases power, prolongs engine life and rides more quietly in a motorhome than the standard front gas engine. Diesel pusher type A motorhomes are 30 feet or longer. One manufacturer, Sellers, has produced a gas pusher model.

8. Home-style furniture and appliances from seven-foot sofas to side-by-side refrigerators, even dishwashers, icemakers, washer/dryers and vanity tables, are turning up in many motorhomes and travel trailers. Corian-type countertops with self-sinks and plugs to expand work space, linoleum or vinyl easy-clean bath and kitchen floors and pantries with fitted storage slideouts make cooking a breeze. Wet bars, undersink water filters, built-in vacuum cleaner systems and garbage disposals can also be spotted on some models. Across the board, freestanding dining room furniture is beginning to replace the dinette and island beds, especially in queen- size, are becoming standard.

9. Outdoor options include gas grills installed in storage areas; radios, tape decks and TV sets built in as outdoor entertainment centers; a hand-held hose for washing off muddy shoes, sandy kids or pets outdoors.

10. More super-deluxe motorhomes, many of them motor coaches built on a bus shell, are showing up at RV shows and on lots. They cost $200,000 to $700,000 or more, depending on options and extras. Here you can expect cushy carpeting, pale leather upholstery, a large TV set on the dash, perhaps a second smaller one in the bedroom and a back-up TV for the driver as standard equipment. Most are from 36 to 40 feet but may go as long as 42-1/2 feet or even 45.

RV MANUFACTURERS AND WHAT THEY MAKE

The following are the leading North American manufacturers of type A motorhomes, type B van campers, type C mini-motorhomes, travel trailers, fifth-wheel trailers, truck campers and folding camping trailers.

If there is a manufacturer in your vicinity who produces an RV type you're interested in seeing, you might want to call and ask if it's possible to tour the plant. You could also request brochures from the company, or get the name of a dealer in your area so you could visit the lot and see the latest models. Some manufacturers also provide a video of their travel products for a modest fee or deposit.

"U" preceding the company name means "Uninspected"; the authors have not yet inspected that company's RVs.

ABI LEISURE PRODUCTS

726 Broad Street East, PO Box 10B, Dunnville, Ontario, Canada N1A 2X1
☎ *(905) 774-8891*
This Canadian company manufactures travel trailers and fifth-wheels under the Award label, distinguished by sleek aerodynamic styling and good towability. They claim gas mileage averaging 13.5 mpg for a 30-foot Award travel trailer pulled by

vehicles such as Ford Explorer, Jeep Cherokee or Buick Roadmaster. In lengths from 23 to 34 feet, the travel trailers have good storage and numerous bedroom options in the stylish interiors. Fifth-wheels offer a choice of rear kitchen or rear lounge, and queen or twin beds.

Airstream travel trailer at Los Angeles RV Show

AIRSTREAM, INC.,

419 West Pike, Jackson Center, OH 45334,
☎ *(513) 596-6111*
One of the best-known names in RVs, Airstream began manufacturing its classic travel trailers 60 years ago. That famous design was recently honored by the Franklin Mint with a working miniature replica. Now part of the Thor Industries group, Airstream manufactures travel trailers in lengths from 21 to 34 feet, priced from around $25,000 to $58,000, as well as motorhomes and van campers.

The mid-range Land Yacht LE label with great storage inside and out is available in 30- and 34-foot gas models. A Land Yacht widebody diesel pusher starting at $126,000, as well as standard width gas and diesel Land Yacht motorhomes are also part of the line.

Airstream Classic type A motorhomes, starting at $123,000, have the familiar curved lines, and standard features such as leveling jacks, water purifier and pantry built-ins; they come in either gas or diesel pusher models.

They also produce Land Yacht Clipper bus-style motorhomes. A new series of Airstream LE Cutter widebodies introduced at Louisville included a built-in toaster-oven to complement the usual microwave. The Airstream 190 type B camper van on a Ford chassis has a small tub/shower, toilet, four-burner stove with oven and microwave, a refrigerator with a small freezer and good storage in the $45,000 range.

ALFA LEISURE, INC.

13501 5th Street, Chino, CA 91710
☎ *(909) 628-5574*
Under the Alfa label, this company produces travel trailers and upscale fifth-wheels, many with slideouts and/or basements, well-planned kitchens, some with Corian counters and 18-inch dishwashers. Homelike furnishings such as big comfortable loungers, built-in glass curio cabinets and entertainment centers make them particularly appealing to snowbirds and full timers.

The Alfa Gold label is an upscale luxury model; we saw one model that has two double refrigerator/freezer combinations, a boon for full-timers.

A new See Ya! entry-level fifth-wheel with slideouts, spacious kitchen and optional garden tub comes in traditional decor offered in "country" or "formal" styles.

U - AMERICAN TRAVEL SYSTEMS

21746 Buckingham Road, Elkhart, IN 46516
☎ *(219) 294-2117*
Based in the heart of RV manufacturing country, this company manufactures fifth-wheel and travel trailers under the labels Capri, Ledger, Royal Voyager, Vacation-Aire and Vagabond.

AUTO-MATE RECREATIONAL PRODUCTS

150 West G Street, PO Box 831, Los Baños, CA 93635
☎ *(209) 826-1521*
Auto-Mate makes deluxe fifth-wheels and travel trailers, many with slideouts and/or basements. Their high-profile fifth-wheel allows full standing room in the front bedroom, with some models containing extras such as ceiling fans, built-in water filters and an outside removal door for built-in kitchen garbage can. A mid-profile model is available as well.

BARTH, INC.

PO Box 768, State Road 15 S, Milford, IN 46542
☎ *(219) 658-9401*
Under the Barth label, this Indiana company manufactures top-of-the-line type A motorhomes with elegant furnishings in leather, natural handcrafted woods and ultrasuede. Thoughtful details like pull-out pantry shelving, large showers, built-in bedroom TV sets, wood floors in galleys and vinyl floors in bathrooms are part of the basic decor in these tasteful, well-made motorhomes. Prices are between $150,000 and $180,000 on the Monarch models, which are 31 to 37 feet.

BEAVER COACHES, INC.

20545 Murray Road, Bend, OR 97701
☎ *(800) 423-2837*
This top-of-the-line Oregon manufacturer of type A motorhomes, recently partnered with Oregon-based Safari, turns out elegantly handcrafted vehicles under the Marquis label with a choice of wood cabinetry comparable to fine furniture, as well as luxuries like swivel leather chairs, dressing room with lighted makeup table, washer/dryer, bathroom vanity table with stool, icemakers and separate water closet with solid door. The slightly less expensive Patriot models are almost equally grand.

BIGFOOT INDUSTRIES INC.

3405 43rd Avenue, Vernon, BC, Canada, V1T 8P5
☎ *(604) 549-4222*
A versatile company, Bigfoot manufactures affordable fifth-wheels, travel trailers, type C mini-motorhomes and truck campers under the Bigfoot, Bigfoot Lite and Oakland labels. The latter is a design especially for cold-weather camping with the line's own Fibercore Wall System insulation. Their 17-foot gaucho-bed travel trailers have all the basics, including galley and bath with shower, for an entry-level towable. Some models have linoleum flooring throughout, practical for hard-use camping. Their truck campers are sturdy and laid out for a maximum of comfort in a minimum of space.

BLUE BIRD WANDERLODGE

PO Box 1259, One Wanderlodge Way, Fort Valley, GA 31030
☎ *(912) 825-2021*
Some of these type A motorcoaches list at $500,000 or more when all the luxurious options are added—huge basements, white leather cockpit chairs piped in blue

leather trim, European-style high gloss kitchen cabinets, big showers in ultra-luxe bathrooms, garbage disposals, side-by-side refrigerator freezers—what's not to like?

Blue Bird Wanderlodge with basement storage bins open

The diesel pusher 40-foot model has an instrument panel that looks like an airplane cockpit. Their 42-1/2-foot diesel pusher prototype, listed at $550,000, was exhibited at the shows last fall to great acclaim. A more modestly priced BMC diesel pusher, a mere $300,000 or so, features all-steel body construction and a 102-inch widebody design.

BORN FREE MOTORCOACH, INC.

Highway 169 North, PO Box 39, Humboldt, IA 50548
☎ *(800) 247-1835*
The Born Free type C mini-motorhome comes in several President models from 21 to 26 feet. Sturdy and well made, the Born Free has options for a rear side bed and side bath or a larger rear bath and a sofa that makes into a bed. Two swivel chairs and a pullup table with drink holders make a nice TV watching or card-playing spot.

The company's new "built for two" model in 19, 21 and 23 feet is compact enough for all national park campgrounds; prices start at under $45,000.

Designed to sleep two in comfort with a size small enough to offer ease in handling, the design features sofa twin beds with folding, removable pedestal table between them, a full galley and bath. The company is proud of its awards over the years for safety, design and fuel economy.

CARRIAGE, INC.

#5 Industrial Park, PO Box 246, Millersburg, IN 46543
☎ *(219) 642-3622*
This Indiana company produces Royals International top-of-the-line fifth-wheels with great kitchen features like dishwasher, Nutone food center, side-by-side refrigerator/freezer with ice and water dispenser, washer/dryer, pull-out spray kitchen faucet and kitchen cabinets fitted with storage carousels.

They also make some cushy, slideout fifth-wheels under the Carriage label and the affordable but handsome Carriage Commander. Carri-Lite Emerald fifth-wheels and Carri-Lite Cashay travel trailers show good workmanship and traditional decor. Their Callista, Cove and Cruiser mini-motorhomes have a contemporary exterior styling that should appeal particularly to younger buyers, with some cabover areas furnished with an entertainment center instead of the usual bed; the latter has been moved to the rear as twins or an island queen bed.

Interior, Royals International fifth- wheel by Carriage

CHALET RV MFG. INC.

829 9th Street, San Jacinto, CA 92583
☎ *(714) 487-2440*
Chalet A-frame folding camping trailers are well furnished for comfortable camp living, with undercounter refrigerator, two-burner cooktop and dinette. The model we inspected at the Los Angeles show, which listed at $8500, had no toilet or shower.

COACH HOUSE

208-D Warfield Avenue, Venice, FL 34292
☎ *(800) 235-0984*
These well-built type B van campers contain many extra features for easy living, from slideout pantry storage to optional entertainment center with color TV and VCR. The Dodge chassis models have an exterior height of eight feet with recessed floor, so a six-foot person can stand inside, but the vehicle can still be stored in most carports or garages.

Self-contained toilet and shower on some models, holding tanks and an optional generator let you camp comfortably without hookups. GMC and Ford chassis are also available. Some models get up to 17 mpg, they claim. The four big passenger seats convert to two single beds.

COACHMEN INDUSTRIES, INC.

601 East Beardsley Avenue, PO Box 3300, Elkhart, IN 46515
☎ *(219) 262-0123*
One of the largest and most respected companies in the industry, Coachmen is notable for well-built RVs in every type category and more than 30 different model names. One company representative calls them "the Volvo of the RV industry" for their longevity. We were particularly impressed with their new widebody Destiny type A motorhome with leather cockpit chairs and big TV under the dashboard.

All the type A motorhomes are basement models. The mid-range Santara type A slideout model has many fitted kitchen features and space for an icemaker and washer/dryer. Their entry level Catalina motorhome offers a variety of floor plans.

Coachman's Maxxum fifth-wheels are spacious, comfortable and traditionally styled, while its Royal label towables offer a high quality livability for the price.

Interior wide-body type A motorhome Intrigue by Coachmen with southwestern upholstery fabric

The Catalina and Leprechaun standard and widebody type C mini-motorhomes feature cabover bunks and some rear double beds, sturdy pan drawers under the cooktop and an undersink drawer for cutlery. Catalina Lite towable travel trailers also offer some good entry-level buys.

Coachmen Saratoga vans have bath, galley and twin sofas that convert to queen-sized bed. Viking folding camping trailers feature large kitchen and dinette areas. We also liked their Coachmen Sport 110SE truck camper with an optional foldout hide a bed just right for a child, when not in use, it fits above the dinette area out of the way.

The company's type A and C motorhomes, fifth-wheels and economy and mid-range travel trailers were all cited as best buys by *Consumers Digest* magazine in 1994. At press time, Coachmen was in the process of acquiring Georgie Boy, a major type A motorhome manufacturer (see below).

COBRA INDUSTRIES

2766 East College Avenue, PO Box 124,Goshen, IN 46527
☎ *(219) 534-1418*

Another very large company, Cobra produces all RV types in one or another of its eight subsidiaries in Indiana, Texas and California. Their Rockwood XL folding camping trailers offer good entry-level prices and some toilet/shower options, and the Wildwood by Rockwood travel trailer has some models with an island queen at the front and a bunkhouse with three or even four bunks at the rear, an excellent floor plan for a big family.

Cobra also manufactures some mid-range fifth-wheels for full-timers, including one 35-foot model with a built-in desk for computers, double slideout and big side-by-side refrigerator/freezer for under $35,000 list. The Sandpiper 25-foot fifth-wheel slideout is a good budget vehicle with generous storage, island bed and cedar-lined closet.

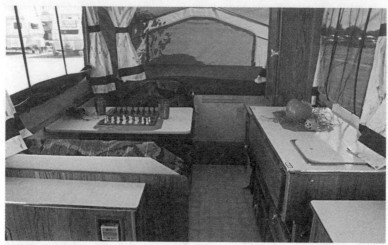

Interior, Rockwood folding camping trailer

The company's Summit travel trailer features a super slide, one big slideout for both sofa and dining table as opposed to earlier versions which used two smaller slide-outs. Sierra and Salem labels are entry level travel trailers.

The company's Passport type C mini-motorhome also fits into the entry-level price range, as does the slightly less expensive Seven Seas. In type A motorhomes, Cobra produces Monterey, the Regent by Rockwood and Bayport by Rockwood, all with gas and diesel pusher models available, from 23 to 34 feet, at entry-level to lower mid-range prices.

Interior Cobra Sierra travel trailer with slideout

COLLINS

1635 North 30th Street, Springfield, OR 97478
☎ *(800) 888-6295*
A division of Safari, Collins produces fifth-wheel travel trailers in the $30,000 to $50,000 bracket, some of them under a Lite label from 26 to 30 feet with widebody cabins, others 29- to 33-foot widebody models in regular fifth-wheels. Slideout fit-

ted pantries, the option of rear kitchen or rear living room and twin mirrored night-stands are among the amenities.

COLUMBIA NORTHWEST, INC.

1 Main Street, Mammoth, PA 15664,
☎ *(412) 423-7440*
The unique A-Liner label folding camping trailers are pyramid-shaped and can fold up or down in less than 30 seconds. They come in three basic styles: spa, dinette and bunkhouse. The spa model features a full-sized Jacuzzi tub with a double bed base that slides over the tub plus a big table with dinette seats, cooktop, sink, under-counter refrigerator and heater at a list price of around $12,000.

The dinette model has two seating units that make into beds, around $11,000, while the bunkhouse model has additional sleeping units at around $9000.

The A-Lite model for two unfolds into half a pyramid or right angle triangle, with double bed and dinette table, and is priced around $7000. All have cooktops, solid state walls, cathedral ceiling, a compartment for an optional travel toilet, enclosed storage space and radius windows with tinted glass. They can be towed by most automobiles.

COUNTRY COACH, INC.

210 East Sixth Street, Junction City, OR 97448
☎ *(800) 654-0223*
These stylish and elegant type A motorhomes have Corian-type kitchen and bath-room counters with cutouts of the same material to fit over sinks and cooktop to create one long solid work counter. With handsome wood cabinetry, stall shower, built-in TV/VCR in the bedroom, leather swivel chairs and freestanding wood din-ing table and chairs, they'd provide a very posh full-time home.

The Coach Tender is a small electric vehicle that can be stored in large basement areas of motorhomes such as this Country Coach.

To demonstrate the size of their basement storage areas, they showed one model with a compact golf cart/minicar tucked away to ride inside. (To find out about the minicar, see "Nuts and Bolts, Seven Great Gadgets and Gizmos.")

Country Coach models range from the $190,000 Garnet to the $485,000 Concept. Intrigue includes an insulated skylight, clothes hamper and tub/shower combina-tion; Affinity's 102-inch widebody is available with light or dark oak, walnut, cherry or whitewashed ash interior cabinetry; and Magna packs a lot of high-style living into a 34-foot widebody.

COUNTRY COMFORT CORPORATION

21279 Protecta Drive, Elkhart, IN 46516
☎ *(219) 522-3377*
This Elkhart company manufactures fifth-wheel and travel trailers under the Country Comfort label. Their entry-level widebody fifth-wheels are very livable with good-looking traditional decor, including glass-door breakfronts, shower stall with skylight and full-length bedroom mirrors. They make 11 different models in fifth-wheels from 33 to 40 feet.

U - CUSTOM CAMP VANS & SERVICE, INC.

7575 Jurupa Avenue, Riverside, CA 92504
☎ *(909) 359-3443*
This California company produces type B van campers as well as multi-use van conversions.

DAMON CORPORATION

52570 Paul Drive, Elkhart, IN 46514
☎ *(219) 262-2624*
Damon produces the handsome Inverness type A motorhome with dark cabinetry, wood dining table, Corian-type counter and self-sink with built-in cutlery drawer and pantry pullout as one of its top-of-the-line models, along with the Intruder type A with wide body, slideout and basement models. Less expensive labels in the type A fleet include Challenger and Ultrasport, while the Frontier Flyer is an entry-level motorhome at under $50,000. Damon's Ultrasport type C mini-motorhome offers the option of cabover bed or an entertainment center with or without a pullout child's bunk; the 30-foot widebody lists around $54,000.

We liked the Hornet label bunkhouse model travel trailer with a separate bedroom for the kids with its own small dinette for games and wardrobe for storage, plus a slideout island double bed for adults at the opposite end. A smaller type C mini-motorhome also carries the Hornet tag.

The Damon Escaper fifth-wheel models are cushy and comfortable with good built-in storage, big kitchens and furnishings like those in a suburban house, especially appropriate for full-timers or snowbirds.

U - EXCEL TRAILER COMPANY, INC.

5111 Grumman Drive, Carson City, NV 89706
☎ *(702) 885-0808*
Excel produces fifth-wheel and travel trailers under their own Excel label and Silverado by Excel.

U - FEATHERLITE MFG., INC.

Highway 63 and 9, PO Box 320, Cresco, IA 52136
☎ *(319) 547-6000*
Econolite and Featherlite label fifth-wheel trailers are produced by this Iowa-based company in one of their four Iowa manufacturing plants in Cresco and Nashua.

FIRAN MOTOR COACH, INC.

PO Box 482, 58277 SR 19 S, Elkhart, IN 46515
☎ *(219) 293-6581*
Firan manufactures upper mid-range type A motorhomes under the Europremier label with extras like marble-floored baths, vinyl foam padded ceilings and L-shaped Corian-counter kitchens. They also make the less expensive Westhaven line, which nevertheless has luxury details like side-by-side refrigerator/freezers, picture windows and two sofa living/dining set-ups.

Firan's entry-level label is Raven, with a widebody 31-foot diesel pusher with L-shaped sofa and high-low dining/coffee table, which costs in the neighborhood of

$64,000. A slideout version of the same offers the option of a hide-a-bed sofa or an entertainment cabinet.

Their Covington type A is another option for mid-range buyers at $64,000 for a 31-foot motorhome with island queen bed and street-side bath.

We were particularly impressed with the Firan Ultrastar as a winter RV for skiers, with an Arctic pack included, along with plentiful storage for skis, electronic heating for all systems and extra-thick injected urethane foam insulation. The sleek, low-profile vehicle with curved aerodynamic styling lists at around $73,000.

FLEETWOOD ENTERPRISES, INC.

3125 Myers Street, Riverside, CA 92503
☎ *(909) 351-3500; for brochures or videos, contact them at*
PO Box 92919, Milwaukee, WI 53202-0919
☎ *(800) 444-4905*
Fleetwood, with divisions in nine states and one Canadian province, is North America's largest manufacturer of RVs. Fleetwood's top-of-the-line type A motorhomes are the American Eagle, listing around $225,000, and the slightly less expensive American Dream, both in gas or diesel models. Expect extra touches such as leather sofas and cockpit chairs, cedar-lined closets, icemakers, Corian-type counters, side-by-side refrigerator/freezers and island beds. The Eagle electrical system includes a 2000-amp inverter that can convert battery power for appliances without needing hookups or a generator.

Other Fleetwood type A motorhomes include the mid-range Southwind and the Pace Arrow, including a model decorated with the distinctive Route 66 fabric and a retractable dash TV. At the entry-level range are Bounder, Flair, Coronado, American Flyer and the new Southwind Storm; the model B 28 on the latter offers a compact half-dinette facing the cockpit TV and a crosswise queen bed.

Fleetwood's type-C mini-motorhomes under the Montara Tioga label are good for big families, with an entry-level design with four bunks in the rear in addition to a cabover bed, so nothing has to be made up or converted at bedtime; the cost is around $48,000. Also in type C is the new Tioga Walkabout and the sturdy, easy to handle Fleetwood Searcher Jamboree; we drove one of the latter on the Alaska Highway (see "Driving the Alaska Highway").

Savanna 30-foot travel trailer by Fleetwood

The well-known Coleman folding camping trailers are also part of the Fleetwood family, and offer 16 different models, including a top-of-the-line hardwall Hattaras model with E-Z crank stabilizers, built-in cassette toilet and hot water shower for $11,000.

In travel trailers, Mallard is a popular entry-level candidate, with one $12,000 model with queen-sized bed for parents and a second bedroom with bunks, bath and wardrobe. The company's travel trailers go upscale from Mallard through Wilderness, Prowler, Terry (the flagship for 50 years and middle of the line), Savanna, Westport and Avion.

The top-of-the-line Avion fifth-wheel lists around $50,000 with slideouts, entertainment center, island bed and lavish bath and kitchen. The Westport label, also upscale, has big wardrobes, slideouts and L-shaped kitchens; some offer two doors on opposite sides of the unit.

Fleetwood truck campers are designed particularly for sportsmen as the names suggest, with the new lightweight Angler that is available in both softsided and hardsided models. The rugged Caribou and Elkhorn models offer luxury in camp and a tough on-the-road attitude.

FORETRAVEL, INC.

1221 NW Stallings Drive, Nacogdoches, TX 75961

☎ *(409) 564-8367*

Top-of-the-line luxury type A motorhomes under the Foretravel Grand Villa Unihome label have Corian-type kitchen counters and dining-table tops, stall shower, choice of rich wood cabinetry in light or dark shades, big closets, space for washer/dryer, built-in TV/VCR in bedroom, slideout undersink storage and huge basement storage areas. Prices start around the $380,000 mark and escalate, depending on size. The Foretravel Unicoach provides the same deluxe features, including built-in vacuum cleaner, CB radio, drinking water filter, icemaker and trash compactor as standard issue.

FRANKLIN COACH CO., INC.

South Oakland Avenue, PO Box 152, Nappanee, IN 46550

☎ *(219) 773-4106*

Fifth-wheel and travel trailers under the Franklin name are homey and livable with an option of L-shaped kitchens and some floral, feminine interiors that stand out refreshingly against the standard sea of velour upholstery.

Travel trailers from 19 to 35 feet have rear bedroom bunk options good for large families, garden tub models, and even a choice of exterior styling— their classic black and gold stripe or a contemporary multi-color stripe.

GEORGIE BOY MANUFACTURING, INC.

69950 M 62, Edwardsburg, MI 49112

☎ *(800) 521-8733*

Recently acquired by Coachmen, Georgie Boy is a major producer of type A motorhomes under such labels as Cruise Air, Cruise Master, Encounter, Swinger and Pursuit. Both traditional and motorcoach designs are offered, along with some widebody, diesel and slideout models. Details such as underbed drawer storage, wood-floored dining rooms and tub/shower combinations enhance the appeal. Pursuit is an entry-level label with several standard floor plan options.

Interior, kitchen in Cruise Air type A motorhome by Georgie Boy

GET-AWAY INTERNATIONAL MFRS., INC.

9400 River Drive, Richmond, BC, Canada, V6X 1Y9
☎ *(604) 270-1152*

Well-crafted van campers that can carry commuters during the week and hunters, fishermen or campers on the weekend, Get-Aways come with easy-clean interiors in four different models. We like the round table that plugs into the floor to access the four big swivel chairs in the 505-4 Get-Away, which also has a toilet, optional shower and TV, sink, undercounter refrigerator, cooktop and microwave. A rear dinette makes into a bed.

The Commander Travel Van would make a good ski RV with ski storage space in an optional watertight locker. Get-Aways have a base price from around $45,000.

GLENDALE RECREATION VEHICLES

145 Queen Street, Strathroy,Ontario, Canada N7G 3J6
☎ *(519) 245-1600*

Under the Golden Falcon and Travelaire label, Glendale, a sister company to Firan, offers travel trailers with slideouts, fifth-wheels under the Presidential, Golden Falcon and Travelaire tags, and Type C motorhomes under the Royal Classic brand. Their Presidential fifth-wheel series includes models with side-by-side refrigerator/freezer, washer/dryer connections and freestanding dining table.

U - GO VACATIONS INDUSTRIES

66 Mohawk Street, Brantford, Ontario, Canada N3S 2W3
☎ *(519) 759-5652*

This Canadian company produces type B van campers, type C mini-motorhomes and truck campers, as well as multi-use van conversions.

GREAT WEST VAN CONVERSIONS INC.

Box 33, Group 6A, RR1B,Winnipeg, Manitoba, Canada R3C 4A3
☎ *(204) 338-9303*

Founded in 1976, this Canadian company produces type B van campers on a Dodge chassis under the aerodynamic Classic Sport and spacious Classic Supreme labels. Corner or side baths with flush toilet and optional vanity or shower also contain rear dinettes with sofa beds or side sofas that convert to sleeping accommodations. Furnace, three-way refrigerator, stainless steel sink, swivel captain's chairs, cooktop and stainless steel kitchen sinks are included as standard equipment, with options such as electronic water heater, color TV, rear music center and roof air-conditioner also available.

GULF STREAM COACH, INC.

PO Box 1005, 503 South Oakland Avenue, Nappanee, IN 46550
☎ *(219) 773-7761*

Gulf Stream's current decor colors are Wedgewood, Rainforest and Acorn, an option in all their RVs, and type A diesel units carry generators in front of the coach with basement storage below. Both type A and type C motorhomes are well-planned and livable. The top-of-the-line Tour Master widebody diesel type A offers huge storage areas, a lavish optional outdoor entertainment center with color TV and 12-volt party cooler, glass stall shower, eye-level microwave, wet bar and mirrored wardrobe with bifold doors.

Interior type A Sun Stream motorhome by Gulf Stream

Scenic Cruiser offers slideouts in both gas and diesel pusher models. The company's Sun Voyager and Sun Stream type A mid-range models average around $80,000 with bedroom TVs, freestanding dining tables, some basement, slideout and diesel models; the latter are higher-priced. Generally, the space and storage are good, with well-planned kitchen and dining areas and solid oak cabinetry.

Type C widebody mini-motorhomes under the Conquest label have well-arranged kitchens with handy undersink drawers and plenty of space and storage. The Yellowstone Capri offers a good type C model for families with four bunks and a cabover bed at $50,000. The Ultra limited edition type C mini-motorhome opens up with a "glide-out expando" slideout. Kingsley is the label for fifth-wheels with two distinctive interiors, traditional Country Manor and contemporary Mirage Ivory.

HARMAR INC.

58456 County Road 3 South, 46517, Elkhart, IN
☎ *(219) 294-1269*

This Indiana manufacturer makes truck campers, travel trailers and fifth-wheels, the latter available in both basement and non-basement models with rubber roofs and some slideouts.

HAWKINS MOTOR COACH, INC.

1610 South Cucamonga Avenue, PO Box 3189, Ontario, CA 91761
☎ *(909) 947-2512*

Top-of-the-line type A motorhomes with the Special Edition Hawk label feature leather cockpit seats, Corian-topped tables, pullout pan drawers under the cooktop and heavy-duty pantry slideouts. A glass stall shower and island bed with built-in bedroom TV, wood kitchen floor and back-up TV monitor give these diesel pushers a lot of class. The more affordable HMC Hawk is diesel-fueled, with swivel recliners, cruise control, Corian counters and cedar-lined closet. HMC's Aerosport label is also upscale, with features included in the basic price that are extras with other lines, such as coffee makers, built-in blenders, icemakers, Corian countertops and freestanding dining table and chairs. Some Special Edition Aerosports have built-in kitchen water filters.

HI-LO TRAILER CO.

145 Elm Street, Butler, OH 44822
☎ *(419) 883-3000*

This innovative company produces several labels of telescoping travel trailers, including the TowLite, a super-lightweight, low-profile vehicle with a list price ($12,000) competitive with upper-level folding camping trailers and a lot of comfort items from full bath to full-sized sofa bed and galley.

FunLite has low-profile, lightweight towing and an automatic lifting system with six-year limited warranty that raises the trailer in 12 seconds.

Top-of-the-line Hi-Lo looks like any good travel trailer inside with little to tip you off that it telescopes. A full galley with dinette across the way, spacious bathroom and island bed make the living comfortable in this easy-tow vehicle. Any of them can be stored in your garage; they fold down to 69 to 74 inches, depending on the model.

Holiday Rambler type A motorhome with slideout

HOLIDAY RAMBLER CORPORATION

65906 State Road 19, PO Box 465, Wakarusa, IN 46573
☎ *(219) 862-7211*

Holiday Rambler produces high quality type A and type C motorhomes, fifth-wheels and travel trailers under the Aluma-Lite, Imperial, Endeavor and Navigator labels.

The top-of-the-line Imperial type A motorhome has been redesigned with slideout, widebody and fiberglass exterior replacing the former aluminum skin. One model offers a roll-top desk as an option, along with a kitchen snack bar and four chairs in lieu of a dining table.

The handsome, upscale Navigator offers features like a built-in vacuum cleaner system, convection browning oven, wood-floored kitchen and bedroom TV.

The mid-range Endeavor type A offers optional bathroom tile flooring, colored bathroom fixtures and bedroom TV sets. The company's light aluminum frame and an all-new design is featured in both the Imperial fifth-wheels and the Aluma-Lite fifth-wheels and travel trailers; all provide a variety of floor plans with slideouts.

HOME & PARK MOTORHOMES

100 Shirley Avenue, Kitchener, Ontario, Canada N2B 2E1
☎ *(800) 663-0066*
Roadtrek Motorhome Vans offer 170, 190 and 210 models in Versatile, Independent and Popular floor plans. The 210 Popular, for instance, has bath, galley, a dinette that converts to a king-sized bed and a unique combination of shower/ wardrobe that has to be seen to be believed. A round dining table snaps into the floor with folding petal leaves for the four swivel passenger chairs. The base price is around $50,000.

U - HOMESTEADER, INC.

1520 Cedar Lane, PO Box 320, New Tazewell, TN 37825
☎ *(615) 626-9040*
Tennessee-based Homesteader produces travel trailers and aluminum-skin fifth-wheels at entry-level prices under Homesteader labels.

HONORBUILT INDUSTRIES, INC.

1200 West 10th Street, Minneapolis, KS 67467
☎ *(800) 342-6234*
Honorbuilt manufactures type B van campers and type C mini-motorhomes under the ElDorado label. The latter contain larger storage areas, a new cabover bed design, an aluminum galley subfloor and larger galley windows. Various rear bedroom, rear bath, corner bath and island queen bed designs are available. Bathroom skylights are optional. The price range is around $53,000. The type B van camper, around $42,000, offers a toilet and shower in some models, along with sofa bed, cabover bed and galley.

U - HORIZONS, INC.

2323 North Jackson, Junction City, KS 66441-2288
☎ *(800) 235-3140*
This Kansas-based company manufactures fifth-wheel and travel trailers with a lot of custom options and sells directly from the factory.

HY-LINE ENTERPRISES INC.

21674 Beck Drive, Elkhart, IN 46516
☎ *(219) 294-1112*
Hy-Line travel trailers offer a choice of fabrics in nicely furnished units from 22 to 32 feet. Numerous bedroom, bath and kitchen options mean the buyer can virtually design his own unit. A fifth-wheel under the same label has washer/dryer, slideout, bunkhouse in back and bedroom in front. Other floor plans offer rear kitchens or living rooms in the 28- and 34-foot models.

INTERNATIONAL VEHICLES CORP.

PO Box 459, 200 Legion Street, Bristol, IN 46507
☎ *(219) 848-7686*
Under the Falcon and Horizon labels, Intervec turns out type B van campers above and below the $50,000 mark with toilet, tub/shower, refrigerator and some sunken floors so six-footers can stand upright in the center of the vehicle. The Falcon 190

is a good model for a small family, with a choice of rear or side bathroom, dinette or sofa beds with portable table, two- or four-passenger swivel chairs, galley and TV. The Horizon label also appears on the company's compact and tightly-planned mini-motorhomes.

ITASCA

605 West Crystal Lake Road, PO Box 152, Forest City, IA 50436
☎ *(515) 582-3536*

This division of Winnebago Industries manufactures type A motorhomes with gas or diesel, including a Sunrise 32-foot diesel in limited edition Route 66 decor ($74,000) with livable denim-and-chambray-style fabrics many buyers will find more appropriate to the outdoors than the standard velours.

Snowbirds and full-timers may be interested in the 34-foot diesel pusher or the 34- or 37-foot gas model of the Suncruiser with a spacious slideout and a choice of mulberry or sandstone interiors.

An entry-level 25-foot Itasca Passage at $36,000 has an overhead bunk in the cockpit big enough for a child, as well as two optional overhead bunks in the bedroom above twin beds.

Spirit type C mini-motorhomes offer a lot of sleeping options in limited space with cabover bed supplemented by a rear double bed. Sundancer type C includes options with outdoor entertainment area, cabover entertainment area and swivel chairs with pull-up table.

JAYCO, INC.

58075 SR 13 S, PO Box 460, Middlebury, IN 46540
☎ *(219) 825-5861*

This reputable company dates back more than 25 years, and produces folding camping trailers, fifth-wheel and travel trailers, truck campers and type C mini-motorhomes under its Eagle and Designer Series, Jayco and Starcraft labels.

A widebody mini-motorhome with crosswise sofa and extension table for snacks and dining, a spacious kitchen, split bath and island queen bed lists around $57,000 under the Eagle label, while a Designer almost the same size provides a dinette and two swivel chairs with a pull-up game table between them. Handsome wood cabinetry, slideouts and garden tubs are options in the company's affordable Designer label fifth-wheel and travel trailers, while Jayco Jay, Designer and Eagle series folding camping trailers, some with shower and toilet, may cost up to $15,000. The Eagle travel trailer has a roomy front storage compartment that can hold skis or golf clubs for sports-minded RVers; some also come with bunkhouse bedrooms.

K-Z, INC., SPORTSMEN

9270 West US 20, Shipshewana, IN 46565
☎ *(219) 768-4016*

Under the Sportsmen label, this company produces fifth-wheel and travel trailers and truck campers. New models include the Sportracker, a compact folding camping trailer displayed in the Louisville show. Their travel trailers range from 18 to 40 feet, their fifth-wheels from 20 to 35 feet. Practical vinyl floors, sturdy construction that can handle the rugged backwoods and good towability make these vehicles especially good for hunters, fishermen and outdoorsmen. No-nonsense interiors pack in all the necessary components for an outdoor holiday in the smaller travel trailers, while larger fifth-wheels offer slideouts, gracious living rooms and spacious kitchens.

KING OF THE ROAD

553 Front Street, PO Box 553, Russell, KS 67665
☎ *(800) 255-0521*

King of the Road builds deluxe fifth-wheels including a top-of-the-line slideout basement-model with double porcelain sink, fitted pantry shelving, 18-inch dishwasher and spacious kitchen that offers all the comforts of home. The new tandem slideout makes living room space twice as open as a single slideout.

The Knight model slideout is a lavish entry-level fifth-wheel with washer/dryer option, side bath, island queen bed and swivel rockers. Furnishings like glider-recliners, island desks, slideout pantry baskets, lighted vanity tables and ceiling fans make these RVs appealing to full-timers. A video of the company's products is available for $9.95 by calling the 800 number above.

KIT MANUFACTURING COMPANY

412 Kit Avenue, PO Box 990, Caldwell, ID 83606
☎ *(800) 859-0344*

This Idaho company, which started by selling teardrop, prefabricated travel trailers back in 1945 that could be built from a kit, now produces fifth-wheels and travel trailers under labels that include Road Ranger, Cordova, Companion and the new Sportsmaster. Big, comfortable horseshoe-shaped dinettes, good kitchen storage that includes heavy-duty pan drawers under the cooktop, and eye-level microwaves make these vehicles comfortable for short- or long-term camping. Road Ranger fifth-wheel bedrooms have a vanity shelf with mirrors that open to reveal a window in back.

U - KROPF MANUFACTURING CO., INC.

58647 SR 15, PO Box 30, Goshen, IN 46527-0030
☎ *(219) 533-2171*

This Indiana company, based in the heart of the RV manufacturing area, turns out custom-made fifth-wheels.

U - L.E.R. INDUSTRIES, INC.

19475 US 12 E, Edwardsburg, MI 49112
☎ *(800) 537-8267*

This Michigan manufacturer makes van campers under the L.E.R. label.

LAKE CAPITAL CORP.

3701 SE Naef Road, PO Box 68305, Portland, OR 97268
☎ *(503) 653-1160*

This Oregon company produces Komfort-label fifth-wheel and travel trailers at entry-level prices. A 28-foot travel trailer at around $24,000, for instance, has a slideout living room, an island queen bed, split bath, good kitchen work space and built-in entertainment center. Fifth-wheels range from 24 to 32 feet, and a special series of Lite Models includes 15- to 25-foot travel trailers and 22- and 24-foot fifth-wheels.

LANCE CAMPER MFG. CORP

10234 Glenoaks Blvd., Pacoima, CA 91331
☎ *(818) 897-3155*

Lance builds three classes of truck campers: the Lance label, which has been called the Cadillac of campers; the mid-range Squire, just as sturdy but with less luxurious fittings; and the budget-range SquireLite, made especially for short- or long-bed full-size lighter duty trucks. New models include a family-sized Squire 9000, a lightweight SquireLite 185 for lighter weight trucks with six- or eight-foot beds, and the Lance 945, a fully equipped 11-foot camper. One model we liked was a 10-foot Squire 8000 truck camper with an extended cabover bed, a window to the truck cab, three-burner stove, double sink, U-shaped dinette and bath with shower unit. There's an optional generator available, along with optional heated holding tanks for cold weather camping. Also new is a white aluminum roof. List price for the Squire 8000 is $12,400. Other models with options range up to $21,000.

LAZY DAZE, INC.

4303 East Mission Blvd., Pomona, CA 91766
☎ *(909) 627-1103*
Lazy Daze claims to have built the first type C mini-motorhome in the United States back in 1966, and certainly their models contain some of the most versatile features we've seen, including their unique Converta-Seats that change easily from sofa-type seating to dinette banquettes, as well as angled hanging space in bedroom shirt closets that allows deeper hanging length but still leaves a narrow nightstand area below. A double-thick shower door conceals extra canned-goods storage, and built-in pantry fittings add storage where you'd never expect it. Even the 22-foot model is big enough for two to travel in comfort, and the 26-foot and new 30-foot model with island bed are quite spacious. Base prices start at $42,250; buyers can purchase directly from the factory.

LEISURE TRAVEL VANS LTD.

7th S #764, PO Box 189, Gretna, Manitoba, Canada R0G 0V0
☎ *(204) 327-5871*
The two-seater Freedom widebody from Leisure Travel Vans is spacious and convenient for a couple and has various rear sleeping options from foldout king-size sofa bed to twin beds that double as dinette seats. Outside tables with gas stove connections let you prepare meals inside or out. The vehicles fit in a garage, can seat up to seven and sleep four, and contain shower and toilet options. The price is around $53,000.

MARATHON COACH INC.

91333 Coburg Industrial Way, Coburg, OR 97408
☎ *(800) 234-9991*
The Marathon with its base price of $642,000 was the big show-stopper at the LA RV show. A lavish 45-foot motorhome conversion of a Prevost Le Mirage XL with granite floors, mirrored walls, big carousel wardrobe closet, angled queen-sized island bed, round glass-walled shower and mirrored ceiling with halogen lights, this state-of-the-art RV has to be seen to be believed. With a diesel generator and powerful inverters, the coach is all-electric, with no propane gas anywhere. The cooktop is halogen, the kitchen counters Corian and the cabinetry high-gloss European-style with rounded edges. The cockpit with its leather seats and intricate panel of push-buttons resembles an airplane's. While test drives indicate a fuel consumption of seven mpg, operating economy is the last thing to worry about if you can afford this super-deluxe vehicle.

MARATHON HOMES CORP.

22471 Pine Creek Road, PO Box 1302, Elkhart, IN 46515
☎ *(219) 294-6441*
Marathon Homes produces fifth-wheels, travel trailers and type C mini-motor-homes under the Marathon and Olympian labels. Travel trailers and fifth-wheels, some with double slideouts, offer large kitchen workspaces, a variety of options including rear bath, twin or queen beds and dinettes and sofas that convert to beds.

MONACO COACH CORPORATION

325 East First Street, Junction City, OR 97448
☎ *(800) 634-0855*
Monaco produces top-of-the-line type A motorcoaches under the Crown Royale, Dynasty, Executive and Signature labels, plus the new Monaco Windsor motor-coach motorhomes that come in 32-, 34- and 36-foot lengths.

Monaco's vehicles are distinguished by their generous use of leather upholstery, backup TV as a standard feature, glass-fronted wood cabinetry, cedar-lined closets, vinyl tile galley flooring and Corian countertops, some with molded self-sinks. Dynasty features a choice of 96- or 102-inch widebody designs. The interiors can only be described as posh with a lush, cushy feel. Buyers can choose solid wood cabinets in oak, silver pine or walnut, side-by-side refrigerators, washer/dryer options in some models, icemakers and water purifiers. Prices go up to $335,000 for the Crown Royale label.

NATIONAL RV, INC.

3411 North Perris Blvd., Perris, CA 92571
☎ *(909) 943-6007*

National RV manufactures Dolphin and Sea Breeze type A motorhomes and fifth-wheels. A 34-foot turbo-diesel widebody Dolphin type A motorhome with sofa and facing love seat, wood table that can raise to dining height, L-shaped kitchen with generous workspace, side-by-side refrigerator, convection oven, island bed and plentiful closet area carries a list price of $112,000.

Sea Breeze fifth-wheels come in 29- to 36-foot lengths, all with slideouts and added niceties like swivel loungers, ceiling fans and rear kitchens with two windows.

The 92-inch wide Tropi-Cal "new generation RV" introduced several seasons ago has sleek styling, low profile, an entry-level price, good weight distribution and increased gas mileage.

NEWMAR CORPORATION

355 North Delaware Street, PO Box 30, Nappanee, IN 46550-0030
☎ *(219) 773-7791*

This season Newmar, which continues to introduce slideout innovations, debuted flush floor slideouts, which eliminate the slight rise between main body and slideout, in its London Aire and Kountry Aire motorhomes. Newmar's top-level Kountry Aire, mid-range Kountry Star, affordable Mountain Aire and entry-level Dutch Star are type A motorhomes, while London Aire and Dutch Star are diesel pusher models with slideouts.

The company also produces Kountry Star and American Star travel trailers and fifth-wheels, as well as London Aire, Kountry Aire and Mountain Aire fifth-wheels. Craftsmanship is excellent in this line with its handmade wood cabinetry, wood galley floors and hidden-leaf extendable dining tables.

NU WA INDUSTRIES

4002 Ross Lane, PO Box 808, Chanute, KS 66720
☎ *(316) 431-2088*

Hitchhiker and Nu Wa are the labels for this company's fifth-wheel and travel trailers. Hitchhiker II deluxe model fifth-wheels feature glide-out bedrooms, new this year, while all 102-inch widebodies have completely enclosed underbelly and heated washer/dryer connections.

An eye-catching brochure photograph of a three-quarter-ton pickup truck atop a Nu Wa SnowVilla fifth-wheel emphasizes the line's pride in its solid construction and engineering skill. While the pickup was perched atop the fifth-wheel for six hours, employees ran the glide-out in and out successfully.

The name SnowVilla seems to indicate that the company markets this fifth-wheel for snowbirds and full timers, and certainly this model is appropriate with its living room glide-outs, large kitchens with easy-clean linoleum floors, and a glide-out bedroom with queen island bed that offers a lot of walk-around space.

Interior, type A motorhome by Odessa with slideout

ODESSA INDUSTRIES, INC.

2208 Middlebury Street, PO Box 188, Elkhart, IN 46515
☎ *(219) 293-0595*
Odessa's Overland motor coach is an upscale, elegant type A motorhome with handsome exterior styling, Tivoli undercounter lighting, side-by-side refrigerator, icemaker, dishwasher, Corian kitchen counters, even an appliance garage for mixer or food processor. Bathrooms are big with some mirrored sliding-door wardrobes that open from either bathroom or bedroom side. The new 41-foot model has custom graphics interior designs. The Odessa label designates a new mid-range line with slideouts, while the Lextra label is a small entry-level type A with easy handling and fuel efficiency in 24-, 26- and 28-foot models.

Interior type A motorhome with Tivoli lighting, Odessa Overland with slideout

U - PETERSON INDUSTRIES, INC.

Rural Route 2, Box 95, Smith Center, KS 66967
☎ *(913) 282-6825*
This Kansas company produces fifth-wheel and travel trailers under the Excel, Legacy and Knoble Esquire labels.

Attendees at the Louisville RV Show inspect a Pla-Mor Wind River model designed to load and carry small vehicles or large furniture inside.

PLAY-MOR TRAILERS, INC.

Hwy 63 South, Westphalia, MO 65085
☎ *(800) 752-9667*
Travel trailers and fifth-wheels under the Play-Mor label incorporate many unique design features and special models.

A Pla-More Wind River travel trailer adapted for disabled RVers with hydraulic lift for wheelchairs and good negotiating space inside.

Their Wind River 2350 model travel trailer equipped for wheelchair users, for instance, was exhibited in Louisville. It featured a motorized lift unit for the wheelchair and extra-wide doors and plentiful space inside to maneuver the chair into the bathroom, the bedroom and up to the galley work areas.

Another special model is the Play-Mor Timber Creek Sport Cargo model with a back-loading ramp for a small vehicle, snowmobile or ATV, or big pieces of antique furniture from flea markets. Flip-up gauchos fold up or down against the wall to make room for cargo; the model is available in both fifth-wheel and travel trailer, from 21 to 37 feet. One model can carry a full-sized auto in the cargo area. The company also makes some neat little 15-foot travel trailers with everything a young family would need for a start-up RV.

PLEASURE-WAY INDUSTRIES LTD.

302 Portage Avenue, Saskatoon, SK, Canada S7J 4C6
☎ *(306) 934-6578*

Pleasure-Way's well-planned type B van campers come in four basic models: the SRL with L-shaped dinette seating that turns into a double bed; the VRL with private enclosed bathroom and rear living room/double bed; the STW with twin sofa beds at the rear; and the MPL with four seats (that turn into two single beds) up front and L-shaped dinette in the rear. All have flush toilet, optional color TV, wardrobe closet, full kitchen and huge storage areas big enough for golf clubs or fishing tackle.

The STW offers a lot of luxury for its $45,900 tariff, with sink, shower and small tub in a molded bathroom unit, rear twin beds, built-in TV/VCR and full galley with refrigerator, microwave and two-burner cooktop. All units also have easily accessible holding-tank dump attachments located in the running board rather than underneath the vehicle.

U - RED-E-KAMP, INC.

3401 Etiwanda Avenue, Mira Loma, CA 91752
☎ *(909) 685-0151*

Van campers and type C mini-motorhomes are produced by this California-based company under the Red-E-Kamp label.

U - REVCON MOTORCOACH, INC./ OFFROAD MOTORCOACH, INC.

17422 Pullman, Irvine, CA 92714
☎ *(714) 955-5340*

This California company produces type C mini-motorhomes under the Revcon Trailblazer label.

Rexhall Rexair type A motorhome with awning

REXHALL INDUSTRIES, INC.

25655 Springbrook Avenue, Bldg 1, Saugus, CA 91350
☎ *(805) 253-1295*
Rexhall makes type A gas and diesel pusher motorhomes under the Aerbus, Rexair and XL Limited labels. Rexair and Aerbus come in both 96-inch standard and 102-inch widebody models with some slideouts, workable U-shaped kitchens, side-by-side refrigerators, hardwood galley floors and an easily accessible holding-tank dump hose in the basement storage area rather than underneath.

In some models, dining areas have been put into the living room with folding adjustable tables between the sofas, opening up more walking-around space. On the mid-range Rexair XL widebody (listing at $68,700 for the 36-foot model), cook-tops are recessed to allow the microwave to be positioned at eye level for ease and safety.

U - RITTER ENTERPRISES, EMPIRE RV

59140 County Road 3, Elkhart, IN 46517
☎ *(219) 522-8548.*
Fifth-wheel and travel trailers are produced under the Empire label.

SAFARI

30725 Diamond Hill Road, PO Box 740, Harrisburg, OR 97446
☎ *(800) 458-8735*
This Oregon company attracted a lot of looky-loos at the LA RV show because their exhibit used life-sized, stuffed-toy African animals, African music, jungle foliage and fountains. Makers of very high quality type A motorhomes with sophisticated, contemporary designs, Safari sells vehicles from entry-level prices in their Trek models to mid-level Saharas ($135,000 range) and top-of-the-line Serengeti and Ivory models ($170,000-$185,000). Their even more deluxe Continental motor coaches with chassis by Magnum start at over $200,000.

Furnishings are leather and hand-rubbed woods, with some African-patterned bedspreads and other lovely fabrics and upholstery. First-time buyers concerned about handling ease might check out the 24-foot Trek model with Safari's patented Electro-Majic bed which lowers from the living room ceiling at the push of a button to make a comfortable king-sized bed.

Both spacious rear bath and bunkhouse models are available in 24- and 28-foot vehicles, as well as a new office version for RVers who work on the road with computers. Inverters and solar panels make the vehicle practical for wilderness camping, and the $75,000-area price tag puts it in the upper entry-level class. Both gas and front diesel Chevrolet chassis are available, as well as a diesel pusher for the 30-foot model.

U - SCI SPORT-CAM INDUSTRIES

9306 Weston Avenue, Schofield, WI 54476
☎ *(715) 355-1257*
This Wisconsin manufacturer produces truck campers under the Sport-Cam label.

SERRO TRAVEL TRAILER CO.

450 Arona Road, Irwin, PA 15642-9512
☎ *(800) 466-6747*
Scotty, with its familiar black Scottish terrier logo, now nearly 40 years old, is the brand name for Serro's type C mini-motorhomes, which come in Hilander and Dakota models. Compact bathrooms and galleys contain the necessary components, and some of these trim vehicles can get up to 18 mpg on the road. The queen-sized cabover bed in many models has been supplanted by an island queen bed in the rear of the new 2900RQ Hilander.

A driver's side air bag (the one that protects the driver, not the leveling of the RV) is an industry first, says Serro, which is also proud of the anti-lock brakes on the

Dodge Ram chassis. Travel trailers under the Scotty label come in super lightweight models 14 to 20 feet, mid-sized lightweights from 19 to 29 feet and fifth-wheels are available in 21-, 24- and 26-foot lengths.

SELLERS MOTOR CORP.

601 North Old State Road 15, PO Box 398, Milford, IN 46542
☎ *(219) 658-3020*
Sellers makes type A motorhomes under the Land Cruiser Lx and Wakeechee labels, including a unique gas pusher (rear-mounted gas engine) with economy torque. The company also has a couple of innovative design features for a motorhome; a rear kitchen model with great livability in a 25-foot model with a sofa that makes into a bed, and a 34-foot rear lounge model with a queen-sized sofa bed that opens up at bedtime, leaving plenty of walk-around room at other times. Very traditional interior styling, solid oak cabinets and some L-shaped kitchens and sofas are also available.

SHADOW CRUISER, INC.

13861 County Road 4, Bristol, IN 46507
☎ *(219) 825-1000*
Shadow Cruiser turns out sleek and practical hardside and fold-down truck campers with a lot of furniture and storage in a small, well-planned area. Their nine-and-one-half-foot hardside, for instance, packs in a cabover bed, double sink, dinette with sofa, three-burner stove with oven, bath with shower and generous storage for under $10,000.

A nine-foot folding unit has most of the same amenities except for the shower. When closed, this unit is only five feet four inches high, as easy to fit into a garage or carport as to tow down the highway. Their trim travel trailers and fifth-wheels are also aerodynamically sound, with silhouette trailers at 13 feet nine inches and 17 feet nine inches, and fifth-wheels from 21 to 29 feet.

Interior, Shasta fifth-wheel 300 FL travel trailer

SHASTA INDUSTRIES

14489 US 30, PO Box 631, Middlebury, IN 46540
☎ *(219) 825-8555*
A division of Coachmen Industries, Shasta, which started business back in 1941 building mobile military housing, is a familiar name to longtime RVers. Their new Travelmaster label widebody mini-motorhome made its debut in Louisville with an option of cabover bed or entertainment center with slider bunk, along with tub/

shower combinations, split baths and island queen beds. Shasta label mini-motor-homes provide a variety of options within six standard and widebody configurations, and Shasta fifth-wheels offer stand-up front-kitchen models with slideout living rooms and wrap-around couches, split baths and rear bedrooms in the $25,000 range.

U - SIERRA MOTOR CORPORATION

4341 Pine Creek Road, Elkhart, IN 46516
☎ *(219) 293-6026*
Sierra label type B van campers are produced by this Indiana company.

SKAMPER CORPORATION

State Road 15 N, PO Box 338, Bristol, IN 46507
☎ *(800) 348-7563*
Folding camping trailers, truck campers, fifth-wheels and travel trailers are all produced under the Skamper label. The company's new Prime entry-level folding camping trailer was introduced at the Louisville show with vinyl tent fabric, indoor/outdoor LP stove and unique single-crank raising system. Two equipment packages plus various options are available with the Prime, with prices starting under $4000.

Interior, Nomad fifth-wheel travel trailer by Skyline with slideout

SKYLINE CORPORATION

2520 By-Pass Road, PO Box 743, Elkhart, IN 46515
☎ *(800) 348-7469*
Skyline manufactures fifth-wheel and travel trailers under the Aljo, Layton, Nomad, Skyline and Mountain View labels. We especially like the Nomad bunkhouse models for families with kids or teens because it has a small dinette for games in the room with the bunk beds, plus a split bath, big closet, slideout living room and island double bed for the parents. The unit is around $22,000.

Other Nomads, designated compact trailers, range from 16 to 23 feet, cost from $8000 to $14,000 and can be pulled behind a Ford Explorer.

Aljo Limited compact travel trailers start as small as 16 feet and go up to 23 feet; a 22-foot Limited with front bedroom, sofa, dinette, kitchen and bath goes for around $13,000.

Deluxe travel trailers and fifth-wheels under the Layton and Aljo Deluxe labels have homelike interiors in oak or chestnut finishes, easy-clean vinyl kitchen floors and wall coverings and generous storage space.

Mountain View fifth-wheels with their extra-large water and holding tanks are good for full timers. The company's Weekender all-weather truck camper has heated and insulated holding tanks and a cabover queen bed with clothes hampers, wardrobe closets and TV shelf all incorporated into the area, which provides room to sit up without bumping your head. The 11-foot ten-inch rig also has a big dinette, galley and bath for around $18,000.

SPORTSMOBILE

425 North Minnewawa, Clovis, CA 93611
☎ *(209) 322-1562*
Sportsmobile's RB 30 type B van camper has an optional penthouse bed in its pop-up model that sleeps two more people upstairs in addition to those in the main body. It offers an optional shower and Porta Potti. Their 4 x 4 cruisers can be built on a Ford, Dodge, Chevy or GMC van and drop-shipped to a 4 x 4 converter, then trucked to Sportsmobile for the interior conversion. Total work time is 90 to 120 days from the order filing. Some 40 interior plans are available, or you can design your own.

STARCRAFT RV, INC.

536 Michigan Street, PO Box 458, Topeka, IN 46571
☎ *(800) 945-4787*
This company, a division of Jayco, makes folding camping trailers in both standard and widebody deluxe models. The Starmaster XL 1224 is a top-of-the-line vehicle with built-in toilet and shower, portable cooktop that cooks inside or out, refrigerator, sink and dinette. It sleeps up to 8 and lists at around $8800.

Starcraft's Leisure Star 280 fifth-wheel is a good family entry-level model with front bed and rear bunkhouse and bath, while Luma Star travel trailers incorporate slide-outs, optional Route 66 upholstery on the dinette and other popular features.

SUNLINE COACH COMPANY

245 South Muddy Creek Road, Denver, PA 17517-9773
☎ *(717) 336-2858*
Sunline fifth-wheel, travel trailers and folding camping trailers fit into the entry level and affordable bracket, with many compact but livable model options. Some two-door travel trailers, rear corner bed and bath travel trailers and fifth-wheel slideouts are available, all with very traditional interiors.

SUN-LITE, INC.

PO Box 517, Bristol, IN 46507
☎ *(800) 327-7684*
Sun-Lite's Hideaway and Sun-Lite label is seen on folding camping trailers, truck campers and travel trailers. The Eclipse travel trailer is lightweight but tough, tele-scoping into a six-foot eight-inch vehicle that can be towed by minivans and some smaller cars. It's a combination hardside and folding camping trailer with a screened Sun-Porch created by Sun-Lite added to the rear as a patio. Bunks, a dinette, TV set, full galley, shower and toilet make this lightweight entry very livable.

SUNNYBROOK RV, INC.

11756 County Road 14, Middlebury, IN 46540
☎ *(219) 825-5250*
Fifth-wheel and travel trailers from SunnyBrook have a light aluminum structure and good craftsmanship, with a choice of blue, teal or sandstone interiors, well-designed kitchens and some bunkhouse models. Aimed at fastidious older RVers, SunnyBrook's vehicles feature solid oak cabinetry, one-piece molded lavatory tops with extra-large sinks that are easy to keep clean, and traditional furnishings and styling. Built-in storage drawers under rear island queen beds, etched glass in overhead cabinets and magazine and spice racks are among the added details.

TETON HOMES

PO Box 2349, Mills, WY 82644; 3283 North 9 Mile Road, Casper, WY 82604
☎ *(307) 235-1525*
Top-of-the-line fifth-wheels made by Wyoming's Teton Homes and Summit
Homes top the wish list for many full timers because of their luxurious interiors and
great storage space. A Best Buy commendation from *Consumers Digest* in 1994 in
the premium price category went to Teton's $85,000 Denver III 40-foot wide-
body, available in the Royal, Grand or Prestige series.

These fifth-wheels are ideal for full timers or snowbirds who like to set up and stay
for a while in one location because they offer just about anything you can think of
in the line of comfort—slideouts that open the living room into a 15-foot-wide area
big enough for entertaining, water purifiers, shower/tub combinations, built-in TV
and entertainment centers, a secretary's desk, huge wardrobes and washer-dryer
connections.

Royal and Grand are 102 inches wide, while Prestige models are 96 inches. A dazzling array of floor plans and options lets you virtually design the unit yourself, a
boon for full-timers. Optional Arctic Pacs and storm windows make them a possibility for reverse snowbirds as well.

THOR INDUSTRIES

419 West Pike Street, Jackson Center, OH 45334
☎ *(513) 596-6849*
Well-known labels like Airstream, Dutchmen and Four Winds are all subsidiaries of
Thor, which produces fifth-wheels, travel trailers, type A and C motorhomes and
type B van campers under 18 or so different models and brand names. The company
is the second largest manufacturer of RVs in North America.

Residency by Thor is a big handsome series of type A motorhomes in the $75,000
and up range, with picture windows, breakfast bar with stools in some models, nice
kitchens and bath dressing tables, and, in one popular model in Louisville we suspect was created just for the show, a "fireplace" complete with pine mantel decorated for Christmas with Mr. and Mrs. Santa Claus in residence.

A Dutchmen label fifth-wheel caught our eye in Louisville because it had an extra
half-bath to complement its rear bunkhouse as well as the usual full bath adjacent to
the forward bedroom, a real boon for a big family. Dutchmen type A motorhomes
are well-planned with many fitted storage details.

Four Winds XL type A motorhomes fall into the $70,000 average range. Lower
mid-range Four Winds type C mini-motorhomes come in standard and widebody
models, with rear kitchens or bedrooms with island queen beds.

Thor also produces entry-level Columbus and Pinnacle type A motorhomes, Cita-
tion label fifth-wheels with slideouts, Electra travel trailers and fifth-wheels, Chateau travel trailers, fifth-wheels and Chateau Sport type C mini-motorhomes.

TIFFIN MOTOR HOMES, INC.

Golden Road, PO Box 596, Red Bay, AL 35582
☎ *(205) 356-8661*
This Alabama company turns out upscale motorhomes under the Allegro, Allegro
Bay and Allegro Bus labels. The Tiffin Allegro Bay type C mini-motorhome was
termed a Best Buy by *Consumers Digest* in 1994, cited for its choice of gas or diesel
engine on a Ford chassis, steel frame construction and rubber roof.

The Allegro Bus 102-inch widebody diesel pusher offers an extra-long kitchen work
counter, gold gooseneck faucets, slideout sofa and dining area, side-by-side refrigerator and icemaker, and, in a model we saw in Louisville, a handsome, white silk
taffeta headboard for the island queen-sized bed. The list price is around $185,000.

Allegro Bay's gas model on a Ford or Chevrolet chassis ranges from 30 to 37 feet with options of slideouts, split or side bath, Corian-type kitchen counter and self-sink and dinette or fixed dining table with freestanding chairs. The Allegro wide-body retails at $112,000 in the 34-foot length, with L-shaped kitchen and sofa, coffee table that converts to dining and a large TV at floor level in the cockpit.

One of Tiffin's most popular options is a barbecue grill mounted on slides in an undercoach storage area that lets you cook outdoors anywhere anytime.

TRAILMANOR, INC.

PO Box 130, Lake City, TN 37769

☎ *(615) 426-7426; area code changes to (423) September 1995.*

Telescoping travel trailers that fold down for easy towing and storage are the specialty of this Tennessee company, which claims up to 16 mpg on a 30-foot Trail-Manor towed with a Chevy Astrovan. The vehicle comes in seven models with lengths from 25 to 33 feet when set up. For towing, the RV lowers to only five feet high and telescopes so that the length is reduced as much as one-third. Setup takes only two minutes, and it looks as stylish as other travel trailers with a hardwall bathroom with tub/shower combination, an optional slideout living room, and permanent beds at one or both ends. Prices range from $13,000 to $26,000.

TRAIL WAGONS, INC.

1100 East Lincoln Avenue, PO Box 2589, Yakima, WA 98907

☎ *(800) 552-8886*

Under its Chinook label, the company produces van campers and truck campers. The Chinook Concourse, built on a Ford chassis, has a dinette, sofa, kitchen with stove, refrigerator/freezer, stainless steel sink and bathroom with shower and toilet, for a list price of around $53,000.

The Chinook Premier SE is a sturdy, maneuverable vehicle built on a Ford chassis that has everything already in place; a seating/sleeping area, bath with toilet and shower, and kitchen, ideal for two people. It can park on a city street with ease. Four different models offer a choice of lounge area with sofa and two chairs, twin beds, sofa and dinette or lounge and double bed. The vehicle lists at around $49,000.

TRAVEL LINE ENTERPRISES, INC.

25876 Miner Road, Elkhart, IN 46514

☎ *(219) 264-3127*

Indiana-based Travel Line produces fifth-wheel and travel trailers under about a dozen different labels, including Astro Star, Celebrity, Country Charm, Elite, Impala, International, Kountry Comfort, Royal Stewart, Spartan, Sun Aire and Whispering Pine.

TRAVEL SUPREME, INC.

66149 State Road 19, PO Box 610, Wakarusa, IN 46573

☎ *(219) 862-4484*

Fifth-wheel and travel trailers under the Travel Supreme label are aimed particularly at the full-timer market, with a combination of practical but attractive furnishings in several colors and wood finishes, including bleached oak, golden oak and walnut. Design pluses include slideouts, rich fabric tones, built-in cutting boards, Corian-type counters and sink plugs, hutch and entertainment centers, dressing tables and ceiling fans. The price range goes up to the $70,000 area for a 40-foot fifth-wheel with contemporary design, triple slideout, freestanding dinette, pullout kitchen faucet hose, dishwasher and four-burner stove.

Interior, Travel Supreme fifth-wheel travel trailer

TRIPLE E CANADA LTD.

PO Box 1230, Winkler, Manitoba, Canada R6W 4C4
☎ *(204) 325-4361*
This Canadian company produces stylish and well-made type A and C motorhomes and fifth-wheel trailers. Top of their type-A motorhome line is the Empress, available in three floor plans with gas engine or diesel pusher. The basement model has an L-shaped kitchen and freestanding dining table, wood floor in the kitchen and bath, island bed with bedroom TV set, big built-in wardrobe and a unique swing-out pantry with storage in both the door and the pantry proper. The craftsmanship throughout is lovely.

Their mid-range Commander, which comes in five floor plans, is also a basement model with an optional driver-side door and a handy cutlery drawer built in under the dinette table.

The entry-level Embassy, which caught our eye with a big hinged desk on the co-pilot's seat for maps and papers, has a low-profile but generous storage space. Four different sizes and floor plans are offered. Triple E's Regency type C mini-motorhome has a full-sized slideout pantry, island queen bed, a full-through storage compartment underneath big enough for skis, along with an optional winterization package. The Emerald fifth-wheel offers three models with full slideouts, three without, in lengths from 26 to 31 feet.

U - TURTLE TOP, DIVISION OF INDEPENDENT PROTECTION CO., INC.

67895 Industrial Drive, New Paris, IN 46553
☎ *(219) 831-5680*
This Indiana company produces type B van campers under the Turtle Top label.

USA MOTOR CORPORATION

1730 West Bike Street, Bremen, IN 46506
☎ *(800) 872-5450*
USA manufactures compact type A motorhomes under the Europa label in two sizes, 23 and 27 feet, and three floor plans. Deluxe and well-constructed, they feature either a side bath and rear bedroom on the 27-foot models or a rear bath and bedroom in the 23-foot model. Interior height is six-feet-three-inches, and the cockpit seats swivel into the living area, which contains a sofa/bed in all three versions. Dining is on a folding, pullup table in front of the sofa, and a third swivel chair is included in the 27- foot models. Prices begin around $57,500.

VANGUARD INDUSTRIES OF MICHIGAN INC.

31450 M-86-West, PO Box 802, Colon, MI 49040
☎ *(616) 432-3271*
Palomino label folding camping trailers and truck campers offer high quality for the price. The TXL-SC folding camping trailer provides a lot of amenities for under $10,000, including toilet and shower, two full beds, dinette that can convert to additional sleeping area, three burner stove that can be used indoors or out and undercounter refrigerator. The company's Fold-A-Wall construction technique on the TXL series gives a hard-sided finish to an easily telescoped camping trailer.

The soft-sided Mustang version includes many of the same features, but with a Porta-Potti and optional shower, while the Stallion and Pinto versions are mid-range. The Colt and Yearling are entry-level models, as the nomenclature implies. A front storage area is easily accessible while on the road, and an optional screen room attaches to the folding unit in minutes for additional living space.

VERI-LITE, INC.

22540 Pine Creek Road, PO Box 339, Elkhart, IN 46516
☎ *(219) 295-8313*
Veri-Lite, known for its truck campers, has also entered the travel trailer arena with a lightweight, compact unit compatible with one-half-ton pickups and rear-wheel-drive minivans. Listed at around $17,000, the model 242 travel trailer offers 13 different floor plans, with master bedroom, sofa/bed, kitchen and fully enclosed bath, along with stereo, heating, air conditioning, microwave and slideout fitted pantry.

The company's sturdy truck camper comes in models from eight and one-half to 12 feet, and features strong 100 percent laminated construction and rubber roof. The 12-foot model, the line's most popular, is built for a three-quarter-ton heavy truck with an eight-foot bed. Model 980 can be put on a one-ton truck. Veri-Lite also devoted considerable legal work to obtain the familiar Real-Lite brand, which had disappeared from the market, and is introducing the Real-Lite laminated year-round unit with block foam insulation, which is particularly popular in Alaska. These units retail in the neighborhood of $16,000.

VOLKSWAGEN/WINNEBAGO

☎ *(800) 444-8947* for the name of your nearest Volkswagen EuroVan dealer
The joint venture from these two notable companies has produced the new Euro Van Camper, which made its long-anticipated debut at the LA RV show. Intended to replace the classic Westphalia VW camping van, the EuroVan is sleek and stylish with a list price of $30,750, a businesslike and understated gray interior, pop-up roof, full galley, rear seat that converts to double bed and removable center row bench seat. There's a tall wardrobe closet, optional furnace and plenty of storage but no built-in toilet or shower. An optional kit with awning and a freestanding tent that hooks up to the van is also packaged to enhance the camper's options. The Eurovan can seat up to six adults and sleep four people, two in the optional bunk in the pop-up roof. The unit is 80 inches high with the pop-up closed, small enough to fit in most garages and parking facilities.

WESTERN RECREATIONAL VEHICLES, INC.

3401 West Washington Avenue, PO Box 9547, Yakima, WA 98903-0547
☎ *(509) 457-4133*
Under the Alpenlite label, Western manufactures fifth-wheel trailers, truck campers and travel trailers. The Alpenlite Odessa nine-foot truck camper with U-shaped dinette, three-burner stove, microwave, compact bath unit and queen-sized cabover bed offers all the basic comforts for around $17,000, but 10- and 11-foot models are also available.

Alpenlite's fifth-wheel provides slideouts in three of its five models, with well-planned galleys and generous storage space. Some built-in entertainment centers, freestanding dining tables and split baths are included, along with bedroom TV jack and shelf.

R.C. WILLETT CO., INC.

3040 Leversee Road, Cedar Falls, IA 50613-9702
☎ *(800) 367-3910*

Northstar and Texson are the labels for this Iowa truck camper manufacturer who offers a variety of low-profile pop-up campers and campers with wrap-around rears for short-bed trucks. Some models contain toilet and shower as standard equipment, and an Arctic Pak for four-season camping can be snapped quickly into place. When closed for travel, the pop-up models are seven feet high or less. A four-corner mechanical or hydraulic jack system makes separating your camper from your truck quick and easy. Special fishing pole bins safely carry rods or other long gear up to seven feet.

WINNEBAGO INDUSTRIES, INC.

605 West Crystal Lake Road, PO Box 152, Forest City, IA 50436
☎ *(515) 582-3535*

Just as Frigidaire became a generic term for refrigerators, Winnebago is often used to refer to all RVs. This 35-year-old Iowa company produces high-quality type A and C motorhomes, as well as the unique Rialta, built on a Volkswagen chassis, that looks and handles like a van camper. The company also worked in cooperation with Volkswagen to produce the EuroVan Camper . The Rialta, at just under 21 feet, is packed with all the usual motorhome features—compact galley, dinette that makes into a bed, molded bathroom unit with train-style pulldown lavatory, and two reclining passenger seats behind the cockpit that make into a bed—and lists at around $45,000.

The Winnebago Warrior is the entry-level type A motorhome (the 25-foot version is around $38,000), good for a couple or, with the optional fold-down bunks, a family with two children.

The popular Minnie Winnie type C mini-motorhome comes in standard or widebody 28- or 29-foot lengths with 36 different floor plan possibilities, while the Mini-300 type C ranges from 21 to 28 feet with 10 floor plan combinations. The 28-foot model, for instance, lists around $46,300.

In type A motorhomes, the Adventurer widebodies in the $60,000s and the Brave in the $50,000s are good upper-entry or lower midlevel buys available in either gas or, when over 30 feet, in diesel pusher models. Winnebago's top-of-the-line type A motorhome is the new 37-foot Luxor widebody diesel pusher, listed at $185,000, with Corian kitchen counters, many custom kitchen fittings, big mirrored wardrobe, sectional sofa with ottoman and spacious bath, and a Thetford telescoping drain for quick, clean waste removal.

Under the upscale Vectra label, priced from $86,000 to $125,000 or more, the company turns out gas or diesel models in 31- to 35-foot lengths with options like leather cockpit seats, patio entertainment center, heated holding tanks with easy-access sewer line connections, dishwasher and bedroom TV with remote control.

XPLORER MOTOR HOME DIVISION, FRANK INDUSTRIES, INC.

3950 Burnsline Road, Brown City, MI 48416
☎ *(810) 346-2771*

Back in 1958, Ray Frank starting building motorhomes in his barn in Michigan, first under the Frank label, then under the Dodge MotorHome brand in 1963 with an all-fiberglass body. Today his low profile motorhomes and van campers under the Xplorer label include a "New Think Small" rear engine, diesel-powered motorhome. The 235X van camper is fully self contained with a seven-foot 10-inch height and 6-foot interior headroom. Rear twin beds, bath, galley, swivel chair, folding table and swivel seats in the driving compartment offer full livability for two people.

APPENDIX:
FIELDING AWARDS

The following awards of distinction are presented for outstanding merit in design, decor and livability for the recreation vehicles in each category. The Fielding Picks select specific models that project particularly outstanding qualities of livability within each category.

FIELDING AWARDS OF DISTINCTION

OUTSTANDING TYPE A MOTORHOMES

Top-of-the-Line...with prices to match
$200,000–$500,000 plus

BEAVER COACHES, INC.	Marquis
BLUE BIRD CORP.	Wanderlodge
COUNTRY COACH, INC.	Affinity
	Magna
**FIELDING PICK	Concept
FORETRAVEL, INC.	Grand Villa Unihome
	Foretravel Unicoach
HOLIDAY RAMBLER CORP.	Navigator
MARATHON COACH	Marathon
MONACO COACH CORP.	The Dynasty
	The Crown Royale
	The Executive
SAFARI	Continental

OUTSTANDING ENTRY MODELS TO THE SUPER DELUXE

Only $150,000 to $200,000

BARTH, INC.	Monarch
**FIELDING PICK BEAVER COACHES, INC.	Patriot

71

OUTSTANDING ENTRY MODELS
TO THE SUPER DELUXE

Beaver Patriot

COACHMEN INDUSTRIES, INC.	**Destiny**
COUNTRY COACH	**Garnet**
	Montage
FLEETWOOD ENTERPRISES, INC.	**American Eagle**
	American Dream
GULF STREAM COACH, INC.	**Tour Master**
	Friendship
HAWKINS MOTOR COACH	**Aerosport**
	Hawk
**FIELDING PICK	
HOLIDAY RAMBLER CORP.	**Imperial**
ODESSA INDUSTRIES, INC.	**Overland**
**FIELDING PICK	
SAFARI	**Ivory**
	Serengeti
TIFFIN MOTORHOMES	**Allegro Bus**
WINNEBAGO	**Luxor**

OUTSTANDING MID-RANGE MOTORHOMES
$75,000 - $150,000

AIRSTREAM	**Airstream**
DAMON CORP.	**Inverness**
FIRAN MOTOR COACH, INC.	**Europremier**
GEORGIE BOY MANUFACTURING	**Encounter**

OUTSTANDING MID-RANGE MOTORHOMES

GULF STREAM COACH, INC.	Scenic Cruiser Sun Voyager
NEWMAR CORP.	Dutch Star Mountain Aire
REXHALL INDUSTRIES, INC.	Rexair Aerbus
SAFARI	Trek Sahara
THOR INDUSTRIES	Residency

FIELDING PICKS IN MID-RANGE MOTORHOMES

COACHMEN INDUSTRIES, INC.	Santara 360 MBS
DAMON CORP.	Intruder 350B
FLEETWOOD ENTERPRISES, INC.	Southwind 36AD
HOLIDAY RAMBLER CORP.	Endeavor LE 33D
ITASCA	Suncruiser 34 RQ pusher
NATIONAL RV	Dolphin 634
NEWMAR CORP.	Kountry Aire 3451
SAFARI	Trek 2830
WINNEBAGO	Vectra 34 RA

OUTSTANDING ENTRY LEVEL MOTORHOMES

Affordable values below $75,000

COACHMEN INDUSTRIES, INC.	Catalina
DAMON CORP.	Frontier Flyer Ultrasport
FLEETWOOD ENTERPRISES, INC.	American Flyer Southwind Bounder Pace Arrow
GEORGIE BOY MANUFACTURING	Pursuit
ODESSA	Lextra
TIFFIN MOTORHOMES	Allegro Bay Allegro

FIELDING PICKS IN ENTRY LEVEL MOTORHOMES

FIRAN MOTOR COACH, INC.	Raven RV 346
COBRA/ROCKWOOD	Regent 325
THOR INDUSTRIES	Four Winds XL 34WL Dutchmen 34 QC

FIELDING PICKS IN ENTRY LEVEL MOTORHOMES

TRIPLE E	**Embassy A29**
WINNEBAGO	**Adventurer WQ**
	Brave 29RC
	Warrior 25RU
ITASCA	**Passage 25RU**
	Sunrise 32 RQ

OUTSTANDING VALUES IN VAN CAMPERS TYPE B

AIRSTREAM, INC.	**Airstream 190**
COACH HOUSE	**Coach House**
COACHMEN INDUSTRIES, INC.	**Saratoga**
	RD Model Van
INTERNATIONAL VEHICLES CORP.	**Falcon**
	Horizon
**FIELDING PICK	
GET-AWAY INTERNATIONAL	**505-4 Get-Away**
LEISURE TRAVEL VANS	**Two-Seater Freedom Widebody**
**FIELDING PICK	
PLEASURE-WAY	**STW**
HOME & PARK MOTORHOMES	**Roadtrek 210 Popular**
TRAIL WAGONS	**Chinook Premier**
XPLORER MOTORHOMES	**Xplorer**

OUTSTANDING TYPE C MINI-MOTORHOMES

BORN FREE MOTORCOACH, INC.	**President**
COBRA INDUSTRIES	**Seven Seas**
COACHMEN INDUSTRIES, INC.	**Santara**
	Catalina
DAMON CORP.	**Hornet**
	Ultrasport
FLEETWOOD ENTERPRISES, INC.	**Jamboree**
	Tioga
GULF STREAM	**Conquest Classic**
HONORBUILT INDUSTRIES, INC.	**ElDorado**
SERRO TRAVEL TRAILER CO.	**Scotty**
	Hilander
SHASTA INDUSTRIES, INC.	**TravelMaster**
TRAIL WAGONS	**Chinook**
TRIPLE E	**Regency**
ITASCA	**Sundancer**
	Spirit

FIELDING PICKS IN MINI-MOTORHOMES

CARRIAGE INC.	Callista 2854
INTERNATIONAL VEHICLES CORP.	Horizon 2801
JAYCO	Designer D2830 Designer D2940WB
LAZY DAZE	Lazy Daze 30'
COBRA/ROCKWOOD	Viper V-28QB
SHASTA INDUSTRIES, INC.	TravelMaster 275 WB
THOR INDUSTRIES	Dutchmen 27/Bmt
WINNEBAGO	Minnie Winnie 29 WU Mini 300 28 RQ

OUTSTANDING MODELS OF FIFTH-WHEELS

ALFA LEISURE	Gold
AUTOMATE	AutoMate
**FIELDING PICK CARRIAGE INC.	Royals International Carriage
COACHMEN INDUSTRIES, INC.	Royal Maxxum
DAMON CORP.	Challenger Escaper
**FIELDING PICK FLEETWOOD ENTERPRISES, INC.	Avion Westport
GULF STREAM COACH, INC.	Kingsley
HOLIDAY RAMBLER CORP.	Imperial
JAYCO	Designer
**FIELDING PICK KING OF THE ROAD	King of the Road
**FIELDING PICK NEWMAR CORP.	Mountain Aire London Aire Kountry Aire

OUTSTANDING MODELS OF FIFTH-WHEELS

Newmar Mountain Aire

NU WA INDUSTRIES, INC.	Hitchhiker
	SnowVilla
	Snowbird
TETON HOMES	Royal
	Grand
	Prestige

FIELDING PICKS AT ENTRY-LEVEL IN FIFTH-WHEELS

CARRIAGE, INC.	Carri & Lite
	Emerald 631 RKS
COUNTRY COMFORT CORP.	Country Comfort 3301 RK
FLEETWOOD ENTERPRISES, INC.	Terry 21 L 5B
KIT MANUFACTURING CO.	Road Ranger 23 CF
LAKE CAPITOL CORP.	Komfort 26 F
NU WA INDUSTRIES, INC.	Discovery 29 1/2 RK
SKYLINE	Layton 2975
TRIPLE E	Emerald
WESTERN RV, INC.	Alpenlite

OUTSTANDING VALUES IN TRAVEL TRAILERS

**FIELDING PICK	
ABI LEISURE	Award
**FIELDING PICK	
AIRSTREAM, INC.	Airstream Excella
	Airstream Classic

OUTSTANDING VALUES IN TRAVEL TRAILERS

**FIELDING PICK BIGFOOT	BigFoot Lite
COBRA INDUSTRIES	Sierra Summit
COACHMEN INDUSTRIES, INC.	Royal
FLEETWOOD ENTERPRISES, INC.	Savanna
FRANKLIN COACH COMPANY	Garden Tub Models
**FIELDING PICK HOLIDAY RAMBLER CORP.	Aluma-lite
HY-LINE ENTERPRISES	Hy-Line
K-Z INCORPORATED	Sportsmen
KIT MANUFACTURING CO.	Companion
**FIELDING PICK LAKE CAPITAL CORP.	Komfort
NEWMAR CORP.	American Star Kountry Star
SUNNYBROOK	SunnyBrook
WESTERN RV	Alpenlite

OUTSTANDING ENTRY LEVEL TRAVEL TRAILERS

COACHMEN INDUSTRIES, INC.	Catalina
**FIELDING PICK FLEETWOOD ENTERPRISES	Prowler Mallard Wilderness

Fleetwood Wilderness

JAYCO, INC.	Eagle

OUTSTANDING ENTRY LEVEL TRAVEL TRAILERS

SERRO TRAVEL TRAILER CO.	Scotty
SKAMPER CORP.	Skamper
**FIELDING PICK SKYLINE CORP.	Aljo
SUNLINE COACH COMPANY	Sunline

OUTSTANDING TELESCOPING TRAVEL TRAILERS & FIFTH-WHEELS

**FIELDING PICK HI-LO TRAILER CO.	Hi-Lo FunLite Tow-Lite

Hi-Lo Trailer Co. Tow-Lite

SUN-LITE, INC.	Eclipse
TRAILMANOR	TrailManor
FUNLITE	Fifth-wheel Model

FIELDING PICKS FOR FULL-TIMERS

COBRA INDUSTRIES	35' fifth-wheel slideout
DAMON CORP.	Escaper 40RL
KING OF THE ROAD	King of the Road F37CLMAX
NEWMAR CORP.	Mountain Aire 40 WRKD
NU WA INDUSTRIES, INC.	SnowVilla SE 33 RK BG
SKYLINE	Nomad 2955 FBS
TETON HOMES	Louisville III 37'
TRAVEL SUPREME	Travel Supreme 40' SBSS

OUTSTANDING MODELS OF TRUCK CAMPERS

BIGFOOT INDUSTRIES	BigFoot
COACHMEN INDUSTRIES	Sport
FIELDING PICK **FLEETWOOD ENTERPRISES, INC.	Caribou

Fleetwood Caribou

FIELDING PICK **LANCE CAMPER MFG.	Lance Squire
SHADOW CRUISER, INC.	Sky Cruiser Highway Cruiser
SKYLINE	Weekender
FIELDING PICK **VERI-LITE, INC.	Veri-Lite
R.C. WILLETT CO, INC.	Texson Northstar
WESTERN RV, INC.	Alpenlite

OUTSTANDING MODELS OF FOLDING CAMPING TRAILERS

COACHMEN INDUSTRIES, INC.	Viking RV
FIELDING PICK **COBRA/ROCKWOOD	Rockwood
FLEETWOOD ENTERPRISES, INC.	Coleman Folding Trailers
FIELDING PICK **JAYCO	Designer
SKAMPER	Skamper
Entry level	Prime

OUTSTANDING MODELS OF FOLDING CAMPING TRAILERS

STARCRAFT RV, INC.	**Starcraft**
VANGUARD INDUSTRIES, INC.	**Palomino**
WESTERN RV, INC.	**Alpenlite**

FIELDING PICKS DESIGNED FOR FAMILIES

Winnebago's Warrior 25RU and Itasca's Passage 25RU have options of overhead bunks in the bedroom which can also be used for storage.

Lextra by Odessa is a compact entry type A motorhome with an optional bunk available in the 24' model.

Fleetwood's type C motorhome Montara Tioga 27V has four bunks in the rear, plus the cabover bed and ample dining area, listing around $48,000.

Fleetwood's Prowler 29S travel trailer has a bunk bed option and is a good entry model listing around $15,000.

Franklin Coach Company has a series of bunkhouse models with three or four bunks in the rear, or bunks and dinette, or bunks and a rear bath. Models range from 30' to 35'.

Safari's Trek models 2820 and 2420 have a bunkhouse area in rear as well as their retractable Electro-Majic king-sized bed.

K-Z Inc. has 25' and 27' fifth-wheel models with a double bunk and bath in the rear in addition to the cabover bed forward.

Starcraft's Leisure Star 280 CK fifth-wheel is priced as a good entry model with a front bed and a rear bunkhouse and bath.

SunnyBrook RV has a bunkhouse model in their light aluminum structure fifth-wheels. Models are well engineered and designed.

Thor Industries' Chateau Sport 25-5LH fifth-wheel is an entry level model with bunk beds and a rear bath in addition to the regular front bed area.

Thor's Dutchmen 35' FW 2B DSL goes it one better with a second half-bath and bunkhouse in rear along with a full bath and bedroom forward of the kitchen/living room area.

Travel Supreme's fifth-wheel 21-1/2' model 215F has a double bed forward, dinette, sofa/bed and kitchen midway, and the bath opposite a pair of bunk beds in the rear. It is a good entry level model for a family.

Damon's Hornet travel trailer bunkhouse model has a slideout, and island double bed, great for teens and larger kids. The split bath has two solid doors.

Hy-Line's travel trailer has bunkhouse models with two or four bunks plus double bed in 30' and 32' lengths. One has the main bed near the bunks, another with it as far away as possible.

KIT's travel trailer 232 T has three cross bunks in the rear and one overhead bunk up front plus a sofa that makes into a queen bed. Good for a large family of kids at an entry list price under $16,000.

Thor's Electra 29' ZB travel trailer has three bunks staggered over each other in a separate room to the rear with an island queen bed, sofa, dinette and kitchen forward.

FIELDING PICKS DESIGNED FOR FAMILIES

Skyline's Nomad travel trailer has a great bunkhouse area in the rear with a small game table/dinette plus split bath, slideout living room, kitchen and island double bed listing under $24,000.

Coachmen's Sport 110 SE truck camper offers a handy fold-out hide-a-bed just right for a child. When not in use, it fits above the dinette area out of the way. This model also includes a full kitchen and bath and queen-sized cabover bed with overhead storage cabinets for a lot of living space in a compact area.

OUTSTANDING AERODYNAMIC DESIGN
A plus for stability and gas mileage

The sleek design of **Airstream's Land Yacht motorhomes**, Classic travel trailers and Pinnacle motorhomes from Thor Industries adds mileage to every gallon of fuel.

National RV's Tropi-Cal, an entry level motorhome with a low profile, has holding tanks and appliances between wheels for better weight distribution, offering increased gas mileage.

The **Award fifth-wheels and travel trailers** produced by Canada's ABI Leisure have been designed to create an airflow that increases stability on the road with less drag and easier handling.

Shadow Cruiser's fifth-wheel has an interesting aerodynamic profile which aids control and lessens drag. It does, however, sacrifice headroom over the bed area as a result.

Shadow Cruiser produces folding truck campers which lower the traveling profile and reduce drag and sway in addition to their hard side truck campers.

R.C. Willett's Texson truck campers have pop-up variations that lower the closed height to 66 inches, yet are fully equipped. An optional snap-up Arctic Pak is available for cold-weather camping.

SPECIAL MENTION

Firan's Ultrastar for its well insulated, electronically heated systems suited especially for skiers and winter sports travelers.

Sellers Motor Company's Land Cruiser LX is a 34' gas pusher that produces better economy and torque. Another model features an L-shaped kitchen in the rear, unusual in a type A motorhome.

The "Route 66" interior design used in **Itasca's Vectra** and the racing motor speedway theme in **Winnebago's Brave** are a refreshing variation from the floral and velour fabrics so prevalent in motorhomes.

Some of **Safari's Trek** motorhome models (standard on 24' and 28') have a king-sized Electro-Majic bed that lowers hydraulically from the ceiling above the living area, letting a shorter vehicle offer all the living space of a much larger one.

USA's Europa is a compact type A with the maneuverability and flexibility of a van. The 27' model has kitchen, bath, sofa, swivel chair and queen-sized bed. Interiors have a sleek European style design.

The **Rialta van-like motorhome** is a compact 21' with kitchen, mini-bath, dinette that converts to a double bed plus additional seats that convert to beds.

SPECIAL MENTION

"Built for Two" by Born Free is a compact 21' motorhome that fits in your driveway, parks easily and will be acceptable in all national parks. With twin beds, kitchen, and fold-away dining table, it's list priced at $46,661.

Sportsmobile's Cruiser RB-30 van has the usual compact amenities but adds a unique pull-down penthouse bed in its pop-up models to add two additional sleeping berths.

Volkswagen/Winnebago's EuroVan Camper, which replaces the classic Wesphalia VW camping van, is sleek and stylish, with a base list price of $30,750. It has a pop-up roof, galley, rear seat double bed, removable center-row bench seat, but no toilet or shower. The vehicle can seat up to six adults.

Play-Mor's Timber Creek Sport Cargo model has a unique rear-door loading ramp with space inside for a vehicle or other large cargo along with the living quarters of a normal travel trailer or fifth-wheel.

Play-Mor's Wind River 2350 has been specially adapted for the disabled traveler with a motorized loading platform lift and space inside to allow a wheelchair to maneuver easily in the living area and bathroom.

Shadow Cruiser has a 13'9" silhouette travel trailer reminiscent of those pulled behind cars in the 1950's, but it has all the modern styling of the 90's and comes in at a list price under $15,000.

Columbia Northwest has produced an A-Liner pop-up folding camping trailer with three models: a standard with two dinettes that convert to double beds, range and sink; a storage bunk model which offers a dinette/double bed with two bunks, one which can be used as storage area; and a unique hot-tub model that offers a two person hot tub which when covered turns into a bed.

SPECIAL AWARD FOR OUTSTANDING DESIGN

Airstream travel trailers from Thor Industries carry the sleek exterior reminiscent of the past but maintains the same classic elegance and craftsmanship inside with rich polished wood, countless built-in storage details and tasteful decor.

RENTING OR BUYING?

For a first-time RV traveler, renting a unit of the same type you're thinking of buying can be an invaluable help in making up your mind. Just be sure to allow enough time—a week is the minimum, two weeks are better—to get comfortable with the day-to-day logistics of handling it on the road and hooking it up in the campground.

Our own first RV experience was a six-week lease on a 27-foot motorhome because of a book assignment that required us to visit more than 100 remote ski areas all across the United States. If we'd only been renting it for a few days, we'd probably have turned it back in and said RVing was not for us. (See "Life on the Road, First-Timers' Diary".)

When they heard about our plans, well-meaning friends regaled us with their experiences. A West Los Angeles bookstore owner took her family out for a month, but they only used the RV for travel and sleeping. "We never cooked a single meal inside," she said. "It seemed too complicated."

A couple from San Diego had tried a rented motorhome for two days, then, frustrated by slow road speeds, turned it back in and set out in their Mercedes 300 SL instead. But even that's a record compared to a short-tempered D.C. lawyer and his wife, who rented an RV for a weekend and gave it up less than an hour into the trip.

Note that in none of these cases did the user give the vehicle the old college try.

One interesting way to test the livability of an RV for your family, especially with several kids, is by checking into Fort Wilderness Campground Resort at the Walt Disney World Resort in Orlando, which rents lodging in Fleetwood park trailers, similar to travel trailers, in the resort. Although you won't be able to road-test the vehicle, you can determine how well your family fits into an RV. Reserve by calling ☎ *(407) 827-7200* or contacting a travel agent.

INSIDER TIP:

Reserve a rental RV at least a month in advance, three months during peak vacation time. If planning to rent in Alaska, reserve six to 12 months ahead.

WHEN TO RENT RATHER THAN BUY

1. When setting out on your very first RV journey.

2. When considering replacing your current RV for a totally different type.

3. When you and your family can only take a two-week vacation once a year but want to do it in an RV. That way you can test-drive different models every year, and when the time comes to buy, you'll have plenty of experience.

4. When you want to travel several weeks far from home, say a distant part of the U.S., or take a camping trip in Europe. (For more about the latter, see "RVing Abroad.") Popular fly-and-drive packages are available from many rental companies.

5. When you want to drive the Alaska Highway (see "Driving the Alaska Highway") or down Baja (see "Bouncing Down Baja") in one direction only and/or without subjecting your own vehicle to inescapable wear and tear.

INSIDER TIP:

Get a detailed list of what furnishings are included in your rental so you'll know what necessary items you have to supply. It may be easier to bring things from home than spend vacation time searching for them on the road.

WHERE AND HOW TO RENT

A great many rental RVs are booked by European and Australian visitors to the U.S. who want to be able to see our national parks or drive along the coast of California.

The most common unit available for rental is the motorhome , either the larger type A or the type C mini-motorhome , which accounts for 90 percent of all rentals. Prices begin at around $450 a week.

Use of the generator is not usually included in the fee. You would need it only for operating the ceiling air conditioning, microwave oven and TV set in a place without electrical hookups, and the dealer will know how much time you've logged by reading the generator counter, usually located by the on/off switch.

When you find a company that rents travel trailers, you'll find they usually require that you furnish your own tow vehicle, hitch and electrical hookups on the tow vehicle.

Some companies offer a furnishings package with bedding, towels, dishes, cooking pots and utensils for a flat price of around $50 per person.

Be sure you're provided with a full set of instruction booklets and emergency phone numbers in case of a breakdown. Best of all is to have a 24-hour emergency 800 number in case of a problem.

When in doubt, ask a fellow RVer what to do. They're always glad to help but sometimes hesitant to offer for fear of offending. No matter how much you bustle around like you know what you're doing, the veterans in the campground can spot a goof-up a mile away.

Some RV campgrounds offer on-site rentals for people who want to confine their camping to that area while perhaps checking out the livability of a unit.

Several helpful publications that list rental companies all over the U.S. and Canada are available from Recreation Vehicle Rental Association (RVRA) at ☎ *(800) 336-0355*. *Who's Who in RV Rentals* is a 32-page annual directory that lists companies with addresses, phone numbers and prices. The 1994-95 edition, for example, carries one European company, nine Canadian companies and 269 U.S. companies listed by city and state or province. Accompanying the $7.50 publication is a companion booklet, *Rental Ventures*, with additional helpful information. Write to them at *RVRA, 3930 University Drive, Fairfax, VA 22030-2525*.

Your local yellow pages should also carry a listing for rentals under "Recreation Vehicle - Rentals."

Cruise America, the largest rental company, with more than 150 outlets, has added more budget items such as camping vans, fully equipped travel trailers and fold-out truck campers with compact pickups to tow them, to answer the requests from European campers in America, who are responsible for one-half to two-thirds of the company's rentals.

Carl's Acres of Trailers in Ontario, CA, claims to have the largest trailer rental department in the U.S., offering folding camping trailers from $250 a week and travel trailers from $400 a week. No rentals are made to anyone under 25 years of age. Renters supply tow vehicle, hitch and electrical connections. A cleaning deposit is required and forfeited if the vehicle is not returned clean; the company has its own dump stations for emptying holding tanks.

Many rental companies offer free airport pickup and return, so long as you notify them ahead of time of flight number and estimated arrival time.

Before setting out, be sure the dealer demonstrates all the components and systems of your unit, taking careful notes, and, just as with rental cars, check for dents and damage from prior use before leaving the lot.

Finally, if you fall in love with your rental vehicle (as we did ours) you may be able to negotiate a purchase price that would subtract your rental fee from the total. If the vehicle is a couple of years old, the price should be even lower, since most dealers get rid of vehicles after two or three years.

One source for low-priced used RVs is Cruise America's RV Depot lots which sell previously rented units at discounted prices, along with a 12-month, 12,000-mile warranty and free emergency road assistance for a year. Call ☎ *(800) 327-7799* and ask for national fleet sales.

INSIDER TIP:

Normally, insurance on a rental RV is not covered on your personal automobile insurance, so ask your insurance agent for a binder that extends your coverage to the RV for the full rental period. Many dealers require the binder before renting you a vehicle.

FIVE MONEY-SAVING RENTAL TIPS

1. Check prices with several companies before making a decision, then establish exactly what the lowest-priced rental will include, such as free miles, amenities like dishes and linens and breakdown service.

2. Try to plan your trip for shoulder season or off-season, which may vary seasonally, depending on the rental area.

3. Check in advance to see if your own automobile insurance agent will cover your rental insurance; he can usually do it more cheaply than the rental company. (See "Inside Tip - Insurance.")

4. Try to plan a loop trip from the area where the rental unit is based to avoid drop-off charges. On long, major journeys such as Alaska or Baja California, you may wish to pay the drop-off charge and fly back rather than repeat the arduous drive back to the beginning.

5. The more units a rental company has, the wider your range of choices, but if you're flexible about what sort of rig you rent, you may be able to negotiate a better price if the selection is limited.

INSIDER TIP:

Read your instruction sheets and checklists through at least once before setting out, then daily before hooking up and unhooking until you know the whole routine. Otherwise, you may—as we did that first time—drive miles out of your way to an RV dealer to find out why your generator doesn't work, only to learn it never works when your gas level drops below one-quarter of a tank.

TEN BIG RENTAL COMPANIES

1. Cruise America—☎ *(800) 327-7799* with 4000 units nationwide

2. Go Vacations—☎ *(800) 487-4652*, with 12 locations

3. El Monte RV Center, ☎ *(800) 367-2120* in Orlando, FL; ☎ *(800) 367-2201* in Santa Ana, CA, with 950 units

4. Carl's Acres of Trailers—☎ *(909) 983- 2567* in Ontario, CA

5. Moturis Inc.—☎ *(800) 292-7655*, in Hawthorne, CA, near LAX w/300 units; also in San Francisco w/400 units

6. Road Bear Intl.—☎ *(818) 865-2925* with 100 units in Agoura Hills, CA

7. Nolan's RV Center—☎ *(800) 232-8989*, with 120 units in Denver, CO

8. Western Motor Coach—☎ *(800) 800-1181*, 95 units in Lynnwood, WA

9. Canadian RV Rentals—☎ *(604) 530-3645*, 120 units in Vancouver, BC

10. Global motorhome Travel—☎ *(800) 468-3876*, motorhome rentals in Europe

INSIDER TIP

Just as in car rentals, be sure to establish how many free miles you get and what the cost per mile is beyond that daily or weekly limit.

INSIDER TIP:

You'll save money by renting off-season rather than in peak season. We found when checking rental prices that different companies had different "peak season" dates.

WHERE TO SHOP FOR RVS

RV SHOWS

Dozens of national and regional RV shows are held annually, most during the winter months. These make especially safe hunting grounds for three types of people: looky-loos who have no idea what they want but are not about to succumb to the first smooth-talking salesman they encounter; well-researched potential buyers who know exactly what they want and are ready to make a deal; and RV owners who want to see the latest technical and design innovations but are basically happy with their existing rig.

The action gets hot and heavy during the last day or two of a show when it's possible to stumble across an offer you can't refuse. On the other hand, if you're susceptible to super-salesmen, tread carefully or you may be driving a brand-new rig home from the show.

Besides acres of new RVs to explore, a show usually presents seminars on how to "full-time" or where to travel, an oriental bazaar of esoteric gadgets from no-snore pillows to salad-makers (as well as a lot of helpful and practical items), and entertainment from Dixieland or country music musicians to a walk-through virtual reality module.

For a free listing of RV shows, contact the Recreational Vehicle Industry Association (RVIA), *Dept. SL, PO Box 2999, Reston, VA 22090*, or watch your local newspapers for a show in your area.

RV DEALERS

Check the yellow pages for local RV dealers and spend an afternoon walking around the lot looking at various types of vehicles and mentally moving into them. The dealer can usually provide you with a brochure to take home and study, which will detail all the features, along with floor plans and specifics about the vehicle's features.

Don't worry about taking up time if you're not ready to buy yet. Sooner or later you will be, and dealers are accustomed to the allure of a new and unfamiliar RV both to "wannabe" and veteran owners.

Expect the best buys in December and January, when dealers want to get the previous year's still-new models off the lot to make room for the new year's models.

INSIDER TIP:

RVs that carry the RVIA Seal clearly affixed to the vehicle in the vicinity of the doorway are certified by the manufacturer to comply with 500 safety specifications for fire and safety, plumbing and electrical systems and LP gas systems established under the American National Standards Institute. The Recreation Vehicle Industry Association, representing builders of more than 95 percent of all RVs sold in the U.S., makes periodic unannounced plant inspections to assure members maintain an acceptable level of compliance.

WHERE NOT TO SHOP FOR AN RV

Avoid parking lot and campground "distress" sellers who give you a spiel about bad luck and desperate need for cash. A nationwide group of con artists who call themselves Travelers make a big profit selling cheaply made travel trailers, which also serve as living quarters and office headquarters for numerous other scams.

Be extremely careful buying from any private party unless you know a great deal about the RV you're considering and can make a clear-eyed evaluation of it before signing the deal. If it looks beat up and shows wear and tear inside and out, walk away. Chances are, if the owner has treated the superficial areas badly, the critical working systems you can't see are also flawed. Remember, with motorized vehicles, you're buying both a used car and a used house.

FIVE PRECAUTIONS BEFORE BUYING A USED RV

1.   Take a long test drive watching gauges closely, and check out all systems personally from toilet flush to water pump and heater. Look particularly for dry rot in any areas with wood, or water stains that may be signs of leaks.

2.   Ask the owner very direct and specific questions about all systems in the vehicle.

3.   Ask a knowledgable friend, or better still, hire an RV mechanic to a look at the vehicle.

4.   Check out the current value in a Kelley or NADA blue book; your bank loan officer should have current copies.

5.   Check comparable models and prices at a dealer's lot to have a price comparison.

INSIDER TIP:

Interest on a loan to purchase an RV is deductible as second home mortgage interest as long as the unit contains basic sleeping, cooking and toilet accommodations.

INSIDER TIP:

Renting out your own RV to others to help defray costs of ownership may appeal to you. If you decide to try it, check the costs of upgrading your insurance policy to cover any liability, and see if a local dealer might add it to his rental fleet for a share of the profits.

CAMPGROUNDS AND RV PARKS: WHERE TO SLEEP

Mini-motorhome in a tree-shaded campsite near Anacortes, WA

The answer to the question of where to sleep in your RV is, "Almost anywhere." There are more than 16,000 campgrounds in the United States that can accommodate RVs, some offering hookups, others for self-contained or "dry" camping.

A few are free, many more are lavish resorts that may cost $25 a night and up for full hookups, cable TV, phone service, spas, swimming pools, tennis courts, playgrounds and miniature or par-three golf courses.

If you prefer ranger hikes and scenery to horseshoe pits and pancake breakfasts, head for one of the 29,000 campsites in our national parks and monuments. The national forest service has 4000 developed campgrounds in 155 forests, and the Bureau of Land Management oversees 270 million acres of scenic outdoor sites, many with free camping.

For watery wonderlands, check out the Corps of Engineers projects, with 53,000 campsites near oceans, rivers and lakes, with fishing, boating, swimming and water-skiing on tap.

Bird-watchers can overnight in many of the nation's wildlife refuges to get the drop on feathery friends, and game watchers can take advantage of the optimum spotting times of dawn and dusk. (See "FYI: Campground Guides" for how to get a full listing of wildlife refuge camping, as well as guides for all the other campgrounds.)

INSIDER TIP:

A good way to begin is to get a free booklet about camping by calling toll-free ☎ *1-800-47-SUNNY.*

CAMPGROUND GLOSSARY

Hookups—umbilical cords that connect your RV with electrical power, water and sewer service

Full hookups—a site furnished with all three connections

Partial hookup—a site furnished with one or two of the three connections

Dump station—also called sanitary dump, disposal station, and so on; where an RV dumps the gray water and black water from its holding tanks

Gray water—waste water from the sinks and shower

Black water—waste water from the toilet

Pullthrough—a campsite that allows the driver to pull into the site to park, then pull out the other side when leaving, without ever having to back up, a boon for beginners

Boondock—to camp without electrical or other hookups

Propane or LPG—liquefied petroleum gas used for heating, cooking and refrigeration in RVs

Three-way refrigerator—an RV refrigerator/freezer than can operate on LP gas, electrical hookup or gas generator

Dual electrical system—an RV that can run its lights and other electrical systems on 12-volt battery power, 110 AC electrical hookup or gas generator

INSIDER TIP:

Many older campgrounds, especially in state parks, may have 15- or 20-amp electrical hookups, for which modern RVs with a three-prong plug will need an adaptor. When we first encountered this, we happened to be at a Texas state park which loaned out adaptors, but we soon acquired one of our own. You can use the lower amperage so long as you remember not to run the air-conditioner, microwave and TV set at the same time. Otherwise, you'll blow a fuse.

CAMPSITES: THE GOOD, THE BAD AND THE UGLY

As backpackers, we would set up camp at any clearing that didn't have too many rocks where we were going to spread out the ground cloth and sleeping bags.

As tent campers, we looked for scenery, shelter and seclusion, but not too far away from the water source and facilities.

Now, as RV campers, we have a long list of Ls:

Location

We want to be away from the highway and campground entrance and not too near the swimming pool, bath facilities, garbage dumpster or playground.

Large

It must be big enough to back our 27-foot motorhome in and park it, and still have space for chairs, table and charcoal grill.

Level

There's a lot of running back and forth to check spirit levels inside and outside the vehicle; sometimes we have to wedge wooden blocks under the tires until that pesky little bubble hits the center.

(What happens if it's not level? Something dire and expensive befalls the refrigerator.)

Length

The umbilical cords from the vehicle to the electric, water and sewer connections, where applicable, must reach comfortably.

Look out

for any low-hanging branches or wires that could damage the roof air-conditioner or TV antenna; for a potentially noisy neighbor; for wet or marshy ground that could mire us down if it should rain all night.

A rustic private campground on Michigan's Upper Peninsula

A campsite may or may not contain a picnic table, grill or fire ring. What is critical for tent campers becomes an added luxury for an RVer, who already has a table, chairs and cookstove inside the vehicle. While we all want to overnight in the very best campgrounds, we find that campground ratings, for example those in the popular *Trailer Life Campground/RV Park & Services Directory*, do not always seem to relate to us. The guide, issued annually, rates campgrounds very specifically according to a detailed form that scores in three areas, facilities, cleanliness (particularly of toilets and showers) and visual or environmental appeal.

Since we always use our own toilet and shower facilities, we are not concerned with the campground's, and we rarely if ever take advantage of a TV lounge, swimming pool, Saturday night dance or children's playground. Therefore, for us, a highly rated campground may have less appeal than a remote area in a national forest or state park, or a simpler family-run park in the country.

Occasionally in both private and state park campgrounds you may encounter what we call a "parking lot" design, with rows of paved spaces fairly close together. The up side is that you're usually level and don't have to spend time checking spirit level bubbles and putting ramps under tires. The down side is that your dining room window may be two feet away from your neighbor. The saving grace is that with an RV you can close your curtains or blinds, turn on some soft music and be all alone in the universe.

On the other hand, we are always thrilled to find those enlightened campground owners who have spent extra time and money to create terraced areas with landscaping that gives a sense of space, light and privacy.

While we frequently are at odds with the campground ratings, we find the directories, especially the one from *Trailer Life*, invaluable when traveling, particularly when we're making one-night stands and need to find a place to overnight. Being able to call ahead for reservations is also helpful; you won't have to drive five miles off the route only to find there are no campsites left.

A luxurious private RV park in Bend, OR

Careful reading of an entry can also tell you the site width, important if you have an awning or slideout; if there are pullthroughs; if you can expect any shade trees; if the campground is open year round or only seasonally, and if there's a dump station on the premises.

A list of sources for campground guides is under "FYI" at the end of this chapter.

INSIDER TIP:

A family of four can vacation in a family campground for less than $200 a week, and a snowbird can spend the entire winter in a full-service warm-climate resort for less than $2000, according to the National Association of RV Parks and Campgrounds.

10 WAYS TO SAVE MONEY ON CAMPGROUNDS

1. Never pay for more park than you'll use. Posh playgrounds with swimming pool, spas, tennis courts and miniature golf are usually pricier than simple, clean mom-and-pop campgrounds. The latter are adequate for an overnight stay. If there is a charge per hookup, take the electric and forgo the water and sewer unless you really need them.

2. Remember you can camp without hookups comfortably for several nights as long as you don't insist on using the TV, air-conditioner or microwave. Read a book or listen to a tape for entertainment, and cook on your gas cooktop or outdoors on a grill. You'll still have running water, lights, refrigeration, heat and hot water for dishes and shower.

3. If you're on a tight budget, watch out for campground surcharges such as extra fees for running your air-conditioner or hooking up to cable TV, or "extra person" charges for more than two people when you're traveling with your kids. Some of the campgrounds which accept pets may also levy a fee on Fido's head.

4. Join membership clubs that offer a discount to member campgrounds, such as KOA (Kampgrounds of America) and Good Sam, which usually discount 10 percent. KOA promises the discount whether you pay by cash or credit card; Good Sam usually grants the discount only if you pay cash. In most cases you can join up right at the campground when you register.

5. If one of you is over 62 and applies for a free Golden Age Passport with proof of age at a national park visitor center, your vehicle enters the park, national monument, recreation area or wildlife refuge free, and gets a 50 percent discount on overnight camping areas administered by the federal government.

6. Look for free campgrounds such as those in the southwestern desert administered by the Bureau of Land Management. (For details, see "The California Desert" under "On The Cheap: Cutting Costs on the Road.")

7. County, city and national forest campgrounds range from free to considerably less expensive than most privately-owned campgrounds, although they do not often offer the luxury of hookups. Invest in a current campground guide or request a state tourism office's free campground listings to find them.

INSIDER TIP

Always stop at the tourist information offices when you enter a new state on an interstate. You can pick up everything from maps to campground booklets to individual flyers for private RV parks that may offer a discount for visitors—all of it free.

8. If you arrive late at a campground, ask about staying overnight self-contained in an overflow area at a reduced price. Some owners are amenable, some are not. If they're already full, however, you lose any negotiating power you may have had.

9.   Stay longer than a week and you can negotiate discounts, usually from ten to twenty
     percent or even more, depending on the season and length of stay.

10. If you're interested in staying a long time in one area, consider volunteering as a
     campground host where you can camp free and may pick up a bit of pocket change
     as well in exchange for performing specified duties on the premises. (See "How to
     Become Campground Hosts" in this chapter.)

INSIDER TIP:

*California State Parks have instituted something called Enroute Camping, in
which self-contained RVs may stay overnight, from sunset until nine or 10
the next morning, in the day parking lot for the park's basic camping fee.
These parks are located primarily along the coast and designated with RV
profile signs.*

*A swap meet at Quartzsite, AZ, Bureau of Land Management desert
campgrounds where thousands congregate in winter*

THREE WAYS TO CHECK OUT CAMPING
WITHOUT A TENT OR RV

Check into a Kamping Kabin at a nearby KOA (Kampgrounds of America)
campground. These one- and two-room rustic log cabins with porches and
double beds plus bunk beds can sleep four for $20-$30 a night. It's a good
introduction to camping, especially for families with kids.

You do need to bring your own bedding, lantern and cooking utensils,
however. The fee includes use of the campground's toilet and shower facilities, pool, playground, laundry and store. The Kabins do not have bathrooms, but an outdoor grill and picnic table are provided. Get a full list of
locations from KOA (see "FYI").

Call around to the campgrounds in your area or the area you'd like to visit
and ask if they have any rental RV units available. Sometimes a popular area
may offer RVs already in place and hooked up and available for rent by the
night. To get campground guides, see "FYI".

Book the family into Fort Wilderness at Walt Disney World in Orlando, where lodging is available in Fleetwood park trailers with full kitchens and baths, similar to travel trailers but set in place for a season or longer. The cost with air conditioning, swimming pool privileges, cable color TV, cookware and housekeeping services is around $200 a night for a party of six with two adults. It's a good idea to reserve well ahead ☎ *(407) 827-7200.*

INSIDER TIP:

RV campers drive an average of 5900 miles a year, spend 44 nights on the road and spend an average of $102 a day on a 13-day vacation.

CAMPING WITH KIDS

Children make great campers.

Veteran RV writers Don and Pam Wright in their book *Camping with Kids* (Cottage Publications, 1992, $9.99; available from RVIA Publications Division, *PO Box 2999, Reston, VA 22090-0999*) suggest involving children in the preliminary planning, assigning regular duties at the campsite, assigning seats in the car or RV en route to the campsite, and curfew and campfire times, taking into consideration any special evening events from ranger talks to movies and dances at the campground. Each child (the Wrights have four) was also assigned a last-minute duty at home before leaving, whether locking doors and windows or removing perishable food from the refrigerator.

Even infants can happily go camping. The Wrights recommend taking along a backpack for a toddler or a chest pack for an infant for hikes, as well as a folding stroller and playpen, mosquito netting and baby guardrail for the bed to use in camp. A baby seat that clamps to a picnic table will also allow the child to participate with the rest of the family at meals or game time.

Sunscreen to protect a baby's delicate skin is essential, along with a gentle insect repellent like Avon's Skin So Soft skin lotion. (That works for adults as well; we've used it successfully in buggy places like the jungles of Honduras.)

INSIDER TIP:

While we know plenty of veteran RVers who think nothing of parking free overnight at a highway rest stop, a truck stop or supermarket parking lot, we would never consider it ourselves. Campground fees are a modest enough investment in security and peace of mind. Besides, the poor truckers, unlike RVers, have few other options when they need to take a rest. Why take up their space?

AIN'T MISBEHAVIN': CAMPGROUND ETIQUETTE

1. Anything marking a campsite, from a jug of water on a picnic table to a folding chair set out in the parking space, means that site is occupied and the campers are temporarily away in their car or RV. You may not set it aside and move into the site.

2. Teach your kids never to take a shortcut across an occupied campsite, but to use the road or established pathways to get where they're going.

3. Never let your dog roam free in a campground. It should be walked on a leash and exercised in a designated pet area.

4.   Avoid using your generator whenever possible, even within designated generator-use hours, to keep from disturbing other campers with the noise and fumes. If using electrical appliances such as microwaves and TV sets is that important, go camping in a private campground with hookups.

5.   Avoid loud and prolonged engine revving in the early morning and late evening hours.

6.   Don't play radios, TVs or boomboxes loudly at any time in a campground. Many of your fellow campers are there to enjoy the peace and quiet.

7.   Never ever dump waste water from holding tanks, even gray water, on the ground. While some old-timers claim it's good for the grass, it can also contain virulent salmonella bacteria if raw chicken has been rinsed in the sink, or bits of fecal matter from showers and diapers. This matter can be transferred to anyone touching or stepping on contaminated ground. Gray water, like black water, belongs only in a dump station.

8.   Do not cut trees for firewood. Most campgrounds sell firewood at special stands or the camp store. Even picking up or chopping dead wood is forbidden in many parks.

9.   Never leave aluminum foil, aluminum or glass cans or bottles or filter-tipped cigarette butts in a campground fire ring or grill. They do not burn but remain as litter. And never crush out cigarettes on the ground without picking up the butts and putting them in the garbage.

10. Don't leave porch or entry lights on all night in camp; they may shine in someone else's bedroom window.

WINTER CAMPING

Winter camping in Grand Canyon National Park

Some of our best freewheeling adventures have been in winter in snow-covered campgrounds in national parks such as the Grand Canyon and Bryce Canyon, as well as various ski resorts. Skiers who want to make a budget trip to the snow but enjoy some of the best ski mountains will find that many ski areas permit free, or low-cost, self-contained RV parking overnight in their parking lots—Killington and Aspen Highlands, for example—while other resorts such as Breckenridge, Deer Valley and New York's Holiday Valley have RV hookups or year-round RV campgrounds at or near the site. California's Sierra Summit has free RV hookups for skiers.

Many RVers enjoy snowmobiling, sledding, cross-country skiing, skating and ice fishing in winter. Besides being able to stay toasty-warm with a propane heater that does not require a hookup, winter RVers can enjoy hot meals, hot showers and a snug, cozy feeling despite ice and snow all around.

We've found winter a good time to visit and photograph national parks, particularly in the southwest where a light dusting of snow highlights the vivid red canyons and green pines. Another bonus is the wildlife, particularly deer and elk, that come down into lower elevations in winter for better feeding. (See "Southern Utah's National Parks Country.")

10 TIPS FOR COZY WINTER CAMPING

1. Don't connect your water hose to an outdoor faucet overnight unless you want to create a 12-foot Popsicle. Use water from the RV's supply and refill when necessary.

2. Add antifreeze to holding tanks to keep drains from freezing.

3. Don't park under trees where branches heavily weighted with snow and ice could break off and fall on your RV.

4. Watch battery strength; the colder it gets, the faster it will discharge.

5. When using a propane heater, open one window slightly for fresh air; we use the window above the kitchen sink.

6. Leave the bathroom door open at night so the heat from the main living area can circulate inside this normally unheated room.

7. Keep a pair of après-ski boots handy for good traction on even short walks through the snow, especially to a photo opportunity.

8. Carry chains or have snow tires for your tow vehicle or motorized RV.

9. Don't let snow accumulate on the refrigerator roof vent or exhaust ports.

10. Drive with extreme care. Even an experienced driver will find handling a motorhome or pulling a towable trickier in snow and ice. A heavy motorhome can be difficult to stop on an icy surface.

INSIDER TIP:

A toll-free telephone number for campsite reservations in national forests, ☎ (800) 280-2267, is supposed to be in effect through 1995, although the line is usually busy or applicants wait on hold for a long time. Biospherics, the operator, suggests callers attempt to reach them early or late in the day or on Sundays, but never on Saturdays. The line is operative Monday through Friday from 9 a.m. to 9 p.m. (Eastern Standard Time) and Saturdays and Sundays 11 a.m. to 7 p.m.

HOW TO BECOME CAMPGROUND HOSTS

Energetic retirees or full-timers on a budget can camp free and sometimes pick up a little extra income as well by volunteering as campground hosts or work campers. In theory, it's a great idea—living in your RV in a lovely campground with free hookups, maybe even with your pick of sites.

In practice, however, veterans of a season's work seem to either love it or hate it. Some mutter darkly of being treated like migrant labor, while others describe it as a highlight of their lives. A lot depends on how thoroughly you check out the campground and its management ahead of time and how realistic you are about doing hard and sometimes unpleasant chores like cleaning toilets and showers or telling a noisy camper to turn off his generator at curfew.

If campground hosting sounds like something you may want to do, here's how to get started:

Apply well ahead of time. Veterans of the program suggest a year in advance is not too early.

Learn about job openings in RV publications under "help wanted" or from a newsletter called *Workamper News*, published six times a year in Heber Springs, Arkansas, by Greg and Debbie Robus. Subscriptions are $23 for one year, $42 for two. Call ☎ *(800) 446-5627* weekdays between 9 a.m. and 5 p.m., Central Standard Time, for more information or a subscription.

Good Sam Club members can also apply through that organization's Campground Host Program, *Box 6060, Camarillo, CA 93011,* ☎ *(800) 234-3450*. The application form requires your name, Good Sam Club membership number, address, telephone, type and size RV, first, second and third choice of states as a work area, months available for work, and the period of stay, a minimum of 60 days. In addition, they ask if you would consider working the entire season, what RV hookups you require and any special considerations you wish to add.

You could also volunteer in campgrounds by contacting the National Forest Service, U.S. Department of Agriculture, *PO Box 2417, Washington, DC 20013*; the National Parks Service, *18th and C Street NW, Washington, DC 20240*; or the Bureau of Land Management, Public Affairs Office, *1800 C Street NW, Washington, DC 20240*.

You should apply to several campgrounds, using a resume that should include both personal and business references. Some ads ask for a recent photograph, which many applicants think shows possible discrimination because of age, physical appearance or condition. Many campgrounds prefer a couple to a single person, or require a single person to work 30 to 40 hours a week rather than the 15 or 20 a couple would work.

If you get a positive response, ask for references from the campground managers so you can interview people that have worked previously for them. Check privately owned campgrounds with the local Chamber of Commerce or Better Business Bureau.

One cautionary note: Out-of-state workers who volunteer for California campgrounds are required to register their motor vehicles, including RVs, in California since live-in volunteers are considered to be gainfully employed.

INSIDER TIP:

Six percent of all traveling dog owners take their pets with them on vacation, but only one percent of cat owners do, according to the Travel Industry Association of America.

10 OWNER TIPS FOR CAMPING WITH PETS

1. One cat owner suggests keeping the cat's litter box in the shower or tub, encased inside a 30-gallon plastic trash bag. Put the bottom of the box in the trash bag, dump a 10-pound bag of kitty litter inside, and snap on the litter box cover. The same owner carries a folding cat cage so her pets can enjoy the outdoors.

2. Put a throw rug or two on top of the carpeting in a motorhome to protect it from little cat (or dog) feet. These can be taken out and shaken when necessary, and washed and dried in the campground laundry.

3. Owners get into lively debates about whether to keep dogs and cats sheltered in air-line-type kennel crates when the RV is in motion, or to let them lie about on the floor, furniture or dash. The lie-about school suggests the pet could protect itself better from possible injury in an accident if he's free, while the kennel crowd (many of them professional dog handlers) assert just as doggedly that the pet (and the driver) are much safer enclosed en route.

4. Always carry plastic baggies to pick up after your pet, even in camping and hiking areas (or should we say, especially in camping and hiking areas?)

5. Never leave your pet alone in the RV for more than 10 minutes in any weather, and less than that in summer when heat can cause great discomfort or even death.

6. Feed a pet, especially one susceptible to motion sickness, at night only, so it will have digested the food before the next day's drive. Give only water during the day, preferably bottled water, which you have introduced at home several days before leaving.

7. Check in a campground guide (see "FYI" at the end of this chapter for a list of them) to ascertain whether the campground will accept pets. While many do, some assess a surcharge and all require that dogs be kept on a leash. When in doubt, call ahead.

8. Bring familiar bedding and toys for the pet, and spend some time regularly for about a week ahead of setting off on its first trip just sitting with your pet in the RV to help accustom him to it.

9. Bring along your pet's shot records and extra leashes and collars, as well as flea treatment products that will kill not only live fleas but eggs and larvae as well.

10. Good Sam Club members can take advantage of the club's Lost Pet Service. They provide a tag imprinted with a toll-free number to call so your pet can be returned during rather than after the trip.

MEMBERSHIP CAMPGROUNDS

Membership campgrounds and resorts are sort of like time-share condos, meaning that once an RVer is a member, he can stay at any of the areas participating with the group. Joining something of this sort has to be weighed carefully against the initial cost, the amount of time you'll stay in the various resorts (note the locations and your access to them) and the amenities they offer.

For example, we recently checked out two upscale membership RV resorts affiliated with Outdoor Resorts of America in the Palm Springs area (see "The California Desert, Ten Campground Oases", for details), the older of which is owner-operated and mostly owner-occupied. We were quite impressed with the cleanliness and security, as well as the landscaping. A great many expensive motorhomes and fifth-wheels, as well as a few more modest travel trailers and mini-motorhomes, are parked seasonally or permanently on the sites, many of them owned by southern Californians who use them as a weekend home in the desert.

While a few owners make their sites available for overnighters or transient RVers, most seem to keep their vehicles based there. The base lot price in the newer park limited to motorhomes is $36,900 to $51,900 for a 35-by 69-foot site, plus a monthly fee of $180.

There are about 450 membership resorts nationwide for RV travelers who want a range of indoor and outdoor activities. Most sell memberships for a one-time fee, much like a country club, plus an annual or monthly fee. One such company, Thousand Trails/NACO, based in Bellingham, Washington, and owned by U.S. Trails in Dallas, Texas, estimates it has 150,000 members in North America, with about 10,000 using the campground chain year-round as full timers.

Members who use the campgrounds for fewer than 50 nights a year pay no surcharge, said a spokesman for Thousand Trails, while those who use them more than 50 nights a year pay a $2 fee for each additional night. Except during peak travel seasons, RVers can usually find a spot without advance reservations.

In general, the spokesman said, the cost of joining a membership campground has dropped considerably from a peak of $5000–$10,000 a few years ago. Thousand Trails members currently pay $1500 membership with annual fees of $429.

INSIDER TIP:

Thousand Trails/NACO membership campgrounds offer potential members a chance to try out their product with no obligation to buy or attend a sales presentation. A two-night stay in any of the company's 62 campgrounds costs $10. Call them at ☎ (800) 288-7245 for details and reservations, which may be made up to 90 days in advance.

On all membership campgrounds, memberships can be sold after a specified period of time, but it appears to be a buyer's market with a lot of members opting to sell.

Because some membership resorts in the past have been plagued by bankruptcies and undelivered promises, potential buyers should check with the local Better Business Bureau, the state attorney general's office and members of the prospective resort before signing up or making a payment.

Avoid resorts that use high-pressure sales tactics and promise big prizes for buyers who sign up right away. And be wary of resorts that seem reluctant to provide information unless you make a personal visit. If you're interested in buying someone's membership, check the classified ads each month in RV magazines such as *Trailer Life* and *MotorHome*.

INSIDER TIP:

A recurring scam affecting persons advertising campground memberships for sale goes like this: An individual contacts the seller, says he has a buyer, then sends an official-looking contract with buyer name and purchase price by Federal Express. All the eager seller has to do is send back a certified check for $500 or so by return Federal Express. You can guess what happens next—nothing.

FYI: CAMPGROUND GUIDES

Trailer Life Campground/RV Park and Services Directory, covers 12,500 campgrounds in the U.S., Canada and Mexico, $21.95, at bookstores, camping stores, or write *PO Box 6060, Camarillo, CA 93011*

Wheelers RV Resort & Campground Directory, Print Media Services, *1310 Jarvis Avenue, Elk Grove Village, IL 60007*, $12.95

Woodall's Campground Directory, *28167 North Keith Drive, Box 5000, Lake Forest, IL 60045-5000*, $16.95

ARVC, National Association of RV Parks & Campgrounds, *8605 Westwood Center Drive, Suite 201, Vienna, VA 22182*

KOA, 615 campgrounds in the U.S., Canada and Mexico will give you the guide free, or send $3 for annual guide from Kampgrounds of America Executive Offices, *PO Box 30558, Billings, Montana 59114-0558*

Yogi Bear's Jellystone Park Campground Directory, Leisure Systems, Inc., *6201 Kellogg Avenue, Cincinnati, OH 45230*. Free.

National Forest Service, 4000 campgrounds. Write to U.S. Department of Agriculture Forest Service, Public Affairs Office, *PO Box 96090, Washington, DC 20090-6090*. Free.

National Park Camping Guide, 440 campgrounds, $4 to *U.S. Government Printing Office, Supt. of Documents, Washington, DC 20402-9325*. Ask for stock # 024-005-01080-7.

Bureau of Land Management, 270 million acres of public land. Ask for camping information from BLM, Department of Interior-MIB, *1849 C Street NW, Room 5600, Washington, DC 20240*. Free.

U.S. Army Corps of Engineers, 53,000 campsites near oceans, rivers and lakes. For a list of district offices that can supply data, write Department of the Army, U.S.A.C.E., Regional Brochures, IM-MV-N, *3909 Halls Ferry Road, Vicksburg, MS 39180-6199*

National Wildlife Refuges, 488 refuges. For a list of those that permit camping, write for "National Wildlife Refuges—A Visitor's Guide," U.S. Fish and Wildlife Service, Publications Dept., *4401 North Fairfax Drive, Room 130 (WEBB), Arlington, VA 22203*.

GETTING READY TO HIT THE ROAD

The first time we set out in an RV—it was to be a six-week journey—we devoted as much attention to it as the Allies planning the Normandy landing, with about as much success as Napoleon at Waterloo.

These days, we can decide on the spur of the moment to go away for a few days, pick up the RV keys and set out.

It's not that we've gotten more organized or efficient over the years, just that we've managed to squeeze everything we could possible need—and a few impulse buys we didn't—into the motorhome and find a place to store it.

MAKING A LIST, CHECKING IT TWICE...

It's a good idea for beginning RVers to make up some sort of check list to follow when packing for a trip, preparing the vehicle for a trip or when setting up and breaking up camp. Some veterans suggest laminating the list, then checking off the items in grease pencil or erasable felt pen so it can be wiped clean to use again.

If you don't want to write out your own, the *"RV Check List"* from MAR-COX Products, *Box 7815, Moreno Valley, CA 92552, ☎ (909) 242-1248*, covers all the preparation and safety details in a three-ring binder ($11.95) or a paperback with spiral binder ($8.95). Add $2.95 for shipping, deduct $2 by adding your Good Sam membership number.

LEARNING YOUR VITAL STATISTICS

Our lack of technical knowledge was most frightening the first time we encountered a narrow, rickety, one-lane bridge near New Harmony, Indiana, with a small sign noting its weight limit was five tons. But how much did we weigh? We didn't know. Finally, since there was no way to turn around and go back, and the traffic was beginning to build up behind us, we gingerly inched our way across, holding our breaths until we made it.

Later, we studied the brochure that detailed our floor plan and learned that our maximum weight, fully loaded and with passengers, could be just over 12,000 pounds, or six tons.

The moral is, memorize your height, weight and width before getting behind the wheel.

ROAD GLOSSARY

GVW or Gross vehicle weight—total weight of a fully-equipped and loaded RV with passengers, gas, oil, water and baggage; must not be greater than the vehicle's GVWR.

GVWR or Gross Vehicle Weight Rating—the amount of total loaded weight a vehicle can support; determined by the manufacturer, this amount must not be exceeded.

Dry weight—the weight of the RV without fluids such as gas, oil and water added.

STOCKING THE LARDER

A cook's kitchen on the road may have fresh herbs and a food processor.

Because we use our RV year-round, we keep it stocked with non-perishables which are always ready to go and need only be supplemented with fresh food, ice and water before setting off for a weekend. But since even canned goods should not be stored for a long period of time, we mark the date of purchase on top of each can with an indelible marker and use them up in order of age.

Particularly in warm weather, we try to avoid leaving open cardboard packages of crackers, flour or cornmeal in the RV. We usually store small amounts of dried beans, rice and grains in screw-top jars or plastic zip-lock bags, along with coffee beans and sugar. Open bottles of olive oil, mustard or mayonnaise are brought back home at the end of each outing, to be replaced by another small, unopened container on the next trip. All wines are returned home at the end of every trip, but liquors can usually be stored in the vehicle between trips.

Because we both enjoy cooking for ourselves after so many years of dining out, we include among our permanent equipment a food processor, spice rack and pots of fresh herbs (which go back home between journeys).

A large, French enameled cast-iron soup pot, which doubles as a spaghetti pot, is the biggest item in our cookware collection. It is accompanied by several smaller, non-stick enameled cast-iron skillets and pans, a small whistling teakettle, an earthenware teapot that always travels in an old-fashioned, padded tea cozy and several Pyrex microwavable measuring cups and dishes.

For eating, we have a set of sturdy French bistro plates, soup bowls and wine glasses, plus two oversized ceramic mugs that fit nicely into the beverage-carrier on the cockpit dash. New dishtowels double as place mats and/ or napkins, then become dishtowels after a few washings. We try to avoid using disposable paper products, preferring to recycle.

Our large wooden cutting board doubles as a cooktop cover when we're traveling; it keeps the burners from rattling. In the microscopic work space between the double sink and cooktop, we have the food processor, electric can opener, knife block, spice rack, wooden box with cooking utensils and glass canning jar of coarse salt.

A DOZEN DELICIOUS, QUICK AND EASY ONE-POT MEALS

The following are some of our favorite quickly assembled meals after a day of driving or hiking, made with ingredients that are easy to keep on hand. Each involves one pot and a few simple preparation steps. On some, there are vegetarian and/or low-fat adaptations of the original recipe.

1. QUICK TORTILLA SOUP

2 to 4 servings

The cook controls the spiciness in this dish with the ratio of enchilada sauce to chicken broth.

Combine in a saucepan:

1 8-ounce can enchilada sauce

1 to 2 14-ounce cans of low sodium, low fat chicken broth (for milder flavor, use more broth)

1 15-ounce can of beans, drained and rinsed (black, red or pinto beans)

2 seeded and chopped fresh tomatoes

Heat thoroughly, then stir in:

the kernels cut from 2 ears fresh corn that have been shucked and washed

Stir and let warm through briefly. Remove from heat and serve with any or all of these optional toppings: corn chips, grated cheese, sliced green onions, fresh cilantro, cooked chicken breast slivers.

2. EASY FRIED RICE

2 main- or 4 side-dish portions

With planned-ahead leftover cold cooked rice, this is a tasty hot main dish that takes less than 15 minutes.

Arrange in large nonstick frying pan:

4 slices bacon chopped in one-inch pieces. Cook over medium heat until the bacon browns, then remove the pieces of bacon to drain on paper towels, leaving the fat in the pan.

Still over medium heat, in the same pan, saute until tender but not browned:

1 green pepper, seeded and chopped

2 green onions, washed, trimmed and chopped

2 TB fresh Italian parsley, washed and chopped (optional)

Stir in:

2 cups cold cooked rice

Continue stirring until heated through. Then pour evenly over the top of the mixture:

2 beaten whole eggs, blended with 2 TB bottled soy sauce

Cook over medium heat, stirring constantly, until eggs are no longer runny.

Sprinkle the cooked bacon on top and serve at once.

VARIATION: LOW FAT FRIED RICE

Omit the bacon from the recipe above. Instead, lightly spray the pan with no-stick cooking oil or heat 1/4 cup vegetable or chicken broth in the pan. Saute the vegetables and follow the recipe above until the addition of the eggs.

Instead of two whole eggs, add one whole egg and two egg whites beaten with the soy sauce.

3. THREE-BEAN TUNA SALAD

4-6 portions

For lunch on a warm day after a hike, this is ideal.

In mixing bowl, combine:

1 15-ounce can each of kidney or white cannelini beans, black beans and garbanzo beans, drained and rinsed in cold water

Add:

1 6-ounce can of solid tuna in water, well-drained

1/4 cup finely chopped red or green onions

2 TB minced parsley, basil, oregano or other fresh herb (optional)

Juice of one large lemon or lime

1 to 2 TB olive oil

Toss gently and serve atop lettuce leaves.

Can be prepared as much as a day ahead and refrigerated, tightly covered, until serving time.

4. EASY LOW-FAT OVEN FRIED CHICKEN

4 portions

This is good hot or cold or in sandwiches. We sometimes make a double recipe and refrigerate part of it for another meal.

Rinse and pat dry:

4 boneless, skinless chicken breasts, about one pound

Marinate for 30 minutes in a mixture of:

1/2 cup vermouth, dry white wine or chicken broth

1 minced clove of garlic

Remove from marinade and dip each piece in a mixture of:

1/2 cup bread crumbs

2 TB cornmeal

1/2 tsp each cumin, ground cayenne pepper, and crumbled dry sage or thyme

Arrange in baking pan that has been sprayed lightly with no stick cooking oil and bake at 450 about 20 minutes or until no longer pink inside.

5. CAMPGROUND PIZZA

6-8 slices

A special lunchtime treat for a lazy day in camp.

Preheat regular oven to 475.

Following baking directions on the package, put on a baking sheet or large piece of heavy or doubled aluminum foil:

1 large prepared pizza shell (Boboli and Contadina are two brands in the non-refrigerated deli section of the supermarket)

On the shell, smear:

1 envelope (6-8 ounces) of prepared pizza sauce

Top with some or all of the following:

thinly sliced tomatoes

thinly sliced onions

thinly sliced regular pepperoni or low-fat turkey salami

grated low-fat mozzarella, mixed with

nonfat mozzarella if desired

Cook following baking directions for the shell, usually 10-12 minutes, and serve at once.

6. MICROWAVE FISH DINNER

2 main dish portions

We like this when we're driving along the coast and spot a fish market.

In a Pyrex pie dish, arrange side by side in the center:

2 skinless, boneless fresh fish fillets or steaks

Around the edges of the dish, arrange:

1 cup finely diced, unpeeled red potatoes

On top of the fish place:

1 cup thin spears of fresh asparagus or zucchini

Sprinkle lightly with:

Salt and white pepper to taste

The juice of 1/2 to 1 fresh lemon

Then drizzle across the top:

1-2 TB olive oil

Cover tightly with plastic wrap and microwave at high for 11 minutes. Serve with slices or chunks of fresh sourdough bread (optional).

7. REST AREA HUEVOS RANCHEROS

2 portions

On a driving day, we like to start early in the morning with only some fruit or juice and a cup of tea, then stop later at a highway rest area for something more substantial. This dish takes less than 30 minutes from the start of cooking through cleanup after the meal.

In a nonstick skillet, sprayed with no-stick cooking oil, saute:

2 to 4 corn tortillas

When hot, remove to serving plates.

In the same pan melt:

1/2 T butter

Fry over easy or as preferred:

2-4 eggs

Put the cooked eggs atop the tortillas. Then add to the same pan:

1/4-1/2 cup prepared salsa or canned enchilada sauce

Heat through and spoon atop eggs.

LOW FAT HUEVOS RANCHEROS

Warm the tortillas without oil in a nonstick skillet, at the same time poaching the eggs in water in a second pan. Remove tortillas, put drained poached eggs atop and spoon over the heated salsa as directed above.

8. QUICK POSOLE

4 to 6 portions

This low-fat version of a full-meal, traditional winter soup from Mexico and New Mexico is easy to put together and good enough for guests. It's even better reheated the next day.

In a large soup pot, put:

2 pounds of boneless, skinless chicken thighs, chopped into one-inch pieces

2 quarts chicken broth, canned or made from bouillon cubes or powder

3 cloves minced garlic (optional)

1 yellow onion, peeled and chopped

1 teaspoon ground New Mexico chili (optional)

1 sprig fresh thyme or oregano or

1 tsp dried thyme or oregano

Simmer for an hour or so, then add:

2 14-ounce cans of white or yellow hominy, drained and rinsed.

Simmer until heated through. Serve in soup bowls with any or all the following toppings:

thinly sliced raw radishes

thinly sliced green cabbage

diced avocado

prepared corn chips

lime wedges

chopped red or green onions

sprigs of fresh cilantro

9. EGGPLANT PARMESAN

2 to 3 main dish servings, 4 to 6 side dish servings. This dish can be prepared in a regular oven or a 650-watt microwave.

In a baking dish combine:

1 medium eggplant cut into 1/2 inch slices

2 seeded, diced fresh tomatoes

1 to 2 cloves minced garlic

2 TB chopped fresh basil or parsley (optional)

1 TB olive oil

Cover tightly with aluminum foil and bake in 400 degree regular oven one hour.

Uncover and sprinkle with:

1/2 cup grated mozzarella

2 TB freshly grated Parmesan cheese

Return to oven and bake five minutes or until cheese has melted.

To prepare in a microwave oven, put the cheeses on top of the eggplant/tomato mixture, cover tightly with plastic wrap and microwave high for 5 minutes.

10. ONE-POT GARLIC SPAGHETTI

2 to 4 portions

This vegetarian dish contains heart-healthy olive oil and garlic. Spraying the cooking pot before adding the water keeps the spaghetti from sticking to the bottom, making the pan much easier to wash. If you spot some fresh basil in the market (or are carrying a pot of it), you could opt for the Pasta with Pesto variation at the end of this recipe.

Spray a very large cooking pot with no-stick cooking oil, fill with water and add 1-2 TB salt.

When water is boiling rapidly, add:

1/4 pound of dry spaghetti for each serving. Cook until al dente (just soft enough to bite through easily but not soft and flabby), then drain and rinse with hot water. Wipe out the spaghetti pot with a paper towel and return to the heat.

Put in:

1/4 cup olive oil for two portions, 1/2 cup for four

4 to 6 cloves of minced garlic

Cook until garlic begins to sizzle, then stir in minced fresh parsley, basil and/or oregano (optional) to taste.

Return spaghetti to the pot and toss over heat until warmed through. Serve at once with optional freshly grated Parmesan cheese. A big green salad goes well with this, along with fruit and cheese for dessert.

VARIATION: PASTA WITH PESTO

Prepare pesto sauce ahead of time or while pasta is cooking.

In blender or food processor, finely chop:

3 cloves garlic

1 cup fresh basil leaves (can use part basil and part fresh parsley)

When chopped, pour over:

2 TB olive oil

Blend thoroughly. Prepare spaghetti as directed above, toss with the pesto and serve.

11. FRENCH VEGETABLE SOUP

6 to 8 portions

This soup from the south of France is incredibly delicious, although it is simple and easy to make. It is even better with a spoonful of pesto (see the recipe directly above) stirred in just before serving.

In a large soup pot combine:

2 quarts water or chicken broth

2 cups unpeeled red or new white potatoes chopped into 1/2 inch cubes

2 cups green beans, cut into 2-inch pieces

2 to 3 zucchini, washed and sliced

2 cups tomatoes, seeded and chopped into small pieces

Bring to a boil, lower heat, cover and simmer for one hour.

Then add:

4 ounces dry spaghetti, broken into short pieces

1 15-ounce can garbanzo beans or cannelini beans drained and rinsed

Cook until spaghetti is tender, season to taste with salt and pepper, then serve in wide soup bowls.

Top each portion with optional grated Parmesan cheese or pesto sauce.

12. MICROWAVE POLENTA WITH MUSHROOMS

2 to 4 portions

This trendy Italian dish technically takes two pots, one for the microwave and one for the top of the stove. We like this when we find fresh wild mushrooms in farmers' markets or supermarkets. The microwave eliminates all the tedious stirring from the traditional recipe, as well as cutting down the time considerably. Any leftovers can be put in a dish or small loaf pan and refrigerated to slice and saute later for a side dish.

To make the polenta, put in a Pyrex microwavable bowl or large measuring bowl:

4 cups water

1 cup yellow cornmeal

1 tsp salt

Microwave uncovered for 12 minutes, stirring once about halfway through.

Remove from microwave and let stand 3 minutes, then spoon onto serving plates.

While the polenta is cooking, prepare the mushroom sauce. Clean, trim and slice:

1 pound wild or cultivated mushrooms, preferably a mix of several such as oyster, Portobello, chanterelle or shiitake

In a large nonstick skillet, melt:

1 TB unsalted butter or margarine

1 TB olive or other cooking oil

Over medium heat, saute the mushrooms until tender and lightly browned, about 5 to 8 minutes.

Remove and keep warm. In the same pan in the drippings, saute:

1 clove garlic, peeled and minced

2 to 3 TB fresh sage leaves, chopped, or

1 tsp dry sage

Spoon polenta on warm serving plates, and top with mushroom sauce and herbs.

DON'T DRINK THE WATER

When there's no bottled water available in the fishing villages of Fiji or the mountainside inns of the Himalayas, we brush our teeth with scotch whiskey. We veto street-food vendors in Madras, Mazatlán or Manhattan, and always skip summer shellfish salads, rare hamburgers, and anything with custard in it.

As veteran world travelers, we're cautious—some of our friends say overly-cautious—but with a schedule that requires us to be on the road 60 percent of the time, we can't risk getting sick even for a day.

So before setting out on the first of our long RV journeys, we decided to stick with bottled water for drinking and cooking and using bags of commercial ice whenever we're on the road, using the campground water supply and the surplus stored in our tank only for washing and flushing. While most of the city water in North America is probably safe to drink, a constantly changing mineral content when you're making one-night stands can throw your system off. We pick up two or three gallons at a time at a supermarket, convenience or campground store, put one in the galley and the others below in outside storage, and store a 10-pound plastic bag of ice cubes in the freezer.

People who have a restricted sodium intake would also be wise to use sodium-free bottled water, which is available in most supermarkets, since the sodium content of water varies widely from one campground area to the next.

Another solution for RVers who don't want to buy ice and water is the use of a water filter either permanently installed in the kitchen sink or temporarily hooked up to the hose system when filling the tank initially.

Even more thorough is a water purifier that not only removes sediment from the water the way a filter does, but also takes out bacteria and delivers a clean, good-tasting drinking water. (We use one in our kitchen at home for drinking water and the icemaker, but the cost is such that for the RV we'd just as soon stay with bottled water for daily use.)

A new series of low-cost water treatment and disinfection equipment for boats and RVs has been introduced by **Whitewater Technologies**, *Box 37, Salem, SC 29676,* ☎ *(803) 944-6541.* They offer under-counter and counter-top models in various sizes.

We also saw, at the Los Angeles RV Show, a Rexhall motorhome that was equipped with an optional water exchange, with which you could separate your own fresh water source for drinking and cooking and use the campground plug-in source for washing and flushing only.

It's wise to use biodegradable toilet paper and holding-tank chemicals, both available from camping supply stores and many campground stores.

Follow the RV instruction booklet or the directions on the chemical container.

When you're driving every day, you rarely need to use your water heater, since the engine heat keeps the water hot.

SHOULD YOU SLEEP BY THE SIDE OF THE ROAD?

While more than half the states permit some overnight parking in highway rest areas, except where posted, we feel there have been too many recent incidents of violence in these areas and would not consider parking overnight in our RV in a rest area, shopping mall parking lot or by the side of the road. Some of our friends frequently do, however, and consider us money-wasting wimps for insisting on overnighting at a secure private or public campground only.

SHOULD YOU CARRY A GUN IN YOUR RV?

If you want to start a lively argument around a campground, try this as an opener. We personally would never carry a firearm of any sort in our motorhome, but then we would never have one at home, either. While many frequent and full-timing RVers agree, just as many others disagree, sometimes vociferously.

Even in the U.S., according to *Trailer Life Campground/RV Park and Services Directory*, 34 states require a license to carry a concealed handgun and 17 states require a license to carry a handgun openly.

Entering Mexico with a firearm of any sort can land an RV owner in jail, and did, in one famous case in 1993. Veteran RVer Paul Musser of Big Bear, California, had bought a semiautomatic rifle at an Arizona gun show and stowed it, along with 500 rounds of ammunition, under the couch in his travel trailer. When the Mexican police found the AK-47 in the trailer and a pistol in his truck, they confiscated the vehicle, firearms and ammunition, and put Musser in jail in Hermasillo. Jailed in May, he spent months incarcerated with no bedding or regular meal service, both optional luxuries the prisoner's family members are expected to pay for, before his attorney could bring the case to trial. (See "Bouncing Down Baja.")

Despite our feelings that our motorhome is indeed our home, the law in many states considers the RV a motor vehicle when moving and a home only when parked in camp. Therefore any firearms carried must be unloaded and the bullets kept separately from the weapon when in transit.

Firearms are also prohibited in many state parks.

If we did choose to carry a firearm, we would make it a point to keep abreast of the regulations in every state, which can differ radically the minute you cross a state line.

Besides the annually updated *Trailer Life Campground/RV Park & Services Directory*, which gives a rundown on handgun regulations in every state and Canadian province under "Rules of the Road and Towing Laws," an article in the July 1994 *Trailer Life* magazine detailed the question fully and fairly. For a faxed copy ($7.95), call FYI Xpress at ☎ *(800) 955-5293.*

SHOULD YOU CARRY A CELLULAR PHONE IN YOUR RV?

We always do, but it provides almost as much frustration as assistance. The places we like to drive and camp are frequently if not always in a borderline or "no service" area, even though we have (and are willing to pay a sizable sum for) a Follow Me Roaming system that theoretically can forward our calls to almost anywhere in the U.S. and Canada we happen to be. Our editors have been able to reach us in the wilds of British Columbia or when we're driving down an interstate in west Texas, but can't seem to get through to us when we're on a two-day outing in San Diego or Santa Barbara counties, only a hoot and a holler from our Los Angeles base.

We find it most helpful for dialing ahead for a campground reservation or for returning business calls we've picked up from our answering machine when the campground or highway pay phones are too noisy. And we would certainly be happy to have it in case of an emergency, which we have not yet had to deal with.

The technology leaves something to be desired, with voices fading in and out when you're in a fringe reception area. The cost is almost prohibitive, because you pay for connecting to the roamer system as well as the elapsed time for any calls whether incoming or outgoing.

A 1185-page guide promising all you need to know about roaming is available for $19.90 from **Communications Publishing**, *Box 500, Mercer Island, WA 98040, (800) 927- 8800*. It includes areas with maps, rates, instructions on sending and receiving for many cities and roaming agreements.

If you are reluctant to invest in a cellular phone, be aware that most private campgrounds and many public campgrounds have a pay phone on the premises.

AIN'T MISBEHAVIN': ROAD ETIQUETTE

1. Don't hog the highway; pull over at turnouts or into slow-moving lanes to let vehicles behind you have a chance to pass. In some states it's against the law for a slow-moving vehicle not to allow vehicles in back of him to pass at the first opportunity when five or more are trailing him.

2. Keep in the right lane except when passing a car, and when you do pass, make sure you have the speed and space to do it quickly and easily.

3. As with your car, dimming your RV headlights for an approaching car is a must. It is also a good idea to do the same when driving into a campground after dark.

4. It seems customary to make a friendly wave to an oncoming RV as you meet, particularly if it's a make and model similar to your own.

5. Always signal your intention to turn or change lanes well ahead of time so the driver in back of you has plenty of warning. Your vehicle is not as agile as those around you.

WHAT KIND OF WARDROBE IS RIGHT?

Like most RVers, we have a wardrobe always stowed in our motorhome that can cover any situation we may encounter on the road, from an impromptu dinner in a fine restaurant to an outfit for cold-weather camping or white-water rafting.

Since wardrobe and drawer space is fairly limited, except on the largest motorhomes and fifth-wheels, you'll want to confine your carry-along wardrobe to a few carefully selected basics, adding seasonal or special apparel when the journey requires it.

We concentrate on basic clothing that is machine washable, stretchable with elastic waists and a comfortable but loose fit, in styles and colors that will harmonize with the other items in the closet. For cold-weather camping, even parts of the California desert in winter, a set of silk long underwear is invaluable to wear under the sweatshirts and pants. A loose cotton gauze or linen shirt and a pair of shorts is always on hand for unusually hot weather, like the heat wave we encountered in New England last summer.

A spare pair of hiking or jogging shoes is handy to have, along with a comfortable pair of slippers to wear in the evenings after outside chores are finished. We each take one pair of slightly worn but acceptable dress-up shoes, along with one business or evening outfit, in case of an important appointment en route. Anyone planning to use the public showers in the campground should also take a pair of rubber shower shoes.

Several changes of underwear, socks and pajamas, along with a bathrobe, are folded and tucked into nightstand drawers beside the bed. We even carry spare bottles of prescription medication and a full supply of toiletries so we can slip away on the spur of the moment and find everything we need aboard the RV.

Knit clothes that can be folded and stacked rather than put on a hanger take up less room and don't need ironing. We often take travel- or sample-size toiletries, stowing them at home in a special "Winnie-box" ready to be taken along on the next RV trip.

On our initial six-week journey, we took far too many clothes, forgetting that a lot of campgrounds have laundromats and that items of clothing can be worn more than once. The other thing to remember is that in a campground nobody pays much attention to what anyone wears anyhow.

LIFE ON THE ROAD

One of the authors at work on her computer on the road in Zion National Park

After nearly 20 years on the road as travel writers, we've traveled by just about every mode of transportation known to man, including hot-air balloons, elephant backs and dugout canoes. But our lives changed three years ago when we set out for the first time in an RV, a leased 27-foot Winnebago Brave motorhome, on a six-week trip to visit more than 100 remote ski areas all over the U.S. for a computer service guidebook.

In an earlier life, as film and television actors, we had spent many long days in RVs changing clothes and studying scripts—they are routinely used as dressing rooms on film locations and studio sound stages—but we had never been in one that moved. The size we selected is a compromise between how large an inside and how small an outside we can deal with. Here are some notes from that first time on the road, all of them written in the passion of the moment.

EXCERPTS FROM A ROAD DIARY, or
IF WE CAN DO THIS, ANYONE CAN

August 12

At the California dealer's where we are leasing the motorhome, a young man named Daryll with sun-bleached shoulder-length hair and a Persian Gulf War T-shirt walks us through it, saying how easy everything is and how nothing can go wrong. We nod wisely and make frantic scribbled notes like "circuit breaker and fuses in bedroom" and "generator runs off gas tanks" and "water pump switch off while moving." When he leaves us alone for a while, we go into a frenzy of measuring and diagram-drawing.

August 14

The day before we are scheduled to leave, we lay out newspaper sections on the floor of our apartment folded to fit the measurements of the RV's cupboards and set out the items we intend to put there, then pack only those items in a box labeled for that section.

August 15

Unfortunately, life isn't that rational and orderly. On packing day, we are forced to double-park in our crowded urban neighborhood and relay boxes of books, cartons of pots and pans and hangers of clothes back and forth from our apartment to the street, one of us keeping a constant eye out so nothing is stolen, and dumping them anywhere there is space, most of it on the plastic-wrapped mattress and in the bathroom shower.

When Daryll saw us off this morning, he turned on the generator so the rooftop air-conditioner can cool down the interior and chill the refrigerator and freezer, but has neglected to tell us whether to keep it on while we're driving, or turn it off. Somewhere we remember him saying it's capable of running 16 hours straight with no problem, so we leave it on.

The soothing noise from the air-conditioner drowns out many of the small crashes and thuds from the back as our possessions settle in on their own, with only an occasional loud thunk causing us to glance furtively backward.

August 15 from the driver's seat:

The first impression is that you're way above the traffic and at the same time divorced from the road itself. Suddenly you realize you're looking down at the middle of the lane and half your vehicle is in the next lane. To keep from slipping over into an adjacent lane, you have to hug the left lane line. The back of the vehicle seems to have a mind of its own and wants to turn at a shorter distance than the front end. I soon learned to make wide turns, particularly to the right. Another problem is that at any bump or rut, the vehicle leans to the right or left, then rolls back to the other side. My fingers and arms are stiff after a couple of hours from white-knuckling the wheel.

August 15, nightfall

It is after dark when we stop for gas in Kingman, Arizona, and Harry goes into a state of shock as he watches the numbers on the tank turn and turn and turn, as gallon after gallon flows in, until the pump turns off automatically at $50 and the tank still isn't full.

Exhausted, we agree it's time to stop. Just in front of us, between the gas station and the freeway, is an RV campground—we can see the sign—but we cannot figure out how to get to it since a used car lot and a strip mall are in the way.

(It is about now that we give up the fantasy of waking to birdsong and the breeze wafting through the pine trees.)

Not far away we find a second campground and something better than birdsong—a space called a "pullthrough," which means we can drive the motorhome in one side, plug it in, then drive out the other side the next morning without backing up.

In desperation we begin to speed-read the instruction manual and learn that it is necessary to turn off the generator before plugging in the electricity. That part is a snap—our plug fits into the campground's receptacle.

We make a long, fruitless search by flashlight through all the outdoor storage bins for a hose so we can hook up the water connection. (Harry is positive Daryll pointed one out, but Shirley thinks he has remembered the sewage hose instead, and Harry thinks that maybe we should get a divorce, right now, tonight, or at least go check into a motel with running water. As it turns out, we have plenty of water in the storage tanks without having to use the external hookup.)

We studiously ignore the sewage hookup. The refrigerator has been turned down to the coldest setting—obviously Daryll wanted it to get chilled quickly—and we find frozen romaine, frozen eggs and frozen chicken breasts inside. Instead of a gourmet dinner, we settle for soup warmed in the microwave.

Stunned, almost stupid with exhaustion, we wash the dishes, close the blinds and curtains, and move back to the bedroom to make up the bed. Clearing it is easier than we expect, since most of the gear piled on the bed has already fallen onto the floor.

We raise the mattress to remove its plastic cover, and the hinged supports lock into the open position, leaving the bed firmly set at a rakish 45-degree angle. By this time we probably could have slept in it anyhow, but we get out the toolbox and unscrew the supports so we can flatten the mattress again. Somehow we manage to simultaneously make up the bed and fall asleep in it...

August 16

The skies have opened up in the high desert of western New Mexico, dumping so much water in the streets of Socorro that the intersections are flooded ankle-deep. Although our campground guidebook promises there is an RV park in town, we spot the flickering light of a Motel 6 just ahead and with no discussion whatsoever, pull in just behind a battered truck camper from Texas. If the veterans can't weather the storm, we mutter, we amateurs can't be expected to. We check into a $29-a-night room.

August 17

The sun comes out. We stop at a hardware store and buy a water hose, which we hook up, but for some reason it never fills the tank. Later we realize we hooked the water hose to the outside connection that feeds water directly into the system. While we're still not able to make the TV work, we've gotten very good at plugging in the electric, once we realize our large three-prong plug has to fit into a three-prong 30-amp receptacle.

We studiously ignore the sewage hookup.

August 18

While checking out the ski resort at Crested Butte, we make a left turn uphill into the parking garage of the Grande Butte Hotel, which causes the tow-bar connection at the rear of the motorhome to drag and stick fast in the asphalt. The concierge arrives and says a Greyhound bus got stuck there only last week, and should she call the tow truck again? Harry congratulates himself on taking out auto club emergency insurance, and the tow truck duly frees us from the driveway. We vow never again to turn into a hotel driveway that heads uphill.

August 19

In the ski town of Breckenridge, we spot a locksmith standing beside his truck talking to a pretty blonde, and ask if he could help us get into our outdoor storage area, because either the lock is broken or the key doesn't fit. The locksmith takes one look at the key and says we're using it upside down. From then on it works. At Dillon Reservoir, we settle down to lunch beside the lake, opening a couple of the roof vents for air, when a sudden gust of wind tears across the roof of the motorhome and takes off one of the white plastic roof vents. Harry chases it down and climbs on the roof to replace it, just as the rain begins. At a nearby gas station, we buy a roll of silver duct tape and batten it down. We vow never again to open the roof vents on a windy day.

August 20

We get lost in Kansas City looking for Arthur Bryant's famous barbecue restaurant, so it is once again after dark when we check into a small RV campground in the town of Independence, where a kindly campground manager with a flashlight loans us a sewage hose (ours is too short for the hookup) and talks us step-by-step through the dumping procedure for the holding tanks, which have reached their capacity. The same helpful manager shows us where to push a black button that activates the TV set.

Harry, I don't think we're in Kansas any more.

August 27

It is almost with a sense of relief that we return to Winnie (for some reason we have begun calling the vehicle that lately) after staying overnight in the lavish West Virginia country cottage of some friends. Their gardens are lovely, their hospitality warm, but Winnie has become home.

August 29

It has taken us two weeks to discover why the bedroom in the back of the motorhome was getting so hot while we were traveling, then cooled down once we stopped for the night. It turns out that Harry had kept a control switch on the dash to the left side, thinking it was off, when the left side actually activates the low fan of the bedroom heater.

September 1

There is a great comfort in riding along listening to the sounds in the motorhome behind us. We recognize the sharp clatter of the cutlery drawer suddenly swinging open, the more subdued sounds of the mug of wooden utensils spilling onto the stove top, the rolling thud of the canned food swaying back and forth in its bin, the rattle when the bedroom blinds have come unhooked from their pins and are randomly swaying, the bump when a camera forgotten and left on a chair falls off into the floor and breaks a wide angle lens, the swishing sound of the cardboard box with its water jugs sliding on the plastic floor covering. (We did not remove the plastic over the carpeting, figuring that was one way to keep it cleaner inside.)

After we have the bed supports repaired, the bed develops a mind of its own and pops up occasionally while we're in transit as if to have a look around.

September 15

We drive into Yellowstone, suddenly aware of how special it is to travel in a motorhome like this with wide scenic views through the big windows and high seats as if looking down from a bus. Huge herds of bison shamble around in the roadway, in no hurry to move along, and our vantage point is ideal for photographing them. We stop for lunch by the Yellowstone River in a grove of trees, their leaves turned golden, make lunch and for the first time talk about perhaps buying a motorhome of our own.

September 27

Partly because we despair of ever having to unpack Winnie, we buy her from the dealer. That was nearly three years and 50,000 miles ago. When not on the road, she resides on the roof of a parking garage in Van Nuys, California.

AN ODE TO BUBBLE WRAP

Mel Brooks in a comic routine as "The 2000-Year- Old Man" lauded plastic wrap as the greatest invention of the past two millenniums, but we'd have to say bubble wrap is a close second, at least in the wonderful world of RV cupboards.

The cylinder-shaped bubble wrap containers that come around bottles in airport duty-free shops make great sleeves for mugs and glasses, while the flat sheets that come in packing boxes are easy to slide between plates or pots and pans to protect them. You can also buy commercially produced plastic foam sleeves for glasses and pan protectors in camping supply stores such as the Camping World chain.

Alternately nesting baskets and metal bowls keeps down the clatter from the cupboards as well. Lining the bottoms of drawers and cupboards with waffle-patterned rubber matting, available by the yard at RV dealers and camping stores, makes a non-skid surface for dishes.

We store fragile items like tulip-shaped champagne glasses in their original boxes and use other boxes or shaped styrofoam packing protectors that come around appliances to wedge them firmly in the cupboard. Whenever possible, we use real dishes and utensils and cloth napkins that are recycled instead of disposable paper and plastic products.

EIGHT MONEY-SAVING TIPS FOR THE ROAD

1. Shopping at roadside fruit stands or farmers' markets will usually net the freshest and the cheapest local produce, plus the chance to have a chat with some locals.

2. Watch for pick-your-own farms and orchards in season where a few minutes of work can save a lot of money on luxuries like fresh raspberries and cherries. One national park campground in Utah is set in the midst of fruit orchards where campers pick their own. (See "Southern Utah's National Parks Country, Ten Campground Oases.")

3. Pick up local newspapers or free throwaways in towns where you overnight and use the ads and supermarket discount coupons to save grocery money.

4. If you see a local gas station having a price war with a neighboring station, turn around and go back and fill up your tank. You'd be surprised how many times that happens along the road.

5. Some gas stations charge more when you use a credit card than when you pay cash. Keep your eye out for stations that list the same price for credit or cash. If there's no sign that says so, ask before filling the tank.

6. Spend that extra bit of money for regular engine and vehicle upkeep on a long haul. This saves a lot of money in the end.

7. When overnighting in campgrounds that charge based on hookups and facilities used, opt for the most basic, since RVs are designed to be self-contained. (For more campground money-savers see "Campgrounds and RV Parks: Where to Sleep.")

8. Buy out of season (antifreeze, for instance, in summer) and in quantity. When canned or paper goods are on sale in bulk, buy two or three for the house and two or three for the RV.

HOW TO GIVE BACKING-UP DIRECTIONS WITHOUT DESTROYING YOUR MARRIAGE

Whenever possible, request a drive-through campsite and postpone as long as possible the agony of a back-in site.

When no drive-throughs are available, we prefer to start with a quick confab about the broad general aims of the driver, particularly in regard to where the RV will end up, along with some general observations about the presence of boulders, picnic tables and low-hanging tree limbs. Unfortunately, if the vehicle is blocking campground traffic, the prologue step has to be eliminated.

It is critical to establish a mutual signal that means *Stop Immediately Before You Back into That... (Truck, Tree, Utility Post, Fence, or Fire Grate)*.

The first step is for the signaler to learn to stand where he or she can be seen by the driver in the side mirror. The same rule applies here as for cameras: If you can see the mirror, the mirror can see you.

Next, the signals should be clear and decisive. The fewer signals that are used, the simpler it usually becomes. We use a two-hand beckoning signal for "keep coming back," a right-hand signal to move toward the right, and a left-hand signal to move toward the left. Too many signals or verbiage simply confuses the issue.

If all else fails, you still have three options: Invest in a closed circuit TV backup system that shows the driver exactly what is behind him as he backs— expensive but effective (although these, too, have their limitations); a CB radio system with one unit in the cockpit and the second a hand-held model; or buy an OHRA Walkphone, a walky-talky crystal-controlled system good for a three mile area in flat land that does not require a relay closing. Call **OHRA Corporation** in Torrance, California, at ☎ *(310) 212-3196*. Motorola also makes a two-way radio with a two-watt transmitter good for a two-mile line of sight, $299 at Camping World.

NUTS AND BOLTS

Into each book some miscellaneous information must fall and here's where loose and leftover data falls in ours:

CABLE TV

Many private RV parks offer cable TV connections as an option, usually with an added dollar or two on the nightly fee. If you don't have a built-in exterior cable connection, you can use a length of coaxial cable hooked to the campground connection at one end, then routed through a window to your RV's TV set. You can also use an alternative outdoor entertainment area hookup as the connector. It's best if you carry your own cable, since the campground does not often provide it.

CARAVANS AND RALLIES

RVers who would prefer to travel or camp with a group can join up with any number of like-minded people for a paid vacation tour that they make in their own rig instead of a tour bus, or a friendly get together with other owners of the same brand of RV. Caravans are the RV equivalent of a group tour with structured itineraries, sightseeing, communal meals and many group social functions.

Popular caravan destinations include Mexico, Alaska and New England at autumn foliage time. To find out about caravan and club tours, read general monthly RV publications such as *Trailer Life* and *MotorHome*, available by subscription or from most magazine racks; or *Family Motor Coaching Magazine, Highways* (for Good Sam Club members) or other club or RV manufacturing company publications.

CLUBS

American Sunbathing Association, for nudist RVers, has RV parks in many states. For information, call ☎ *(407) 933-2064.*

Baby Boomers, for RV enthusiasts born between 1940 and 1960. *Write PO Box 23, Stoneham, CO 80754.*

Escapees Incorporated, founded in 1978 by veteran RV writers Joe and Kay Peterson, is a support system for full timers. Membership numbers more than 33,000. Members have pooled resources to build their own nonprofit RV parks across the country, as well as creating a new CARE program that provides parking facilities and support services for temporarily or permanently incapacitated full timers. ☎ *(409) 327-8873.*

Family Motor Coach Association, *8291 Clough Pike, Cincinnati, OH 45244,* ☎ *(800) 543-3622,* is for owners of self-propelled, self-contained vehicles with cooking, sleeping and permanent sanitary facilities in which the living quarters can be accessed directly from the driver's seat. Members number around 170,000 families, each with its own ID number. The group provides a handsome monthly magazine and other benefits, including insurance. Costs are $35 for a family, including initiation fee and first year dues.

Good Sam Club, ☎ *(800) 234-3450*, is a broad-range club with insurance, campground affiliates, financing and other services. Members number nearly a million, and the club also has special-interest chapters for hobbyists, computer aficionados, singles, the deaf and others.

Handicapped Travel Club, for disabled individuals who enjoy traveling and camping, also welcomes the nonhandicapped. *4500 Tennessee Avenue, Chattanooga, TN 37409.*

Loners on Wheels, now 25 years old, is a club for single RVers, numbering around 3000 widowed, divorced or never-married members. While members who subsequently give up traveling alone turn into nonmembers, they are welcomed back at special anniversaries and rallies. Write *PO Box 1355, Poplar Bluff, Missouri 63902*, for more information.

RV Birdwatchers Club, with caravans for birders, ☎ *(812) 295-2729.*

RV Elderhostel, study groups for RV owners at universities or on the road in caravans along a historic route. Contact Elderhostel at *80 Boylston Street, Suite 400, Boston, MA 02116,* ☎ *(617) 426-7788.*

Vagabundos del Mar, a club of RV travelers who spend a lot of time in Mexico, and also provide Mexican auto insurance and information on RV parks south of the border. ☎ *(707) 374-5511.*

Wandering Individual Network, for single RVers born after 1926. The group has a newsletter and rallies. *PO Box 2010, Sparks, NV 89432.*

COMPUTER ON-LINE SERVICES

On-line RV bulletin boards on computer services such as Prodigy allow RV enthusiasts or "wannabe" RVers to exchange dialogue, give helpful hints and discuss the pros and cons of the various vehicle brands.

DISABLED RVers

RVing, like cruising, makes an enjoyable and easy vacation for disabled travelers, particularly those in a wheelchair, so long as the camping units are configured to take care of the chair's width and turning radius and are free of steps or level differences inside. Among manufacturers providing equipment for disabled RVers are Foretravel, Play-Mor and Winnebago, listed in "RV Manufacturers: Who Makes What." For a complete list, contact RVIA (see "Driving Tips" in this chapter).

Clubs for disabled RVers include **Handicapped Travel Club**, *667 J Avenue, Coronado, CA 92118*, and Accent on Information, *PO Box 700, Bloomington, IL 61702,* ☎ *(309) 378- 2961.* The latter publishes booklets and magazines for disabled travelers.

DRIVING SCHOOLS

While most confident (or overconfident) drivers pick up RV-wrangling fairly quickly, here is one place to get really professional RV driving skills:

RV Driving School, *1512 E. 5th Street, #149, Ontario, CA 91764,* ☎ *(909) 984-7746.* Instructor Dick Reed has 20 years of RV driving experience as well as being a teacher of truck and RV driving. He covers use of mirrors, driving defensively, courtesy, backing into campsites, safety checks and braking and control. Students may learn on their own rigs or his. He also offers driving seminars at the Los Angeles RV Show each October at the Fairplex in Pomona.

DRIVING TIPS

To combat glare, fog, snow or oncoming headlights when driving after dark, slip on a pair of yellow glasses (sold in ski shops as ski goggles) or clip a pair over your regular glasses.

The AARP (American Association of Retired Persons) puts out an excellent booklet called *Safety in RVs: A Moving Experience*, that is available free from RVIA, *PO Box 2999, 1896 Preston White Drive, Reston, VA 22090*. They point out various ways driving an RV is different (not more difficult) than driving your family car. Adjusting to the vehicle, taking care in inclement weather, and anticipating difficult situations ahead are stressed in the booklet. A separate chapter on towing and a detailed explanation of equipment and how to handle emergencies is also included.

FINANCING

Because RV buyers are generally considered more reliable for a loan than car buyers (only 1.39 percent of all RV loans are delinquent), loans are easier to get. Check with banks, savings and loan associations, finance companies, credit unions or the RV dealer. Loans for big new RVs typically range from 10 to 12 years, even 15, with many asking a 20 percent down payment or less. A few lenders may require a 25 percent down payment. Financing packages for used RVs are usually for up to eight years. Interest on the loan is deductible as second home mortgage interest so long as the unit contains basic cooking, sleeping and toilet accommodations. To get free IRS publications detailing interest information, call ☎ *(800) 829-3676* and request Publication 936, Home Interest Deduction, and Publication 523, Selling Your Home. *The RV Money Book* by Bob Howells (Trailer Life Books, 1992, $29.95, also available from RVIA, address previously given) offers detailed information on buying, selling, financing and insuring RVs.

FULL-TIMING

While we've spent many months at a time in our motorhome, we've never been on the road without our home, bank, post office and telephone answering machine taking care of business.

Anyone seriously considering living full-time in an RV with no other home base should read one or more of the current books out on the subject—*Full-Time RVing* by Bill and Jan Moeller (Trailer Life Books, 1993, $19.95), *Fulltiming: An Introduction to Full-Time RVing* by Gaylord Maxwell (1991, GSC Mail Forwarding, *PO Box 404, Agoura, CA 91301, $8.95)* and *Living Aboard Your RV* by Janet Groene and Gordon Groene (Ragged Mountain Press, 1993, $15.95). All three are also available from RVIA (see address under "Driving Tips").

SEVEN GREAT GIZMOS AND GADGETS

1. **Solar charger units**—solar panels that can be installed atop an RV to keep batteries charged with energy from the sun; comes in all sizes from a unit to keep coach battery charged with trickle charger to a power kit good for 60 amp hours a day, from **Solar Electric Specialties**, ☎ *(707) 459-9496*

2. **Coach Tender stowable runabout**—a golf cart-like electric vehicle that is 23 inches high and can be stored in the basement cargo areas of large motorhomes; around $8000; ☎ *(503) 683-1930*

3. **The California Room**, an add-on screen- and-awning living area that can be attached to an RV to add an outdoor eating or sleeping area complete with optional privacy or rain panels, **Shademaster**, *El Cajon, CA,* ☎ *(800) 367-1791* or *(619) 448-5310*. A similar unit made in Florida could be dubbed the Florida room, **Fiamma Inc.**, *Orlando,* ☎ *(407) 672-0091*

4.   **EZ Lift for disabled** pickup, van or mini-motorhome drivers has a 300-pound lift capability and a seat platform with wrap-around safety arm; the driver (or passenger) simply rides the unit up or down and swivels into the vehicle seat. **Mobility Products**, *Houston, TX,* ☎ *(800) 972-5438*

5.   **Cycle Sac**, a waterproof sack with Velcro closing big enough to fully enclose two bikes on an RV bumper and protect them from dust, rain, rocks, mud and snow. About $115, **Cycle Sac**, *Hamilton, MI,* ☎ *(313) 455-0922*

6.   **Indoor-outdoor Rain-Er-Shine Grill** lets you cook outdoors over charcoal or indoors over your gas cooktop, about $75, **Talisman Marketing**, ☎ *(800) 866-2922*

7.   **Jumbo sun visor extension** for big Type A motorhome windshields, swings from front to side, swivels or flips down, about $30 from **Hackley Marketing**, *Geneva, IL,* ☎ *(708) 232-6640*

INSURANCE

We were very pleasantly surprised to find our RV insurance was very affordable, even in costly southern California. Safe driving records, a shorter use period during the year and slightly older drivers on the average mean less risk for the insurer. Before buying, check your own automobile insurance carrier as well as specialized RV insurance carriers such as **Good Sam Club's National General,** ☎ *(800) 847-3450, extension 5784*; **Foremost Insurance Company**, ☎ *(800) 545-8608*; **AARP Insurance**, ☎ *(800) 541- 3717*; **Alexander & Alexander** (Family Motor Coaching Association), ☎ *(800) 521-2942*; **Caravanner Insurance**, ☎ *(800) 423-4403*; and for Mexican insurance, **Sanborn's**, ☎ *(512) 686-3601*. Towing insurance in case of a breakdown is a good idea; in many cases, AAA members can extend that company's towing coverage to their RV. For a more extensive discussion of coverage and insurers, see *The RV Money Book* (under "Financing").

MODEL YEAR

Until recently, RV manufacturers often produced motorized units that carried split model year information between the RV unit and the chassis. Ours, for instance, is a 1993 motorhome unit on a 1992 Chevrolet chassis. Problems from arguments about whether or not a warranty is in effect, to which *Blue Book* value should be applied when the RV is up for sale have cropped up frequently. But in 1994 for the 1995 model year, under the urging of the RVDA (Recreation Vehicle Dealers Association) most manufacturers agreed to set August 1, 1994, as the uniform introductory year for 1995 models. Some of the remaining manufacturers unable to comply for one reason or another in 1994 have agreed to comply in August 1995. While the agreement does not yet include all manufacturers, a substantial number have apparently concurred, making it simpler for a buyer to know which year's model he is getting. A full agreement is still in the future.

SPEEDERS BEWARE

While exceeding the speed limit is never laudable, it can also be extremely inconvenient for residents of California, Alaska, Hawaii, Montana, Oregon, Michigan and Wisconsin, states that are not signatories to the Non-Resident Violators Compact.

What it means is that drivers with license plates from these seven states are subject to having their driver's license confiscated and being required to go to the nearest office of a judge, sheriff or justice of the peace to appear before an officer, post bond and/or pay a fine. If said officer is not available, the individual may be jailed until a court appearance can be arranged, which may be several hours later.

SIX OFF-THE-WALL TIPS
FOR RV AILMENTS

1. To remember to lower your TV antenna before pulling out of the campground, put some sort of label or tag—one RVer suggests a spring-loaded clothespin—on the antenna crank in the travel position. When the antenna is up, put the same tag or device on the gear shift or steering wheel. Then as you prepare to move out, the item will remind you the antenna is still raised.

2. When stuck in snow, mud or sand, suggests one Canadian RVer, use two strips of metal plasterer's lath, available in hardware stores, approximately 10 by 30 inches each, either in front of or behind the drive axle wheels to extricate the vehicle. The lath can be hosed off and stored flat to be re-used as many times as needed.

3. To get rid of mice, tuck sheets of Downey fabric-softener around the sofa, under the sinks and near the furnace.

4. Spray white vinegar on the electrical connectors for a tow vehicle when lights or turn signals fail to work.

5. When sensors on holding tanks for gray and black water do not read properly, a Prodigy on-line Bulletin Board subscriber suggests filling the problem tank half full of water and adding a half-cup of Dawn liquid dish detergent before leaving home, then emptying the tank on arrival at the campground. He suggests repeating the technique if the first effort doesn't fix it.

6. A Nevada man reminds us of the hero in *The Accidental Tourist* with his washing suggestion: put hot water, dirty clothes, soap and a tennis shoe (to act as agitator) in a large beverage cooler and strap the whole thing to the rear bumper of the motorhome. At lunchtime, empty the soapy water in an appropriate spot, refill the cooler with clean water, and drive on into the afternoon. In camp, set up a clothesline and hang the clean laundry out to dry.

RVing ABROAD

PART ONE: FOR VISITORS COMING TO THE UNITED STATES

At the headquarters of Cruise America, the largest RV rental company in the U.S., salesmen estimate that at least 70 per cent of the rentals are made to Europeans, primarily Germans, who want to tour parts of the western United States.

The favorite well-worn loop takes visitors from Los Angeles to Las Vegas and the Grand Canyon, Death Valley, Yosemite National Park, San Francisco, then back down the coast highway to Los Angeles.

We meet them in campgrounds and RV parks all over the southwest, and sometimes wish we could take them by the hand and show them some of the colorful sidelights as well. By adding a few days, they could complete their basic loop but still veer off into some of the RV adventures in the second part of this book—the off-the-wall corners of the California desert, the spectacularly beautiful and uncrowded national parks of southern Utah, the culturally rich Ozarks and the country/pop music phenomenon that is Branson, Missouri, Texas and its Rio Grande Valley and Big Bend, or the Black Hills of South Dakota with its rich Native American cultural heritage. So we've tried to cover some of that ground in the section that follows.

Some differences Europeans may notice first in camping in the United States is that Americans like their campsites farther apart, and may have fewer made-to-order services such as restaurants or pizza parlors or even bakeries in a campground.

The natural friendliness and curiosity of Americans may strike some Europeans as overly inquisitive. Be prepared to answer where you come from and what it's like there.

In many parts of the American west, private property is a concept that is taken seriously. Ranchers worry about damage to their land or livestock escaping or being injured, and they have their property fenced and posted with signs forbidding entrance, camping, hunting, fishing or gold panning. Always heed these signs and never trespass on private property.

In many U.S. campgrounds, both public and private, a campground host is on duty; the residence is usually marked with a sign or banner. Feel free to ask questions of the host about the area for sightseeing, shopping or dining out.

American campgrounds may seem to have more rules than the ones in Europe. For example, generator hours (when you may operate a gas-driven generator when your RV is not plugged in) are usually posted, and campers are asked not to use them at any other time.

Not many Americans speak other languages, so it's helpful to have more than a smattering of basic English to drive around rural areas of the west. Being able to decipher regional accents will also be helpful, and Americans won't mind being asked to speak more slowly. A lot of Americans can hardly understand each others' accents as it is.

Since Europe has a generous share of supermarkets, there's little adjustment when it comes to shopping, but Europeans will find American liquor laws confusing if they want to buy a bottle of wine for dinner in some parts of Texas or Utah.

But we think Europeans will get a great deal of pleasure out of our vast open spaces, our magnificent scenery, and the natural friendliness of Americans. And most of our friends, particularly from Germany, really enjoy American beef.

So hit the side roads and back roads, pardner, in some of our wonderful parks and wilderness areas, and take along a bag of charcoal and a grill. First thing you know, they'll think you're a native.

PART TWO: FOR AMERICANS TRAVELING ABROAD

For most American RVers, the first foreign country visited is usually our neighbor to the south, Mexico, or to the north, Canada. (For more about RVing in Mexico, see "Bouncing Down Baja". RVing in Canada's British Columbia and Yukon Territory appears in "Driving the Alaska Highway," while the maritime provinces of eastern Canada are covered in "The Lobster Coast: New England and the Martimes.")

But people dedicated to the mobility, flexibility and freedom of RVing soon begin glancing at destinations even farther field. Here are some good possibilities.

EUROPE

Summer is peak season for travel in Europe, when rental units need to be reserved well ahead of time. The cost per week for a mid-sized unit (what we would call a mini-motorhome) verges around $1000 in summer, but drops off slightly for the shoulder seasons of spring and fall when the roads are less crowded and the weather may actually be better. (When we lived in Europe, October was our favorite travel month all over the Continent.) A value-added tax is usually levied on top of the basic rental rate. More than 25,000 Americans each year see Europe by rental RV, most in vehicles they have booked before leaving home.

The standard RV unit in Europe is somewhat smaller than in the U.S., although many American manufacturers are now producing mini-motorhomes and travel trailers for European buyers since a former Yugoslavian manufacturer went bankrupt with the political collapse of the country several years ago. The smaller size copes well with narrower roads that cover some of the most scenic parts of the Continent, as well as offering fuel efficiency for the admittedly expensive gasoline.

While it is possible to bring your own RV unit by cargo vessel from the U.S., it's economically infeasible unless you plan to spend a very long time touring. If you do decide to ship your own vehicle over, you'll need to deal with a customs broker who can do the paperwork and arrange the shipping.

Some American RVers swap vehicles with European RVers. One company that makes arrangements, if you're interested in this, is the **Vacation Exchange Club**, *PO Box 650, Key West, FL 33041,* ☎ *(800) 638-3841.*

Diesel fuel is easy to find in Europe, but propane is not as readily available as in the United States.

It's a good idea to get an International Camping Carnet from the **Family Campers and RVers Association**, *4808 Transit Road, Building 2, Depew, NY 14043-4906,* ☎ *(716) 668- 6242.* While it's not required everywhere, it lets you leave your carnet rather than your passport at the campground registration desk overnight. Purchase of the carnet also usually includes liability insurance while you are in the campgrounds.

While an International Driving Permit is also not essential, it might be a good idea to carry one in case of an accident. Contact your local automobile club for more details or the American Automobile Association, ☎ *(407) 444-7000.*

You'll be able to take your RV aboard train flatbeds through the tunnels in the Alps or on ferries to cross major bodies of water.

Traveling through the European countryside is relatively simple and scenic, except perhaps for the hedgerows of England, Ireland and Scotland, thick hedges eight or 10 feet tall that line the narrow, curved roadways and block all views of oncoming traffic.

On European expressways like Germany's autobahn, you'll have little problem so long as you remember to keep in the slow lane except when passing a vehicle. Otherwise you may get a shock when a BMW appears on your rear bumper out of nowhere, flashing his lights and clocking in at 100 m.p.h.

If it's your first trip to Europe, you'll undoubtedly want to include the major cities, but sightseeing can be difficult since there's hardly anywhere to park a camper unit legally and they're too big for parking garages. The best bet is to book a campsite in a suburban part of the city near public transportation and commute by bus, train or subway to your daily sightseeing.

Standard rental units in Europe may have no toilet or shower facilities, or include a detachable cassette toilet that has to be lifted out manually from a cabinet on the outside of the vehicle to be emptied in special dump stations at most gas stations and some campgrounds. Gray water is commonly run off into a street grate or even onto the ground.

Mid-sized vehicles with built-in hot water shower, space heater and flush water toilet or portable chemical toilet are also readily available, especially in Germany. These run abut $150 a day in high season and sleep two adults in a double bed made from dinette seating, plus two children (or small, friendly adults) in a cabover bed. The toilet unit is removed from its storage area by an outside door and can be emptied in any public toilet facility.

You may find your unit scantily furnished if at all. Sometimes the renter must provide bedding and frequently needs to add even the most basic items to the sparse supply of pots and utensils.

Many European campgrounds have morning milk and bread delivery, restaurants or pizzerias, saunas, pools, tennis courts and discos. What they usually lack is space for individual sites. Instead, you'll usually find yourself wedged in cheek-by-jowl with your (usually) friendly neighbors in a parking lot configuration. Campsites average around $10 a night; some have group or individual electric hookups, sometimes individually metered. The charge may be a flat fee or one based on how much electricity you use. Drinking water is available from taps in the campground, but not always conveniently near the campsite. You almost never find a sewer hookup. Sometimes the electrical hookup may be one post in the center of the campground with wires leading back in all directions to individual caravans.

Public toilet facilities at campgrounds vary considerably country to country; the farther east you drive, the more basic they become, culminating in the popular two- blocks-for-your-feet-and-a-hole-in-the-floor.

And don't expect restrooms at the frequent rest areas along Europe's superhighways. You'll find a picnic table and some bushes at most.

Some European campgrounds provide coin-operated laundry facilities; otherwise, look for a local laundromat. (When we lived in Europe, the first word we learned in seven languages was "laundromat.") Some places will accept your laundry in the morning, let you go about your sightseeing while they wash, dry and fold it, then you pick it up in the afternoon.

Because the lodging infrastructure in the former eastern European nations has not caught up with the west, some visitors find visiting these places by RV to offer the most comfort. Insurance is a major consideration, however. Be sure to coordinate your itinerary plans with your insurance coverage.

So long as you're on the Continent, you can pretty much travel anywhere from northern Norway to Greece, southern Portugal to Poland, with relatively short and simple ferry connections and traffic moving on the right in the same familiar pattern as back home. But if you want to include the British Isles, you'll probably be better off renting your RV in Britain, where the vehicle is designed to be driven on the left side of the road.

Global Motorhome Travel in Manhattan Beach, CA, ☎ *(800) 468-3876* or *(310) 318-9995,* can reserve an RV to be picked up in Germany, Holland or France (the latter two countries are more expensive on the daily rate) at prices from around $100 to $250 a day, depending on season and size of vehicle, including unlimited mileage, value added tax and full insurance.

If you want to travel in an RV with a group in Europe, contact **Overseas Motorhome Tours**, *222K South Irena Street, Redondo Beach, CA 90277,* ☎ *(800) 322-2127.*

England's Caravan Club, *East Grinstead House, East Grinstead, West Sussex RH19 1UA, England,* puts out a campground directory in English for all of Europe. High quality Michelin road maps for Europe can be purchased at kiosks and newsstands in France, at many bookstores all over Europe or in map or travel bookstores in the United States before you leave. *Europe by RV* by Dennis & Tina Jaffe (Globe Pequot Press, 1994, $14.95) gives not only a good rundown on things an RVer needs to know about Europe, but also suggests a variety of itineraries with campground and driving information.

10 TIPS FOR TOURING EUROPE BY RV

1. Don't try to do the whole Continent in a one, two or three week trip. Instead, concentrate on one region, say Scandinavia or The Netherlands, where RV camping is very popular, or France, which is extremely friendly to RVers, or the British Isles.

2. If you're traveling in July or August, avoid those areas where the Europeans themselves vacation—the French Riviera, for example, or the beaches in any country—unless you really love crowds. Portugal can be extremely hot in summer, as is the interior of Spain; save both countries for spring or autumn journeys. On the other hand, summer is the best time for Scandinavia and the Baltics because the weather is mild. Germany is great in the autumn.

3. Buy food for meals in local street markets, bakeries and butcher shops. You'll get a double pleasure from it—sampling local products and having a dialogue in sign language or a different language. If you really are inhibited about trying to get along in another language, shop in the supermarkets which are everywhere now. You'll find the same see-through plastic packaging you're accustomed to at home with no need to converse with anyone.

4. Contact the foreign government tourist offices in the United States for the places you're planning to visit (most have an office in New York and/or Los Angeles) and ask for maps, campground directories and other travel information.

5. Because some campgrounds have a center post with all the electrical connections snaking off it, you may want to carry your own 25-meter cable roll, available from most hardware stores; be sure it's manufactured for outdoor use. Your own electric appliances such as hair dryers and irons are usually 110-volt and will not work on the 220-volt power generally used in Europe. If you bring your own rig from North America, you'll also need a step-down transformer to change the current. These are not always readily available.

6. Germany and France have begun building some official free camping sites for RVs to encourage tourism; they are usually identified with a motorhome picture on a sign.

7. You will be able to use credit cards in many parts of Europe, in gas stations and on some toll motorways and tunnels. If you use pay phones often, you should invest in plastic "phone cards," available at the local post office or telephone company, which eliminates the need to carry coins.

8. In France, look for specially designated RV parking areas that may also provide a dumping station and fresh water supply. They are identified by motorhome pictographs.

9. In Britain, the speed limit for motorhomes is 70 m.p.h. on the motorways, 60 m.p.h. on surface roads, and 30 m.p.h. in towns. Trailers longer than 23 feet or wider than seven and one-half feet are not permitted.

10. Just as in North America, RVers should take care when camping in parking lots, on deserted beaches or by the side of the road.

JAPAN

Japan has taken a major interest in RVing in the past few years, with unit size the critical factor. One model particularly popular with Japanese RVers is the Shadow Cruiser T-139 travel trailer with an optional fold-down upper bunk for a child and a skylight with cover. The wonderfully compact 13-foot 9-inch trailer, designed for a small tow vehicle, has a shower and Thetford cassette toilet, water heater, two-burner cooktop, twin bed sofa/dinette combination, TV cabinet, wardrobe and optional microwave, stereo and air conditioning.

In Japan, RVers get a permit only by coming in with both the travel trailer and the tow vehicle, which are licensed as one. If a driver is caught driving the travel trailer with something other than the approved tow vehicle, there's a huge fine.

KOA (Kampgrounds of America) recently opened its first franchised campground in Japan, the Okayama Central KOA in southern Japan near Kobe. The year-round facility has 100 sites in a rural farm setting, plus pool, tennis courts, a miniature zoo, food service and a Karaoke Kabin. (Karaoke is an electronically sophisticated version of the sing-along, with acoustic background music and the printed lyrics projected on a screen in front of the singer.) The Japanese division of KOA promises a system of campgrounds throughout Japan in the near future aimed at both Japanese and foreign tourists.

AUSTRALIA

RVing, or caravanning, is a major holiday activity in Australia, whose residents also make up a major RV rental market in the United States.

Australia is a huge country, comparable in size to the United States, but without our network of fast interstate highways. To explore even the nearest edges of the Outback, you'd need a four-wheel-drive vehicle and an extra supply of gasoline, since service stations may be 150 miles apart.

Rental campervans or folding tent trailers rent for around $350 a week; small motorhomes are generally available for around $450–$650 a week. Look for a company that offers an unlimited kilometer rate. Units are generally furnished with the basics, but some dealers rent an amenities package for a surcharge.

Just as in the U.S., it's a good idea to make advance reservations in the popular areas like Ayers Rock and the Blue Mountains. Camping is especially popular on the pretty little green island of Tasmania, which has superlative fresh shellfish, historic Port Arthur and the fascinating little Tasmanian devil, best seen in commercial parks or zoos.

Australian RV rentals can be arranged in the U.S. with the following agencies: **Explorer Motor Caravans**, ☎ *(800) 558-0872*; **Newman's Sunseeker Caravans**, ☎ *(800) 252-4616* in California or ☎ *(800) 421-3326* for the rest of the U.S., ☎ *(800) 624-4349* for Canada; **Holiday Motorhome Rentals**, ☎ *(800) 231-1468* in the U.S., ☎ *(714) 675-7306* in California, and ☎ *(714) 675-2250* (collect) in Canada.

Some larger parks have on-site RVs for rent by the night as well. Although there are no RV campgrounds within the city limits of Sydney, you'll find several in outlying areas such as Rockdale, Ramsgate and North Ryde, all about 10 miles from the center.

Fielding's Australia by Zeke and Joan Wigglesworth is a handy guide with an RV angle for touring Australia.

NEW ZEALAND

This green, friendly, English-speaking, two-island country makes an ideal RV destination for a two- or three- week holiday. Roads are good and relatively uncrowded, the scenery is magnificent—especially the South Island's fjords and national parks and the craggy Mackenzie sheep country.

Camping is permitted virtually anywhere in New Zealand other than in specifically posted "no camping" areas. In addition, there are motor camps and campgrounds everywhere, since camping and "tramping" (hiking) are the favorite holidays of the Kiwis themselves. In most motor camping areas, you can expect to find communal kitchens, flush toilets, hot showers, laundry, perhaps a store, swimming or mineral pool and TV lounge. Campsites are priced around $5 a day per adult and are usually limited to a seven-day stay.

Rental campervans that sleep up to six people are generally furnished with gas cooktop, refrigerator, heater, shower, running water, dishes and bed linens. High season runs from December through March (remember, this is the southern hemisphere where the seasons are reversed). Costs start at around $50 a day for a low season rental of a camper van for two with unlimited kilometers, and escalates rapidly for larger vehicles and in high season. Insurance and deposit are extra.

The largest New Zealand RV rental company is Maui Campas, with offices in Auckland and Christchurch. Mount Cook Line and Suntrek also rent RVs. To get more information, call ☎ *520-1404* in Auckland. In most cases, you can pick up your RV right at the Auckland airport. Your U.S. travel agent or the rental companies can make the booking for you before you leave North America. Read the fine print; some roads around the islands are off limits for RVs.

If you're an auto club member and have your card along, the Auckland office of the Automobile Association at the corner of Albert and Victoria Streets will supply free maps and campground guides, as well as towing and accommodations guides.

Chains of private campgrounds throughout New Zealand include Top 10 Group and Kiwi Camps, and most have similar facilities to American private campgrounds, with laundromats, recreation room, showers and toilets and communal electric kitchens with sinks. Some also have bars and restaurants.

Do note the eccentric housetrucks on the highways of New Zealand, whimsical vehicles with shingles, bay windows and flower boxes, looking something like the homemade hippie camping vehicles of the 1960s and 1970s.

A good driving/RV guide to take throughout the country is *Fielding's New Zealand* by Joan and Zeke Wigglesworth, with more than a thousand detailed listings of places to go and things to see and do.

TEN FREEWHEELING RV ADVENTURES

Driving the Alaska Highway
Catch a salmon, snap a grizzly bear, make a wager with Diamond Tooth Gertie in the midnight sun of the Klondike. Brave this legendary road with its frost heaves and lurking caribou and you too can wear a T-shirt saying, "I Drove the Alaska Highway."

Bouncing Down Baja
Hit Baja's ten best beaches, catch a billfish or be caught by a giggling marlin, splurge on fresh shrimp and bump into a boojum along the thousand miles of Baja California's notorious Transpeninsular Highway.

The California Desert
Learn to drive a race car, get lost in the Barstow Triangle, sip a date milkshake, and see the Strippers' Hall of Fame in sunny Southern California, where Palm Springs eternal and Death Valley comes alive.

The Black Hills of South Dakota
Go dancing with wolves where the buffalo roam, gaming in Deadwood where Wild Bill met Calamity Jane, see the wonders of Wall Drug Store and the profiles of presidents, check the Crazy Horse carving, catch a trout, pan for gold, learn Lakota in these magical hills.

The Lobster Coast: New England and the Maritimes
Find the twelve best lobster spots, take a walk on the beach, see how Twinkies get those gooey white centers, drill with an 18th century French soldier, shop for Cape Cod antiques, lift a glass where "Cheers" got its start, see the Salem witch trial and salute a snowbird in the Anne Murray museum.

The Ozarks and Branson, Missouri
Slip into a Hot Springs spa, dine with Carmen Dragonwagon, buy a made-to-measure chair, join in some picking and singing on the courthouse steps in Mountain View or head for Branson, which boasts more visitors than the Grand Canyon.

Cruising the Florida Keys
Meet Hemingway's six-toed cats, celebrate Doris Day Night, catch a crocodile, dive with dolphins, heft a bar of gold from a sunken treasure ship,

chew on a conch or spend the night in an undersea motel in this wacky, watery wonderland.

Along the Rio Grande

Follow this lazy river as it delineates the border between Texas and Mexico, learn the law west of the Pecos, meet a beer-drinking goat, hike the Chisos, compete in a jalapeno-eating contest and see where Wolfman Jack beamed out rock 'n roll to the teens of an earlier America.

The Blue Ridge Parkway and Skyline Drive

Drive Cook a country ham, take a hike, paddle your own canoe, see a Civil War battle recreated, tap your toes to down-home fiddlers at the world's largest fiddling convention as you follow this famous scenic drive along the ridge of the Appalachians.

Southern Utah's National Parks Country

Ride a mountain bike on the Slickrock Trail, float on a houseboat past ancient Anasazi settlements, photograph some awesome arches, raft the Colorado and taste a pickle pie amid the west's most magnificent terrain.

DRIVING THE
ALASKA HIGHWAY

The beginning of the Alaska Highway in Dawson Creek, British Columbia

The Alaska Highway kept the Japanese from invading the North American mainland during World War II, helped Alaska achieve statehood in 1959 and, more recently, set off a flourishing bumper sticker and T-shirt industry with lurid illustrations around the theme, "I Drove the Alaska Highway."

Alaska is where people relish Spam and line up on highway roadkill lists for a chance at the next moose struck down by a car, where Warren G. Harding drove a golden spike to mark the completion of the Alaska Railroad in 1923, and where the most powerful earthquake ever to hit the North American continent struck on Good Friday in 1964, a 9.2 on the Richter scale which lasted an incredible five minutes.

It's where you can stand in mud up to your knees and have dust blow in your face, where mosquitoes are as big as hummingbirds and where you won't be considered a real Alaskan until—to paraphrase the locals in more polite terms—you've wrestled a grizzly, urinated in the Yukon and had an amorous encounter with a bear.

It's where Arco tapped a $10 billion oil reserve at Prudhoe Bay in 1968 and Exxon spilled 11 million gallons of it off Valdez in 1989, where Russia established an outpost in the 19th century, and a historical marker at a creekside bordello describes the area as a place where the salmon and the fishermen both came upstream to spawn.

It was where "wannabe" gold miners headed for the Klondike by any means they could, crammed into any boat that could float and some that couldn't, where salesmen brought their inventory, gamblers their cards and dice, women their bodies for sale or their scrubboards and sadirons for labor. And all of them intended to get rich.

"They didn't build a city here; they found gold. That's the whole story of Alaska."

Ruth Allman, Alaska pioneer

FREEWHEELING ALONG THE ALASKA HIGHWAY

Rocky Crest Lake, near Muncho Lake on the Alaska Highway

While this mighty motorway still strikes fear into the hearts of travelers, it's tamed down considerably since its asphalt surface was more or less completed a couple of years ago. The main attraction to the freewheeler is a combination of end-of-the-world roadways peeling off it at intervals and the incredible scenery—craggy peaks capped with perpetual snow, hanging and calving glaciers, golden midnight sunsets, swirling acid-green northern lights—and wildlife—grizzly bears, moose, caribou, bald eagles, sometimes wolves—waiting to be discovered along the way.

The first challenge in driving the Alaska Highway is to get to the starting point, the famous Mile 0, located in Dawson Creek, British Columbia, 817 miles north of Seattle on the western access route, or 867 miles northwest of Great Falls, Montana, on the eastern access route.

Eighty percent of the Alaska Highway is in Canada, which is why some people still call it by its nickname "the Alcan." Despite losing their box office billing in the official name, the Canadians got a good deal because in 1946, after the war that created its construction, they bought their share at half what it cost to build.

The precise length of the Alaska Highway keeps changing as engineers straighten out its notorious curves. The original, or historic, mileposts are still used as addresses by the business and residents along the highway. Contemporary mileposts reflect the present distances, while in Canada kilometer posts are also in service.

Another point of contention is where the highway actually starts and stops. The milepost for Historic Mile 0 is in Dawson Creek, British Columbia, and the true terminus is in Delta Junction, Alaska, because a road connecting Delta Junction and Fairbanks already existed. Most Alaska Highway travelers, however, consider Fairbanks the real end of the highway, after which they usually head south via Denali National Park and Preserve to Anchorage.

Denali means "the high one" in the language of the local Athabascan peoples, and the name has been given to the former Mount McKinley National Park, which was named in 1917 for an assassinated president who never saw it. The four-million acre park, slightly bigger than the state of Massachusetts, includes a wilderness area and a national preserve; sport hunting, fishing and trapping are allowed in the latter by state permit.

Denali State Park is located southeast of the national park area, bisected by Parks Highway, which is named for George Parks, a territorial governor in the late 1920s, not for the fact that two major parks lie along it.

INSIDER TIP·

Always top off your gas tank when you pass an open station. Sometimes a station ahead may be closed for the day or gone out of business. Our closest call came on the Klondike Highway when we had to drive 269 miles between open stations and finally rolled into Dempster Corner on the fumes. Another time, we turned around and drove 20 miles back to buy gas at a station we had passed up, because the one we were headed for was closed.

A CRASH COURSE IN SPEAKING ALASKAN

Sourdough—anyone who's been in Alaska longer than one season, as in "Sour on Alaska without enough dough to get out"

Outside—anywhere that isn't Alaska; generally the lower 48 states

Native—not just anyone born in Alaska, but only those with Eskimo, Aleut or Indian blood

Cheechako—newcomer

The Bush—any place reached by plane instead of road or Alaska ferry

Permafrost—the permanently frozen subsoil that covers much of the state

BUILDING THE HIGHWAY

When Japan bombed Pearl Harbor in December 1941, it didn't take long for the U.S. government to look at a map and see that the narrow Bering Strait that separated the westernmost spot in North America—in Alaska—from the easternmost spot in Asia—in Siberia—was only 36 miles across. With the Japanese navy lurking close to North American shores, even invading the Aleutians, and Russia an ally who desperately needed supplies, the United States decided its Corps of Engineers should construct an inland road to Alaska. Because timing was important, trainloads of U.S. soldiers and equipment began arriving in tiny, remote Dawson Creek before any agreement was signed with Canada. All told, 33,000 men would work on the road that year, 11,000 of them U.S. Army troops, and some 200 would die in the subzero temperatures and hazardous working conditions.

The surveyors were just steps ahead of the bulldozers that winter of 1942, sinking into the mud and the permafrost below it. Not much attention was paid to grades or curves. As the surveyors pointed to what they perceived as the horizon, the bulldozers followed in their footprints. The original 1422-mile road was built in only eight months and 12 days.

Canadian construction crews cleaned up and straightened out the roadway for the next several years, but the Japanese threat in Alaskan waters had subsided. By 1949, the road was open to traffic, and paving continued sporadically until the last stretch was more or less covered by macadam in 1992. Drivers today still encounter long rough stretches undergoing construction.

When to go: While the highway is open and maintained year-round, RV visitors will find mid-May to late September best. The "season," according to the locals we met on our mid-May trip, had not yet begun, which meant we could find empty campsites late in the day. On the other hand, a few lodges and service stations along the way had not yet opened for the summer. Try to avoid July and August, when RVs are almost bumper-to-bumper along some stretches of the highway.

What to take: Binoculars, cameras and plenty of film, a world-class mosquito repellent, sunscreen, and good maps. Fishermen will want to carry fishing gear for lake trout, northern pike, Dolly Varden, arctic grayling and five species of Pacific salmon. Spin or bait-cast fishing and/or fly fishing rods and tackle capable of handling fish up to 30 pounds are recommended by the experts.

For the RV, experts suggest spare parts such as fan belt, oil filter, air filter, radiator hose and heater hose. Mud flaps or "eyelashes" for the back are a good idea to keep gravel and mud from splashing all over the rear window. We took a basic tool kit and an emergency medical kit, neither of which we had to open.

What to wear: Although we took along ski-weight down parkas and heavy-soled hiking boots, we never donned either. Walking or jogging shoes were adequate on the short trails we hiked. But dedicated hikers and climbers should carry specialized equipment. A raincoat and umbrellas are a good idea, since it can rain or even snow, but don't be surprised to find Fairbanks sunny and hot. Dress is casual all over Alaska, so typical RV outfits will pass muster anywhere (except on a cruise ship if you take the Alaska Highway Cruise package).

INSIDER TIP:

Our 1994 21-foot Fleetwood Jamboree rented from Alaska Highway Cruises averaged six to seven miles per gallon on the Alaska Highway, less than our larger 27-foot Winnebago type A motorhome usually gets. We drove a total of 3100 miles in May, 1994, spending approximately $600 on gas and about $500 on food and beverages for two.

DRIVING TIPS

Expect to drive with your headlights on. In this part of Canada the law requires it, and in times when dust is billowing, you'll be glad the oncoming traffic is visible through the clouds.

Don't try to "make time" on the road; it can make you crazy. We saw too many RVers limping into camp exhausted at nine p.m.; they kept driving because the sun was still high in the sky. Even if you drove your RV hell-for-leather, ignoring loose gravel, buckled roadways and potholes, you'd miss a lot of the scenery and the wildlife, two of the most important reasons for being there.

The eastern access route for the Alaska Highway goes from Great Falls to Calgary, across Alberta to Edmonton and northwest to Dawson Creek.

The western access route sets out from Seattle, north on I-5 to the Trans-Canada 1, east to Hope and north via either the fast new Coquihalla Highway or the slower route 97 to Cache Creek, Quesnel, Prince George and Dawson Creek.

10 CAMPGROUND OASES

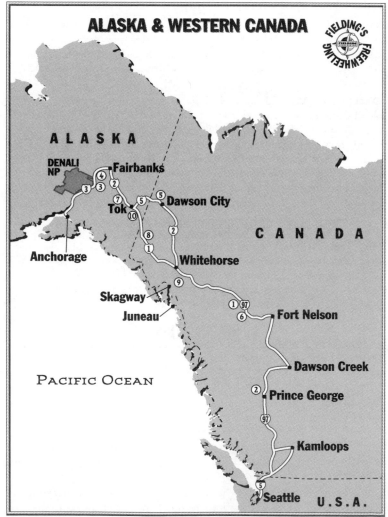

1. **Liard River Hot Springs Provincial Park**, Mile 496, is the most popular park along the route, with its 53 sites filling up by noon (no reservations). Besides handsome,

tree-shaded spots spaced well apart, the camper will find free firewood and hot springs for soaking away travel aches, but no RV hookups. Playgrounds, heated rest rooms, wheelchair accessible toilet. Bears sometimes prowl the area.

A campground at Tabor Lake near Lake George on the Alaska Highway comes with its own pets.

2. **Log House Restaurant and Campground**, Tabor Lake, near Prince George, is a clean, well-run campground with 24 sites, electric connections and water but no sanitary dump available. There's an excellent dinner restaurant on the hill above the RV park, also operated by proprietor Richard Gunther, plus a float plane base, cottages and fishing, as well as good bird-watching. (We spent much of our stay transfixed by the antics of a pet Canada goose and her wild boy friend who flies in for the summer, and two pair of horned grebes on the lake.) Reservations accepted, ☎ *(604) 963-9515.*

3. **Riley Creek Campground**, Denali National Park, with 102 well-separated and tree-shaded sites not far from the railway station. No reservations. After mid-June, any empty sites in the campground are usually filled the minute the previous tenant pulls out. Flush toilets, piped water in summer, sanitary dump station but no hookups, 14-day maximum stay. An overnight or two at Denali will allow time to get a spot on the popular park service shuttle bus that goes 66 miles into the wilderness, where private vehicles are not allowed.

4. **River's Edge RV Park**, off the Parks Highway in Fairbanks, has 170 sites with full and partial hookups, a sanitary dump station, laundry, showers, and free shuttle service to attractions such as the sternwheeler *Discovery* and the Alaska Salmon Bake. On the Chena River with fishing and boat ramp. For reservations, call ☎ *(800) 770-3343.*

5. **In downtown Dawson City**, Gold Rush Campground is the best bet, although its main appeal is its location, within easy walking distance of the sights. Some electric connections, a sanitary dump station and narrow, parking lot-type sites are what you'll find; reserve well ahead if you want a spot in midsummer, ☎ *(403) 993-5247.*

6. **Muncho Lake Provincial Park**, Mile 437 and 442 on the Alaska Highway in BC. The lake's icy waters are a gorgeous blue-and-turquoise color from a combination of copper in the rocks and glacial runoff. There are 30 sites, 15 in each location,

with piped water, firewood, boat launch, fishing and hiking. Caribou, moose and sheep are sometimes seen here, and bears may frequent the area. No hookups, no reservations.

7. **Moon Lake State Recreation Site**, on the Alaska Highway at Mile 1332 west of Tok, 15 campsites amid the trees by a beautiful lake, toilets, piped water, boat launch. No hookups, no reservations.

8. **Westmark RV Park, Beaver Creek**, AH Mile 1202, has 65 sites with electric and water hookups, adjacent to the Westmark Inn if you want to treat yourself to a meal or two out. Lounge, laundry, gift shop, showers, wildlife display, sanitary dump. To reserve ahead, call ☎ *(403) 862-7501.*

9. **Tagish Lake Campground**, Yukon Government, on Tagish Road near Tagish Bridge, famous for great lake trout fishing. The campground itself has 28 sites with firepits, tables, piped water, toilets, kitchen shelters, fishing and occasional bears. No hookups, no reservations.

10. **Tok Sourdough Campground and Pancake House** in Tok, two miles south on the Anchorage highway, specializes in sourdough pancakes. The RV park adjacent has 58 sites, 34 with electric hookups, 36 with water and 16 with sewer hookups. Sanitary dump station, laundry, showers and flush toilets. Cafe, gift shop, walk-through museum of Alaskan artifacts, car wash. To reserve, call ☎ *(907) 883-5543.*

> ### INSIDER TIP:
> *The biggest enemy your vehicle has in Alaska are "frost heaves," irregular bumps where the pavement has buckled or sunk because of permafrost melting and refreezing. Spots may be marked with little red flags by the roadside, but sometimes the wind takes them away. If the white center or side lines look squiggly ahead, slow down.*

ON THE ROAD IN NORTHERN BRITISH COLUMBIA

Once past Calgary on the eastern access road or Kamloops on the western access road, urbanites need to make an important mental adjustment. There are no more cities until Whitehorse, Yukon Territory, just a series of small towns separated by as much as eight hours of driving through gorgeous, uninhabited scenery.

While those places with serious names and major crossroads you've been looking at on the map all day may not be what you expect by the time you finally arrive, the inhabitants are generally friendly and helpful.

Dawson Creek is where most of the Alaska Highway drivers stop coming and going to trade war stories, especially at service stations, car washes, RV parks and the town's major drinking and dining spot, the venerable Alaska Cafe. This is where you photograph your RV in front of the Mile 0 Alaska Highway sign, take a look at one of the three competing pioneer villages and admire the big red grain elevator that doubles as art gallery and tourist information office.

In Fort Nelson, as we were running out of reading and cocktail materials, we found an office supply store that had a treasure-trove of second-hand paperback books sold at half the cover price and a liquor store that had a sparse and pricey inventory. Less exciting was a highly advertised "European deli" with a meager supply of meats and cheese but doing a land office business in microwaved burritos.

The world-famous Sign Post Forest at Watson Lake, BC, on the Alaska Highway, has some 20,000 signs from all over the world.

Watson Lake, on the Yukon border, has a unique sign forest (see "Ten Off-the-Wall Attractions" in this chapter), a 1940s "Stage Door Canteen" musical (in summer) and a modest supermarket. Campground Services RV park offers 140 sites, full and partial hookups and a coin-operated car/RV wash to get rid of the top layer of road dust. Don't worry about street addresses—the whole town is laid out in a strip along the highway.

The "lodges" so grandly promoted by highway road signs before you get there usually turn out to be very basic roadside cafes with a straggle of cabins in the back and a gas tank out front, and a cashier/waitress who also sells fishing licenses, pumps gas, makes beds and does the home cooking in her spare time.

Whatever the roadside food lacks in flavor, it more than makes up for in volume. We fussy freewheelers were glad our RV had a kitchen.

INSIDER TIP:

We make it a habit never to assume any piped campground water is potable, using it only for the kitchen and bathroom. We drink bottled water and use prepackaged ice, which is available almost everywhere along the route in Alaska and northern Canada, where tap water sometimes comes out in shades of brown.

Never drink water from a stream or lake, no matter how pristine it looks. The parasite giardia, which can cause extreme intestinal upset and is impervious to antibiotics, is present in Northern Canada and Alaska waterways.

10 GREAT NORTHERN HIGHWAY SPLURGES

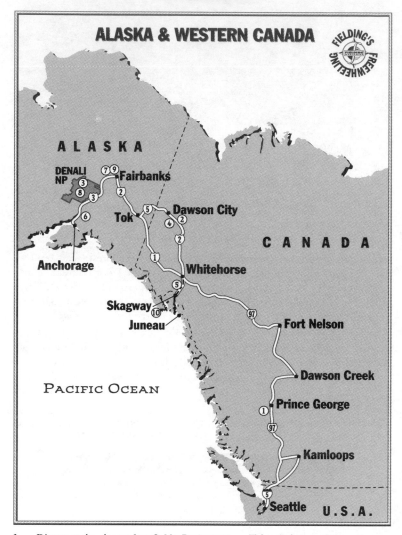

ALASKA & WESTERN CANADA

FIELDING'S FREEWHEELING

ALASKA

DENALI NP

Fairbanks

Tok

Dawson City

Anchorage

Whitehorse

CANADA

Skagway

Juneau

Fort Nelson

PACIFIC OCEAN

Dawson Creek

Prince George

Kamloops

Seattle U.S.A.

1. Dinner at the elegant **Log Cabin Restaurant** on Tabor Lake near Prince George, BC, ☎ *(604) 963-9515,* where host Richard Gunther will show you his astonishing collection of antique stoves and sewing machines, plus Indian artifacts, stuffed and mounted black bears and wolves, and everything else you could imagine. The food is Continental with a German accent (Gunther is from Berlin) and dinner begins with a bottomless tureen of homemade soup.

2. An evening of gaming at **Diamond Tooth Gertie's** in Dawson City, especially rambunctious at the end of the season when all the locals are trying to win enough money to head south for the winter.

3. An overnight or two at the appealing if archly rustic **Kantishna Roadhouse** at the end of the road inside Denali National Park lets you go on guided hikes deep in the

park. A special permit is necessary to drive in, but there's the park shuttle bus or, if you're in a hurry, a resort airstrip for a Denali air shuttle. Reserve well in advance, ☎ *(800) 942-7420.*

4. A performance of the **Gaslight Follies** in Dawson City's 1899 Palace Grand Theatre brings together a surprisingly professional cast; it's far less corny than the similar show in Whitehorse.

5. A three-hour excursion aboard the summer-only, narrow-gauge **White Pass & Yukon Railway** from Skagway to the White Pass Summit and back. There's also daily afternoon service from Skagway to Whitehorse with a morning return. Built in 1899, the train has one of the steepest railroad grades in North America.

6. A dinner of rare white King salmon (all the rage in Anchorage during its very brief season) at that city's **Simon & Seafort's Saloon**, preceded by fresh King crab and followed by the house's brandy ice, a concoction of vanilla ice cream, brandy, Kahlua and creme de cacao.

7. In northern craft shops, look for rare and costly **qiviut**, the soft underwool of the musk ox, gathered when it's shed each spring and woven into warm, feather-light gloves, scarves, caps and sweaters, or seek carved soapstone pieces, ceremonial wooden masks or last season's trendy ulus, fan-shaped chopping knives with wood handles.

8. On a clear day, fly over **Mt. McKinley** and the Susitna Valley, where glimpses of moose, bear, foxes and eagles are common, then land in Talkeetna, staging area for climbers who tackle the high peaks of the Alaska Range. Call Sky Trekking Alaska, ☎ *(800) 770-4966* for details.

9. Dine at the colorful **Pump House Restaurant** on the banks of the Chena River, two miles southwest of Fairbanks on Chena Pump Road, now a national historic site crammed with gold rush-era artifacts.

10. Park the RV in Valdez and take an all-day cruise of Prince William Sound aboard the **Glacier Queen**, with close-up views of vast Columbia Glacier, cliffs with nesting kittiwakes and glimpses of marine mammals. Call Gray Line Alaska at ☎ *(800) 544-2206* for details.

> ### INSIDER TIP:
> *Stock up your RV with any esoteric items before you get into the woods. You'll be able to find basic groceries, towing services, RV repairs and telephones along the road, but if you want to prepare a bouillabaisse with your freshly-caught fish, take your saffron and Sauvignon Blanc along with you.*

THE YUKON

Around Dawson City they joke, "This isn't the end of the world, but you can see it from here."

This is a destination for North Americans with a yen to wander, nagged by an insatiable restlessness to see what lies at the end of the road. It is written in the faces of men wearing rumpled plaid shirts and blue jeans as they climb out of dirty, mud-streaked RVs and 4-by-4s with license plates from Florida, New Brunswick, Texas, California and Ontario. They have made it to the place where the Yukon and the Klondike Rivers meet, to the fabled city of gold and the end of the infamous Trail of '98.

Coming to Dawson City is like meeting a childhood idol or your favorite movie star three or four decades after the fact and being surprised to find the old dear is still alive, let alone lively enough to dance a fandango and tell a couple of salty tales.

Weary buildings in Dawson City await restoration by Parks Canada.

Far from being some saccharine gold rush Disneyland or horsehair-stuffed historical monument, Dawson is alive and kicking. Under the aegis of Parks Canada, where "money is always iffy," the town is slowly being renovated. Some buildings like the splendid Palace Grand Theatre, the old post office, the Arctic Brotherhood Hall (now Diamond Tooth Gertie's Casino) and Madame Tremblay's store have been restored. Others, sagging and unpainted, lean wearily against each other waiting their turn, looking as if they won't last much longer.

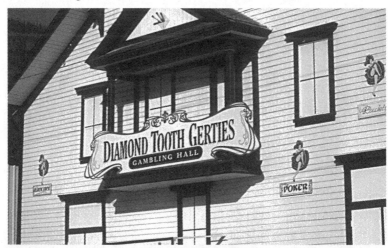

Diamond Tooth Gertie's in Dawson City has Yukon's only legal gambling.

Some of the wilder goings on from earlier years were not in evidence last summer. The "Miss Nude Yukon" contest had faded into obscurity and the Eldorado's famous Sour Toe cocktail—a pickled human toe tossed into a beer mug of champagne—has tamed down and moved over to the Keno Lounge in the Westmark Inn. But the annual Great International Outhouse Race and Bathroom Wall Limerick Contest is still on the Labor Day weekend agenda.

Today Dawson's biggest gold mine is Diamond Tooth Gertie's Casino, the only legal gambling casino in the Yukon.

> ### INSIDER TIP:
>
> *An advance-ticket purchase for the ARA Tundra Wildlife Tours ($45) into Denali National Park is a boon for anyone who hasn't a day or two to wait for space on the free park shuttles; call them at ☎ (907) 683-2215 in summer, ☎ (907) 276-7234 in winter.*

FAIRBANKS

In 1902, when the Klondike excitement had quieted down a little, a prospector named Felix Pedro discovered gold in the Tanana Valley near present-day Fairbanks, and a new rush was on. The prospectors and gamblers from Dawson hurried west to the new boom town, rode the crest of the newest wave, then crashed in the depression that followed.

Vestiges of those days can still be seen in Alaskaland, not as commercial as its name sounds, where the history of the gold mining days is re-created. The town's original cabins, a replica Indian village, the Crooked Creek & Whiskey Island railroad with its little steam engine, and the sternwheeler *Nenana*, one-time star of the Yukon riverboats, are all on display.

From Fairbanks, you can take a paddlewheeler day cruise along the Chena and Tanana Rivers or a motorcoach excursion along the Dalton Highway following the Trans-Alaska Oil Pipeline farther into Prudhoe Bay than private vehicles can go.

You can find a Fairbanks branch of every fast-food outlet known to man.

The turn-off to downtown Chicken, Alaska, from unpaved route 5.

10 TOP SIDE TRIPS

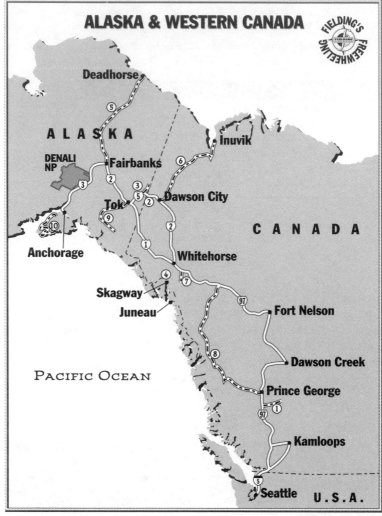

1. From Quesnel, BC, take route 26 over to the Cariboo Gold Rush town of Barker-
    ville, in its heyday the largest city north of San Francisco and west of Chicago. More
    than 125 original and restored buildings, many of them occupied by costumed
    docents, are open, including Lung Duck Ton Chinese restaurant, Eldorado Gold
    Panning, The Wake-Up-Jake Restaurant, McPherson's Watchmakers Shop and
    Cameron & Ames Blacksmith Shop. An historic stage stop called Cottonwood
    House is also on the route; the round trip from highway 97 is 100 miles.

2. The Top of the World Highway (Yukon route 9) from Dawson City to Eagle is 146
    miles of unpaved, white-knuckling terror you'll talk about for years, especially if you
    go early in the season when half the roadway is still covered with ice and snow.
    There are no guard rails and few markers to let you know whether you're still on the
    roadway or have ventured off onto a side road that peters out in the tundra. Eagle,
    where author John McPhee set much of his classic *Coming Into the Country*, is an

optional destination at the end of the rough, narrow road. There's been a trading post here for gold miners since the 1880s, and today Eagle is populated by some 150 pioneers, curmudgeons and refugees from urban life.

3. The Taylor Highway from Eagle to Tetlin Junction is 161 miles of rough road, with the biggest metropolis en route being the town of Chicken with its population of 37. There's a saloon, a cafe, a gas station and two gift shops where you can buy T-shirts with slogans like, "I got laid in Chicken, Alaska." The old gold mining town itself is off the main road and closed to visitors except on a daily guided walking tour or gold panning venture in summer. The original settlers wanted to name it after the ptarmigan, the plump little edible grouse that was a dietary mainstay, but since they couldn't spell it, they called the town Chicken instead.

4. Klondike Highway 2 from Whitehorse 99 miles south to Skagway, via Carcross (short for Caribou Crossing), looks nothing like the precipitous trail, lake and river route followed by the prospectors of '98, most of them ill-equipped cheechakos who were required by the Northwest Mounted Police to carry a ton of supplies to the gold fields. A few had horses, a few more "sled dogs" that were usually poodles or terriers dognapped from Seattle back yards, but most had to carry the stuff on their backs in relays, caching it along the trail and doubling back for more. Skagway, at the end of the road, is the town where sharpies like gambler Soapy Smith and his cronies fleeced the innocent. The two-lane paved road is asphalt-surfaced and fairly wide.

5. The rough, gravel-surfaced Dalton Highway to Prudhoe Bay takes you across the Arctic Circle, the Brooks Range and the Continental Divide, but you'll have to stop a few miles short of Prudhoe Bay itself; the oil companies limit access. The 414-mile road was constructed to build and service the Alaska pipeline, and there are very few services available along it. Check on road conditions and how far you'll be able to drive before setting out. Last year it was open only to Dietrich Camp, about half-way.

6. Canada's 456-mile Dempster Highway crosses the Arctic Circle at Mile 252 after striking north from Dawson City and Klondike Highway 2. Final destination is the Northwest Territories' Inuit village of Inuvik, with 57 days of midnight sun beginning May 24 each year. The gravel road, with some slippery clay surface sections, also requires two ferry crossings; the most feasible time to go is between mid-June and the end of August. Black flies and mosquitoes are also a problem, so take plenty of repellent. You may spot wolves, caribou, grizzly bears, moose, eagles and gyrfalcons. Allow two days in each direction to drive this tough tundra route. Government campgrounds are spotted along the road, but few services are available. Stop for gas whenever you see a station open.

7. Atlin Road, Yukon/BC 7. From Jake's Corner, Mile 836, turn south for a spectacular 58-mile scenic route to Canada's Little Switzerland, with snow-capped mountains, lakes with good fishing, and a good chance of spotting moose or grizzly bears. The all-weather gravel road is fairly good although winding, and slippery in wet weather.

8. The Cassiar Highway, BC 37, drops south from Mile 726 west of Watson Lake down to the Yellowhead Highway 16. It's also possible to use the Cassiar as an alternate to the Alaska Highway between Prince George and Watson Lake. A lot of adventuresome drivers prefer this route, which they liken to driving the Alaska Highway back in the fifties and sixties. There are some stretches of gravel instead of road and services are few and far between, but the scenery from hanging glaciers to snow-capped mountains is stunning.

9. Chitina, the gateway to Alaska's 13-million acre Wrangell-St. Elias National Park and Preserve, is reachable by 33 miles of paved road from the Richardson Highway between Tok and Valdez. Only small RVs or four-wheel drive vehicles without trailers should attempt the next 58 unpaved, steep and sometimes slippery miles of the road into McCarthy, but the effort is worth it. The privately-owned copper company town of Kennicott, now a ghost town, can be visited by hikers crossing the Kennicott River via hand-operated cable tram (wear thick gloves). Guided glacier walks, Kennicott tours, back-country hikes and horseback riding are available in McCarthy.

10. Drive south from Anchorage along the Turnagain Arm, keeping an eye out for whales, and stop at Alaska's top ski resort of Alyeska (the lifts take you sightseeing in summer) and the Portage Glacier with its self-guiding nature trail to the ice worms. If time permits, you can keep going south to the town of Seward or take the Sterling Highway to Homer and the Kenai Peninsula.

INSIDER TIP:

Don't attempt to drive down to the Kenai Peninsula on a summer weekend; it's bumper-to-bumper traffic heading south from Anchorage on Friday afternoons and heading north on Sunday nights and Monday mornings.

ANCHORAGE

In the Bush, they like to say, "The nicest thing about Los Anchorage is that it's only 30 miles from Alaska."

People who don't know Alaska usually visualize Anchorage as an icy outpost in the wilderness populated by moose, grizzly bears and bush pilots. True, you will find moose and bears—most often in the Anchorage Zoo—and plenty of bush pilots taking off from and landing at Lake Hood. But the first time we arrived there, on a July day, it was warmer and sunnier than Los Angeles and bright with summer flowers. On our most recent May visit, however, it was cold and windy and socked in with fog.

Earthquake Park still shows graphically the results of the 9.2 earthquake on Good Friday in 1964, when two huge chunks of earth fissured and dropped 20 feet in an instant. "It looked like chocolate pudding somebody had been dragging their fingers through," one eyewitness said.

A statue of Captain James Cook looks out on Turnagain Arm, so named when the captain told his first mate William Bligh, later to command the *Bounty*, to turn around again when it turned out not to be the Northwest Passage he was seeking.

The fine Anchorage Museum, in a stylish building with a frieze of stylized Alaskan designs across the top, displays an excellent collection of contemporary Alaskan and Native arts and crafts.

GOING FOR THE LONG HAUL

If you want to stretch out your Alaska RV adventure for a full, freewheeling summer, follow as many of the 10 side trips as you can squeeze in and weather permits. In spring and fall, check ahead on weather conditions since there could be a late thaw and some roads still closed by snowpack in spring. We were snowed in one August day in Dawson City when an early storm dumped so much of the white stuff the roads were closed.

> **INSIDER TIP:**
>
> *One expert says, If you encounter a bear while out on a hike, don't turn and run because he may give chase. Instead, walk backward to get away, facing the bear and continuing to talk in a normal tone. ("Nice bear, nice bear"?) Above all, "do not imitate bear sounds or positions, even if they sound funny to you."*

HITTING THE HIGHLIGHTS

With only a two-week vacation, you can still see a lot of Alaska, especially if you fly in and pick up an RV there. Anchorage is the center of RV rentals; call Clippership Motorhome Rentals at ☎ *(800) 421-3456* or ABC Motorhome Rentals at ☎ *(800) 421-7456* for prices, making sure to weigh the unlimited mileage rate against per mile fees.

Alaska Highway Cruises, ☎ *(800) 323-5757*, has a 12-day program that lets you fly to Anchorage, pick up an RV, drive to Denali and Fairbanks, take the Alaska Highway to Tok, the Taylor Highway and Top of the World Highway to Dawson City, then the Klondike Highway to Whitehorse and Skagway. At Skagway you pick up a cruise ship that cruises Glacier Bay, calls in Sitka and returns you to Vancouver for a flight home. The whole package starts at $2295 per person, double occupancy, plus airfare to Seattle, and includes the cruise with all meals and entertainment, a fully furnished rental RV, campground reservations and fees. You buy the gas and food.

10 AUTHENTIC FAR NORTH
TAKEOUTS AND TREATS

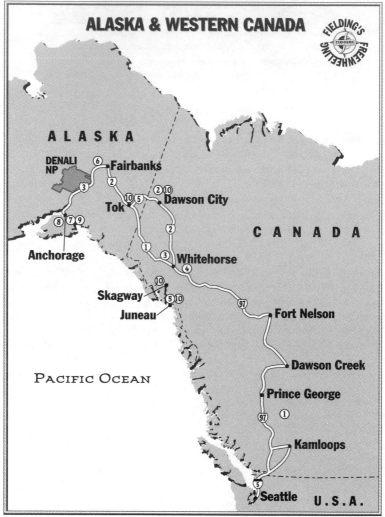

1. **Whole wheat or sourdough bread** from the Goldfields Bakery or Chinese dim sum from Lung Duck Tong restaurant in Barkerville, a historic gold rush town near Quesnel, BC.

2. **The Klondike mud pie** at T.J.'s Grill in Dawson City.

3. The Braeburn Lodge **superburgers** (one is big enough for two) or their famous "gianormous" (but not particularly tasty) cinnamon buns, Mile 55.6, Klondike Highway.

4. Halstead's original **Yukon rhubarb pie**, three miles west of Teslin on the lake, Mile 807.

5.   Juneau-brewed **Alaskan Beer** or **Alaskan Pale Ale** from the Alaska Brewing Company. Its Alaskan Amber has already been twice voted the most popular brew at the Great American Beer Festival in Colorado, and its only been around since 1986.

6.   The **reindeer stew and Alaska Dungeness crab** at the Malamute Saloon, eight miles west of Fairbanks at Ester Gold Camp. At night it includes the price of the show, a recitation of Robert Service poems like *The Shooting of Dan McGrew.*

7.   The **smoked salmon and reindeer sausage** packaged to go at The Alaska Sausage & Seafood Company in Anchorage.

8.   The **Double Musky cake** at the restaurant of the same name in Girdwood, south of Anchorage near Alyeska, with its layers of pecan meringue, brownie-like chocolate, chocolate mousse and cocoa cream frosting.

9.   Get some **Alaska Wild Berry chocolates** and check out the flowing 20-foot chocolate waterfall at the company's new Anchorage outlet. Filling options include wild rosehip, elderberry, salmonberry, high bush cranberry and lingonberry.

10. **Sourdough pancakes** almost anywhere, but they're especially good in Dawson City's Midnight Sun and Skagway's Klondike Hotel. In Juneau's Baranof Hotel, they're the size of Frisbees and accompanied by sturdy reindeer sausages, and in Tok you can camp next door to them at the Sourdough Campground. (See "10 Campground Oases.")

INSIDER TIP:

One of the best places to spot caribou is by the side of the road, oddly enough. They stand around morosely by signs and at road junctions as if waiting for a bus. Mountain sheep, too, like the roadsides.

A caribou crosses a side road off the Alaska Highway.

WILDLIFE WATCH

When you're on an African safari, you get into an eager pattern of wanting to check off the trophy animals first, and the same thing is true in Alaska. The first time you see a caribou, you hit the brakes, grab the cameras and shoot away. The second time, you take a minute to frame and focus, the third time you don't bother unless the light is right and the animal close enough, and after that, you say, "Oh, it's just another caribou."

We never got sated with moose sightings on our May trip, perhaps because spring is calving time. In early fall, however, plenty of them come down into the lower meadows in Denali. Pulling over to cook breakfast at a rest stop on the road between Denali and Anchorage, we saw a moose cow browsing at the edge of the trees and managed to snap a couple of shots before she gave us an aggrieved look and ambled back into the woods.

A close sighting of a porcupine in the wild, waddling up a bank with his silver-tipped quills aquiver, or a bald eagle in the roadway snacking on road kill is just as exciting as seeing the big animals. And unless you're unusually quick or patient or the animal very slow, your memory will be clearer than your photograph.

Our first good day of wildlife spotting was on an early morning transit of the Crooked River Nature Corridor south of McLeod Lake in British Columbia, with a wolf, deer and great blue herons spotted in quick succession. We were too late in the season to catch the trumpeter swans who winter here.

Hummingbird-sized mosquitoes—aka Alaska's state bird—in a campground at Fort Nelson were next, too large, fortunately, to get through the window screens of the RV.

An early morning roadside sighting of a black bear a few miles north of Fort Nelson did not net any photographs. He spotted us first so all we saw was his backside disappearing into the woods.

There were great caribou sightings at Stone Mountain Park, right past a huge sign warning, Caribou in the Roadway. The indigenous Stone sheep in Stone Mountain Park, colored cream and brown and bigger than Dall or Rocky Mountain sheep, can be glimpsed looking down from craggy rock cliffs or photographed as they gather by the roadside to lick salt deposits.

To spot the two-legged wildlife, head for Fly by Night Club in Anchorage, where the Spam hors d'oeuvres are free if you order a bottle of Dom Perignon champagne, and "The Whale Fat Follies" break up the locals. The house jazz band is called the Spamtones and the phone number is ☎ *279-SPAM.*

At the Howling Dog Saloon 11 miles north of Fairbanks, you can play volleyball all night long in June and July by the light of the midnight sun. A rock'n roll band drops in on weekends.

10 OFF-THE-WALL ATTRACTIONS

ALASKA & WESTERN CANADA

1. The **world's largest chopstick manufacturing plant**, Fort Nelson, BC, at mile 278.1, turns out six million pairs of the wooden utensils a day; tours by appointment only.

2. The **collection of 3600 billed caps** stapled to the ceiling at Toad River Lodge, Mile 422, makes an intricately textured soundproofing.

3. **The Sign Post Forest** at Watson Lake, Mile 612, started in 1942 when a homesick GI from Illinois working on the highway put up a road sign to his home town, has grown to some 20,000 signs from all over the world.

4. **The "Teslin taxi"** in the little Tlingit town of Teslin, where photographer George Johnston had a 1928 Chevrolet shipped up by barge, despite the fact there were no roads. George built a three-mile road for summer use, then put chains on the taxi and drove it across the frozen lake in winter. See the restored vehicle in the George Johnston Museum, ☎ *(403) 390-2550.*

Ice crystals at Teslin Lake

5. **Action Jackson's Bar** in Boundary, Alaska, on the Top of the World Highway at the Alaska/Canada border. One of Alaska's first roadhouses, it was manned for years by its eponymous owner with six-shooters strapped to each hip. Restless citizens used to drive the 70 miles from Dawson City on a Friday or Saturday night for the action; they were rarely disappointed. Today it has no liquor license.

6. **The Bird House Bar** in Indian, 27 miles southeast of Anchorage on the Seward Highway, collapsed during the 1964 earthquake and is half-buried but still in business. A giant blue bird head faces the highway and everything inside is on a slant.

7. Chetwynd, **the chainsaw carving capital of the world**, with its distinctive three bears, heroic loggers and other rustic road sculptures, on BC's highway 97 at the junction of route 29.

The Chainsaw Carving Capital of the World is in Chetwynd, BC, on the Alaska Highway. These bears are only one of the town's many exhibits.

8. **North Pole**, on the Richardson Highway 13 miles south of Fairbanks, is where letters to Santa Claus are delivered by the U.S. Post Office. If you don't want to see the elves at Santa Claus House, you could arrange a tour of the nearby MAPCO oil refinery instead.

9. **The big black-and-white tripod** that is put on the Nenana River ice in winter, connected to a clock. When the ice breaks up enough in the river to drag the tripod cable and stop the clock, lottery ticket holders who guessed the closest date and time share a prize that can run up to $180,000. A hint to would-be winners: The ice usually breaks up some time between mid-April and mid-May.

10. Hyder, **"the friendliest ghost town in Alaska,"** off the Cassier Highway straddling the Canadian border at Stewart, where people traditionally pin a dollar to the wall in the Glacier Inn in case they pass through again in the future broke and in need of a drink. The bars here are open 23 hours a day.

ON THE CHEAP: TRIMMING COSTS ON THE ROAD

The type of RV you choose to drive can make a big difference in expense on the road. The best gas mileage and greatest route flexibility comes from a four wheel drive truck camper with a cabover sleeping and cooking unit, but you'll sacrifice some of the comforts a type C or type A motorhome can provide. (This quandary inspired a popular bumper sticker that says, "Sure it gets lousy gas mileage for a car, but it gets great mileage for a house.")

Staying in government campgrounds without facilities is much cheaper than private campgrounds with hookups. Parking by the side of the road is cheapest of all, if you're in an area where you feel safe. (See "Getting Ready to Hit the Road, Should You Sleep by the Side of the Road?")

Food is expensive in the north, so stock up with as many provisions as you can in the gateway cities to the south.

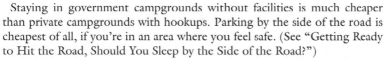

FYI

Contact the Alaska Division of Tourism, *Dept. 901, PO Box 110801, Juneau, AK 99811,* ☎ *(907) 465-2010* or *FAX (907) 536-8399* for a free booklet called Alaska State Vacation Planner.

Tourism British Columbia, *Parliament Buildings, Victoria, BC Canada V8V 1X4,* ☎ *(800) 663-6000,* provides a lot of free material about the province, including maps, campground guides and other specialized information.

Tourism Yukon, *PO Box 2703, Whitehorse, YT Canada Y1A 2C6* ☎ *(403) 667-5340* can also provide material including maps and campground guides.

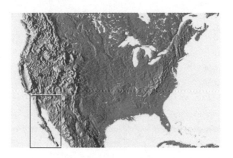

BOUNCING DOWN BAJA

A comfortable campground south of Ensenada in Estero Beach (see 10 Campground Oases #1) looks onto a lagoon where wading birds are often seen.

Baja is where John Wayne, Desi Arnaz and Bing Crosby used to go fishing and Orson Welles, Prince Ali Khan and Mickey Rooney used to come partying in the fifties, where boxer Jack Dempsey ran a hotel and bar during Prohibition, and where Raquel Welch got married.

Back in the 1840s, the United States offered to purchase Baja California in a $25 million package with California, but after conquering it during the Mexican-American War decided it wasn't worth keeping. In 1864, a cash-poor Benito Juarez leased two-thirds of the peninsula to an American named Jacob P. Leese for purposes of real estate development, but the lease was cancelled when Leese turned out to be a fraud.

For many Americans, particularly Californians, the bumpy highway down the long, skinny Baja Peninsula is a rite of passage, no matter that the once almost-impassable highway has been paved (if not always well maintained) since 1973 and that, despite a number of closed or abandoned service stations along the way, the danger of running out of fuel is less than it once was.

Who makes the rite of passage? Based on our observation, a lot of people, many of them young men.

> *One after another, the motorcyclists zipped past our 27-foot motorhome so fast we might be standing still—not the hulking cliche bikers of legend but trim, yuppie riders on touring bikes, wearing helmets and neatly zipped red leather jackets. Later, there were the bicyclists, two young men pumping diligently along a roadway that runs endlessly into the Vizcaino Desert with no shade in sight as far as the horizon.*

> *And on our way back north, when we turned off the highway to return along some crisscrossed sandy trails to a favorite beachfront picnic spot, we found ourselves behind a driver in his late thirties in a brand-new four-wheel-drive vehicle loaded with a surfeit of shiny new camping and fishing gear. He wasn't sure where he was going, he told us, just somewhere to camp and fish, but he planned to spend a month or more along the road—and when he hesitated, the unspoken phrase "to find myself" hung in the air for a moment.*

As for the rest of us, Baja has its own unique attractions—isolated beaches, fresh shrimp and abalone, world-class fishing, charming colonial towns still living in an earlier time, and, for driving the highway, a strong sense of pride and accomplishment. Anybody with the price of a plane ticket can get to Los Cabos; freewheelers do it the hard way.

ON THE ROAD

Paving was finally completed on Baja California's notorious Transpeninsular Highway in 1973, and the next year the former territory won statehood, divided into Baja California (or Baja California Norte) and Baja California Sur.

INSIDER TIP:

While the 1060-mile Highway One is covered, more or less, with some form of macadam, it is also deeply scarred by potholes, rutted by vados (dips or washes) in the roadway, and often studded with unmarked topes or vibradores (speed bumps) exactly the same color and texture as the roadway.

The frequent curves are labeled peligroso (dangerous), not only because they rarely have guard rails but also because the long-distance buses and overloaded trucks coming at you at top speed are usually in the middle of the road.

It starts off impressively at the border if you opt to bypass Tijuana and take the toll road south to Ensenada (tolls for our motorhome came to $15), a smooth divided highway with frequent ocean views. Your RV will purr along at top speed, and you'll find yourself thinking, "This is gonna be a piece of cake."

Only after you get south of Ensenada do you see the real road you'll be driving, rough despite its paving, filled with potholes and dropping off precipitously on the shoulders as if someone has been nibbling at the pavement.

Don't expect to make more than 40 miles an hour anywhere along the route, and sometimes considerably less.

Warnings of washouts or bumps may be marked by clusters of whitewashed rocks or an occasional empty plastic water jug, less often by red plastic traffic cones which are apparently a rare commodity on the peninsula. Watch for wandering animals in the road and don't drive after dark.

You'll buy gas in liters (four equals a little more than one gallon) and count distances in kilometers (10 kilometers equals six miles), because Mexico uses the metric system. When shopping, a kilo equals 2.2 pounds, and a hundred grams is about a quarter-pound.

You'll need Mexican vehicle insurance, a tourist card and proof of citizenship (passport, birth certificate or voter registration; a driver's license is not acceptable.)

> **INSIDER TIP:**
>
> *The 2000-mile round trip cost us $800 in gasoline and tolls for our 27-foot Winnebago Brave motorhome, which averages around nine miles to the gallon.*

Because our gas tank holds 60 gallons, we were able to make the journey without needing to carry extra gasoline containers. The longest single stretch we had to drive without lead-free gasoline (*magna sin* in the green pump) available was the 219 miles between El Rosario and Guerrero Negro, plus the 84-mile side trip over to Bahia de Los Angeles and back.

> **INSIDER TIP:**
>
> *Never, never, never drive at night, because big trucks whose drivers know every bump and curve come barreling down the road at high speed, hitting any cows who happen to be standing there, which is what those vultures you see perched on the cactus are waiting for.*

When to go. Spring and fall months offer the best temperatures, because it can be too cool to swim in the north in winter, and very hot inland in summer in the south. However, the climate is fairly dry, so if summer is the only time you can go, you shouldn't be too uncomfortable. Just make sure your RV or four-wheel drive van is air-conditioned. From Christmas through February or early March is the high season in Los Cabos, when hotels are full and prices at their highest.

What to wear. Comfortable, all-cotton clothes are best, along with a couple of bathing suits, since the beaches along the way are tempting. If you plan to stay in one of the resort hotels at Cabo San Lucas, you may want to take along some dressier resort clothing; otherwise, don't bother.

What to take. Insect repellent, cameras and film, binoculars, detailed road books and maps. Bottled water and clean, commercially produced ice are available along the route, as are very basic groceries, but it's a good idea to take along as much food as you can comfortably pack. For the RV, a tool kit, spare fan belts, hoses and filters are a good idea. Some of the mechanics along the way are good at jury-rigging spare parts if something breaks down.

What not to take. Under no circumstances should you carry a firearm of any kind into Mexico; it is against the law. Not long ago, a longtime RVer and traveler to Mexico was found in possession of a firearm in his vehicle and summarily thrown into jail.

INSIDER TIP:

We found Jack Williams' The Magnificent Peninsula *a detailed and helpful kilometer-by-kilometer log. He updates it every couple of years. It's usually in bookstores, but you can order it by calling* ☎ (415) 332-8635.

A ROAD GLOSSARY

Magna sin—lead free gasoline (usually designated by a green highway sign and a green pump at Pemex stations)

Vibradores—speed bumps

Vado—dip in the road

Curva peligrosa—dangerous curve (when this sign appears, it signifies a *serious* curve)

Cuoto—toll

Autopista—superhighway (don't expect to see this south of Ensenada)

Llantera—tire repair shop

No Rebase—no passing

Alto—stop (often interpreted by local drivers as 'yield')

"No hay magna sin hoy"—"No lead-free gas today," a phrase you may hear at any station along the highway when your tank is running low

Moonrise on the Sea of Cortez at the Bahia de Los Angeles

BAJA ADVENTURES

Several eco-tourism companies offer natural history expeditions around the Sea of Cortez, led by naturalists who also organize hiking, snorkeling and diving. Oldest is **Baja Expeditions**, ☎ *(800) 843-6967*, in La Paz, who also book summer, one-day diving and snorkeling trips to Los Islotes, where there's a sea lion rookery. **Sea Trek**, ☎ *(800) 934-2252*, provides five-day kayak trips for both beginners and experienced kayakers in the bays north of Loreto. **Biological Journeys**, ☎ *(800) 548-7555*, can take you on a variety of trips, and **Oceanic Society Expeditions**, ☎ *(415) 441-1106*, in San Francisco, leads both boating and camping expeditions.

> ### INSIDER TIP:
> *While it takes little or no time to cross into Mexico at Tijuana, the wait coming back into the United States can be an hour or more. Consider crossing back into California at Tecate, southeast of San Diego, or Mexicali, south of Calexico. Both connect to I-8.*

TIJUANA AND THE BORDER

If you're headed south from California on I-5, you'll cross the border at Tijuana, and will find plenty of insurance offices on the U.S. side of the border. For our 27-foot motorhome, we paid $100 for Mexican auto insurance for seven days. Baja California is relatively simple for RV drivers, but if you cross into the mainland, you will have to get an auto permit, which requires posting a bond commensurate with the value of the vehicle. New regulations allow the use of a credit card for this purpose. While tourist cards are required for visitors spending more than three days or going farther south than a prescribed area around the border, we never managed to get one, and nobody in Baja ever asked for it. Agricultural inspections also occur in several spots along the Baja Highway; the inspectors may ask to look in your refrigerator and pantry.

Tijuana is the foreign city most visited by Americans, and is the fourth largest city in Mexico with more than a million people. Tijuana Cultural Center with sight-and-sound show, museum and IMAX scenic film offers one good introduction to the country. Mexitlan, a 3.4-acre architectural theme park with 150 scale models of Mexico's most famous sites, is another. Here you can visit miniature versions of the silver city of Taxco, Mexico City before the conquest or the famous Maya ruins of Yucatán.

Shopping is another major Tijuana attraction (so long as you remember labels are not necessarily what they seem), along with horse and dog racing, jai alai and bullfighting.

INSIDER TIP:

The Green Angels (Angeles Verdes) are government employees who patrol the highway in green-and-white pickup trucks. There are always two, and one usually speaks English. They carry spare parts, gas, oil and water and make minor repairs free of charge; you pay only for the parts. If you have a breakdown, you should not have to wait more than a few hours before they find you. You can also dial toll-free ☎ 91-800-90239 from within Mexico to get English-speaking operators to get help or give advice.

The Green Angels assist a motorist in distress on the Baja highway.

BAJA CALIFORNIA NORTE

About five million years ago, the San Andreas Fault ripped open along the west coast of Mexico, separating the slender, finger-shaped, 850-mile-long Baja peninsula from the mainland. Most people who have only flown over it think of the peninsula as one big desert flanked by beaches on both sides, but there are also huge boulder fields around Cataviña, lush groves of palm trees around San Ignacio, and a spine of mountain ranges almost the length of the peninsula.

Through much of Baja, the air is clean and sparkling clear, the sea and sky intensely blue. You may run into local coastal fog in areas marked *Zona Neblina* (foggy zone).

Despite its aridity, Baja California produces a surprising variety of agricultural products. Baja has been producing wine grapes since they were introduced in 1687 by the Jesuits. The Santo Tomás Winery south of Ensenada was founded in 1888 in fields where vines had been planted a century before.

INSIDER TIP:

You can go on a tour and tasting in the Bodega de Santo Tomás in the middle of Ensenada daily for a small fee, or sample the company's finer wines in their wood-paneled restaurant, La Embotelladora Vieja, built in a converted aging shed

Past Santo Tomás, the agricultural Camalu Valley produces tomatoes, peppers and squash. The tourist town of San Quintin and its beaches can be crowded, but farther south Pacific waves splash on beaches empty except for the shadows of swooping pelicans and gulls.

Bright red splotches on the hillsides turn out to be drying red chile peppers. To eyes accustomed to easier terrain, the cactus begins to take on a life of its own after a day or two, turning into trees and people and distant landmarks. In the Cataviña boulder fields, a tumble of smooth granite stones sets off the prickly flora as if ordered up by a set designer for Hollywood westerns. Especially weird are the knobby gray elephant trees with their peeling, scaly bark.

INSIDER TIP:

When you see a rare billboard in English that says the highway is "designed for economic development, not high-speed driving," you can be sure the road ahead will improve.

The beautiful spit of sand at El Requeson on Bahia de la Concepcion

10 BEST BEACHES

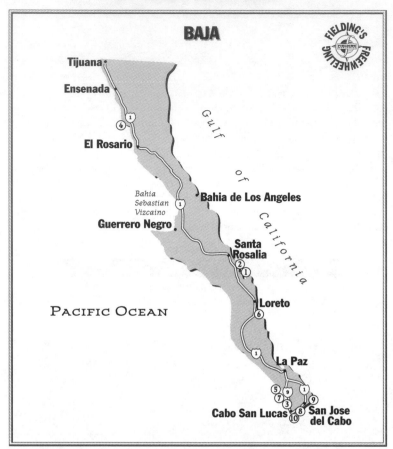

1. **El Requeson** on Bahia de la Concepción is unbearably alluring, a sugar-white curved sandspit with intensely blue water on both sides, bright blue sky beyond. Self-contained camping is permitted; there's usually someone collecting a fee.

2. **Playa Santispac** on sheltered Bahia Coyote, a part of the larger Bahia de la Concepción, lies just off the highway with a steep road downhill to the beach that should not be attempted by larger RVs and trailers. Palapas provide shade, and a person is on hand to collect a parking fee at this very popular beach. A natural hot spring can be found a short stroll away.

3. **Playa de Amor**, Cabo San Lucas, where you can hire a local boatman to take you, your lover and a picnic lunch to this sandy beach and cove tucked into the rocks where the waters of the Pacific meet the waters of the Sea of Cortez. Have him come back to pick you up several hours later; don't pay in advance. And don't expect to have the beach all to yourself, especially when a cruise ship is in port.

4. South of San Quintin, a sand road crosses one-quarter mile or so over to the cliffs and dunes, where flocks of pelicans and seagulls may be your only company. If you find the right sand road into the dunes, you can look back toward San Quintin and see surfers and swimmers on the beach to the north, then look down at **an empty, nameless beach** below.

An empty beach south of Quintin makes an ideal lunch stop for an RV in Baja.

5. **Playa San Pedrito**, about four miles south of Todos Santos on route 19, then 1.6 miles down a dirt road, has a large grove of coconut and Washingtonia palms and a nice sandy beach. Don't plan to swim, however; as with most beaches near the cape, the surf can be rough.

6. **El Juncalito**, south of Loreto and off the highway via a half mile dirt road, has sand, palms and a quarter-mile beach with some phosphorescence in the water. A fishing village nearby offers *pangas* (open boats with outboard motors) for rent.

7. **Playa Los Cerritos**, off highway 19 south of Todos Santos via a 1.4-mile road, a sheltered beach with good surfing and views of the coastline.

8. **Santa Maria Beach**, on a secluded cove by the Twin Dolphin Hotel between Cabo San Lucas and San Jose del Cabo, good for swimming, snorkeling and diving. One catch: It's a public beach but reached by crossing through Twin Dolphin's private property; beach-goers are not permitted to park in Twin Dolphin's lot.

9. **Pueblo La Playa**, also sometimes called La Playita, about a mile east of downtown San Jose del Cabo, has traditionally shared its stretch of beach with local fishermen and a seafood restaurant that buys its catch fresh from the boat. Catch it while you can; there's a big resort development in the works.

10. **Medano Beach**, in Cabo San Lucas, a busy, popular beach right in town with water-skiing, jet-skiing, snorkeling, canoeing, sailing, windsurfing. A beachside restaurant called The Office serves grilled snapper or shrimp in garlic sauce and the view is of the rock arch at Land's End.

INSIDER TIP:

As a rule of thumb, the RV parks throughout Baja do not provide picnic tables at hookup sites. The electricity is most often 15 amps, inadequate to operate air conditioning simultaneously with TV or microwave oven. We paid an average of $10 a night for campsites with hookups. Parking without hookups usually averaged $5. U.S. currency is accepted all over Baja California.

11 CAMPGROUND OASES ALONG THE BAJA HIGHWAY

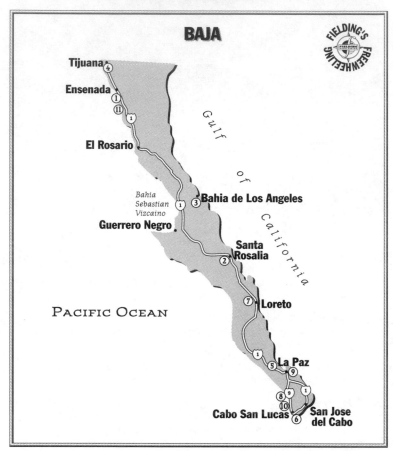

1. **Estero Beach Hotel and Resort RV Park**, six miles south of Ensenada off highway one in Estero Beach. Gate-guarded resort with hotel, swimming pool, outdoor restaurant with lounge and music, sailing, windsurfing, jet-skis and water-skiing, snorkeling, diving, fishing. There are 68 full hookup sites, many by the estuary with good wading-bird watching. Fire pits, flush toilets, showers. For reservations dial ☎ *011-(526) 676-6230*.

2. **El Palomar RV Park**, south of Santa Rosalia, newly opened, on a hilltop with showers, hookups, coin laundry, recreation room with pool table and a restaurant and bar. Palapas for shade, fenced, gates closed at night, very friendly and hard-working owners.

3. **RV Park Brisa Marina**, 1.8 miles from Bahia de Los Angeles on a very rough track (it can't be called a road), marked by roadsigns that advertise "150 spaces," this derelict camp was once a government RV park. Now signs say "Parking $5" and there are no working hookups, plumbing or water connections. It's a quiet place by the Sea of Cortez with incredible moonlit nights, concrete pads for chairs and folding tables and plenty of level space for parking. Sometimes someone comes out from the village to collect, sometimes they don't.

The new El Palomar RV Park south of Santa Rosalia

4. **Oasis Hotel and RV Resort**, 15 miles south of Tijuana on the toll road to Ensenada, 126 paved spaces with full hookups, patios, brick barbecues and cable TV, nine-hole golf course, tennis, swimming pool, spa, store, sauna, laundry, weight room. No tents. Reservations ☎ *(800) 462-7472* or *011-52-(661) 332-53.*

5. **Oasis de Aripes** at El Centenario, north of La Paz, hot showers, swimming pool, English spoken, clean and well-kept. At the water's edge with a restaurant on the premises.

6. **Villa Serena**, 3.6 miles north of Cabo San Lucas on highway 1, new and very plush with full hookups, laundry, pool, dramatic ocean view.

7. **Tiapul Trailer Park**, 16 miles south of Loreto near a nautical park development with marina. Mostly seasonal or permanent resident Americans, with only 31 transient spaces in an overflow gravel lot. The park itself has flush toilets, showers, swimming pool, tennis courts, and lovely landscaping, but overnighters may feel like poor relations.

8. **San Pedrito RV Park**, five miles south of Todos Santos on highway 19, then two miles down a dirt road. 51 RV sites, hookups, showers, flush toilets, laundry room, restaurant, swimming pool and beach.

9. **La Paz Trailer Park**, just south of La Paz, is by the sea with 48 full hookups, swimming pool, clean flush toilets and showers, Jacuzzi, paperback book swap, cable TV, squash court, laundry and restaurant. Call ahead for reservations at ☎ *(112) 2-87-87.*

10. **Vagabundas del Mar**, just north of Cabo San Lucas with 95 spaces, most with full hookups, swimming pool, shade trees, paved interior roads, flush toilers, showers, laundry. Most of the inhabitants are seasonal or full-time residents and members of a club by the same name. To join the club, call ☎ *(707) 374-5511.*

11. **El Palomar Motel and RV Park**, Santo Tomas, on highway one at mile 31, 47 sites, some shaded, 30 with full hookups. Tennis, swimming pool, barbecue pits. Downhill from the road near mission ruins, vineyards and olive trees. Across the road is a restaurant famous for lobster tacos and potent margaritas and a store selling olives from the groves.

BAJA CALIFORNIA SUR

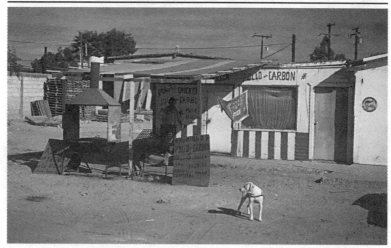

Down Guerrero Negro is an urban metropolis after the first half of the lonely Baja highway.

The Eagle Monument at State Line, the dividing point between Baja Norte and Baja Sur, is stuck right in the middle of the highway, looks like a tuning fork and can be seen for some distance. There's an obligatory stop here at an agricultural inspection station; any home-grown fruits that may have Mediterranean fruit fly infestations will be confiscated.

We noted an attractive new RV park without a name beside the tidy Hotel La Pinta near the junction into Guerrero Negro.

Guerrero Negro is a burst of civilization after the long, dry trek south, replete with pizza joint, disco, *supermercado* and, most importantly, Pemex, at the end of the long road into town. Watch for the unmarked *topes* in town. There's usually a long line at the gas station, so be prepared to wait. The major industry here is salt, hardly surprising since *Las Salinas de Guerrero Negro* are the largest salt flats in the world. You'll see some of the evaporating ponds on the road into town.

A winter side trip to Scammon's Lagoon for whale-watching is possible for four-wheel drive vehicles and smaller RVs but not trailers; see "Seven Swell Side Roads to Explore" later in this chapter.

Charming little San Ignacio, a couple of miles off the main highway, is worth the detour to see the rose-colored Dominican church finished in

1786. The Jesuits had earlier established a mission here in 1728. The *zócalo* (town square) across from the mission is shaded with fine old trees, and there are usually several impromptu RV parks nestled among the date palms on the edge of town.

In Santa Rosalia, the main sight is a prefabricated Eiffel church originally destined to be shipped to Africa, made from galvanized iron to dispel termites. It is cool and graceful and surprisingly modern inside. The one-way streets are wide enough for all but extra-wide RVs. The handsome balconied wooden buildings, made from imported timber, date from the late 19th-century days when a French syndicate built and operated the old copper smelter on the north edge of town.

Lush, tropical Mulege has several RV parks in a canyon down by the river, but they can be close and hot in summer. Rather than stay here, we'd recommend pushing south a few miles to the beautiful beaches around Bahia de la Concepción if you're in a self-contained RV. If you need something organized, RV Park El Coyote, 18 miles south of Mulege, has flush toilets, drinking water and showers.

Looking a little like Puerto Vallarta did a long-ago time, the town draws gringo dropouts, surfers and divers. The mission church here was founded by the Jesuits in 1705 and built in its present style in 1766.

INSIDER TIP:

The worst road surface along the entire route is the stretch south from Loreto most of the way to Ciudad Insurgentes. This is also an area with the most beautiful scenery, so proceeding slowly is a good idea. This was the area where the bumpy road caused a lid from a jar of peanut butter in the refrigerator to come unscrewed and the roll of toilet paper in the bathroom to unwind into a long ribbon on the floor.

LORETO TO LA PAZ

A Baja sunrise on the Sea of Cortez

Loreto's RV parks with hookups can also be hot and close. Las Palmas RV Park is clean and neat, but a solid rock wall separates it from the black sand beach and blocks out any stray breezes. Next door at Loremar RV Park, a motel is under construction by the sea and RVs are relegated to a paved parking lot in back. The third choice, El Moro, is in town in a little fenced lot off a bumpy dirt road with parking spaces outlined in whitewashed stones.

The primary sight in town is the lovely old mission of Nuestra Señora de Loreto, founded in 1697 and the first mission and permanent European settlement in the Californias. The mission was badly damaged by a hurricane in 1829, and the town began restoring it in the last decade.

What used to be the best hotel in town, the Stouffer Presidente Loreto, closed down a couple of years ago for lack of business.

South of Loreto the Sea of Cortez is breathtaking in the light of dawn with the sun rising behind the islands. The road climbs steeply up around torturous curves, with the sawtoothed mountains of the Sierra Giganta plunging straight down into the shimmering, ink-blue sea. Don't spend too much time admiring the scenery, however, since around each one of the curves you can expect to meet a huge truck barreling along well above the speed limit.

In the southern desert, roadside cacti double as billboards with signs tacked on them saying Loncheria, Beer, Tyre Riper (tire repair). Along the sides of the roads, dead animals, mostly cows but some burros and dogs, have been shoved over out of the traffic and lie, still and swollen, legs stretched out taut. The vultures (locals call them *zopilotes*) study them with a proprietary eye but won't start to work until they ripen a bit more. After the feast, there will be nothing left but scraps of desiccated hide. Even the bones disappear.

The splats on the windshield here are not the usual fat bugs but butterflies, both fluttering yellow ones and smaller white ones.

At Insurgentes and Ciudad Constitución, farmers have learned from Israeli agricultural experts how to get optimum yield out of irrigated desert, and the sprawling acres of agribusiness farms sport conspicuously new housing units for farm workers.

La Paz, the capital and largest city in Baja Sur, with a population of around 170,000, has a giant sculpted dove of peace dominating a traffic circle as you enter town, and a neat grid of manageable streets until you get into the old part of town near the waterfront.

This was once a major pearling center. The pearls were first discovered by sailors who survived a mutiny on the ship *Concepción*, sent out by Hernán Cortés in 1535. The greedy Cortés was so pleased at the booty he joined a return expedition personally, claiming the place for Spain and attempting to colonize it with a group of settlers. They stuck it out for three years before giving up for lack of food and water. The area wasn't permanently settled until 1811.

In 1853 an American general named William Walker from the Mexican-American War invaded La Paz on the grounds that it should have been part of the treaty that gave the state of California to the U.S. after the war. Seven months later he left after learning the Mexican Army was on its way and his own government did not support his claim. Undaunted, he went south to Nicaragua, made himself president and ultimately was executed by a firing squad.

South of La Paz, just below the town of Santiago, is a turnoff to the spherical Tropic of Cancer monument, a good place for a "we were here" photo.

INSIDER TIP:

If the children (or adults) get bored on the road, you can play, What's that foodstuff lying beside the road? If it's dark red and you're around El Rosario, it's drying chile peppers. If it's mounds of bright yellow and you're around Ciudad Insurgentes, it's probably cornmeal. If it's white and glistening and you're around Guerrero Negro, it's likely to be salt.

---

10 SPLURGES IN BAJA CALIFORNIA

1. Hit the trendy **Santa Fe Cafe** in gentrifying Todos Santos on highway 19 north of Cabo San Lucas for grilled or steamed fish, super salads and elegant desserts.

2. The seafood platter (one is big enough for two unless you're starving) at **Caesar's** in Loreto, under a big thatched palapa roof near the intersection of Calle Zapata and Calle Benito Juarez.

3. Divers should book an **excursion to the unique underwater sandfalls and 900-foot canyon** first explored by Jacques Cousteau at the tip of Land's End in Cabo San Lucas; bring along your certification. Get tanks and equipment from Cabo Aquadeportes at the Hacienda Hotel or Amigos del Mar across from the Marina.

4. Chow down on **langouste** (spiny lobster) in Puerto Nuevo, 30 miles south of Tijuana off the toll road (exit 44), a village that specializes in a local cooking style that splits them and grills them in oil with garlic and pepper. The most famous are five Ortega family places, including **The Original Ortega Lobster House** from 1954, but all are similar. With the lobster ($15-$30 depending on size) come rice, refried beans, fresh flour tortillas, salsa and chips; cold beer or soda is readily available. Because of area overfishing in recent years, your lobster may be imported.

5. Celebrate your arrival at Cabo San Lucas by checking into the lavish **Hotel Twin Dolphin**, ☎ *(800) 421-8925*, either for a meal like garlic and peppered Brie or Thai grilled shrimp, or even a luxurious stay overnight. The driveway and parking lot can handle your RV, but call ahead since the road into the hotel is unmarked, except for a sign that says Private Property.

6. Extend your visit long enough to take in a healthy and slenderizing week at Tecate's splendid **Rancho la Puerta**, a vegetarian spa with tennis courts, swimming pools and famous early morning walks.

7. The pretty white **Hotel La Pinta** in the middle of Cataviña's boulder fields offers guided expeditions to the prehistoric carved and painted rocks, as well as claiming the best margaritas in the state of Baja California. Technically that covers only the northern half; claimants for the best margaritas in the southern half include the Whale Watcher's Bar in the **Hotel Finisterra**, a quietly romantic spot with a drop-dead view, and the beachfront bar in the lavish **Hotel Cabo San Lucas**.

8. The popular Sunday brunch at **El Molino Trailer Park** in the heart of Todos Santos, in the shadow of a historic sugar mill, unexpectedly elegant with white tablecloths, crêpes, made-to-order omelets, tropical fruit.

9. Take a deep-sea fishing trip for a day from Cabo San Lucas, which boasts the biggest deep-sea fishing fleet in the world. Two local companies you can call ahead are **Solmar Fishing**, ☎ *(800) 344-3349* or **Fishing International**, ☎ *(800) 950-4242*. Expect to pay around $300 a boat for a full day with large boat, guide and tackle, $100 a half-day for a *panga* (smaller outboard).

10. Great new golf courses along the tourist strip between Cabo San Lucas and San Jose del Cabo, including two designed by Jack Nicklaus, one at posh Palmilla Resort, the other at brand-new Cabo del Sol. Call ☎ *(800) 637-CABO*.

INSIDER TIP:

At various intervals along the highway, you may be flagged down by volunteers wearing armbands and collecting money for the Red Cross or other organizations. The easiest thing is to give them some pesos and take the tab they give you for your windshield. It shows you already contributed if and when you drive past again.

LOS CABOS

Los Cabos—the Capes—is a new tourism and marketing name given by the government for the two old settlements at the tip of the Baja Peninsula, sedate and colonial San José del Cabo and kicky, booming Cabo San Lucas.

The 20 miles between the two is turning into a golf course and hotel-lined resort strip far too fast to suit veteran visitors.

Traffic is bumper-to-bumper now on most of Cabo's streets, even those narrow, bumpy sandy lanes that still crisscross most of the town. Our 27-foot motorhome, a palatial shelter along the drive down, turned into a clumsy behemoth in the beeping tourist traffic, especially in the bedlam between the two towns in the vicinity of the modern international airport. Shortly after its completion, the new four-lane road was damaged by a tropical storm, so drivers may find construction repairs going on.

For us, the beginning of the end of Cabo San Lucas' appeal was the first time we sailed into the bay and saw the gigantic, ugly, pinky-orange Plaza Las Glorias, looking like a transplant from Málaga or Marbella, squatting and glowering where there used to be bobbing fishing boats and a view to the hills.

Anyhow, the air is still dazzlingly clear and the sky bright blue.

INSIDER TIP:

Although we were careful and did not get stuck in Baja sand (having weathered being stuck in Quebec mud), that's a potential hazard for RVers who want to camp near the water. Jack Williams in his Magnificent Peninsula *suggests letting some or most of the air out of the tires, which increases the traction. To reinflate them, he says, take along an inexpensive tire pump, available from auto stores, that works off a vehicle cigarette lighter.*

Vultures perch atop a cardoon cactus to survey the landscape.

WILDLIFE WATCH

Along the Baja Highway, coyotes pad calmly along the roadsides like dogs, and birds of prey, mostly turkey vultures with red wrinkled heads and calculating eyes, sit atop tall cardoon cactus to check the terrain for any roadkill.

Porpoises play in the clear blue waters of the Sea of Cortez. In Cabo San Lucas, small boats take you out to the rocky arch and close to pelicans sunning on the rocks and sea lions cavorting in the water or snoozing in the sun.

Between January and March, Amigos del Mar offers trimaran tours for whale watching from Cabo San Lucas. Snorkeling is especially good in Santa Maria Cove near Hotel Twin Dolphin.

The islands in the Sea of Cortez offer fantastic bird-watching, with nesting blue-footed boobies, elegant long-tailed tropic birds, soaring frigate birds, brown pelicans, red-billed Heerman's gulls and royal terns.

As for nightlife, there's not much en route, but when you get to Los Cabos, Van Halen's Cabo Wabo nightclub in Cabo San Lucas is sure to please young rockers with its live bands, as will the tequila shooters at Squid Roe, one of the raucous Grupo Anderson restaurants. Iguana Grill & Bar is back in San José del Cabo with dancing under the stars to live music, and Señor Sushi's in Cabo San Lucas provides good happy-hour people-watching.

INSIDER TIP:

San Diego-based M&M Jeeps rents two-or four-wheel-drive Ford Explorers for a one-way drive up or down the Baja Peninsula with no drop-off fees. You can pick up the vehicle in either San Diego or Los Cabos, and drop it at the other end. Unlimited mileage is part of the deal, and the vehicles have radios, luggage racks and a tow capable of handling a travel trailer or boat. Call them at ☎ (619) 297-1615.

10 OFF-THE-WALL ATTRACTIONS

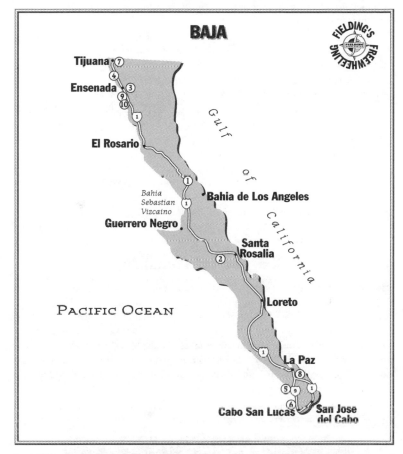

1. The unique **boojum or cirio cactus** found around Bahia de Los Angeles and nowhere else in the world, 30-foot tall stringy vegetable giraffes draped with parasitic mosses, scowling and hunching toward the road like demented animated trees from a Disney cartoon.

2. Infamous **Vado Lester**, between Santa Rosalia and San Ignacio, one of only two highway washouts in Baja that has its own name and danger sign, a red-and-black warning in addition to the usual whitewashed rocks.

3. **Hussong's Cantina** in Ensenada has not gentrified its original sawdust-floor, century-old watering hole despite its new T-shirt and souvenir empire nearby, and it still reeks of disinfectant in the mornings. A newer star on the party-hearty circuit is Papas and Beer around the corner.

4. **The Rosarito Beach Hotel**, dating from the 1920s when it was Hollywood's hide-away, has fiercely devoted fans and equally adamant detractors, but it's sold out on weekends, probably since the days when Mickey Rooney, Ali Khan, Larry Hagman and Vincent Price used to arrive, not at the same time, of course, or even necessarily in the same decade.

5. The midafternoon **panga race** at Punta Lobos beach north of Todos Santos, when local fishermen rev their motors and ride ashore on the crest of the right wave, hitting the sand with boats full of fish.

6. **The Giggling Marlin** in Cabo San Lucas, where the big giggle comes from hoisting bar patrons upside down with a block and tackle to pose for friends' cameras trophy-like beside a cut-out of a grinning fish holding a deep-sea rod.

7. The **sombrero-wearing "zebras"**—burros with painted white stripes—on Tijuana street corners waiting for tourists to climb aboard and be photographed.

8. The **Parque Zoológico** in the town of Santiago south of La Paz has an eclectic zoo that mixes macaws and monkeys with pigs, cows, roosters, a cat and a dog.

9. The former **Playa Ensenada Hotel**, later called the Riviera del Pacifico, opened as a casino managed by boxer Jack Dempsey, which lured movie stars in the early 1930s, but closed when Mexico outlawed gambling in the late 1930s. Rumors say it may have been owned by Al Capone. Now the handsome building, sans the hotel wings, serves as the more sedate Civic Center of Ensenada.

10. **La Fábrica del Erizo del Mar**, the sea urchin processing plant in Uruapán, off the edge of the highway to the east, sends its spiny little products exclusively to Japan. Visitors are permitted.

GOING FOR THE LONG HAUL

If you want to turn snowbird and spend the winter in Baja, you could stay the whole season at a single RV resort (reserve and preferably check it out personally ahead of time, since facilities can change rapidly) or move along at a freewheeling pace, when you are ready, and stopping where you like. A four-wheel-drive vehicle will be invaluable for exploring, although a sturdy pickup with two-wheel drive can accomplish most or all the side roads on our list. You can also rent small boats locally for fishing or book a deep-sea fishing trip out of most Baja seaside towns.

If you want to splurge on your extended trip, plan to spend part of your stay in one of the resorts around Los Cabos.

INSIDER TIP:

Travelers headed for Cabo San Lucas will find the newer, faster highway 19 will cut about 90 minutes off their drive. It follows the Pacific coast rather than going over the mountains through small mining villages. But the latter are so interesting, freewheelers making the round trip should cover them both, one way in one direction, reverse in the other.

SEVEN SWELL SIDE ROADS TO EXPLORE

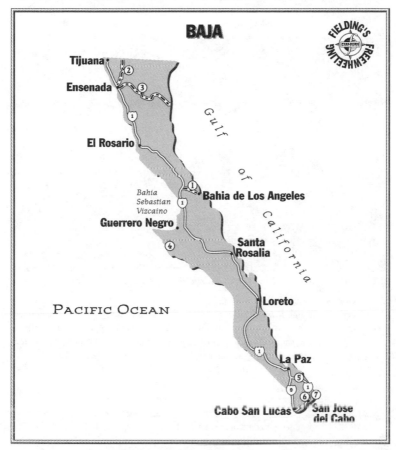

1. Take the road to **Bahia de Los Angeles**, rough in spots with some serious *vados* that have washed out, and lined with acres of spooky boojum cacti. The bay is stark and surreal, flat and smooth as a mirror, dotted with bare islands that shine blue in the gathering twilight, and a full white moon in the blue sky. The town itself isn't cute or historic, just a scruffy fishing town with a half-dozen turkey vultures perched around the dump. RVers who want hookups will find the Villa Vita Trailer Park and adjacent Guillermo's Trailer Park, both little more than waterside parking lots, in town.

2. Route 3 to Tecate from Ensenada takes you into **vineyard country** and past the Pedro Domeq winery, where you can stop and taste or buy the modest local wines. Treats: Olive trees on the hillsides, coyotes along the roadside, very inexpensive clay pottery in Tecate. If you want to cross the border into California, Tecate is simplicity itself compared to Tijuana, where the line of cars is long and slow.

3. The other end of **route 3 between Ensenada and San Felipe**, also paved, will take you up a steep climb (not recommended for those pulling fifth-wheels or long trailers) out of Ensenada. On the downhill side and the second uphill climb you'll see a heavy concentration of barrel cactus. Turn south on highway 5 to the fishing and beach town of San Felipe, which can be rowdy and crowded during holiday week-

ends and spring break. There are a number of RV parks around San Felipe, as well as fishing boats and deep-sea charters. And there is a very loud and lively all-terrain-vehicle crowd using dune buggies.

A deserted RV park on the shores of Bahia de Los Angeles

4. A **whale-watching detour** from Guerrero Negro may produce possible sightings December through May. California gray whales use Scammon's Lagoon as a nursery when the mouth is not silted up too much for them to get in. A 16-mile side trip to the lagoon from the highway south of GN is marked Laguna Ojo de Liebre on a washboard sand road across the desert. Some primitive campsites and whale-watching boats at the end of the road.

5. The drive from the junction of 1 and 19 to Los Barriles at the coast goes through the old **19th century gold and silver mining towns** of El Triunfo and San Antonio, where roadside vendors sell hand-woven baskets and bags of fresh oranges and avocados. The route to the coast over the wooded Sierra Laguna mountains is beautiful. Las Barriles is the windsurfing capital of Baja, with plenty of RV parks with hookups in the vicinity, most of them down washboarded sand roads.

6. **Highway One from San Jose del Cabo to Los Barriles** passes through the little town of Santiago, which has the only zoo in Baja California, and near where the Tropic of Cancer monument is located. Once you are south of it, you're officially in the tropics.

7. The road from Highway One to La Ribera and south to Cabo Pulmo is gradually being improved and paved, although it runs slightly inland from the original dirt East Cape route. Cabo Pulmo has **the best snorkeling and diving in Baja** (partly because it has the only live coral reefs) as well as beautiful beaches, some of which were clothing optional the last we heard. At least one RV park and several areas suitable for self-contained camping are along the route. Ask locally before trying to finish the loop into San Jose del Cabo; the road is heavily washboarded and subject to erosion.

HITTING THE HIGHLIGHTS

It's possible to make a roundtrip drive from Southern California to Los Cabos and back in a week (we've done it), but it doesn't leave much time for fishing, swimming, lazing in the sun and sampling the fresh seafood and local beer. If you only have a week for a round trip, consider going only part way down, say, as far as Bahia de Los Angeles or Bahia Concepción, so you have time to enjoy the water and scenery.

If you have two weeks, you can do the full drive and opt for a couple of the side trips detailed above.

13 TAKEOUT (OR EAT-IN) TREATS

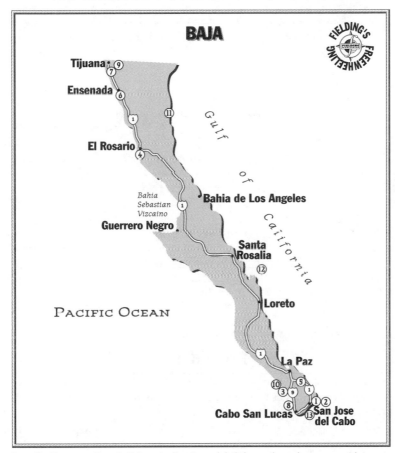

1. La Baguette French Bakery in San Jose del Cabo makes what we consider tasty Cuban-style loaves rather than French, but their **sesame-seed whole wheat bread** is luscious.

2. Sample the local liqueur called **Damiana**, thought to be an aphrodisiac, and served in a special margarita at the classic Damiana in San Jose del Cabo, where fresh abalone is also on the menu.

3. Booths selling **organic vegetables and strawberries** are sometimes open at Rancho Nuevo Villa on route 19 south of Todos Santos at kilometer 60.

4. The **lobster burritos** at Mama Espinoza's in El Rosario are not as good as they were in the old days before the road was paved, but still pretty tasty. Although the cafe is clean and attractive, it doesn't serve alcohol, so get your food to go if you want a cold Tecate to sip along with it.

5.   The bags of **oranges, mangos and avocados** for sale at the roadside booths in the lovely old mining town of San Bartolo.

6.   The famous fried fresh **fish tacos** at Ensenada's fish market, doused with hot sauces and salsas and squirted with fresh lime juice, still cost under $1.

7.   The gigantic **burritos** at Bol Corona on Tijuana's Avenida Revolución between Comercio and Benito Juarez are on sale between 7 a.m. and 4 p.m.

8.   The **octopus tacos** at Supertacos de Baja California in Cabo San Lucas are doused with fresh salsa and rolled up in a hot fresh tortilla.

9.   The original **Caesar salad**, invented by and still served in the restaurant of the Caesar Hotel in Tijuana, will please hold-the-anchovies types; the original recipe does not call for those salty little fish.

10. The **vegetarian pizzas** at Pizzas del Pacífico on Calle Degollado in Todos Santos, to take out or eat at one of tables under the palapa.

11. The fresh **shellfish cocteles** at brightly painted stalls along the main street in San Felipe, tall glasses filled with any combination of shrimp, octopus, and clams in a tart, spicy salsa marinade.

12. Check out the **baked goods** at Villa Maria Isabel RV Park in Mulege, especially the chocolate chip cookies and the cheese onion rolls.

13. Finally, if you can't live another minute without a **cheeseburger**, head for Cabo San Lucas and Pappi's Deli or the Brisa del Mar Trailer Park restaurant at San Jose del Cabo.

FOOD FOOTNOTE

An interesting trend in Baja is the RV or trailer park restaurant, patronized primarily by expatriates but notable stops even for those on a swing through the posh resorts.

El Faro Viejo Trailer Court in Cabo San Lucas, famous for its barbecued ribs, is probably the best-known, but Ruben's Trailer Park on Avenida Golfo de California in San Felipe and El Molino Trailer Park on Calle Rangel in Todos Santos also pack them in. In Mulege, Villa Maria Isabel RV Park has a popular bakery, and Brisa del Mar Trailer Park in San Jose del Cabo claims to make the best hamburgers in Baja.

ON THE CHEAP: TRIMMING COSTS ON THE ROAD

If you're heading for Los Cabos, don't go down in high season—roughly Christmas through Easter—because hotels and restaurants are crowded, prices higher and traffic heavier.

Instead of stopping at RV parks with hookups, ration those out for only when absolutely necessary and stay self-contained in the beach areas for less or even free. You'll find yourself charged even to park at many of the most popular spots around Bahia de la Concepción. There are no accessible free beachfront campsites left on the main road between Cabo San Lucas and San José del Cabo, due to heavy resort development, even though Mexico's beaches are all public. You'll have much better luck finding a place along highway 19 north of Los Cabos, although the Pacific is generally too chilly and rough for much swimming.

FYI

Mexican Government Tourism Office, *10100 Santa Monica Blvd., Suite 224, Los Angeles, CA 90067*, ☎ *(310) 203-8191*, can provide material and answer questions about taking your vehicle into Baja California.

Mexico Hotline, ☎ *(800) 44-MEXICO*, is good for last-minute questions. For road information and updates, call ☎ *(800) 662-MEXI.*

THE CALIFORNIA DESERT

Wildflowers bloom in the California desert between March and May.

Actually, there's not one desert in California, but many—Death Valley's low desert with its sizzling heat records, the Mojave's high desert with its ghost towns and mines, and vast Anza Borrego, the biggest state park in California with 600,000 acres of cactus and canyons. Death Valley and Joshua Tree, previously designated national monuments, were recently turned into national parks by Congress after nine years of petitioning.

And then there's The Desert, Palm Springs and vicinity, where Beverly Hills goes to desiccate, safe and circumspect once again after its own Desert Storm action by former Palm Springs celebrity-mayor Sonny Bono outlawing teen spring-break frivolities and putting Palm Canyon Drive back in the hands of the Waxworks.

It's where 10,000 swimming pools and countless lawn sprinklers, waterslides and misting outdoor air-conditioners turn once bone-dry air damp, where cows are allotted 1000 acres of feeding area apiece to browse on vitamin-rich desert spinach, and where the Charles Manson Family hid out at a rundown movie ranch rehearsing murder and mayhem.

The California deserts gave us date milkshakes, the state's first nudist bed-and-breakfast hotels, the world's first broken sound barrier, 20-mule team Borax and the Twenty-Nine Palms Outhouse Race.

It's where Wyatt Earp retired, where Al Capone took the waters, where Lawrence of Arabia rode his camel across the dunes, where General Patton left his tank tracks and where Paul Newman, Steve McQueen and James Garner learned how to drive race cars.

It's where Elvis and Priscilla Presley honeymooned, where Frank Sinatra lives on Frank Sinatra Drive, where Spiro Agnew hides behind hedges, and where old-time radio favorites Jack Benny, Amos and Andy and Fibber McGee and Molly beamed their shows out to a kinder, simpler nation.

Freewheelers can find the Hullabaloo World Tobacco Spitting Championships in Calico every Palm Sunday, visit an endangered desert pupfish in Anza-Borrego State Park, go to camel and ostrich races in Indio during the National Date Festival in mid-February, and go sand-sailing on a dry lake at speeds up to 70 m.p.h. with no brakes.

When to go: Winter is ideal in California's desert country, balmy and warm days with cool nights. Early spring and late autumn are also good. Summer in the low desert is only for mad dogs and Englishmen, as well as Germans, Swiss and Japanese, who dote on traveling in Death Valley in August when the temperature can top 115 degrees.

What to take: Binoculars, camera and plenty of film, a tripod if you plan to shoot cactus, wildflower portraits or dazzling sunsets. Carry a strong sunscreen and a canteen or water carrier for hikes.

What to wear in the desert: Lightweight and light-colored natural fiber fabrics are best. Stout-soled hiking shoes and tough-fabric pants are essential to repel cactus spikes if you're hiking in cactus country. Winter evenings cool down quickly once the sun sets, so be prepared with a down vest or jacket, windbreaker or heavy sweatshirt. A wide-brim hat, preferably one that can be tied down, is best in the strong desert sun.

FREEWHEELING IN THE CALIFORNIA DESERT

A lazy loop around California's deserts can be made in one long haul or on a series of shorter drives from a central base. From the Palm Springs area, the route fans south and east as far as the Arizona and Mexico borders. From San Bernadino, it radiates east to the Colorado River, northeast to Las Vegas and north to Death Valley. From Lancaster/Palmdale, it runs north into the Owens Valley east of the Sierra Nevada. The whole circuit is about 1000 miles, plus side trips, but can be divided into a number of shorter trips.

Stay on roads and trails at all times, whether driving or walking. The desert terrain is fragile and slow-growing, and one careless off-road driver can destroy vegetation decades old.

GOING FOR THE LONG HAUL

If you want to spend a winter among the snowbirds in the California desert, you could explore all three major desert areas, take a leisurely attack on the 10 side trips, then settle in around the Palm Springs area if you're affluent or on the BLM Lands (see "On the Cheap") if you're strapped.

Most recreation areas, state parks and forest service campgrounds have posted camping limits, often around 14 days, but you can check out, then check in again on a later day. Or you could become a VIP (Volunteer in Parks) and camp free all season long as a campground host. (See "Campgrounds and RV Parks: Where to Sleep, How to Become Campground Hosts.")

HITTING THE HIGHLIGHTS

The Mad Greek in Baker

If you divide your time between Death Valley, the Palm Springs area, Joshua Tree National Park and Anza Borrego State Park, you should get to know the California desert fairly well. Allow four days in Death Valley, then drive south through Baker, Barstow and Calico or detour into Nevada for a Las Vegas or Laughlin fling. Allow two or three days in Joshua Tree, longer if you want to make day trips over into nearby Palm Springs. Anza Borrego State Park is south from Indio and Coachella, then west on route 78 through Ocotillo Wells.

If you're flying in and renting an RV, either Los Angeles or San Diego makes a good base.

10 CAMPGROUND OASES IN THE DESERT

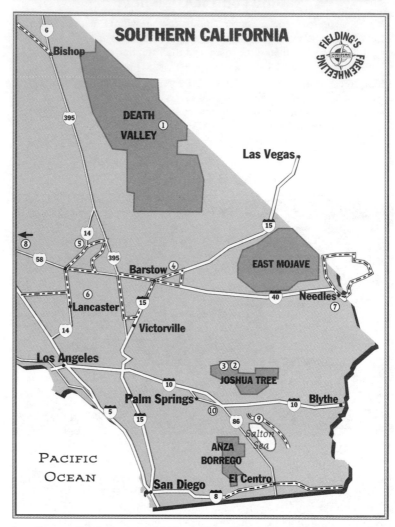

1. **Furnace Creek Campground**, Death Valley National Park, 136 sites, most large enough for an RV, $8 a night, located in the community of Furnace Creek, with spacious campsites looking across open desert terrain, flush toilets, hot showers, fire grates, drinking water and sanitary disposal station, general store, restaurant and propane available nearby. No hookups. Get there early on winter weekends or holidays or you'll be banished to the overflow campground across the road, which has much less ambience.

2. **Jumbo Rocks Campground** in the middle of Joshua Tree National Park near Twentynine Palms, 130 sites, no hookups, no water, pit toilets, free, some evening ranger programs, rock climbing; sites are surrounded by huge boulders. Easiest to find space in winter when nights are nippy; early spring weekends are chock-a-block with rock climbers and desert flower photographers.

3. **Black Rock Campground**, northern end of Joshua Tree National Park, by reservation ☎ *(800) 365-CAMP*, 100 sites with hookups for RVs up to 32 feet long, piped water, flush toilets, sanitary dump available. Good hiking. Open October-May only.

Calico's bottle house

4. **Calico Ghost Town**, a San Bernadino County campground in the canyons just steps away from the commercialized but genuine silver mining town near Baker. 300 sites, 44 with full hookups, some grills, picnic tables, maximum RV length 35 feet, showers, flush toilets, sanitary dump, up to $15 a night with hookups. Reservations essential on weekends, ☎ *(619) 254-2122*. Take Calico exit off I-15 between Barstow and Yermo. Restaurants, shops and attractions in Calico. Groceries, propane and laundry facilities nearby. Families with children, ghost town collectors and rockhounds will especially like the area.

California's beautiful Red Rock Canyon has splendid scenery and a campground.

5. **Red Rock Canyon State Park**, 25 miles northeast of Mojave off highway 14, with 50 primitive sites, no hookups, water and sanitary dump available. No reservations. Ranger campfire programs in summer and fall, hiking trails, dramatic geologic formations, archeological displays at visitor center. Occasional winter snowfalls, cool to cold nights. Nesting falcons, hawks, owls in spring.

6. **Saddleback Butte State Park**, off highway 14, 17 miles east of Lancaster; use Avenue J turnoff. 50 sites, self-contained RVs up to 30 feet, piped water, flush toilets, sanitary dump, no reservations except for groups. Once called Joshua Tree State Park, it has well-preserved stands of Joshua trees, rocky buttes and excellent hiking trails.

7. **Needles Marina Park**, on the Colorado River in Needles, 190 RV sites with hookups, heated pool, hot showers, playground, boat ramp, groceries, gas and laundromat. Water-skiing, boating, fishing, and an 18-hole golf course next door. While you're not exactly roughing it, highly developed parks like this are heaven for some campers. Reservations accepted at ☎ *(619) 326-2197*, $20.

8. **Orange Grove RV Park**, off highway 58 east of Bakersfield at Edison Road, 122 sites nestled in an orange grove, with pick-your-own privileges. Pool, recreation room with big-screen TV, playground, country store, hot showers, air-conditioned restrooms, cable TV, laundry, propane, $23 a night, ☎ *(800) 553-7126*. Nearby: Bakersfield's famous Basque restaurants, like Maitia's.

9. **Fountain of Youth Spa Campground**, Hot Mineral Spa Road near Salton Sea, 15 miles north of Niland off highway 111, 546 RV sites with full hookups, flush toilets, showers, natural artesian steam rooms, hydrojet pools, masseur, church services for Catholics, Protestants, Mormons and Adventists, laundry, barber shop, beauty parlor, propane and groceries. Huge and almost mind-boggling, Fountain of Youth takes no reservations, but if it sounds like your sort of scene, you can call for information at ☎ *(619) 354-1340*.

10. **Outdoor Resorts of America** has two Palm Springs area RV parks, one for motorhomes only, that are well-landscaped, individually-owned sites made available to travelers when space is open. With lavish spa facilities from swimming pools to par-3 golf courses, the full hook-up sites cost around $40 a night. Call ☎ *(800) 453-4056* for the Cathedral City property, open to both motor-driven and towable RVs, or ☎ *(800) 892-2992* for the Indio location, open only to type A and type C motorhomes.

ACTIVE ADVENTURES IN ANZA BORREGO

In the 600,000 acres of the state's largest state park, tent campers can set up almost anywhere so long as they follow the park's guidelines, spelled out in a free publication at the Visitor Center in Borrego Springs. Campers will have to carry their own water in and all trash and garbage back out.

The earth-covered "underground" visitor center provides a good introduction to the flora and fauna of the park, including the endangered desert pupfish.

More organized camping is available at Borrego Palm Canyon Campground, part of the state park system, with full hookups and 30-amp electric capacity. Reservations can be made in advance by calling MIStix at ☎ *(800) 444-7275*. Sites are unshaded and not particularly attractive but the surroundings are pretty. Hot showers and flush toilets are on site, and a self-guided nature trail sets out from the campground area.

The best time to visit is during the winter months. With good January rains, expect to see blossoms in February when the flowering Mojave yucca breaks out in cream-colored bursts from spiny stalks, ocotillos take on sprays of tiny red flowers, and beavertail cactus are topped with big jaunty pink blooms. Check on conditions in advance by calling the visitor center at ☎ *(619) 767-5311.*

East of Anza Borrego off highway 78 is the Ocotillo Wells State Vehicular Recreation Area, where owners of 125s with knobbies can play pretend-moto and new owners of 4x4s can check out the equipment without offending the neighbors.

Bicyclists can contact the **Julian Bicycle Company** *(☎ 619-765-2200)* to join informal bike rides through several canyons in the park. For weekend tours that include camping and mountain bike trips, call **Backroads** *(☎ 800-245-3874).*

Photographers who want to go along in their own vehicle with naturalist/photographer **Paul R. Johnson** on a four-hours-minimum vehicle or hiking tour tailored especially for them can call ☎ *(619) 767-5179;* cost is around $30 an hour.

INSIDER TIP:

RVers should avoid the otherwise very attractive private RV park at Palm Canyon Resort RV Park in Borrego Springs on winter holiday weekends, when so many RVs are crammed together it looks like gridlock.

10 SCENIC SIDE TRIPS

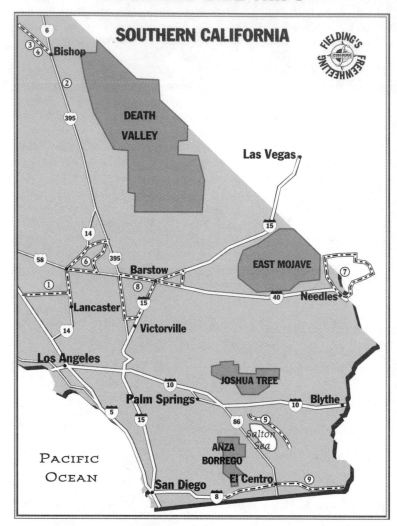

1. **The California poppy trail**, about 50 miles—When the winter has the right amount of rain, early spring looks like Dorothy's dream in *The Wizard of Oz*, except the poppies are orange instead of red. Drive California 138 between Gorman and Lancaster, turning south on Avenue I to the Antelope Valley California Poppy Reserve (☎ *805-724-1180)*. While there's an admission fee to the reserve, you may, as we did last year, see more poppies in bloom along the roadsides than in the reserve itself. Call ahead to determine bloom time, usually best March through May.

2. **The Alabama Hills Loop**, Lone Pine, about 10 miles, unpaved—Make a dusty circle through this whacky terrain where countless good guys in white hats have headed off bad guys in black hats at endless passes, not to mention where Cary Grant's 1939 classic *Gunga Din*, Humphrey Bogart's *High Sierra* and James Stewart's *How the West Was Won* were shot. The rounded, sculpted rocky outcroppings that resemble fantasy animals, castles, temples and skyscrapers are best viewed in early

morning or late afternoon light. If you leave signposted Movie Road, pay close attention to your route or you could get lost forever in this weird place. North of Lone Pine off highway 395.

3. **The road to Bodie**, 13 miles, some of it unpaved—Bodie was one of the rip-roaringest gold towns in California, with some 12,000 residents in its heyday between 1876 and 1880. Today, the remaining houses, school and mines exist in a state of arrested decay preserved by the state park system. Schoolbooks lie open on wooden desks and rusting tins of food line the grocery store shelves. It's best not to attempt the road in bad weather, since the last three miles become a dirt washboard road. Best time to go is summer or early fall. Take highway 270 east off US 395 seven miles south of Bridgeport.

4. **The bristlecone pine forest**—From late June through October, a narrow, winding, paved road is often, but not always, open to an enclave of the world's oldest living creatures, the oldest more than 4300 years old. The tough, twisted trees have only a few limbs but sturdy trunks that grow about an inch a century. From US 395 at Big Pine, turn east on route 168; a sign will be posted within half a mile that will tell you whether the 25-mile road to the trees is open. If you're in a motorhome or towing a travel trailer, you should go no farther than Schulman Grove, where the pavement ends. From here, a ranger station offers maps and self-guiding walking trails lead into the pines.

5. **Along the Salton Sea**—41 miles plus side trips—From Niland to the evocatively named Mecca, route 111 skirts the Salton Sea National Wildlife Refuge, great for spotting Canada geese, snowy egrets, snow geese, pelicans and an occasional glimpse of the endangered Yuma clapper rail. Thousands of migratory birds winter here, filling the air with noise as they chatter or argue back and forth. You'll have to leave the main road at marked intervals and proceed on short, sometimes rough, unpaved stretches to the observation areas.

6. **The desert rat's road to Randsburg**—This offbeat mining town never quite became a ghost town, and today still has a small but hardy population. The Hard Rock Cafe is a piker compared to the Hard Rock Dinner in the town's museum—eggs, pie, sausage, cauliflower, potatoes, even (yes!) hamburgers—all of it actually natural rocks and minerals that look like food. You can swing by California City to pay homage to the endangered desert tortoise at a 38-square mile sanctuary five miles from town; best time to visit is mid-March through May. A loop of roughly 100 miles from the Lancaster area on route 14 could include Red Rock Canyon State Park and Mojave, with its huge grounded fleet of resting or retired jets from commercial airlines near the junction of 14 and 58. The town of Mojave was also the terminus of the 20-mule-team borax wagons from Death Valley.

7. **Along the Lower Colorado River**—A 150-mile loop from Needles can snare you a camping, gaming and watersports excursion, by going first north by US 95 and route 163 to bustling Laughlin, Nevada, where every casino welcomes RVers with open arms. Then head south on state road 95 via Oatman, Arizona, on old Route 66, where wild burros roam the colorful main street. Farther south is Lake Havasu City, Arizona, where London Bridge spans the Colorado. Go west again past Parker Dam into Earp, a minuscule California desert town where the famous marshal retired to try his hand at mining instead of shooting.

8. **The Barstow Triangle**—Despite certain similarities to the more infamous Bermuda Triangle, you won't have to worry about dropping out of sight here so long as you stay off the desert's back roads. Start in the town of Barstow and its Desert Information Center on Barstow Road for a quick read of the Mojave Desert, then check out the Barstow Station, the ultimate curiosity shop built in and around a 1900s

railway station. Head east on I-15 to Yermo and the thriving ghost town of Calico, where mining lore shares the spotlight with archeology and the Early Man site excavated by Dr. Louis Leakey. A few miles east of Barstow on I-40 is the 1860s town of Daggett where you can take a self-guided walking tour. Then head west on route 58 into the triangle, brushing Edwards Air Force Base where space shuttles often land (and some say UFOs as well) at Four Corners before dropping south to Victorville and the ever-popular Roy Rogers-Dale Evans Museum. (For more about the Roy Rogers Museum and Barstow Station, see "13 Off-the-Wall Area Attractions.")

9. **The I-8 to Yuma**—The 171 miles between San Diego and the California border could whiz by in a blur, but not if you take these detours— Desert View Tower at the In-Ko-Pah Park Road exit near Jacumba gives you a great view of what's ahead, plus some eccentric carved stone animals lining the trail; Calexico, separated by a fence from its Mexican neighbor Mexicali, is mysteriously chock-a-block with Chinese restaurants; and the Imperial Sand Dunes Recreation Area draws off-road-vehicle types between October and May. Allow some sightseeing time for the Yuma Territorial Prison, now a state park but once "the hellhole of Arizona."

10. **East Mojave National Scenic Area**—This "wannabe" failed to get full national park honors in the recently passed California Desert Protection Act, ending up instead with a "preserve" status, a designation heavily lobbied for by the National Rifle Association that will allow hunting to continue in this 1.2 million acre high desert reserve. Cattle grazing as well will go on. In Kelso, visit the singing dunes—the sand you dislodge when you walk on a dune makes moaning and humming sounds as it slides. Head north from Kelso on Kelbaker Road to see the cinder cones and lava beds where astronauts trained for the 1969 moon landing. When you join I-40, drive east to the Essex Road exit, then north 16 miles to Mitchell Caverns in Providence Mountain State Recreation Area, where rangers lead tours into the caves and self-contained camping is available. North on Black Canyon Road, Mid Hills and Hole-in-the-Wall campgrounds with 63 sites between them are connected by 11-mile Wild Horse Canyon Road, a scenic unpaved back country byway.

DEATH VALLEY NATIONAL PARK

If publicists had been around during wagon train days, Death Valley would have been named Golden Sands or Shimmering Haze or maybe Rancho Mirage. Instead, it took nearly a century to shake off the bad-mouthing the pioneers gave it. It wasn't until stalwart, sincere Ronald Reagan brought TV's "Death Valley Days" into our living rooms that it became a tourist destination.

Now, as a national park with an additional 1.3 million acres, it's busy even in summer, when European tourists flock here to experience the hottest, driest, lowest, loneliest and so on.

Tent-campers and self-contained RVs (no hookups available) will find comfortable spots to spend a winter weekend at **Furnace Creek Campground** (flush toilets, hot showers, dump station) with shade trees and some privacy. Bigger, less attractive camping areas include **Stovepipe Wells** and **Sunset Campground**, near Furnace Creek Visitors Area. For reservations, call ☎ *(619) 786-2441.*

Bicyclists can tour the mostly-flat terrain of Death Valley quite comfortably in winter. Rain is rare but winds can come up to hinder your progress. Use touring bikes on paved roads, mountain bikes on sandy or rocky routes. The 13-mile paved Artists Palette road (one-way) is particularly scenic, a winding, narrow one with a lot of up and down. A nine-mile paved route from Furnace Creek to Zabriskie Point is best at daybreak, while a seven-mile loop to the sand dunes from Stovepipe Wells is easy any time of day. For an organized tour, call **Backroads** (☎ *800-533-2573*, in California ☎ *415-895-1783*) or **Earth Trek Expeditions** (☎ *800-229-8735*).

INSIDER TIP:

Keep an eye out for the bandit coyotes of Stovepipe Wells, a trio of brazen animals who come out at midday alongside the highway to stop traffic in hopes of scrounging food handouts. Don't encourage them by giving them food or the rangers will banish them to the far-off regions of the park.

WILDLIFE WATCH

Dusk and dawn are the best wildlife-watching times in the desert, especially where there's a water source. But stay downwind so the animals can't smell you.

Besides the bandit coyotes that lurk around all day you might spot the elegant little desert kit fox or the malevolent sidewinder in the sand dunes around Stovepipe Wells at dawn or dusk. Roadrunners are everywhere, looking exactly like the "beep beep" cartoon version.

California's endangered state reptile, the desert tortoise, can often be seen in its own Mojave Desert sanctuary near California City. Chances of sighting one are best from mid-March to mid-June, but if you spot one moving slowly across the highway, don't touch him or pick him up. He'll panic and lose the precious water he's hoarding from those rare winter showers.

One of the best places to see desert bighorn sheep is on the manicured lawns of the posh Ritz-Carlton Hotel in Rancho Mirage. They hoof down from their adjacent hilltop wildlife sanctuary to feast on the foliage, and don't seem to mind tourists and cameras.

Another good spot to look for bighorns, especially rams, is in Anza Borrego State Park on road S-22 between markers 12.5 and 13.5. The best time is in the morning; pull your vehicle off the road completely and do not disturb them.

In Death Valley, you can spot the endangered desert pupfish from a wooden boardwalk at Salt Creek Interpretive Trail off 190 south of Stovepipe Wells.

Both the pupfish and the rare fringe-toed lizard, who can shut off all his body orifices and "swim" through sand dunes, can be found in the Coachella Valley Reserve and may be glimpsed on one of several easy walking trails radiating out from the Visitor Center. Take Thousand Palms Canyon Road off Ramon Road north of I-10 near Palm Springs.

The Living Desert off Haystack Road in Palm Desert has captive and wild-roaming desert species year-round. Look for road runners, quail, desert tortoises, desert pupfish, rattlesnakes, desert kangaroo rats, Peninsular bighorn sheep, coyote, golden eagles, Mexican wolves, bobcats, mountain lions, javelina and rare naked mole rats.

As for that other kind of wildlife, there's not a lot of after-dark action, but daytimes offer just about any extreme you could dream up:

Willow Springs International Raceway, Rosamond, ☎ *(805) 256-2471*, offers an appointment in the fast lane, a chance to watch or take part in fast track racing. You can watch a race, take a lesson on handling your own car from an expert from any of several schools, or book a formula car racing session, just as many movie star drivers have in the past.

Sand sailors head for El Mirage dry lake in the eastern Mojave on a windy weekend afternoon to set up their sand sail craft, a T-shaped tubular frame six feet wide and 10 feet long with a 17-foot mast at the base of the tee. The triangular sail in the right wind lets them get speeds of up to 70 m.p.h.—but there are no brakes. Get there via Avenue P in Lancaster, which turns into El Mirage Road, then turn north on El Medio road (unpaved) five miles to the lake.

How about a free-fall parachute jump with both the parachute and the instructor strapped to your back? Parachutes over Palm Springs, ☎ *(800) 535-JUMP*, calls it tandem parachute jumping, and it looks a little like Superman taking Lois Lane for a whirl. It costs $179 to jump from 8000 feet, or $10 more per thousand feet up to 14,000.

For nocturnal wildlife, **Zelda's Nightclub and Beach Club**, *169 North Indian Canyon Drive, Palm Springs*, ☎ *(619) 325-2375*, boogies six nights a week but never on Sunday. Try **BrewMeisters** in PS at *369 North Palm Canyon Drive*, ☎ *(619) 327-BREW*, for micro-brewed beer and sports bar, and **Cecil's on Sunrise**, ☎ *(619) 320-4202* for rock and roll, pool tables and Sunday night standup comics.

INSIDER TIP:

If you visit Joshua Tree in early to mid-winter or on a weekday, you'll be able to choose a great site on a first-come first-served basis, but if you arrive on weekends or during the prime rock-climbing season in early spring, you'll have to take any vacancy you can find.

THE MOJAVE DESERT

Calico in late afternoon sun

The Mojave is dotted with twisted green Joshua trees which explorer John C. Fremont, never a happy camper, considered "the most repulsive trees in the vegetable kingdom."

Explorers, immigrants and miners alike endured rather than adored the high desert. But latter-day desert rats get rapturous about such ersatz doings as chili cook-offs, tobacco-spitting contests and burro biscuit-tossings.

Cynics forget that Calico, for example, was a real ghost town before it became an artificial ghost town recreated by Walter Knotts of Knotts Berry Farm. Silver was mined there in the late 1880s, and a dog named Dorsey used to carry the mail from Calico to Bismarck a half-mile away.

You may notice the exit markers from I-15 for Zzyzx, where Dr. Curtis Howe Springer, a radio evangelist and health food vendor, developed a health resort for refugees from Los Angeles' Skid Row. After 30 years of tending the urban ill free of charge, the Springers were suddenly evicted by the Bureau of Land Management for trespassing. The site, which was nearly destroyed by vandals during the years, was rescued and restored not long ago by the California Desert Studies Consortium, who welcome visitors.

At nearby Nipton, the four-room Hotel Nipton recalls the days when silent film star Clara Bow and cowboy-actor husband Rex Bell had a ranch nearby. An outdoor hot tub lets you soak under the stars while listening to the mournful whistle of a passing freight train. ☎ *(619) 856-2335*, from $60.

Camping at Joshua Tree National Monument

Joshua Tree National Park is a tumbled wonderland of bizarre boulders and glorious gardens of cactus ideally visited by freewheelers who can tent or stay overnight in a self-contained recreational vehicle; there are no hook-ups or water available. At all but two of the park's campgrounds (Cottonwood and Black Rock Canyon) campers must bring in all the water and firewood they plan to use, and toilet facilities are primitive. Jumbo Rocks, our favorite campground, is also a top draw for rock climbers. Joshua Tree is one of the world's most popular climbing areas, with more than 3500 climbing spots for every degree of ability.

While vehicles of all sorts can negotiate the main roads in the park, four-wheel drive vehicles, motorcycles and bicycles are best for exploring unpaved roads. Rules require all bicycles and motor vehicles to stay on established roadways. Good back country roads include: Pinkham Canyon Road, 20 miles from Cottonwood Visitor Center to an I-10 service road; Covington Flats, which accesses some of the best Joshua tree stands, four miles from Covington Flats picnic area to Eureka Peak; Geology Tour Road, 5.4 miles from Jumbo Rocks to Squaw Tank; or Black Eagle Mine Road, up through the canyons in the Eagle Mountains. Alert freewheelers may spot roadrunners, coyotes, kangaroo rats, jack rabbits, golden eagles and sidewinders.

Birders will find good watching at Cottonwood Spring, while photographers and wildflower enthusiasts will want to set out from there to walk Lost Palms Oasis Trail in early spring to find dozens of native desert wild flowers.

The General Patton Memorial Museum, a marked exit just off I-10 about 50 miles east of Palm Springs, is built on the site of the World War II desert training center. While you won't see George C. Scott lurking around in his Patton uniform, you will see memorabilia, boots and saddles and plenty of free war film footage. Open daily 9–5, ☎ *(619) 227-3227.*

INSIDER TIPS:
FOR OFF-ROAD DESERT EXPLORERS:

—Never head out on back roads in the desert without telling someone where you're going and when you expect to return.

—Carry at least one gallon of water per person per day.

—Carry good detailed local maps (desert access guides are available for $2.50 each from Bureau of Land Management, California Desert District, 1695 Spruce St., Riverside 92507).

—Never trespass on private desert land; some of the "desert rats" don't take kindly to strangers.

—Set up camp at least 200 yards away from a man-made water source for wildlife and no more than 300 yards from the road. Don't set up camp in a wash where flash floods could literally wash you away.

10 DESERT SPLURGES

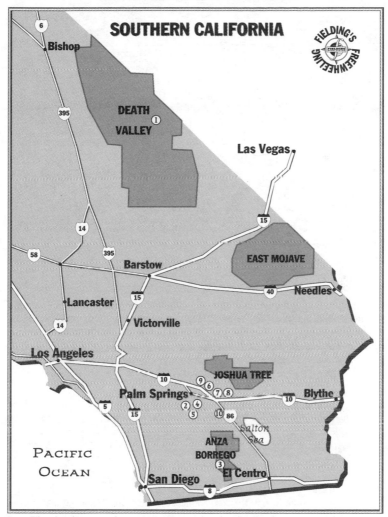

SOUTHERN CALIFORNIA

1. The dazzling, cerulean swimming pool and Palm Garden at **Furnace Creek Inn Resort in Death Valley National Park** looks like a mirage from the 1930s, with stone arches framing distant views of snow-capped mountains beside a lush oasis shaded by palms. ☎ *(800) 528-6387*, from $225 a night for two with breakfast and dinner included.

2. A bouncy jeep ride along private dirt roads with **Desert Adventures of Palm Springs** lends insights into everything from life-styles and rituals of the local Cahuilla tribes to fascinating facts about desert flora and fauna. Try to catch a ride with Morgan Wind-in-Her-Hair Levine, a mile-a-minute talker and one of the company's co-owners. Tours range from one to four hours and cost $35 to $99 for adults. Call ☎ *(619) 864-6530* to book.

Camping in Death Valley's Furnace Creek Campground

3.   Check into a one-bedroom casita at the **Casa del Zorro in Borrego Springs**, dating back to 1940, where laid-back hotel with night-lit swimming pool meets laid-back desert town with two golf courses. ☎ *(800) 824-1884*, from $150 for two.

4.   Sit under the shade trees on the grassy lawn by the pool at the circa-1935 **Ingleside Inn in Palm Springs**, where Howard Hughes used to check in under the name "Earl Martyn," along with Ava Gardner as "Mrs. Clark." In the hotel's Melvyn's Restaurant, you can still dine on 1950s-style martinis, shrimp cocktails and steak while overhearing remarks like, "Sheila, you look wonderful; not even in the light can you tell!" ☎ *(800) 826-4162* (in California), ☎ *(800) 772-6655* (elsewhere), from $100 for two.

5.   Try a villa with tennis court, Jacuzzi and private pool at **La Mancha in Palm Springs**, one of 47 hidden behind tall adobe walls among the jacaranda trees, where management will stock your refrigerator on request, deliver dinner from a choice of local restaurants or send in a masseur who makes house calls. ☎ *(800) 255-1773*, $750 for two.

6.   Book a table for afternoon tea in the hushed purlieus of the posh **Ritz-Carlton, Rancho Mirage**, where, if you linger awhile, you can watch the bighorn sheep who come down from the hills to graze on the lawn. ☎ *(800) 241-3333*, rooms from $300 for two.

7.   Dine in Frank Sinatra's favorite desert restaurant, **Dominick's in Rancho Mirage**, where you can feast on chicken Sinatra, veal piccata, kreplach, fresh Lake Superior whitefish or bread pudding. It's at *70-030 Highway 111*, ☎ *(619) 324-1711*.

8.   If you book a room or dinner at **Marriott's Desert Springs Resort and Spa**, you'll be whisked to your destination by a motor launch that picks you up inside the glass-walled lobby, sails out a sliding glass wall and plies along lagoons to your room or one of the hotel's more distant restaurants. ☎ *(800) 228-9290*, rooms from $260 a night.

9.   Check into a villa at **Two Bunch Palms in Desert Hot Springs**, said to have been Al Capone's desert hideaway, where you can see bullet holes from an earlier time and a 300-yard escape tunnel out to the parking lot. Try to figure out which locations were used for the Tim Robbins film *The Player*, get a facial or massage, take a mud bath or just generally wind down. But don't expect to drive in for a quick look

around; if you're not on the reservations list, a gate guard who could be left over from Capone's days will send you packing. ☎ *(800) 472-8791*, from $125.

10. Luxuriate amid the blooming petunias, pansies, snapdragons and Iceland poppies in the old-fashioned gardens of the 1926 **La Quinta Hotel Golf & Tennis Resort in La Quinta**, with its restored casitas and (alas) all-new meeting and convention facilities. ☎ *(800) 854-1271*, from $85 summer, $235 winter for two.

PALM SPRINGS

Alternate checkerboard lots in Palm Springs belong to the Agua Caliente band of Cahuilla Indians, who control 42 percent of the land in the Coachella Valley and are the richest tribe in North America. To the vexation of state officials, a lavish casino is rumored to be the next major project for the band.

While many of Palm Springs' senior celebrity residents are irreverently referred to as The Waxworks, there's nothing sedentary about the area. You can go sky-diving *(☎ 800-535-JUMP)*, catch a polo match *(☎ 619-342-2223)*, splish-splash in a 20,000-acre wave pool or 500-foot white-water river *(☎ 619-325-SURF)*, go hot-air ballooning over the desert *(☎ 619-568-0997)*, ride the Aerial Tramway from the desert floor to the cool crest of 8516 feet in 15 minutes *(☎ 619-325-1391)* or hit the desert in a covered wagon *(☎ 619-347-2161)*.

For a nostalgic, even romantic, escape, tour the glamorous private estate where Elvis and Priscilla spent their honeymoon back in 1967. **The Alexander Estate**, ☎ *(619) 322-1192*, houses memorabilia of The King and his bride, and you'll probably hear a little *Hound Dog* or *Heartbreak Hotel* in the background.

The Living Desert Wildlife and Botanical Park (closed in summer) exhibits mountain lions, eagles, kit foxes, bighorn sheep and coyotes in habitat displays. The new Eagle Canyon area includes a beautiful mountain lion that can be viewed and photographed through glass, a bobcat, a pair of rare Mexican wolves, and tiny, cuddly kit foxes, who spend their days curled up in glass-windowed rock dens visitors can peek into.

14 OFF-THE-WALL ATTRACTIONS

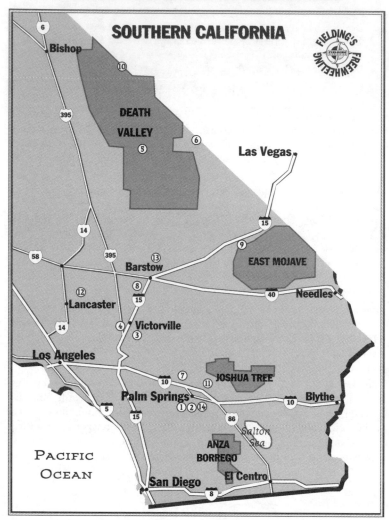

1.   Retired chorus girls aged 50–80 with great gams still kick 'em high at the "**Palm Springs Follies**" in the city's nostalgic Plaza Theatre. Call ☎ *(619) 864-6516* for information, ☎ *(619) 327-0225* for tickets (around $25). Daily matinees at 1:30, nightly performances at 7, winter season only.

2.   The only pair of **nudist bed-and-breakfasts** in the U.S., so far as we know, are in Palm Springs. At **Le Petit Chateau**, south of Palm Springs at *1491 Via Soledad*, ☎ *(619) 325-2686*, rooms range from $68 to $130, depending on size and season. At **Happy Tanner Inn Au Natural**, ☎ *(619) 320-5984*, rooms cost $68 to $89 a night including breakfast and snacks; they prefer you call for the address since they don't like looky-loos. Day rates also available. Don't book unless you're willing to bare.

3.   The **Roy Rogers/Dale Evans Museum** in Victorville is an eclectic compendium of everything the cowboy film stars ever saw, received or touched. A collector's set of

1950s western tableware, a Pontiac decorated with horns, pistols and silver dollars, and dioramas about the family's life are only a minuscule part of the assortment. Roy's horse Trigger and Dale's horse Buttermilk, along with several family dogs, survive as models of taxidermy. ☎ *(619) 243-4547*, $3 entrance fee.

Roy Rogers' horse Trigger announces the location of the Roy Rogers/Dale Evans Museum in Victorville.

4. The **desert poet Miles Mahan** will welcome you to Hula-Ville if you get off I-15 at Amargosa Road southwest of Victorville. His roadside location, where he lives in a faded, decrepit automobile, is named for a 12-foot sign he rescued that depicts a grass-skirted hula girl. You can walk around his bottle trees and read his painted couplets for free, but few escape without forking over $5 for his self-published book of poems.

5. The **moving rocks of Death Valley** skitter along the desert floor at Racetrack Playa, leaving behind a clear trail of their route. Scientists suspect rain-slick clay allows the wind to push the rocks back and forth at speeds of up to two miles an hour, but no one has ever seen them in motion.

6. The ballerina dances for an audience of painted figures if no live ones show up at the **Amargosa Opera House at Death Valley Junction**, where dancer Marta Becket painted in 250 spectators for her dances and pantomimes scheduled on winter weekends.

7. The you-can't-miss-'em **roadside dinosaurs** at Cabazon northeast of Palm Springs on I-10 appeared in the film *PeeWee's Big Adventure* and serve to promote a chow stop at the Wheel Inn, where no less a gourmet authority than Gault-Millau praises the huge helpings of homemade desserts from strawberry shortcakes to bread puddings. While we were not lured by their "famous" cream pies, we adored the gift shop located in the belly of the biggest dinosaur.

8. At **Exotic World, The Strippers' Hall of Fame** at *29053 Wild Road in Helendale*, former headliner Dixie Evans, better known as "the Marilyn Monroe of Burlesque," commemorates the days when disrobing seductively was a work of art for once-famous stars like Lili St. Cyr, Blaze Starr and Tempest Storm. See Gypsy Rose Lee's cape, Jayne Mansfield's dressing room ottoman and an urn with the ashes of Jennie Lee, who started this museum before she died of cancer. Call ahead for an appointment at ☎ *(619) 243-5261*, admission $10.

9. The **world's tallest thermometer** soars 134 feet above the Bun Boy restaurant in the Mojave Desert town of Baker, showing one foot for each degree of temperature, up to the hottest recorded day in history at Death Valley (July 10, 1913). You can see it as you drive along I-15, with the current temperature recorded both day and night. The restaurant dates from 1926, and has a mini-museum about Death Valley in the entrance. The intriguingly named Bun Boy Motel is next door.

10. **Scotty's Castle**, a lavish, $2 million Moorish mansion built by a Chicago insurance executive and his radio evangelist wife, but named for a former performer in Buffalo Bill's Wild West show who also lived there, has an unfinished 270-foot swimming pool, 25 rooms with tapestries and fireplaces and a 26-foot clock tower. Johnson and his friend Walter Scott (Scotty) rejected designs submitted by Frank Lloyd Wright in favor of an unknown architect who did not go on to fame and fortune. Guided tours led by costumed docents are so popular you can expect a wait of an hour or two in season. Scotty died in 1954, and his entire estate consisted of a well-worn cowboy hat.

11. If you've always yearned for the rugged pioneer life, try a **covered wagon tour** through the Coachella Valley Preserve in a genuine bone-crusher of a prairie schooner, with an optional campfire and barbecue also on the agenda, $55 for adults, $27.50 for kids, ☎ *(800) 367-2161*.

This Swiss chalet houses an excellent museum of Native American arts/crafts.

12. A whimsical and eclectic **Swiss chalet Indian museum** filled to the brim with giant kachinas, bird claw fishhooks, grass skirts, some unlikely illustrated Indian legends and a second-story cave is open on weekends only, October through mid-June, *15701 East Avenue M in Lancaster*, ☎ *(805) 942-0662*. It's called Antelope Valley Indian Museum, and was hand-built by a romantic, self-taught artist in 1928.

13. **Barstow Station**, east of town on the I-15 business loop, looks like several small railway cars by the station from the outside, but inside is one huge, rambling shop with an astonishing collection of **great tacky souvenirs** from life-sized plaster of Paris howling coyotes to plastic cactus and personalized mugs for every Tom, Dick and Lupe that happens by. Things dangle from the ceilings and are stacked precariously on random shelves and counters around the premises. A tour bus rest stop, the station also has a McDonald's and various take-out food counters. We were fascinated with the 42 jellybean flavors, including jalapeño, piña colada, buttered popcorn, strawberry cheesecake, cotton candy and toasted marshmallow.

14. Walk through **a giant model of a human heart**, record your heartbeat or step into a pulsating coronary artery to observe plaque formation, all at Heartland, the California Museum of the Heart, in a wing of the Heart Institute of the Desert at *39-600 Bob Hope Drive*, free but voluntary donations suggested. While there, you can catch a healthy snack at the Heart Rock Cafe or watch a heartwarming film at the Happy Heart Cinema.

The hula girl sign shows the off-freeway location of Miles Mahan, desert poet.

ON THE CHEAP: TRIMMING COSTS ON THE ROAD

Ask any snowbird turned desert rat how to live off the land, or rather the Bureau of Land Management, and he'll tell you about "the Slabs" or one of the other Long-Term Visitor Areas in the southern desert.

Here's how it works: You can buy a season permit to camp in one of the LTVAs for $50; that lets you stay in residence for up to seven months between September 15 and April 15. If you only want to spend a few days, you can buy a short-term permit good for seven days that costs $10. Permits can usually be purchased from campground hosts in each camp area.

Don't expect hookups, paved parking (except at "the Slabs," which were once cement pads for military buildings), water or sanitary dump sites. What you get is plenty of desert, some solitude if you wish, and all the warm sunshine you can handle.

The sites are generally located off I-8 or I-10 west of Yuma and in Arizona at Quartzite on US 95 off I-10. The most established areas are Hot Spring, off I-8 east of El Centro at highway 115; Imperial Dam, off I-8 at Winterhaven, then west on Senator Wash Road; Pilot Knob, off I-8 at Sidewinder Road five miles west of Yuma; Dunes Vista, off I-8 at Ogilby Road, 10 miles west of Yuma; La Posa at Quartzsite, AZ, on both sides of route 95; Midland, off I-10 at Lovekin Boulevard; and Mule Mountain, off I-10 at Wiley's Well Road, then north nine miles. To get more information, call the California Desert District Office of BLM in Riverside at ☎ *(909) 697-5200*, or the Yuma District Office in Arizona at ☎ *(602) 726-6300*.

10 GREAT TAKEOUT (OR EAT-IN) TREATS

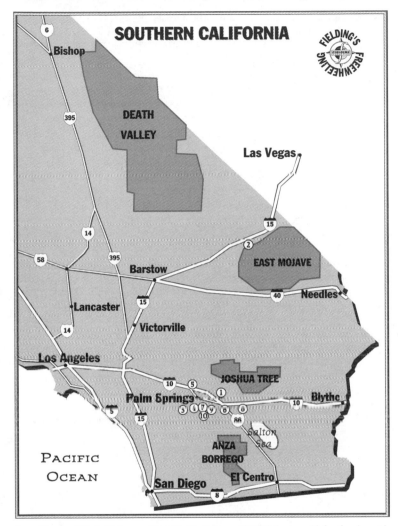

1. The **pan-fried chicken** at Murph's Gaslight at *79-860 Avenue 42*, by the airport in Bermuda Dunes, can be ordered to take out with all the trimmings—black-eyed peas, mashed potatoes, cornbread, hot biscuits, country gravy and fruit cobbler—if you call ahead, ☎ *(619) 345-6242*. It's open 11 a.m. to 3 p.m. and 5 p.m. to 9 p.m. daily except Sundays, when the hours are 3 p.m. to 9 p.m., and Mondays, when the restaurant is closed. You can also feast family-style at a table inside on a first-come first-served basis.

2. Try the half-order of **hummus and homemade pita** bread and the **falafal** sandwich with tahini to go at The Mad Greek's in Baker, where an unautographed photo of Zsa Zsa Gabor hangs over the door.

3. The **cream pies** are what made a hit of Louise's Pantry, since 1946 located in the same spot, *124 South Palm Canyon Drive in Palm Springs*, but the huge, moder-

ately-priced breakfasts are what have people lining up out on the sidewalk these days.

4. **Fresh grilled swordfish, salmon or halibut sandwiches** are $6.95 to eat in or take out at Fish Looie, *68-525 Ramon Road, in a Cathedral City shopping mall*. A combination fishmonger and chef, Looie sells fresh seafood to go, raw or cooked, along with deli-style side dishes.

5. The original recipe for **trail mix**, concocted 20-some years ago by an employee of Hadley Orchard in Cabazon, is still for sale in the freeway farmstand, along with dried fruits and nuts, and what appears to be the world's largest assortment of fruit-and-nut gift packs. Take the Apache Trail exit from I-10 near Palm Springs.

6. Yummy **peanut-butter pie** at Morgans in the La Quinta Hotel, La Quinta, *49-499 Eisenhower Drive, La Quinta*, is surprisingly light and delicate, with a brushing of chocolate on the crisp crust before the filling is mounded on, then topped with whipped cream and sliced almonds. Even in a take-out carton, the pie slice is artistically nestled on a base of chocolate stripes, which helps justify its $3.95 tariff.

7. The **vegetarian enchiladas, burritos, tamales and tacos** at Taqueria, *125 East Tahquitz Canyon Way, Palm Springs*, come with your choice of refried, black or ranch beans and a big dollop of rice. This charming cantina with its bright colors and big patio also features live entertainment and a selection of margarita specialties.

8. **Fresh dates** are harvested between September and mid-December around Indio; check Shields Date Gardens, dating back to 1924, for Royal Medjool-Super Jumbo dates, the world's biggest, *80-225 Highway 111*, open daily. The Oasis Date Gardens *in Thermal on highway 111* give you a free date milkshake at the end of their free 20-minute tour.

9. The **best barbecued ribs in the desert** can be found at Simba's Ribhouse, in a former bank building at *190 North Sunrise Way in Palm Springs*, along with down-home versions of chicken and dumplings, black-eyed peas, barbecued beans, cornbread, hush puppies and sweet potato pie. Call ahead at ☎ *(619) 778-7630*.

10. **Corned beef sandwiches** from Nate's Deli, *100 South Indian Avenue south of Tahquitz Way, Palm Springs*, are virtually guilt-free because the beef is so lean. A big serving of crunchy, fresh, kosher dill pickle slices comes alongside. At a branch deli, Nate's *in Palm Desert at highway 111 and Fred Waring Drive*, evening entertainment is headed up by a lively musical called "Phantom of the Deli."

FYI

Palm Springs Tourism, ☎ *(800) 34-SPRINGS*, and Palm Springs Desert Resorts, ☎ *(800) 41-RELAX*, can provide material and maps of the area.

For general information about the California desert, contact **California Division of Tourism**, *801 K Street, Suite 1600, Sacramento, CA 95814*, ☎ *(916) 322-2881*.

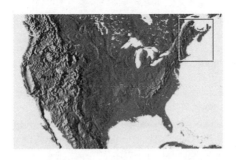

THE LOBSTER COAST: NEW ENGLAND AND THE MARITIMES

RVers enjoy a lobster dinner on board in Freeport, Maine.

As the man who led a lobster on a leash through the gardens of the Palais Royal in Paris explained, "I have a liking for lobsters. They are peaceful, serious creatures. They know the secrets of the sea, they don't bark, and they don't gnaw on one's monadic privacy like dogs do."

Lobsters were served at the first Thanksgiving dinner, and were so plentiful that until this century they were used for fertilizer, fish bait and jail food. The largest lobster ever recorded was 48 pounds with a length of 3-1/2 feet. They are nocturnal and generally eat fish and shellfish. And, as the man said, they don't bark.

Our Lobster Land drive covers the coast of New England and Canada's Maritime provinces of New Brunswick and Nova Scotia.

It was along this North Atlantic coast that Alexander Graham Bell invented the telephone and Guglielmo Marconi sent out the first wireless message across the Atlantic, where Ruth Wakefield baked the first Toll House cookies and Sicily-born Benedetto Capalbo floated the first submarine sandwich in New London, Connecticut. So popular were they during World War II that he supplied 500 a day to the local submarine base, giving what he called a "grinder" its new name.

New England is the birthplace of the graham cracker and the Parker House roll, where Lydia Pinkham's Vegetable Compound "for periodic female weakness" was produced and the birth control pill invented, where Lizzie Bordon took an ax and the Brink's burglars took a powder, where the burglar alarm was invented, Earl Tupper sealed up Tupperware, Clarence Birdseye flash-froze food, and the first snowmobile cranked up back in 1913.

The first Frisbees came from fun-loving Bridgeport, Connecticut, where Robert Mitchum was born and P.T. Barnum lived, only they were originally spelled Frisbies—pie tins from a local bakery with the name stamped on the bottom, that Yale students in the Twenties tossed as a fad.

Saint John, New Brunswick, is where Donald Sutherland was born, MGM's Louis B. Mayer grew up, Captain Kidd raped and pillaged, and the King of Siam's Anna Leonowens retired to found an arts academy. Benedict Arnold was burned in effigy and driven out of town, not for being a traitor— he was a hero to the Loyalists—but for nefarious business dealings.

INSIDER TIP:

It's easy to find out what's going on in New England and the Maritimes. Stop at any tourist information spot, particularly those on main highways at the entrance to a state or province, and you can pick up campground information, times and prices for attractions, maps, and leaflets on everything from local farmer's markets to self-guiding drives or walks—all of it free.

When to go. Summer and fall is prime lobster season, and also when the weather is best. Unfortunately, that's also when everyone else goes. If you go too early in June, you'll encounter the mosquitoes, black flies and no see'ums. Autumn is crowded with what the locals call leaf peepers, arrived for the fall foliage.

What to take. Binoculars, film and camera, rain gear, hiking boots, sun hat, sunscreen and insect repellent. To enter Canada, you should have proof of citizenship such as a passport, birth certificate or voter registration card, because a driver's license is no longer acceptable. Always have a sweater or jacket handy. The Maine coastal weather on a nice summer day is described by author Frances FitzGerald as Baked Alaska, a simultaneous sensation of hot sun and cool breeze. And 18th century Nova Scotia residents were nicknamed "Bluenoses" for bearing up under the cold winters.

What to wear. If you want to mingle at the posher purlieus of New England like Bar Harbor, Nantucket and Martha's Vineyard, wear anything from the L.L. Bean, J. Crew or Land's End catalogues, topsiders without socks, plaid or khaki Bermuda shorts, Oxford cloth shirts and pastel sweaters tied casually around your neck. Otherwise, don your usual RV garb and you'll fit in almost everywhere.

FREEWHEELING IN NEW ENGLAND AND THE MARITIMES

The Lobster Coast route heads north along the edge of Connecticut and Rhode Island, jogs over to Cape Cod, then back up the shore to Boston, Salem and Gloucester, the 18-mile coastline of New Hampshire and the 3500-mile coastline of Maine. (You'll know you're in Maine when all the license plates you see have bright red lobsters on them). Then carry on through New Brunswick's Loyalist and Acadian country to Nova Scotia. Prince Edward Island, which also has very fine lobsters, is reached only by plane or ferry, inconvenient but not impossible for RVers, although a bridge from New Brunswick is under construction for the year 2000 or so. The whole route one-way is approximately 1200 miles, more if you dip into all Maine's picturesque coves and make a loop around Nova Scotia.

Canada's Maritimes offer good driving in most areas for freewheelers, but maneuvering an RV through New England is not always easy. Roads are narrow and often crowded with traffic, especially in summer around Cape Cod or Kennebunkport, and there are not a lot of pullover spots spacious enough for a big rig.

Expect some foggy or misty patches of road along the coast, especially in the mornings, with a drizzle that may go on all day.

The best way to explore most of the towns and villages along the Lobster Coast is to park your RV and set out on foot.

LOOKING FOR LOBSTER
IN ALL THE RIGHT PLACES

Lobster pots off Boothbay Harbor, Maine

A single-minded lobster lover along the Maine coast can cheerfully overlook Bar Harbor day trippers and t-shirt vendors, fudge fairs and ye olde gift shoppes to search out an "early-bird lobster dinner." Before 5:30 or 6 p.m., you can dine on a whole fresh lobster weighing around one and one-quarter pounds for the price of the day, always well under $10. You might even hit a two-for-one lobster special, two one-pounders on the same plate and enough for two. With a little concentration, you can hit a couple of these spots before prices go up for the evening and it's time to get ready for dinner.

A New Hampshire native named Tom Shovan, who later moved to California, claims the all-time lobster-eating record by devouring 61 of the tasty crustaceans at Custy's Restaurant in North Kingstown, Rhode Island.

The peerless Homarus Americanus Northern, or American lobster, has meaty front claws which his warm water cousins lack. We think he also is a great deal more succulent.

Only when driven to desperation (or boredom) should you order lobster prepared any way other than steamed or boiled, except on a cold day, when a lobster stew goes down well, and perhaps at lunchtime, when a lobster roll fills the bill nicely. For the uninitiated, a lobster roll is a top-sliced hot dog bun filled with chunks of cold lobster moistened with mayonnaise or melted butter or both, and sometimes a crunch of chopped celery.

When buying a live lobster, look for the liveliest with a good greenish-brown color. Avoid any that have turned blue. Lobsters can last up to two days out of seawater if you refrigerate them in your RV in a heavy brown paper bag with a few strands of seaweed. Never close it up in a plastic bag, where it will suffocate, or store it in a pot of cold tap water, where it will drown.

To cook a lobster, put several inches of water— preferably sea water—in a pot, bring it to a boil and drop the lobster in, holding him by the underside of the body to keep him from splattering the water, then cover the pot quickly. Listen for the water to boil again, then reduce the heat to keep it from boiling over. The lobster is cooked when all of its shell has turned red, usually in as little as 10 minutes for a small lobster to a maximum of 20 for a large one. Another expert suggests that when the lobster turns bright red and floats, cook for 3 or 4 minutes longer.

The British Society for the Prevention of Cruelty to Animals suggests the most humane way to cook a lobster is to lower it into the pot head first.

12 TOP LOBSTER SPOTS

CANADA & NEW ENGLAND

QUEBEC

St. Lawrence River

C A N A D A

NEW

BRUNSWICK

PRINCE EDWARD IS.

N O V A

S C O T I A

Halifax

Saint John

MAINE

Bar Harbor

Mt. Desert Is.

Portland

N.H.

ATLANTIC OCEAN

Boston

MASS.

Nantucket

CONN.

Martha's Vineyard

R.I.

Bridgeport

1. **Nunan's Lobster Hut**, Cape Porpoise, ME, where the crustaceans are steamed to order in a little water rather than boiled in a lot. A bag of potato chips and a hard roll with butter fill out the lobster dinner tray, a pizza pan. Bring your own beer or wine; finish off with a slice of homemade apple or blueberry pie. Open evenings from 5 p.m.

2. **Beal's Lobster Pier** in Southwest Harbor, ME, serves a shore dinner of soft-shelled lobster, steamer clams, corn on the cob and onion rings. You sit at picnic tables at the end of the pier and feast, after fetching drinks and condiments from a side annex.

3. In Bar Harbor, ME, at Fisherman's Landing, the **Cook House** sells live or cooked lobster by the pound to take out, along with wonderful lobster rolls, fried clams and crab rolls. Of course you don't have to take them any farther than the picnic tables outside the restaurant.

4. **Lobsterman's Co-op**, near the aquarium in Boothbay Harbor, ME, an unpretentious wooden pier with outdoor picnic tables and a choice of hardshell or softshell lobster (defined on a hand-printed sign as "Soft shell = less meat, sweeter taste"). To that definition, we can add "easier to crack open." While fat herring gulls perched on the rail look on, you can devour lobsters with melted butter, a package of potato chips, corn on the cob, fried onion rings, steamed or fried clams and jug wine by the glass or pitcher.

5. **The Gloucester House** in Gloucester, MA, where waitresses call you "dearie" and serve an inexpensive assembly-line clambake with lobster, clam chowder, corn on the cob and watermelon at long wooden tables out back.

6. **Harraseeket Lunch & Lobster Company**, South Freeport, ME, is at a pier on the harbor and won't let RVs in their parking lot when they're busy. There is, however, a boat yard across the way that will let you park briefly if you give them a dollar or two for the time it takes to fetch your steamed lobster, bring it back to the RV and eat it.

7. **Abbott's Lobster in the Rough** in Noank, CT, serves fresh boiled lobster with cole slaw and potato chips at outdoor picnic tables by the water. You can get clams on the half-shell or in chowder, or a lobster roll, if you'd rather.

8. **The Old City Market** in Saint John, NB, sells live or cooked lobsters to take out or ship home, as well as lobster rolls and cooked lobster tails. The paper bags of dark red flaky leaves you see everywhere are dulse, dried seaweed that is a favored local snack and very much an acquired taste. The market dates from 1876 and is built to resemble the inverted keel of a ship. There's a glass-walled solarium next door if you want to eat your lobster here, or head for Billy's Seafood Company in the north corner if you favor a sit-down meal.

9. **Lobster Galley**, in South Haven, NS, on Cape Breton Island north of Baddeck, serves fresh lobster from its own pound, plus a free lesson in speaking Gaelic. Closed in winter.

10. **Mabel's Lobster Claw** in Kennebunkport, ME, where George and Barbara Bush indulge in the peanut butter ice-cream pie, has soft-shell lobster in season (July to November) and lovely lobster rolls to eat in or take out.

11. **The Clam Shack** in Kennebunkport by the bridge has nowhere nearby big enough for an RV to park, but if a passenger hops out and the driver goes on into town and parks for a while (there's often a wait) they can get fantastic lobster rolls to go, or serious baskets of fried clams. They open not-so-promptly around 11 a.m.

12. **The Lobster Pot** in Provincetown, Cape Cod, a funky but pricey two-story clapboard house, serves classic clam chowder along with local clambake dinners, and has takeout chowder and lobster. To eat in, you can sit inside or out on an open deck on the upper level, called Top of the Pot.

THE LOYALISTS AND THE ACADIANS

By the end of the American Revolution, 40,000 Americans loyal to the British Crown had fled north to Canada. Some 14,000 arrived in what is now New Brunswick with land grants for acreage along the Saint John River given to them by the Crown. In 1785, they incorporated their two settlements into the city of Saint John.

Lighthouse along the New Brunswick coast

Meanwhile, to the south in the pretty village of St. Andrew's-by-the-Sea, across the Passamoquody Bay from Maine, other Loyalists put their houses on rafts and towed them over the water to Canada. Kings Landing near Fredricton recreates a Loyalist community from the early 1800s with costumed interpreters. See "9 Living History Sites."

The Canadian Acadians, settled in an area of Nova Scotia, New Brunswick and Maine once called Acadia, are cousins of the Louisiana Cajuns. Descended from French peasant families who were the first European settlers in Canada, the Acadians in 1755 refused to swear allegiance to the British Crown and so were ordered deported. Some fled to other parts of the North Atlantic coast, others south to French-speaking Louisiana. Henry Wadsworth Longfellow dramatized the story in his poem *Evangeline*.

Costumed inhabitant of New Brunswick's Acadian Village

Today the Acadians remaining in English-speaking Canada continue to speak French and to protect their cultural inheritance. The Acadian Historical Village near Caraquet recreates their early settlements. See "Nine Living History Sites."

10 CAMPGROUND OASES

1. **Seaport Campground**, exit 90 from I-95 to route 184, at Old Mystic, CT, has 130 sites and is open March through November. Sites are fairly well spaced, with water and electric hookups and sanitary dump, hot showers, flush toilets, laundry, playground, fishing. Three miles from Mystic Seaport. ☎ *(203) 536-4044* for reservations.

2. On Cape Cod, **Scusset State Beach**, at Sagamore and Sandwich on the Cape Cod Canal near the junction of routes 3 and 6, has 98 RV sites with electricity and water hookups, sanitary dump for registered guests only, a fishing pier, showers, flush toilets and piped water. No reservations, open year round.

3. The state of New Hampshire likes RV campers, so you can find a state park by the sea, **Hampton State Beach** in Hampton, that has 24 sites with full hookups for self-contained vehicles and a seven-day camping limit. No reservations, but you can call ☎ *(800) 258-3609* for more information.

4. In Freeport, ME, for shoppers and lobster lovers, two campgrounds on Casco Bay—**Flying Point Campground**, ☎ *(207) 865-4569*, with 45 fairly spacious ocean-front sites with water and electric hookups, sanitary dump, flush toilets and showers, and **Recompence Shore Campsites**, ☎ *(207) 865-9307*, 100 well-spaced water-front sites, hookups, flush toilets, showers, sanitary dump station.

5. **Mt. Desert Narrows Camping Resort** in Bar Harbor, ME, is on the ocean with some grassy tree-shaded, fairly spacious sites. Swimming pool, video gameroom, playground, laundry, hot showers, and 165 sites with full and partial hookups. They even sell Maine lobster in July and August. ☎ *(207) 288-4782*. Closed in winter.

6. **Blackwoods Campground** In Maine's Acadia National Park requires advance reservations for its 50 sites between June 15 and September 15; call MIStix at ☎ *(800) 365-2267*. Toilets, sanitary dump, no hookups, 14-day maximum stay.

7. **Rockwood Park**, a 2200-acre park right in the city of Saint John, NB, welcomes RVers with 171 sites with electricity and water hookups, 21 with full hookups, and a dump station, flush toilets, showers, picnic tables and fireplaces. Take exit 113 from Highway 1 westbound or exit 111 and route 100 eastbound. With fishing, swimming, a golf course and zoo, the park, only five minutes from central Saint John, makes a good stopover. No reservations.

8. **Fundy National Park** near Alma, NB, has campgrounds with hookups and kitchen shelters. **Chignecto Campground** has 56 electric-only hookup sites and **Headquarters Trailer Court** has 29 full hookup sites. No reservations are taken, but you can call ☎ *(506) 887-2000* for information and road directions.

9. Cape Breton Highlands National Park's **Broad Cove Campground** in Nova Scotia has 83 full hookup sites with flush toilets and showers, fishing, swimming and playground. There's also a fine 18-hole golf course called Highland Golf Links inside the park. No campground reservations.

10. **Louisbourg Motorhome Park** in the town of Louisbourg, NS, near the national historic park, has 39 sites, 20 of them with full hookups. Open June 1 through the end of September. Flush toilets, showers, sanitary dump, fishing, by the ocean. Reservations ☎ *(902) 733-3631*.

INSIDER TIP:

The campgrounds in Nova Scotia that accept reservations can be booked by dialing Check In on a toll-free number, where you can also get travel information. Call ☎ (800) 341-6096 from the continental U.S. and ☎ (800) 565-0000 from Canada.

CAPE COD

The Pilgrims landed at the tip of Cape Cod, where Provincetown is located, before they reached Plymouth Rock, on November 11, 1620. They stayed there for 36 days before crossing Cape Cod Bay to Plymouth.

The famous rock, what's left of it, is shielded under a Grecian colonnade, and a replica *Mayflower* is staffed by costumed personnel.

Things are a bit more crowded these days. Try to avoid arriving on a summer weekend—or any time during the months of July and August—if you want easy driving and a place to park your RV within walking distance of kitschy little Provincetown. Autumn is a beautiful season on the cape and you can have the beaches to yourself.

Traffic on route 28, the southernmost highway across the island, is very slow because the area is built up like a slightly quaint megalopolis. A far better route for freewheelers is smooth-running route 6. Route 6A is the one to take if you like a slow-moving drive through villages with antique shops and country inns.

For 30 miles of protected and beautiful beaches, but no camping, head for Cape Cod National Seashore. Unfortunately, they have only six parking lots (which fill up by midmorning in summer) to take care of vehicles. Those at Nauset Light Beach and Wellfleet's Marconi Beach have steep stairways leading down to the beach. Hiking trails set out from Salt Pond Visitor Center in Eastham, where there's spacious parking for RVs, and Head of the Meadow Trailhead in Truro, both off route 6.

Bicycle trails run along both sides of the Cape Cod Canal, with parking available in the Sandwich Marina area.

Bayside beaches have warmer water and less turbulent surf than the ocean side. Low tide is best for beach hiking because the sand is packed; at high tide you'll be struggling through looser, deeper sand.

THREE THOUGHT-PROVOKING PLACES

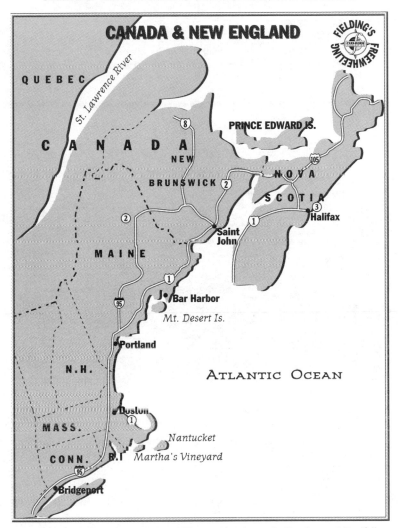

1. **The John F. Kennedy Library and Museum**, by the sea in Dorchester, MA, (follow directional signs from I-93) is open daily except major holidays. Exhibits, films, tapes and slides trace his career and that of his brother Robert F. Kennedy. A half-hour biographical film runs regularly. The striking building design is by I.M. Pei.

2. Maine's 200,000-acre **Baxter State Park** is rugged, primitive and guaranteed to stay pristine forever. Back in the 1920s, Governor Percival Proctor Baxter suggested the legislature acquire Mount Katahdin and its surroundings to be preserved as a park, but the legislators balked at the expense. So Baxter spent the next 30 years buying up parcels of land himself and donating them as park "to be maintained primarily as Wilderness... (and) be 'Forever Wild.'" Roads are gravel or dirt and usually narrow and winding. Self-contained RVs, motorcycles and pets are not permitted inside the park; all overnight camping is by reservation only. Backpackers and hikers will find 175 miles of wilderness trails. Even if you take a 4-by-4 and

drive through the park, you'll have to get out and walk down a trail to see the most spectacular scenery; it's designed that way.

3.   A deck chair and other wood artifacts from the Titanic are among the displays in **The Maritime Museum of the Atlantic**, Halifax, NS. As the closest port to the disaster, Halifax hosted hundreds of funerals for more than 10 days. Today some 150 unclaimed bodies of the victims are still buried in three different Halifax cemeteries. Only five years later, the city faced its own disaster, the Halifax Explosion, when two ships, one of them carrying half-a-million pounds of TNT plus other explosives, collided in the harbor, killing 2000 people instantly and destroying much of the city.

NANTUCKET

A Nantucket Lightship basket purse, a collector's item from the island

On the island of Nantucket, nothing built after the 1920s gets any comment or notice from the local guides. Walking tours meander through the main part of town looking at the shingled houses graying in the weather, the brick houses built by the whaling barons and the newer Federal and Victorian houses. In the early summer, lupine, iris and lemon lilies grow along the walkways, old-fashioned hollyhocks, alyssum, geraniums, hydrangeas and nasturtiums bloom in pint-sized gardens, and rosa rugosa with its big red rose hips thrives in hedges everywhere.

Guides like to point out one house occupied by a writer who had traveled twice around the world before deciding that Nantucket was the best place; he nailed two pairs of shoes by the front door to show his traveling days were over.

Nantucket Island was purchased for 40 pounds by Thomas Mayhew in 1659 from Lord Sterling, who had been given it in a grant from Charles I. After holding onto the property for 18 years, Mayhew sold it for only 30 pounds and two beaver hats, a typical real-estate speculator.

In the Nantucket lexicon, there are two geographical terms—"on-island," which is home, and "off-island," which is where everybody else comes from.

The early Nantucket sailing ships always carried a crew of four young boys ages 13 or 14 in each whale boat, along with a master and a harpooner. The boys did not necessarily choose to go whaling, but in Nantucket, they would not be acceptable suitors for a bride until they had been around Cape Horn and had taken a whale.

NINE LIVING HISTORY SITES

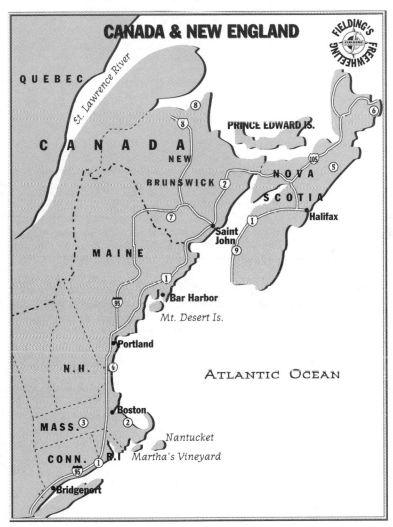

New England and Canada's Maritimes have a plethora of "animated" villages that recreate life in an earlier time. Costumed actors, also called interpreters or animators, usually portray a real person who lived in the village at a chosen time. Some villages are fixed permanently in a given year, and day-to-day life goes on exactly as it would have then. No one seems to mind if you come into their kitchens while they prepare a meal, poke your head in the barn or talk to someone tending a garden or feeding the farm animals. They are happy to pose for pictures as well.

1.   Connecticut's **Mystic Seaport**, exit 90 off I-95, is a restored 19th-century village with whaling ships you can go aboard, costumed craftsmen to chat with and mari-

time artifacts to see. Nearby is an aquarium and penguin pavilion, and plenty of shops and restaurants.

2.   At **Plimouth Plantation** near Plymouth, MA, you can talk with Pilgrims who are still living in the year 1627, tending their crops and remembering in detail their long, cramped sea journey on the *Mayflower*. You'll hear 17 different dialects in the village, reflecting the different places the Pilgrims came from. Hand-crafted items you can watch being made are for sale in the gift shop.

3.   **Old Sturbridge Village** in Worcester County, MA, about an hour inland from Boston, has recreated early 19th century rural life as it existed in 1830, with costumed interpreters, craftsmen, farm animals and the beginnings of industry with shoemakers, coopers, tinners and blacksmiths. Open daily year round except Mondays in winter.

4.   **Strawberry Banke**, in Portsmouth on New Hampshire's 18 miles of coastline, is a 10-acre historic community with 42 buildings, seven that illustrate different time periods in the area's history, plus 17th century herb and vegetable gardens, furnished houses and crafts shops that include weavers, coopers, cabinetmakers, potters and boat builders. Entrance tickets are good for two days. Closed November-April.

5.   **Sherbrooke**, located on Nova Scotia's south coast along highway 7, unlike most of the other villages, has not been moved or reassembled here but is the original 19th century town itself left intact, with tradesmen and craftsmen doing what they did in 1870 when it was a bustling gold town. Thirty buildings make up the village, which is located on the St. Mary's River, one of the best salmon streams in the province.

6.   One of North America's largest historic reconstructions, **Fortress Louisbourg National Historic Park** near Sydney, NS, is for us the most realistic and engrossing of all. It is always the summer of 1744 and the fortress is staffed with scruffy, unruly soldiers (who were to mutiny six months later), French aristocrats in exquisite houses, inns with pewter mugs and earthenware dishes serving 18th century food to visitors. "A moment in time" is portrayed in remarkable detail by a cast of more than 100 in and around the 50 or so buildings. Spend at least half a day; try to arrive first thing in the morning. Buy a loaf of soldiers' bread from the bakery and some farm cheese from the Destouches House to take along on the road (but bring your own plastic bags to take them back to the RV—there was no plastic in 1744). And bring a jacket and an umbrella; the weather can change suddenly along this coast.

7.   **Kings Landing**, on the TransCanada Highway near Fredricton, NB, about 60 miles north of Saint John, is the re-creation of a Loyalist settlement of the early 1800s with more than 100 costumed animators and 60 buildings—farmhouses, mills, churches and inns. You may see Scottish dancing or caber tossing in summer, when the park is open daily.

8.   **Acadian Historical Village**, near Caraquet in northern New Brunswick, about 160 miles north of Moncton, recreates the lives of Acadians between 1780 and 1890 as you walk through time watching costumed residents from fur trappers to blacksmiths at work. A cafeteria and restaurant in the village serve traditional Acadian dishes, which bear no resemblance whatsoever to the food their Cajun cousins cook in Louisiana. Open daily in summer.

9.   **Port Royal Habitat National Historic Park** in NS, about eight miles from Annapolis Royal, is peopled with costumed interpreters, including Samuel Champlain, who recreate the life in one of North America's first European settlements. A French fur-trading post from 1605 is painstakingly reconstructed, using the same primitive building methods as the original.

WILDLIFE WATCH

It always comes a surprise to New England visitors when they learn that there are still plenty of moose in the woods up here, although the only people that seem to run into them do it literally with their automobiles. Throughout New Hampshire, road signs give the running tally of how many moose have been hit by cars during the year.

White-tailed deer are plentiful throughout New England and the Maritimes, as are beavers, raccoons, porcupines and skunks. Black bear are occasionally spotted. The red fox is common in Maine's Acadia National Park but rarely seen by visitors.

With all that ocean, you'll find an abundance of marine life, especially whales. Humpbacks, fin whales and occasionally rare right whales (rare because they were the "right" whale for whalers and therefore virtually decimated) may be spotted, most easily aboard a whale-watching boat. You'll also usually see seals, porpoises and dolphins.

Day cruises go out from Connecticut's Waterford; Maine's Bangor, Boothbay, Lubec, Northeast Harbor and Portland; Massachusetts' Barnstable, Boston, Gloucester, Plymouth, Provincetown and Rockport; New Hampshire's Rye Harbor; Nova Scotia's Cheticamp, Big Bras d'Or and Westport; and New Brunswick's Grand Manan Island, near Campobello.

Pelagic seabirds, those that return to land only for breeding and raising their young, are frequently sighted along the coastline. Look for storm petrels, shearwaters, gannets, guillemots, razorbills and puffins.

The National Audubon Society and the Canadian Wildlife Service have been working on a project since 1971 to return the puffins to Seal Island off Rockland, Maine. The once-thriving colony of birds was almost wiped out around the turn of the century by hunters.

As for nightlife, theater is alive and well in Connecticut year-round, and summer stock thrives throughout New England.

Boston's Bull & Finch Pub on Beacon Street was the prototype of TV's long-running series "Cheers." The city also has several nightclubs and comedy clubs.

Foxwoods High Stakes Bingo and Casino, generally considered the most profitable casino in the United States, is in Ledyard, Connecticut, about six miles north of I-95 on route 117 near Mystic Seaport on the Mashantucket Pequot Indian Reservation. The Pequots were virtually decimated in the 17th century by settlers and militia, but since the casino opened, their numbers, once down to one surviving resident on the reservation, have been increasing.

In the Maritimes, Halifax, Nova Scotia, has a lively pub scene along the waterfront with live music, mostly sea chanteys, and there's usually a rock band playing somewhere. Jazz, folk and bluegrass are popular in Saint John, New Brunswick.

SEVEN SIDE TRIPS

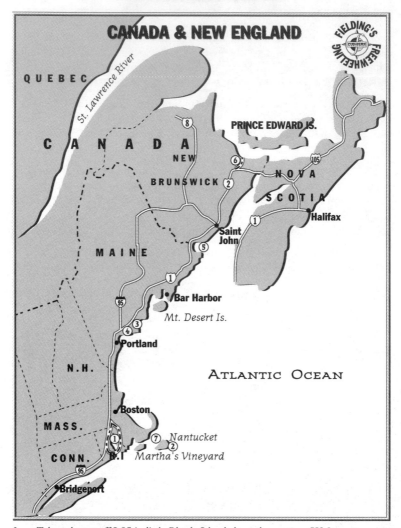

1. Take a detour off I-95 in little Rhode Island along the coast on US 1, across route 138 and over the spectacular Newport Toll Bridge into the elegant city of Newport. This is where Jackie and Jack Kennedy got married, where Claus von Bulow's trial took place, and various Vanderbilts, Astors and Belmonts built 70-room "cottages" in dizzying excess, many of which are restored and open to the public. From here, it's an easy dash up to Fall River, MA, where Lizzie Bordon may or may not have dispatched her parents with an ax. The relics from the trial including the alleged murder hatchet are on display at the Fall River Historical Society. Lizzie was acquitted and lived on in Fall River until her death in 1927. (Extra-wide and extra-long RVs and travel trailers should skip the side trip to Newport since the streets can be narrow and congested.)

2. Leave your RV on the mainland and take a day trip on the ferry to the island of Nantucket from Hyannis via Hy-Line Cruises, ☎ *(617) 778-2602*, then rent a bicycle

when you get there. The town of Nantucket is charming, if chock-a-block with day-trippers like you in summer. Go shopping along the cobbled main street, pausing to see the Whaling Museum and some of the 11 other equally appealing museums. The free public beaches, seafood restaurants, bright flowers blooming in front yards everywhere make this one of New England's prettiest places.

L. L. Bean and factory outlets attract a lot of shoppers to Freeport, ME.

3.   Freeport, ME, formerly famous as the home of sporting goods impresario L.L. Bean, has turned into the factory outlet capital of New England, with around 100 shops, including a vast L.L. Bean emporium open 24 hours a day, 365 days a year. There are several RV campgrounds with hookups in the vicinity if you've shopped till time to drop. See "10 Campground Oases."

4.   Follow the painters through Maine, whose pristine beauty has drawn many artists over the years, including Andrew Wyeth. His famous *Christina's World* was painted at the Olson farm in Cushing, near Rockland. Winslow Homer painted at Prouts Neck, south of Portland, and Edward Hopper's Maine was captured in his light-house paintings at Two Lights in Cape Elizabeth. Hopper also painted with fellow artists George Bellows and Rockwell Kent at Monhegan Island; they followed their former teacher Robert Henri there. Today the island can be visited only on foot; vehicles are prohibited. Take the one-hour ferry trip by mail boat from Port Clyde by reservation only, ☎ *(207) 372-8848.* Do bear in mind that the trip can be rough. It's said Winslow Homer got so seasick on the way over that he turned around and went back home without ever getting off the ferry.

5.   Take the short detour from Whiting, ME, up route 89 and across the bridge at Lubec to Campobello Island, famous as the summer home of Franklin D. Roosevelt, who was vacationing here in 1921 when he was stricken with polio. The house is evocative, even poignant, with FDR's austere bedroom, and the surrounding countryside has a number of wooded and beachfront walking trails where there's a chance of spotting deer, osprey, eagles and, below the rocky ledges by the beach, seals. Herring Cove Provincial Park with 91 campsites is on the island; 40 of the sites have electricity hookups. Take an umbrella if you go walking.

6.   The Acadian shore around northern New Brunswick is great lobster land. Drive north from Moncton (which also has a bore tide) to Shediac, self-proclaimed "Lobster Capital of the World," where you can pick up a crustacean at a stall on the wharf

and cook it yourself in the RV in a pot of boiling seawater, or pop into popular Fisherman's Paradise for table service. The town's annual lobster festival is early July. Acadian towns in this region and the Acadian Historical Museum restaurants serve unique ethnic dishes like *fricots* (stews) based on potatoes and various kinds of meat. A *poulet fricot*, for instance, is a chicken stew; *rapure* is a pie with pork and a potato crust. Look for children selling blueberries by the roadsides in summer.

7. The ferry from Woods Hole to Martha's Vineyard takes walk-on passengers without reservations but vehicles need to be reserved well in advance, ☎ *(617) 540-2022*. Summer weekends can see as many as 80,000 visitors, and traffic and parking are nightmares. RVers would be wise to leave their rigs on the mainland. Chic shopping and fashionable restaurants give the impression of gentrification, but institutions like The Black Dog Tavern by the ferry landing, with its sought-after t-shirts, are still around. Bear in mind a couple of Vineyard peculiarities—beaches are privately owned down to the low tide mark, and Martha's Vineyard is dry except for drinks served at restaurants in Edgartown and Oak Bluff, but you can take your own wine or beer when you're going out to dinner.

MOUNT DESERT ISLAND

Maine's Mount Desert Island (pronounced "dessert") is home to serene and scenic Acadia National Park as well as the overcrowded summer streets of Bar Harbor. Even in August, the climate is fresh and cool.

Landscape painters from the group called the Hudson River School came here in 1844 to paint the scenery, then sold the pictures to wealthy northeast urbanites who in turn traveled to see the places depicted and, in typical robber baron fashion, ended up buying the real estate in their canvases to build elaborate 30-room summer "cottages" patterned after Tudor hunting lodges and Scottish castles.

Summer residents of the island, many of them Boston millionaires, are responsible for preserving the 35,000 acres of land in Acadia National Park and handing it over to the government in 1916. John D. Rockefeller, who disliked automobiles and preferred driving through the parklands in a horse-drawn carriage, commissioned over 50 miles of gravel carriage roads to be constructed. Today hikers, bicyclists and bird-watchers are more in evidence than carriages in summer, and cross-country skiers use them in winter. The 27-mile Park Loop Road for automobiles is accessible for RVs.

Most of the grandiose cottages once built there are gone now, victims of a five-day fire that swept through Bar Harbor in 1947, changing the town's image considerably.

10 SPLURGES

1. A weekend at the Wauwinet on Nantucket, an elegantly understated seaside inn that looks as if it were decorated by Ralph Lauren with Martha Stewart arranging the flowers. The gray shingle inn with its white trim sprawls on a remote, sandy neck of land between Nantucket Harbor and the Atlantic, with sailboats, clay tennis courts, bicycles and a 21-foot launch available for picnics and bay cruises. ☎ *(800) 426-8718.*

2. Go shopping in Nantucket for a classic Nantucket Lightship Basket purse, considered an heirloom that increases in value; prices start at around $350. Or instead, you could pick up some delectable chocolate almond buttercreams in pretty hand-painted tins at Sweet Inspirations on India Street. For some of us, *that's* a splurge.

3. Take a scenic cruise aboard the Islander for the Clambake at Cabbage Island in Boothbay Harbor, ME. Each feaster gets fish chowder, two lobsters, steamed clams, corn on the cob, Maine potatoes and blueberry cake, and there's a full service bar.

Call ☎ *(207) 633-7166* for boat information, ☎ *(207) 633-7200* for the clam-bake.

4. Cut loose for a morning of shopping in Filene's Basement in Boston, where the longer merchandise goes unsold, the lower its price is slashed, until you may end up paying only a quarter of the original figure. After 30 days, however, any unsold item is donated to charity.

5. Take a summer whale-watching cruise out of Hyannis or Provincetown on Cape Cod, from Gloucester, or from Nantucket or Martha's Vineyard. We've seen more humpback whales with the distant Boston skyline as a backdrop than on any number of naturalist expeditions to far-flung corners of the globe. Take cameras, binoculars, a jacket, a securely-fitting or tie-down sun hat and sunscreen.

6. Return to the 17th century at Massachusetts' Plimouth plantation with a period dinner served on Friday and Saturday evenings at the Visitor Center. Vegetables come from the plantation gardens. You eat with your fingers and a knife (forks were not in general usage at the time) and listen to madrigal singers. For reservations, call ☎ *(508) 746-1622.*

7. Book a dinner train ride on the vintage Cape Cod Scenic Railroad, ☎ *(508) 771-3788,* and enjoy a five-course meal on a three-hour twilight ride through 42 miles of the cape.

8. Go antique-shopping along Old King's Highway on Cape Cod, also known as route 6A, lined with countless antique shops, including the biggest, a 135-dealer co-op called Antiques Center of Cape Cod, open daily.

9. Take a day sail aboard a Maine windjammer out of Camden, out among the rocky islands of Penobscot Bay where seals sun themselves on the rocks and porpoises play in the water. Come to the dock at Sharp's Wharf by the Town Landing and sign up.

10. Relive the golden days of summer-long vacations in stylish, old-fashioned resort hotels by stopping off for lunch or tea at the half-timbered 1899 Algonquin in St. Andrews-by-the-Sea, NB, surrounded by manicured lawns, lush flower gardens and a century-old golf course, or at Keltic Lodge (built in 1940 but looking much older) near Ingonish Beach on Nova Scotia's Cape Breton Island.

NOVA SCOTIA'S CAPE BRETON ISLAND

Cape Breton Highlands National Park in the wild and rocky Cape Breton Islands is the northernmost thrust of Nova Scotia into the Atlantic. The poetic headlands are dashed by the surf and softened by morning mists.

A 184-mile loop begins at Baddeck, a tranquil seaside village that was the longtime summer home of Alexander Graham Bell, who is buried here. The Alexander Graham Bell National Historic Park and Museum shows the inventor's energetic and creative mind, which ranged far beyond the telephone into work with the deaf, early aircraft, and conversion of sea water to fresh.

Take the Cabot trail north of Baddeck in a clockwise direction for easier driving, especially if you begin in the morning, to the cluster of towns along the Margaree River that are named after the river. North East Margaree is home to the unique little Salmon Museum with its collection of hand-tied flies, fishing tackle, poaching equipment and a study of the life cycle of the Atlantic salmon.

Follow the river to the coast and you'll encounter a series of French Acadian villages—Belle Côte, Terre Noire, St. Joseph du Moine, Grand-Étang—whose residents still speak the 18th century French of their Norman ancestors. The Cape Breton Acadians show off their regional cooking and handi-crafts at the Cooperative Artisanale each summer. In the tiny downstairs restaurant, local women serve chicken *fricot*, potato pancakes, fish chowder, homemade pies and gingerbread with syrup. In the craft shop upstairs, you can browse among the hooked rugs, wood carvings, handknit sweaters and quilts.

In nearby Belle Côte, a more offbeat craft is being pursued, the Theatre of Scarecrow, a weird assortment of life-sized stuffed figures by the road next to Ethel's Takeout Restaurant.

From Cheticamp, you enter the park itself with its dazzling vistas of lonely beaches and stark cliffs sculpted by the wind and sea. Except for occasional campgrounds and picnic areas, you'll encounter no habitation until Pleasant Bay. Then the road turns inland to the sweeping grandeur of the highlands and distant vistas of the churning sea, interspersed with wooded valleys.

Note Neils Harbour, bright with colorful, painted houses and fishing boats, lobster pots and fishnets. The cottages are usually daubed with what-ever paint is left over from the boats by thrifty fishermen.

A few miles south at Ingonish Beach, a side road leads to the splendid Keltic Lodge. Moody, mist-clouded Cape Smoky lies south of Ingonish Beach, with Wreck Cove, Skir Dhu (Gaelic for "Black Rock") and North Shore, from which you can sometimes see the Bird Islands, protected nest-ing area for cormorants, puffins, petrals and terns. The park's Bog Trail is suitable for wheelchairs.

14 OFF-THE-WALL ATTRACTIONS

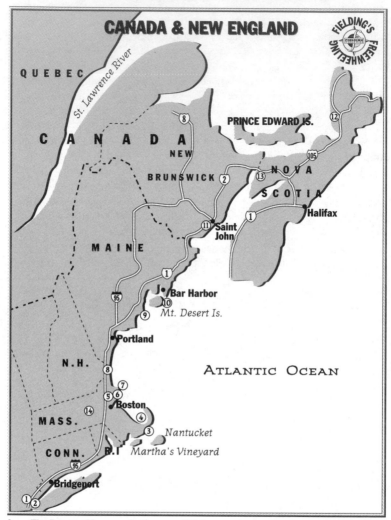

1. **The Barnum Museum**, Bridgeport, CT, has an eclectic collection that includes Tom Thumb's bed, an unwrapped mummy, a coat that Charles Dickens left behind on his American tour, and a 3000-piece hand-carved miniature circus.

2. **United House Wrecking Company** at *535 Hope Street in Stamford, CT*, has 30,000 square feet of antique lighting and plumbing fixtures, furniture and architectural artifacts plus a lot of just plain junk, all of it for sale. They're open daily, Sundays afternoon only.

3. Watch **Cape Cod Potato Chips** being kettle-cooked one batch at a time at Breed's Hill Road in Independence Park near Hyannis, where they turn out 200,000 bags of the crunchy little darlings every day. They'll give you a bag free as you leave. Self-guided tours year-round on weekdays only.

4. In the autumn in Wellfleet on Cape Cod, you can browse among second-hand books and old sheet music, then sit down and sample fresh local Wellfleet oysters and scallops in the unpretentious **Bookstore & Restaurant** on Mayo Beach.

Outside the Salem Witch Museum

5. The **Salem Witch Museum**, located in a former church by Salem Common, recreates the hysteria of the 17th century witch hunts with satanic symbols, taped music, mimed hangings in silhouette and other spooky silliness performed with more enthusiasm than expertise. The audience loves it.

6. Also in Salem, the classy **Peabody Museum** displays an astonishing collection of the curiosities local sea captains brought back home from the exotic East—shrunken heads, stuffed penguins, giant sea clams, ship models, Chinese export porcelain,

Polynesian barkcloth, Japanese warrior costumes and a huge moon bed carved from a single piece of teak.

7. **The Gloucester Fishermen's Museum** in Gloucester is a hands-on exhibit that kids and adults alike enjoy. You can blow a foghorn, sample salt cod, caulk boat seams or haul a longline like a Massachusetts doryman. Most of the guides are retired local fishermen.

8. **The Wedding Cake House**, Kennebunk, ME, is a gorgeously ornamental 19th century house built, it is said, for his new bride by a sea captain who had to go to sea without even having a taste of his own wedding cake.

9. Watch the Red Baron's Fokker Triplane from World War I soar into the sky or listen to the hiss of a Stanley Steamer at the **Owls Head Transportation Museum** in Owls Head, ME. On summer weekends you not only see antique motorcycles, biplanes, automobiles and farm machinery but hear then and smell them—these antique machines are all in working order and cranked up regularly. Visitors may even be offered a ride in a Model T Ford. Call ahead to see which machines are running and when. ☎ *(207) 594-4418.*

10. The nine-wicket croquet tournaments at the **Claremont Hotel** in Southwest Harbor, ME, draw international attention from the croquet circuit; you can watch the action from the big front porch.

11. The **Reversing Falls Rapids** in Saint John, NB, are produced by a phenomenon called a tidal bore. It happens twice a day when high tides in the Bay of Fundy cause the Saint John River to turn back on itself and flow upstream until the bay again drops below the river level and the river reverses itself again. Since the tides here are the highest in the world and the river bed has an underwater ledge, the boiling and surging of the water is dramatic. Best way to watch is from Fallsview Park, near the Reversing Falls Information Center. The highest tides are when the moon is full. Sea kayaking in the bay is the latest thrill around Saint John.

12. For a real Scottish moment on Cape Breton Island, head for the **Glendora Falls Distillery** on highway 19 between Mabou and Inverness, where the only single malt Scotch whiskey in North America is produced. The place is still new and the whiskey still ageing, but you can take a tour.

13. In Springhill, NS, the most popular tourist attraction is the **Anne Murray Centre**, dedicated to the town's top pop singer, whose recording of "Snowbird" might well be the theme song for all winter-escaping RVers. You should be able to find a copy in the gift shop, if you want to spring for the admission fee, on the high side for non-fans, we should think. ("Snowbird" is the only one of her recordings we're familiar with.)

14. If you ever wondered how that sweet creamy glop gets inside a Hostess Twinkie, take a detour in the Boston area to the **Continental Bakery** in Natick, where free tours take you along the assembly line where Twinkies, Wonder Bread and Hostess cupcakes are made. Free samples; wear rubber-soled shoes. Call ☎ *(508) 655-2150* for the four daily tour times and a reservation. Tours are offered on non-holiday Mondays, Wednesdays and Fridays between September and May. Natick is off I-90 west of Boston at exit 13. Take route 30 east and turn right on Speen Street to the bakery parking lot.

STRETCHING OUT YOUR VACATION

If you want to spend more than two or three weeks on the Lobster Coast, you'd better make your plans and arrangements well in advance for July and August. And don't expect to get reduced rates for a long stay in a private campground during the summer; one New Hampshire operator charged us double for the Fourth of July weekend, even though we were in residence for a month, because that's his peak season. As a Cape Cod friend reminded us, they have to make their profits for the whole year in only a few short months.

Add a trip over to Prince Edward Island if you have plenty of time. This sparkling clean, pretty little island is bound to change once the bridge connecting it with the mainland is completed. Two ferry services operate to the island, Marine Atlantic from Cape Tormentine, New Brunswick to Borden, PEI, a 45-minute journey, and Northumberland Ferries from Caribou, Nova Scotia to Wood Islands, PEI, a one-hour trip.

Campsites with full or partial hookups can be reserved in advance in most provincial parks; call Visitor Services at ☎ *(800) 565-0267.* There are also a number of privately-owned campgrounds with hookups. Roads are good and the island's scenery surprisingly varied. Don't miss the community lobster suppers, often sponsored by churches or civic clubs.

HITTING THE HIGHLIGHTS

If two weeks is the maximum time you have for a Lobster Land vacation, you'll still be able to make the coastal drive to Nova Scotia and back from a New York or Connecticut starting point, as well as the journey around Cape Cod, but you might have to miss the day trips to Nantucket and Martha's Vineyard. Allow one week for New England, the second week for Canada's Maritimes.

16 TAKEOUT (OR EAT-IN) TREATS

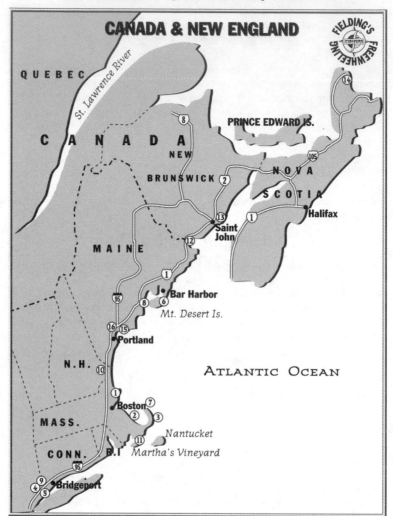

1. The first clam was fried and served, so they say, back in 1916 by Woodman's clam stand in the town of Essex, MA, and today in the same place you can get **clams to go** out or eat in by standing at a counter and watching them fried after you order them. This style of service is called "in the rough" but the delectable clams and their companion onion rings are silky inside, crunchily crusty outside. The **clam fritters** aren't bad, either. In fact, we defy you to drive out of the parking lot past the giant plaster clam without succumbing to the irresistible lure to taste just one.

Woodmans of Essex, it's said, fried the very first clams in New England.

2. **Boston baked beans** and **Indian pudding** are still the mainstays at Boston's Durgin-Park, now located in the gentrified confines of Faneuil Hall Market but still served at long family-style tables by brusque New England matrons. No reservations, no credit cards.

3. **Fried onion rings** at Arnold's Lobster & Clam Bar in Eastham on Cape Cod are extra-special, and the steamed lobster, fried clams, steamers and mussels not bad either. Prices are modest and there's little decor, but the open-air patio and nearby picnic tables among the pines are always filled with happy eaters. Beer and wine are available.

4. Pepe's Pizzeria Napoletana in New Haven claims to have baked America's first pizza back in 1925 when it was called a pie. Pepe's still uses the original brick ovens to turn out the famous **white clam pie**, a tomato-free pizza. It was also in New Haven that Louis Lassen made the first hamburger (so they say) back in 1900, and four generations later Louis' Lunch on Crown Street is still serving them plain on toasted bread, no hamburger buns, ketchup, mayo, mustard or special sauce allowed. Closed evenings, weekends and the month of August.

5. **Dig your own fresh clams** along the Connecticut coast at Cockenoe Island off Westport (☎ *226-8511, ext. 220*), Horseshoe Reef in Groton (☎ *441-6640*), Joshua Cove in Guilford (☎ *453-8000*), and Qulambog Cove in Stonington (☎ *599-4000*). When you buy your town permit, they'll give you a map to the spot. All area codes above are *(203)*.

6. **Afternoon tea** at Jordan Pond Lodge in Maine's Acadia National Park brings popovers and strawberry jam in an old-fashioned garden filled with dahlias, sweetpeas and delphiniums. The island location is called Mt. Desert but pronounced "dessert." Think sweet thoughts.

7. The **classic Portuguese soup caldo verde**, a luscious brew of potatoes, kale and smoked garlic sausage, is one of many dishes brought to Nantucket by Portuguese immigrants. One good place to sample it is at The Elegant Dump Diner, a simple, scrubbed cafe. It's also on the menu at the upscale Jared Coffin House in Nantucket, and at Juventino's Portuguese Bakery in Provincetown, Cape Cod, for take-out.

8. Cappy's Chowder House in Camden, ME, ladles up **clam chowder** by the cup or bowl to eat in or take out, as well as serving bar drinks in Mason jars. This is the town where *Peyton Place* was set. Poet Edna St. Vincent Millay worked as a waitress at the Whitehall Inn nearby during the summer of 1912.

9. Check out the **hot dogs** at Jimmy's at Savin Rock on the beach in West Haven (just west of New Haven) in Connecticut. Famous since 1925, Jimmy's draws a crowd on a hot summer day, so be prepared to queue.

10. Pick your own **fresh raspberries and blackberries** at The Raspberry Farm, Hampton Falls, NH, between July and October, or pick up a freshly baked raspberry pie to go.

11. The **"back door" dinners** from Homeport Restaurant in Meneshma on Martha's Vineyard are a long-standing tradition for locals, who get a regular seafood dinner reduced in price and handed out the back door on a paper plate if they want to dine among the dunes.

12. Ganong's Chocolatier in St. Stephen, NB, just across the border from Maine, is where the **candy bar** was invented when the owner wrapped some slabs of chocolate in waxed paper to take on a fishing trip. Among their unique sweets are "**chicken bones**," crunchy white-striped, cinnamon-flavored logs with a bittersweet chocolate center. Early August the town celebrates a six-day chocolate festival.

13. Tour the **Moosehead Brewery** in Saint John, NB, sample the highly praised brew, then drop by the Moosehead Country Store on Main Street to pick up a Moosehead cap or t-shirt. Call ☎ *(506) 635-7000* for a tour appointment.

14. Try a **lobster burger** and fries at the Chowder House in Neils Harbour, Cape Breton Island, where the boats that brought the lobster in may be anchored in the harbor.

15. The **whoopie pie**, a pair of big cake-like chocolate cookies sandwiched together with fluffy marshmallow cream, is an old Maine treat, usually homemade and always wrapped and ready to go on the cafe counter. Try them at Ogunquit Fish & Lobster in Ogunquit or Harraseeket Lunch & Lobster in Freeport.

16. Sample the descendent of the first carbonated soft drink, **Moxie**, in its tiny Maine headquarters in the town of Lisbon Falls, between Brunswick and Lewiston. Developed in 1876 as Beverage Moxie Nerve Food, it pre-dated Coca-Cola by a decade, and lent its name to the slang vocabulary of the Twenties, when "Moxie" meant "a lot of nerve." Today the little company sells more memorabilia than soft drinks from the store at 2 Main Street at the junction of route 196.

ON THE CHEAP: TRIMMING COSTS ON THE ROAD

First of all, never eat your lobster in a restaurant. You can pick it up at a lobster pound live or cooked. Take a live lobster back to the RV and cook it or refrigerate it until later (see "Looking for Lobster" earlier in this chapter). A hot cooked lobster can be brought back to the RV or eaten on the spot at a picnic table thoughtfully provided by the pound or the town. At many pounds, you'll be able to pick up side dishes and beverages, even beer or wine, to go with your steaming crustacean.

Even though the Canadian dollar is considerably lower in value than the U.S. dollar at this writing, don't get lulled into cutting menu and shop prices in half in your head.

Make the most of admission to living history parks by planning to spend the day, either taking a lunch in with you or buying one (prices are reasonable) in the on-site restaurants. If you have children along, they'll experience new dishes and utensils so interesting they'll forget they never liked such-and-so.

Plan your beach visits for state parks or national parks like Cape Cod or Acadia; many of the beaches in the northeast are private.

FYI

Connecticut Department of Economic Development, Tourism Division, *865 Brook St., Rocky Hill, CT 06067,* ☎ *(800) CT-BOUND,* will send a free Connecticut Vacation Guide.

Maine Office of Tourism, *189 State Street, State House Station 59, Augusta, ME 04333,* ☎ *(800) 533-9595,* can supply you with free material.

Massachusetts Office of Travel & Tourism, *100 Cambridge St., 13th floor, Boston, MA 02202,* ☎ *(800) 447-6277,* also sends out maps and information.

New Hampshire Office of Travel and Tourism, *Box 856, Concord, NH 03302,* ☎ *(603) 271-2666,* mails information.

Rhode Island Tourism Division, *7 Jackson Walkway, Providence, RI 02903,* ☎ *(800) 556-2484,* sends maps and guides.

New Brunswick Department of Economic Development and Tourism, *PO Box 12345, Fredericton, NB E3B 5C3, Canada,* ☎ *(800) 561-0123* for the U.S. and Canada outside New Brunswick, publishes a New Brunswick Travel Guide.

Nova Scotia's Check-In, *Corporatel, Suite 501, 2695 Dutch Village Road, Halifax, NS B3L 4V2, Canada,* ☎ *(800) 565-0000,* can send you free travel information or arrange reservations at hotels or campgrounds.

Prince Edward Island Tourism, Marketing Council Visitor Services, *PO Box 940, Charlottetown, PEI, C1A 7M5, Canada,* ☎ *(800) 565-0267,* publishes a visitors guide and can send any other information you need.

THE OZARKS AND BRANSON, MISSOURI

Basketmaker at work at Ozarks Folk Center

Arkansas is where Hernando de Soto looked for the Fountain of Youth, Jesse James held up stagecoaches, Al Capone got in hot water and saloon-basher Carry Nation buried her hatchet.

General Douglas MacArthur was born here, as was the fictional Lorelei Lee from *Gentlemen Prefer Blondes* (remember Carol Channing in the show—Marilyn Monroe in the film—singing "I'm Just A Little Girl from Little Rock"?). It's where Wal-Mart's Sam Walton started putting his fortune together, where Don Tyson's chickens came home to roost, and where, once upon a more innocent time, every American boy's dream toy, a Daisy air rifle—aka BB gun—was manufactured.

Genial but corny radio comedians of the 1930s and 1940s like *Lum and Abner,* who ran the Jot 'em Down Store in a fictional Pine Ridge, and bucolic Bob Burns perpetuated the hillbilly image of the Ozark dweller for the rest of the nation.

Less friendly and folksy was the image of then-Governor Orval E. Faubus calling up the national guard to keep nine black students from attending Little Rock's Central High School in 1957. (Today Faubus' dramatic hilltop summer house in Huntsville has six rooms that rent out as a bed and breakfast.)

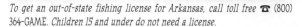

INSIDER TIP:

To get an out-of-state fishing license for Arkansas, call toll free ☎ (800) 364-GAME. Children 15 and under do not need a license.

When to go. Summer can get awfully hot in Arkansas, even in the mountains. Springtime from March through May is ideal, when the dogwoods, redbud and wildflowers are in bloom. The hills come alive with autumn foliage in September with good weather likely through October.

What to take. Hiking boots, fishing tackle, binoculars, camera and film, rain gear, jacket, sun hat.

What to wear. The Ozarks are casual, even at the shows in Branson, to judge by the garb we saw being worn. In spring or fall, you'll want to layer your clothes as the day warms up or cools down. "Clean and decent" is the only dress code around here, along with random instances of "No shoes, no shirt, no service."

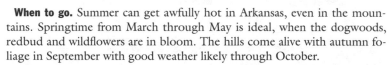

INSIDER TIP:

Jokes you'll hear more than once:

"Arkansas strawberries" are beans,

"Arkansas wedding cake" is cornbread,

and "Arkansas asphalt" is a dirt road.

STRETCHING OUT YOUR VACATION

The Ozarks are an appealing destination to spend more than two weeks exploring. You could settle into a luxurious campground like DeGray Lake Resort State Park (see "10 Campground Oases") and stay for the 14-day limit, then move on for a while and come back in a second 30-day period, with another 14-day stay permitted.

You could sign up for crafts and music classes at the Ozark Folk Center, take a week-long canoe trip along the Buffalo National River or hike some or all the 165 miles of the Ozark Highlands National Recreation Trail. You might even want to learn mountain biking or fly-tying.

If you're a full-timer who likes to settle down for a month or two on a temporary job, we noticed a lot of Help Wanted signs around Branson in shops, hotels and restaurants.

The state itself actively encourages retirees to consider settling in Arkansas, citing its four-season climate and warm hospitality, plus "a quality of life fast disappearing in some other areas."

Woman spinning at Ozarks Folk Center

Take the scenic drives and side trips suggested in this chapter, and take time to chat with the people you encounter. Most people in the Ozarks seem to have both the time and inclination to converse as long you want. You may make lasting friendships.

HITTING THE HIGHLIGHTS

Because the area around the Ozarks is fairly compact, despite the many scenic highways, you could manage to cover most everything in eight or nine days, leaving three days to get to and from this centrally located area. I-40 is the east-west interstate through Little Rock, while I-55 cuts into the eastern edge of Arkansas on its north-south route. I-30 runs diagonally across much of the state, through Little Rock to Texarkana on the Texas border.

This would give you enough time to cover most if not all the suggested side drives. You can't count on making much time in an RV on the roads in the Ozarks, but you could use I-40 or I-30 to cover extra ground. The top towns to visit include Eureka Springs, Hot Springs and Little Rock.

THE OZARKS

For all their remoteness and crags, the Ozarks, among North America's oldest mountains, are only about 2300 feet high. "Our mountains ain't too high, but our valleys sure are deep," the saying goes. Made of limestone and heavily forested, they were named by French trappers, who called them "Aux Arcs" for a local Indian tribe called variously Quapaw, Oo-gaq-pa or O-ka-na-sa, which also gave its name to the state. Needless to say, every explorer spelled it differently, but the spelling that was adopted when Arkansas was admitted as a state in 1836 was from a French explorer named LaHarpe. By 1881, the pronunciation "Ark-an-saw" was dictated by the legislature.

Despite the vast number of authentic craftsmen and musicians that populate Arkansas these days—more than any other state, we would guess—there are still pockets of what one writer calls "painfully quaint," contrived roadside attractions. The natural beauty of the Ozarks, fortunately, even makes these diminish, except in the tackiest of strip mall mayhem.

Perhaps the blessing for latter day visitors is that Arkansas has been so poor all these years. During the Depression, many of the hill people gravitated to the cities to make a living, leaving parts of the Ozarks to revert to wilderness.

In the 1950s, when everyone else was tearing down their beautiful Victorian and art deco buildings to put up characterless "modern" facades, lovely but declining old towns like Hot Springs and Eureka Springs made do with what they had because they couldn't afford not to. Beginning in the 1940s and continuing into the early 1970s, Arkansas was the playground for the U.S. Corps of Engineers, as more and more rivers were dammed, creating 600,000 acres of water area to attract recreational tourism. The sports-fishing season never closes.

The nation's first federally protected river park, the Buffalo National River, so named in 1972, was rescued after a decade of struggle by local and national environmentalists from threatened dam development by the U.S. Corps of Engineers. Today it's a major destination for canoers, kayakers and family float trips.

A loop roughly 700 miles from Hot Springs would go to Fort Smith, Eureka Springs and Berryville, then jog up to Branson, Missouri, back down to Harrison, Mountain Home, Batesville, Stuttgart, Pine Bluff and Little Rock. That covers the main points of interest. Highways throughout the Ozarks are slow and scenic. See "10 Scenic Side Trips."

SPEAKING OZARK

Granny woman—nature-savvy herbal healer

Yarbs—herbs

Greening-up time—when the first wild greens can be harvested in early spring

A mess of sallat—these same greens cooked together in a pot with bacon fat

Vittles—victuals

INSIDER TIP:

All state park campgrounds in Arkansas have water and electrical hookups for RVs, and each park sets aside a limited number of sites available by advance reservation.

---

10 CAMPGROUND OASES

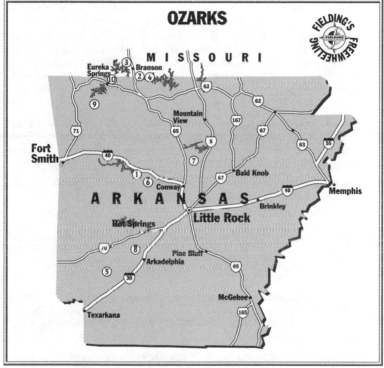

1. **Lake Dardenelle State Park** is a handsome hilltop park by a lake with ducks and swans. The 97 campsites are divided into three different locations; all have water hookups and all but four have electric hookups as well. Seniors get half-price rates. Shade trees, picnic tables, flush toilets, hot showers, fishing, water-skiing, sanitary dump station. It's located near Russellville.

2. If you want to be within walking distance of many of Branson's music theaters or the shuttle trolley, **Pea Patch RV Park and Campground** might do. The 83 sites are close together but all have full hookups and there's a swimming pool on the premises. Flush toilets, showers, laundry. ☎ *(417) 335-3958* for reservations.

3. If trout fishing is what lures you to Branson, check out the **Cooper Creek Campground** and resort on Upper Lake Taneycomo with boat rentals and lighted fishing

docks. There are 91 mostly shaded sites with full hookups, flush toilets, showers, laundry, store and swimming pool. ☎ *(417) 334-5250* for reservations.

4. **Silver Dollar City Campground** in Branson is adjacent to the amusement park, with 134 sites with full or partial hookups. There are flush toilets, showers, sanitary dump, laundry, groceries, swimming pool, playground and waterslide. ☎ *(800) 477-5164* for reservations.

5. **Crater of Diamonds State Park**, Murfreesboro, has 60 campsites with water and electrical hookups, laundry, snack bar, gift shop and hiking trails. Here you can dig for diamonds, amethyst, garnet, jasper, agate and quartz and take home whatever you find. The 35-acre field, the eroded surface of an ancient, diamond-bearing pipe, is plowed regularly to keep moving the stones to the surface. Digging tools are for rent at the park, and the rangers help you with identification. Some advance reservations are accepted, ☎ *(501) 285-3113*.

6. **Petit Jean State Park**, near Morilton between the Ozarks and the Ouchita mountains, has 137 sites with water and electrical hookups, with 24 sites available by advance reservation, ☎ *(501) 727-5441*. Sanitary dump station. The park is named for a legendary French girl who disguised herself as a boy to follow her sailor sweetheart to America. The 95-foot Cedar Falls, a lake with pedal boating and fishing, hiking trails, rustic lodge. Also the Museum of Automobiles, founded by Winthrop Rockefeller, displays various cars in its collection in an ever-changing exhibit. President Clinton's 1967 Mustang convertible is currently on display.

7. **Woolly Hollow State Park**, 50 miles north of Little Rock near Greenbrier, offers 20 campsites near the lake among the trees with water and electrical hookups, grills and picnic tables. Lake swimming, pedal boats, hiking trails, restored 19th century log homestead. Some reservations, ☎ *(501) 679-2098*.

8. **DeGray Lake Resort State Park**, south of Hot Springs near Bismarck, is a huge watersports and fishing resort with lodge, campgrounds, golf, tennis and marina. Its 113 sites have water and electrical hookups, flush toilets, hot showers, picnic tables and grills and sanitary trailer stations. Some sites offer scenic views. Boat rentals, including canoes and catamarans, 18-hole championship public golf course, pro shop with rentals, ranger programs, bicycle rentals, tennis courts, restaurant. Each January bald eagles migrate to the lake. Open year-round. Campsite reservations, ☎ *(501) 865-2801*.

9. **Withrow Springs State Park**, 20 miles from Eureka Springs, offers 25 campsites, 17 with water and electrical hookups. Located in a wilderness area along the bluffs of the War Eagle River, the park has a swimming pool, tennis, snack bar, bathhouse and sanitary dump station. For reservations, call ☎ *(501) 559-2593*.

10. At the north edge of Eureka Springs, **Kettle Campgrounds** is an attractive, family-run private campground with 50 full and partial hookup sites shaded by pine trees, flush toilets, showers, sanitary dump and laundry. They also promise a schedule of pig roasts, barbecue rib events, catfish fries and sloppy Joe nights. The campground can book tickets for the Passion Play, performed nearby, as well as other theaters in town. Ask when you call for camping reservations ☎ *(800) 899-CAMP*.

HOT SPRINGS

Famous nowadays as the town where Bill Clinton grew up, Hot Springs was once the most fashionable watering hole in the midwest, where the notorious (and peripatetic) Al Capone always booked the entire fourth floor in the Arlington Hotel, built in 1925, when he came to take the waters. The ever-restless Hernando de Soto is believed to have ventured here in his search for a fountain of youth.

One of the historic bathhouses in Hot Springs

The eponymous hot springs recycle rainwater that seeps into the ground, makes its way down to heated rock near the center of the earth, then reappears some 4000 years later naturally sterile at a temperature of 143 degrees Fahrenheit. In 1921, the 47-springs area became Hot Springs National Park, the only national park within a city.

A few intrepid souls had been venturing over the rugged mountain trails to soak in the healing waters ever since Jefferson was president, in post-Civil War days arriving by stagecoaches that were sometimes held up en route by Frank and Jesse James or the Younger brothers.

Town growth took off in 1874 when the railroad came in, and soon lavish hotels were being constructed for prestigious visitors, which came to include Theodore Roosevelt, Franklin Delano Roosevelt, Babe Ruth, Andrew Carnegie, Jay Gould and Harry Truman.

But when the gambling, always illegal but tolerated until the late 1960s, was closed down, Hot Springs settled into a quieter, gentler resort without the high rollers. The only action these days is at Oaklawn Park, when the racetrack season runs from late January to mid-April; the track is open year-round for offtrack betting.

Bathhouse Row is a splendid parade of bathhouses and hotels along the city's Central Avenue. Most dramatic of all is Fordyce Bathhouse at 401 Central Avenue, with a statue of an Indian maiden offering a bowl of spring water to De Soto and above her, an 8000-piece stained-glass skylight. Today it serves as the visitor center for the national park. Take a peek into the gymnasium, the 1915 version of a fitness center, with its punching bags, vaulting horses and rings.

The Arlington Hotel is still open with its own bathhouse reserved for guests. The 16-story art deco Medical Arts Building at *236 Central Avenue* was for many years the tallest building in Arkansas. We liked the well-preserved old downtown stores with faded signs like "Uneeda Biscuit 5 cents" painted on brick side walls. The classic revival Mountain Valley Spring Water building won a National Preservation award from the National Historic Trust.

Hot Springs is also famous for its amphibious "ducks," World War II landing craft converted to tourist transportation. Downtown at the "Duckport" you can board one to bop around Lake Hamilton over land and water.

INSIDER TIP:

Note that Hot Springs Mountain Drive is restricted to vehicles less than 32 feet long.

SIX SPECIAL SPLURGES

1. Make a reservation for a six-course dinner at Crescent Dragonwagon's Dairy Hollow House in Eureka Springs for perhaps the best food in Arkansas—but bring your own bottle of wine. Local rainbow trout is usually on her menu of "Nouveau'Zarks cuisine." ☎ *(800) 562-8650.*

2. Book a soak and massage in Hot Springs' classic 1913 Buckstaff Bathhouse, one of the few still open to the public. The usual treatment begins with a relaxing soak in a private whirlpool bath, then a choice of a needle shower or steam cabinet session, a cooldown in cold mineral water, and finally a rubdown. ☎ *(501) 623-2308.*

3. Hit the hamlet of Batesville any weekend year-round, starting Friday afternoons, for America's flea market, 142 booths under one roof and plenty of free parking. On US 167 northeast of Little Rock.

4. Splurge on a hickory-smoked country cured ham (they last for months in a cool, dark place, so you can store it in the RV and take it home) from Hillbilly Smoke House near Rogers, on route 71B in the northwesternmost corner of Arkansas, or Ozark Mountain Smoke House on highway 62 west on Fayetteville. At the latter, you can buy either a half or a whole ham; the half is more perishable. Both vendors also sell dry-cured, hickory-smoked bacon and smoked turkey.

5. Spring for "the works" at the classic old 1901 Palace Bath House in Eureka Springs, restored to its original style. "The works" includes whirlpool mineral bath, eucalyptus steam treatment, clay mask and half-hour massage, for around $40. ☎ *(501) 253-8400* for an appointment. Open daily except two weeks at Christmas.

6. Load up your RV with home-grown fruits and vegetables and homemade jams, cider, candy and Christmas wreaths at the Bunny Patch Country Market two miles

east of Mountain Home on highway 62. They're open daily except Mondays from late March through December.

OZARK FOLK CENTER:
REAL MOUNTAIN MUSIC

"We don't allow counterfeit corn pone around here," folk musician Jimmy Driftwood is reported to have said when asked the difference between the folk music you hear at Mountain View and the Ozark Folk Center, and the hillbilly and country music shows staged elsewhere.

The Ozark Folk Center State Park, the first folk cultural center in the United States, was established in 1973 to preserve the cultural traditions of the mountain region, its music, dancing, handicrafts and folkways. Open from May through October, the center is located in a beautifully wooded mountain area on a curved mountain road that is not difficult for RVs to negotiate. You park in a spacious parking lot at the base and take a free tram ride up a steep hill into the park itself.

Two dozen individual craftsmen are at work in the rustic cabins and outdoor areas, and they spend as much time answering questions and explaining what they're doing as any visitor could wish. Items made are for sale in the individual cabins and in the center gift shop. There's a second country store with some crafts in the parking area as well.

The primitive furniture shop promises, "We measure our chairs to fit our customers." There's a lithographer and photographer, an old-fashioned print shop, candle maker, basket weaver, a chatty lady who makes dolls from cornhusks and dried apples, various potters, spinners, weavers and quilters. There's also a weathered schoolhouse and a splendid Heritage Herb Garden dedicated in 1986 by-then Arkansas first lady Hillary Rodham Clinton. You can sign up for classes from the craftsmen, make special orders or buy crafts directly from them.

Music is presented at scheduled intervals throughout the day, with local musicians and clog dancers, many of them elderly, bantering among themselves before, during and after each tune. No musicians performing at the center or gathering in the town square in the evenings for impromptu hoedowns are permitted to use percussion or electronic amplification, and all musical selections must predate 1937. You may encounter musicians playing mountain dulcimer, autoharp, five-string banjo, fiddle, mandolin or even spoons. Special gospel music concerts are offered on Sunday evenings.

In the center's restaurant, traditional down-home dishes like fried chicken, catfish, country ham and cornbread are dished out family-style, and there's also a snack bar serving barbecue and smoked meat sandwiches, and hot fried apple or peach pies. A 60-room lodge on the premises is open year-round, ☎ *(800) 264-FOLK.* For information about the center, closed in winter, call ☎ *(501) 269-3851.*

The musicians who gather in the evenings on the steps and lawn of the Stone County courthouse in the simple little town of Mountain View are playing for their own pleasure and that of their listeners. Many of them come home from work, eat supper, wash up and come on down for some picking and singing.

10 GREAT LAKES AND WATERWAYS

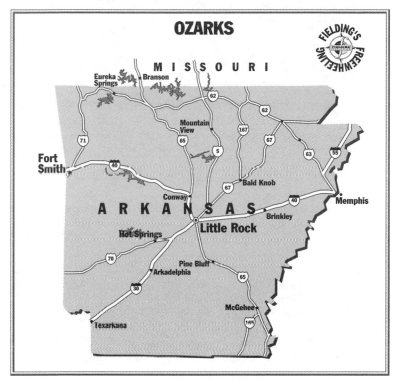

1. **Norfork Lake** near Mountain Home is noted for its clear water, clear enough to please even scuba divers and underwater photographers. Water-sports and hiking are primary attractions. Most of the U.S. Corps of Engineers campgrounds in the area have electrical hookups available, including Bidwell Point, Cranfield, Gamaliel, Robinson Point and Quarry Cove.

2. **Table Rock Lake** near Branson, MO, offers fishing, water-skiing, sailing, canoeing and windsurfing, along with boat rentals, paddle boats and lake swimming.

3. The **Buffalo River** courses its winding way 125 miles through the Ozarks between Buffalo City and Swain, the only major undammed stream in Arkansas. Today it's Buffalo National River Park, a favorite destination for canoeing. You can rent gear from Buffalo Adventures Canoe Rental near the park on route 74 west, ☎ *(501) 446-5406*, for a one-hour or four-hour ride. It's navigable primarily in winter and spring.

4. White water fans find plenty of action on the **Mulberry and Cossatot rivers**, designated for expert canoers and kayakers only. For full canoeing information, call the Department of Parks and Tourism at ☎ *(501) 682-7777* and ask for an "Arkansas Floater's Kit."

5. **Bull Shoals Lake**, on highway 178 where the White River is dammed, is the site of a state park with 85 water and electrical hookups along the river banks and a sanitary dump station on the premises. Fishermen will find "lunker" bass, crappie and bream in the lake, record-size rainbow and brown trout in the river. A trout dock rents canoes and motor boats, and sells bait and tackle.

6. **Lake Ouchita's** 975 miles of shoreline surround one of the best fishing lakes in Arkansas, with bass, crappie, bream, and catfish, as well as stocked rainbow trout, northern pike and ocean stripers. Water-skiers, divers, canoeists and sailboat enthusiasts use the wide open waters and quiet lagoons of this lake. A state park at one end of the lake offers 77 campsites with water and electrical hookups, paved RV sites, picnic tables and grills. Some advance reservations available, ☎ *(501) 767-9366.*

7. **Geers Ferry Lake**, which sprawls with ragged shorelines between Clinton and Heber Springs, is famous for its fishing, including a world-record German brown trout, 40 pounds and four ounces, caught in the Little Red River. Resorts, a rainbow trout hatchery, nature trails, marinas, golf courses, tennis, houseboats and plenty of camping facilities, some with hookups, can be found at the John F. Kennedy Campground north of Heber Springs on route 25, and the Narrows Campground southwest of Greers Ferry on route 16. Both are operated by the U.S. Corps of Engineers.

8. The **Beaver Lake** area on the upper White River near Eureka Springs is convenient to popular tourist areas but also offers world-class smallmouth bass fishing. All but one of the U.S. Corps of Engineers campgrounds in the area offer RV sites with electrical hookups.

9. **Dardanelle Lake** stretches 50 miles along the Arkansas River with 315 miles of shoreline for fishermen and campers. Both state park and U.S. Corps of Engineers campgrounds are located along the lake, five of them—Piney Bay, Shoal Bay, Spadra, Lake Dardanelle State Park and Mt. Nebo—with electrical hookups.

10. The 129-mile-long **Lake of the Ozarks** is the biggest in central Missouri, with some 1300 miles of shoreline, resorts, golf courses and summer homes. It is located in the northernmost part of the Ozarks, some distance north of the main region covered in this RV adventure.

WILDLIFE WATCH

White-tailed deer are plentiful in the Ozarks, and you might even glimpse wild turkeys, especially around Yellville during the October National Wild Turkey Calling Contest.

In Hot Springs National Park, daytime visitors are limited to sightings of squirrels and chipmunks, with an occasional rabbit early or late in the day. However, at night the park is frequented by raccoons, possums, skunks and nine-banded armadillos. Drivers may see gray foxes or an occasional white-tailed deer along the roadways. Also resident in the Ozarks but rarely seen are black bears, cougars and bobcats.

For after-dark action around Branson, when pop and country music shows begin to pall, you can sit in on some live jazz on weekends at Rocky's Italian restaurant.

INSIDER TIP:

Parts of both Arkansas and Missouri are "dry," meaning they have restricted sales or no sales at all of alcoholic beverages, and even in communities where sales are legal, Sundays may be completely dry. Some communities that do permit limited alcohol sales may operate in a "private club" situation, whereby you pay to become a "member" and then can access the bar.

14 OFF-THE-WALL ATTRACTIONS

OZARKS

FIELDING'S FREEWHEELING

MISSOURI

Eureka Springs
Branson ⑦⑧
⑬
②
62
62
⑫
Mountain View
167
71
65
⑤
67
63
55

Fort Smith
⑩⑪⑭ ①
40
67 Bald Knob

Conway
40
Memphis

A R K A N S A S
Brinkley

Hot Springs Little Rock
⑨ ④
⑥
70
③ Pine Bluff
Arkadelphia
65
⑤
30
McGehee
165
Texarkana

1. The bigger-than-life **statue of Popeye** in Alma, Arkansas, a couple of freeway exits east of Fort Smith, salutes "the Spinach Capital of the World." Alma's Allen Canning Company produces 66 percent of all the canned spinach in the United States. SEE the giant Popeye! SEE the world's largest spinach can!

2. The **Daisy BB Rifle Factory and Air Gun Museum** in Rogers offers daily tours of the plant that turns out 65 million BBs a day, as well as the classic air rifle that used to be coveted by every school-age boy.

3. Dig for diamonds at **Crater of Diamonds** State Park near Murfreesboro, about 55 miles south of Hot Springs. A shovel and a bucket are all you need, but if you forget them, the park rangers will lend you equipment. The fee for digging is $4 a day for adults, $1.50 for kids six–12. Since the park opened in 1972, lots of diggers have struck pay dirt, including one who unearthed a 16-carat stone. Bear in mind that dirt doesn't stick to diamonds, so look for clean shiny little pebbles. Any you find, you can take home.

4. If you're curious about animal behavior, check out the **I.Q. Zoo** on route 270 west of Hot Springs, where extremely well-rehearsed animals such as disco-dancing chickens, roller-skating parrots and chess-playing dogs demonstrate their skills. The experts here say it shows how positive reinforcement is the best way to train animals.

5. See the **blacksmith shop** where smithy James Black made **the first bowie knife** at Washington Historic State Park in Washington, where guides in 19th century garb will show you around. The knife, nicknamed the "Arkansaw Toothpick" by Mark Twain, was made for Jim Bowie and patented by his brother Rezin. An example of Bowie's last such knife, believed to have been found on the Alamo battlefield, is on

display at the Arkansas Territorial Restoration in Little Rock. The courthouse here was the Arkansas Confederate Capital during Civil War days.

6. The green duck-feather coat in the **Stuttgart Agricultural Museum**, "Rice and Duck Capital of the World," was made from the feathers of 450 mallards by the late Ruby Abel, a champion duck plucker who stumped the panels on TV's "What's My Line?" and "I've Got A Secret." Located on the Mississippi Flyway, Stuttgart's town slogan is "The duck stops here."

7. **Long's Wax and Historical Museum** in Branson has something for everyone, from a tableau starring Ronald Reagan and Ollie North to Farrah Fawcett standing next to Mahatma Gandhi, along with Hitler and Mussolini, both depicted in coffins, and a two-headed calf.

8. **Dick's Oldtime 5 & 10-cent Store in Branson**, as genuine as the wax museum above is ersatz, dates from 1929 and looks as if it hasn't changed since then. Its wood floors creak and its shelves are still stocked with Evening in Paris perfume, yard goods, popcorn and bubble gum.

9. Dig for crystals in **Mount Ida**, "Quartz Crystal Capital of the World," by going through mine tailings with a pick and shovel, or do it the easy way—buy a crystal from one of the stores along US 270. Maybe you can use it to contact Shirley MacLaine. Mount Ida is about 35 miles west of Hot Springs.

10. **Fort Smith's Belgrove Historic District** preserves the courtroom where "Hanging Judge" Isaac C. Parker sentenced 151 outlaws to death during the 21 years between 1875 and 1896; 79 of them were hanged, many on a unique gallows that could handle six men at the same time and sometimes did. In fairness to Parker, 69 of his deputy marshals were murdered during the same period, which gives a clearer picture of the times. Parker was considered incorruptible and scrupulously fair. The museum is *on Rogers Avenue between 2nd and 3rd Streets*. The gallows is a reproduction, suggesting the original might have worn out.

11. While you're in Fort Smith, visit **Miss Laura's** at *2 North B Street*, the only bordello listed on the National Register of Historic Places. Today a visitor center is located in the famous turn-of-the-century establishment.

12. Burt Reynolds fans will find the real town of **Evening Shade** in Arkansas, although it doesn't look like the fictional town on his TV series. Still, there's a new gym named for the actor in the real town, population 397, and some footage of the turn-of-the-century Victorian area found its way into the series here and there. Look for it on route 167 about halfway between Ash Flat and Batesville in the north-central part of the state.

13. **Sam and Mary Walton's first five-and-10-cent store** is now a museum and visitor center in Bentonville on the square on Main Street. Opened in 1945, the modest store was the beginnings of the Wal-Mart empire, and today is still filled with 1950s and 1960s merchandise. Bentonville is in the northwest corner of Arkansas on US 71.

14. **The world's largest Mr. Peanut**, complete with top hat and monocle, is in Fort Smith. The well-traveled peanut plant went from Brazil to West Africa, then from there to the southern United States, where peanuts were called "goobers."

INSIDER TIP:

Driving a large RV on the steep, narrow, one-way streets in Eureka Springs is not a good idea, especially in summer, except very early in the morning when there's little traffic. Hills are so steep that one church is entered through its bell tower. It's best to park and walk around.

EUREKA SPRINGS

Eureka Springs, Arkansas, has dozens of historic Victorians, many of them turned into bed-and-breakfast establishments.

These long-lost Indian curative springs are believed to have been rediscovered in the 1860s by a doctor, out hunting with his son. The boy's chronic eye infection healed when he washed his face in the water, and his father touted the springs as healing waters, selling "Dr. Jackson's Magic Eye Water" from "Indian Healing Spring."

In the days before antibiotics, this was hot news, and a community grew up quickly around the 63 springs, erecting boardinghouses to bed and feed health-seeking visitors. After the railroad arrived in 1883, construction really took off; more than 50 plush hotels were built in the next three decades.

Famed temperance crusader Carry Nation arrived in 1908 to settle down, naming her home Hatchet Hall after her favorite saloon-smashing tool. She died here three years later.

Today the entire downtown area is listed in the National Register of Historic Places. Streets are steep and narrow, and none of the 230-plus thoroughfares intersect at right angles. Victorian houses painted in lush colors and trims, many of them turned into bed-and-breakfast establishments, perch on the sides of hills either leaning against a rocky backdrop or staring down into a canyon. A house may appear to be one-story from the front but have as many as five stories in back.

Crafts shops, art galleries, superb inns and restaurants make Eureka Springs a romantic getaway for urban honeymooners, and the town has the largest and most upscale collection of bed-and-breakfasts in the state.

The town also has a long association with fundamentalism and the religious right, represented today by the long-running *The Great Passion Play* performed nightly in summer except Mondays and Thursdays, the Anita Bryant Theatre (where summer shows star you-know-who doing a musical autobiography in the first act, a patriotic finale in the second), and a trio of attractions developed by the late Gerald L. K. Smith, a minister nicknamed "the old hatesmith" for his anti-Semitic publication *The Cross and the Flag* back in the 1920s—the 70-foot concrete statue of Christ that can be seen over the treetops, a Bible museum and the Christ Only Art Gallery, with some 500 portraits of Christ.

10 SCENIC SIDE TRIPS

1.   Highway 7 through parts of the Ouchita and Ozark National Forests from Arkadelphia, south of Hot Springs, north to the route 65 connection to Branson, Missouri, cuts a swath through some 200 miles of the most scenic parts of the Ozarks. Roadside shopping opportunities run from sincere arts and crafts to ersatz "silly hillbilly" items suitable only for friends who collect ugly souvenirs. National Forest campgrounds without hookups and private campgrounds with full hookups are plentiful along the route. You go through Hot Springs, past Jessieville's crystal mine, Lake Dardanelle, Russellville, Pelsor with its 1922 general store, rustic Jasper and the beginning of the Ozark Highlands National Recreation Trail, and Pruitt with its "old swimming hole" and canoe launch on the Buffalo River.

2.   Sylamore Scenic Byway of the Ozark National Forest, between Mountain View and Mountain Home on route 5, is a short, lightly-traveled and beautiful route between the Ozark Folk Center and the Bull Shoals Dam area. Drive past small family farms, lushly wooded areas, villages like Calico Rock, and Lake Norfork's crystal clear waters.

3.   I-40 or its parallel US 64 between Conway and Fort Smith covers some fascinating small towns and Arkansas footnotes. Morrilton is the gateway to Petit Jean State Park (see "10 Campground Oases") and its Automobile Museum, currently displaying Bill Clinton's 1967 Mustang convertible; Atkins, "The Pickle Capital of Arkan-

sas" with its fried dill pickles and annual spring Picklefest; the historic Potts Tavern Inn, now a hat museum; Mount Nebo State Park, its campground with RV hookups and advance reservations, ☎ *(501) 229-3655*; Clarksville and its famous peaches; and Altus and the Arkansas wine country (don't expect the Napa Valley!)

4. Ozark Highlands Scenic Byway, 35 miles along route 21 from Clarksville north to Ponca goes through the Ozark National Forest and over Boston Mountain, especially lovely in its fall foliage or spring dogwood bloom. There's an eight-site National Forest campground without hookups at Ozone, a trailhead for the Upper Buffalo Wilderness Area, and a canoe and kayak put-in for the Buffalo National River at Ponca.

5. Arkansas' highest point, a relatively modest 2753 feet, is atop Mount Magazine, with a state park in development and some national forest campgrounds without hookups along 25-mile route 309 between Havana and Paris. The vistas are great.

6. Take a scenic journey by train aboard the Arkansas and Missouri Railroad Company in turn-of-the-century rail cars between Van Buren, on route 71 on the Oklahoma border north of Fort Smith, and Springdale, on route 71B north of Fayetteville. Some rides are three hours, some all day. The train operates between early April and mid-November. ☎ *(501) 452-9582* or, from within Arkansas, ☎ *(800) 364-3255* for information.

7. Arkansas Scenic Highway 74 is famous for its Ozark vistas as it meanders along some 35 miles from Kingston at the intersection with highway 21 (also designated a Scenic Highway) to Fayetteville. There are numerous picnic areas along the way, and the route crosses War Eagle Creek.

8. A 50-mile loop out of Eureka Springs follows route 62 to the historic Pea Ridge National Military Park, where costumed Confederate and Yankee troops recreate the pivotal Civil War battle every March; a detour into Rogers, where the first Wal-Mart store, founded back in 1945, is now a visitor center; and out route 12 to War Eagle Mill, where grains are still ground by water-powered buhrstones for local farmers and sold to visitors, and the Bean Palace Restaurant serves up great breakfasts and lunches; past Beaver Lake State Park; and back into Eureka Springs via route 23 north.

9. The George Washington Carver National Monument south of Joplin, Missouri, southwest of Diamond on county route V off route 71A, preserves the birthplace of the noted agronomist who promoted peanut butter.

10. In Missouri the little town of Mansefield, off US 60 some 40 miles east of Springfield, is the adult farm home of Laura Ingalls Wilder, who wrote the *Little House on the Prairie* series of books that inspired the popular TV series. It was here that she wrote her books about her childhood experiences in DeSmet, South Dakota. (See "The Black Hills of South Dakota.") Adjacent is a museum.

INSIDER TIP:

If getting a country music star's autograph heads your want list for Branson, book a bus tour to the show instead of going in on your own. Many performers will climb on tour buses after the show to sign autographs.

BRANSON, MISSOURI

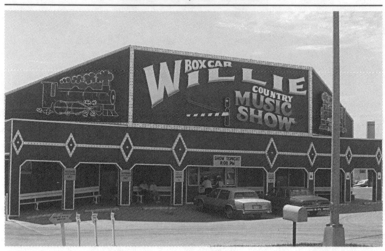

Boxcar Willie was one of Branson, Missouri's first theatrical entrepreneurs.

In 1913, it was a little town by a dam site when the White River was turned into Lake Taneycomo by the Powersite Dam. In the late 1950s, a second dam created Table Rock Lake above Lake Taneycomo, turning the latter into a cold-water lake, ideal for trout.

Now this town of 3706 that nobody ever heard of a few years ago is proclaiming itself "country music capital of the universe," just in case a few banjo-strumming Martians try to get into the act.

Now the second-most visited tourist area in the U.S., with only Orlando ahead of it, Branson has some 34 live-music theaters that play daily matinee and evening shows for the five million tourists who show up in season, from April through the end of October.

After years on the road in one-night stands, country music stars like letting their fans come to them for a change, and are willing to invest a bundle in glitzy theaters in exchange for being able to stay home for a while.

Live country music shows actually began in Branson back in 1960 with the Baldknobbers Hillbilly Jamboree, but after Roy Clark, longtime host of TV's "Hee Haw," opened his own theater in 1983, followed by Boxcar Willie, a down-home comic who whistles train noises while dressed as a hobo, opened his in 1987, things really took off.

Now traffic is usually backed up bumper-to-bumper all day every day along route 76, moving along so slowly that you have plenty of time to see who's playing where through your RV windshield.

Headliners who've performed in Branson read like a Grammy Award show, not only in country music but also in pop—Roy Clark, Johnny Cash, Loretta Lynn, Shoji Tabuchi, Glen Campbell, Wayne Newton, Mel Tillis, Andy Williams, the Smothers Brothers, the Osmonds, Bobby Vinton, Tony Orlando, Boxcar Willie, Micky Gilley, the Oak Ridge Boys and Louise Mandrell. Many have their own eponymous theaters, including Tabuchi, Clark, Vinton, Williams, Orlando, Newton, Tillis and Lynn, and a breakfast or morning show is almost as common as a matinee.

The 1890's Silver Dollar City is a 90-acre amusement park themed to look like an old mining town. (We're just not sure which old mining town.) It began as a traditional crafts village where some 100 costumed craftspeople blow glass, make brooms, weave baskets, grind corn, spin yarn, stitch quilts and throw pots, but has accelerated these days with big-time amusement park rides from high-speed roller coasters to wilderness toboggans that seem designed more to coax money out of family pockets than celebrate the traditions of the mountains. Singer Kenny ("The Gambler") Rogers is one of the owners of the park.

With seven music venues, a dozen restaurants, street vendors, 45 shops, 15 rides, a train, carousels, ferris wheels and balloon rides, the original attraction back in the 1960s when the park was built, Marvel Cave, is all but overshadowed. Of course those 500 steep steps down into the cave might have something to do with its waning popularity as well.

The Shepherd of the Hills, an affectionate novel about the Ozarks written in mountain dialect in 1907 by Harold Bell Wright, has been turned into a summerlong pageant that's been running for more than 30 years with a cast of 75 plus horse-drawn wagons and a burning cabin.

Something to think about—Branson now claims to attract more visitors annually than the Grand Canyon, Yellowstone or Washington, DC.

INSIDER TIP:

The heaviest traffic on route 76 is around noontime, from 6:30 to 8 p.m. and again when the evening shows let out between 10 and 11 p.m. The center lane in the three-lane road is for turning only. You could also leave your RV at one of the campgrounds along the strip and ride the local trolley.

12 TAKEOUT (OR EAT-IN) TREATS

1. The **pit barbecue at McClard's** on Albert Pike in Hot Springs has been called the best in the United States, but McClard's itself simply claims "best in the state since'28." Locals say it's Bill Clinton's favorite. There's a "secret sauce" given to the family in 1928 to settle a $10 debt by a lodger in their motor court. The recipe is still used today and still kept in the family. Try the chopped pork, ribs, fantastic beans, homemade tamales, tangy coleslaw. Decor and table setting is paper and plastic.

2. **Catfish 'N'** in Dardanelle dishes up award-winning fried catfish fillets and hushpuppies along with French fries, coleslaw, pickled peppers and tartar sauce. On our to-go orders, one plate had four catfish fillets, the other five, plus at least half-a-dozen hushpuppies apiece. If you go, skip the so-so French fries in favor of still more hushpuppies. You can also get fried or boiled shrimp and hot fruit cobblers for dessert. It's near the Arkansas River bridge on route 7. Closed Mondays.

3. Curvaceous Dolly Parton-shaped chocolate lollipops at **The Fudge Shop** in Branson, *106 South Business Street*, supplement the more traditional sweet fare that includes fudge, taffy and nut brittles.

4. The **War Eagle Bean Palace** at a working, water-powered grist mill off highway 12 on the War Eagle River serves stone-ground grits with sausage, sausage gravy and biscuits at breakfast, old-fashioned pork and beans with slabs of cornbread at lunch. In the adjacent general store, you can buy the grits, cornmeal, sorghum molasses, hush puppy mix and buckwheat pancake mix turned out by the mill's rollers. A statewide favorite is War Eagle Mill Fish Fry Coating Mix, first developed by radio/TV's "The Sportsman's Friend," Harold Ensley. The mill is open daily until 5 p.m.

from March through December, and on weekends in January and February. It's on highway 98 south of 12E between Eureka Springs and Rogers.

5. Homemade fried pies and heavenly pecan, apple, sweet potato and lemon pies are available whole or by the piece from the **Family Pie Shop** in De Valls Bluff, Arkansas, on route 70 just south of I-40 at exit 202.

6. While you're in De Valls Bluff, cross route 70 to **Craig's Bar-B-Q** for a pork barbecue sandwich topped with coleslaw and accompanied by Ozark-style beans. You get a choice of mild, medium or hot sauce.

7. The **Rockhouse B-B-Q** on highway 7 south of Harrison, Arkansas, boasts that it's been recommended in more than 200 major newspapers in all 50 states. And it is pretty good, albeit cute for a serious barbecue place. Specialties here are loin back pork ribs with pit-cooked beans and jalapeño corn bread. Ask them to add an order of crisp fried onion rings and maybe a Mississippi-style deep-fried dill pickle.

8. **Stubby's Hik-ry Pit Bar-B-Q** on Park Avenue in Hot Springs serves fluffy baked potatoes with its Ozark ham-laced beans and rich, spicy ribs, which are baked with the sauce. Beef outsells pork three to one. Baked beans, slaw and pickles, as well as a side dish of extra sauce, are usually included.

9. **Weidman's Old Fort Brew Pub** in Fort Smith, built by a German immigrant in the 1840s to sell beer to local pubs, has been brightly restored as a brew pub and restaurant. Look for it at *3rd and E Streets.*

10. **Windy City Dogs**, on the Taneycomo lakefront in downtown Branson. The Chicago-style hot dog is a beef frank with jalapeño peppers and a dill pickle spear in the bun; have them put some fried onions on top, then walk over and eat it at the lake.

11. The most famous hamburger in Arkansas, an award-winner for more than a decade, is at the **Whatta-Burger Drive Inn** on *North Arkansas Drive in Russellville.* Locals say it's the "biggest, best hamburger ever to wear a bun."

12. **Edwards Mill** at the School of the Ozarks sells stone-ground grits and funnel cake mix, along with student-baked fruit cakes, apple butter, jams, jellies and preserves, at a gift shop near the school's entrance. All the students here work their way through school by operating the mill or working at the dairy farm. It's in Point Lookout, MO, two miles south of Branson via route 65. The school is open Monday through Saturday and Sunday afternoons from mid-April to October, but closed weekends during winter.

ON THE CHEAP: CUTTING COSTS ON THE ROAD

Penny-pinchers will be delighted with the Ozarks, because prices, especially restaurant meals, are generally much lower than in most areas. What you have to watch out for on this itinerary is to not get carried away buying tickets for too many country music shows in Branson or spending too long with the kids at Silver Dollar City.

Speaking of kids, you'll find big, family-style meals, often "all you can eat," at places like the Old Apple Mill Restaurant on the strip in Branson, and The Mine and Molly's Mill Restaurant in Silver Dollar City, if you don't mind bounteous but predictable buffets.

The other place you'll have to show restraint is shopping, because the handmade crafts are so pretty and appealing.

Plan to catch your own fish for dinner at least part of the time. Then go diamond-digging; who knows—maybe you'll strike pay dirt.

FYI

Arkansas maintains 13 Tourist Information Centers located at all the primary interstate and highway accesses to the state. You can also write to or call the **Arkansas Department of Parks and Tourism**, *One Capitol Mall, Little Rock, AR 72201,* ☎ *(800) NATURAL,* for a copy of the Vacation Planning Kit. Campground guides and state park guides are also available.

For information about Branson, contact the **Branson/Lakes Area Chamber of Commerce**, *PO Box 1897, Branson, MO 65615,* ☎ *(417) 334-4136.* An information packet can be ordered by dialing ☎ *(900) 884-2726,* for a toll charge of around $5.

To get a free Missouri Vacation Packet, call toll-free ☎ *(800) 877-1234.*

CRUISING THE FLORIDA KEYS

Key West sightseeing trolley

Key West is The Last Resort, the t-shirt capital of the world, the place Tennessee Williams called Cocalooney Key. A sign at the end of the dock says "90 Miles to Cuba," and a local mayor once water-skied the distance to emphasize how close it is.

It's where fashion icon Calvin Klein bought a million-dollar Bird Cage, where "tea dancing" doesn't call for white gloves, where Presidents Truman, Kennedy, Nixon and Bush all lodged at the same upscale fishing lodge, Cheeca Lodge, although not at the same time.

The Keys are where the famous 1948 film noir *Key Largo* with Humphrey Bogart and Lauren Bacall was *not* filmed, although the Key Largo tourist office implies it was, but where the 1955 movie *The Rose Tattoo* with Burt Lancaster and Anna Magnani was filmed, much of it in author Tennessee Williams' own house at 1431 Duncan Street, a fact hardly if ever mentioned in Key West.

It's where buccaneers swashbuckled and pirates pirated, where Harry Truman played poker, where ice from the frozen lakes of Maine was delivered by ship until well into the 20th century, where Anna Pavlova danced with the Russian Ballet, and Truman Capote danced with Tennessee Williams.

> ### INSIDER TIP:
>
> *The letters MM, which you'll see throughout this chapter as well as on much printed material about the Keys, stand for Mile Marker, the most commonly used address. The markers are green-and-white signs posted on the right shoulder of the roadway. Miles are measured from Key West (MM 0) to the mainland (MM 126).*

When to go. The weather is warm year-round, but the winter months have the most comfortable temperatures for bicycling around Key West. Late spring brings bright bloom to Key West's streets—bougainvillea, jacaranda and oleander. Summer's muggy temperatures often combine with ferocious but brief thunderstorms; more actual rainfall comes down during fall and winter but rarely enough to bother your sightseeing. Hurricane season is early fall. Spring break can fill the streets of Key West with party-hearty college students; consider yourself forewarned.

What to take. Binoculars, camera and film, powerful insect repellent to combat champion mosquitoes, a sun hat and a good strong sunblock. If you've forgotten your sunblock or are running low, pick up some of the excellent locally-produced Key West Aloe sunblock at their shop/factory on Front Street.

What to wear. Shorts, flip-flops and a tank top or t-shirt is the most common outfit on the streets of Key West on a hot day, but something a little more conservative is appreciated in upscale restaurants and hotels. If you splurge on a meal or overnight at Little Palm Island (see "10 Special Splurges") take some casually elegant resort-type sportswear. Carry a sweater or jacket for rainy days or cool evenings in winter. If you forget anything, you can find plenty of well-made, moderately-priced sportswear manufactured locally.

TALKING CONCH: A KEYS GLOSSARY

Conch ("konk")—a native of the Keys, named for a chewy gastropod that inhabits local waters

Stranger—everybody else in the Keys

Eyebrow house—a dwelling where the second-story roof overhangs the windows

Shotgun house—a long hall you could shoot a bullet through that runs from front to back through a house

Fretsaw—gingerbread trim on houses, much of it applied by ship's carpenters from termite-resistant hardwood

"Square grouper"—what local fishermen call bundled bales of marijuana bobbing in the water, thrown overboard by drug smugglers when the Coast Guard is near

Tourist tree—the gumbo-limbo, whose peeling red-orange bark looks like a bad sunburn

Mangrove—small, broadleaf, evergreen tropical trees growing in marshes or tidal shores with much of their root systems exposed

Hardwood hammock—Not a bed slung between two posts but a dense grove of small hardwood trees growing on a limestone reef in a marshy area at a slightly higher elevation so they form humps

THE OVERSEAS HIGHWAY

The first overland transportation to Key West was an extension of Henry M. Flagler's railroad, called "Flagler's Folly" or "the railroad that went to sea," which covered 25 miles of the distance on land, 75 miles over water.

The aging tycoon's railway began in 1896 when Flagler, content in north Florida's St. Augustine until the freeze of 1894-95 destroyed all the citrus and vegetables north of Palm Beach, decided to move south to get warm. The indomitable Julia Tuttle, a dowager hell-bent on bringing some attention to south Florida, sent a bouquet of fresh orange blossoms to Flagler from her farm, along with an offer to share the land the Tuttles and their neighbors the Brickells owned, in exchange for Flagler extending his railway down to their obscure village on the banks of the Miami River. He did, she did, and the rest is history.

From 1905 to 1912, Flagler took his rail line even farther south along the Florida Keys despite the nay-sayers, running 150 miles of track that connected the Florida mainland with the southern islands. He died shortly after it was finished, secure that his single biggest accomplishment, the famous Seven Mile Bridge, would also be his lasting monument. Although many of the railroad tracks were uprooted by a hurricane in 1935, the bridge remained.

Road engineers were able to use the old railroad pilings to support the 43 bridges of the Overseas Highway, which opened in 1938. While the original bridges and road have been widened or replaced, you can still see some of them, including the first Seven Mile Bridge, as you drive south. In April, the annual Seven Mile Bridge run sets out from Marathon with runners from all over the world.

For RVers, even those towing 40-foot travel trailers, these long, flat, over-water roads are good, free of curves and hills.

The drive from Miami to Key West is three to four hours each way if you don't stop—but if you don't stop, you have little reason to drive down.

INSIDER TIP:

Locals say the most expensive gas in the Keys is at the Sugarloaf Lodge at MM 17.

10 WATERY WONDERS

FLORIDA KEYS

GULF OF MEXICO

Everglades

Homestead

Sugarloaf
Key West *Key*

Florida Bay

Boca
Chica
Key

Marathon   **Islamorada**

Key Largo

Big
Pine
Key

ATLANTIC OCEAN

1.   **John Pennekamp Coral Reef State Park** near Key Largo, part of the Florida Keys National Marine Sanctuary, is a 78-square-mile underwater park made up of reefs like those which formed the keys. The living coral colonies are endlessly fascinating for divers and snorkelers; there are underwater observation rooms and glass-bottomed boats for those who want to keep their heads above water. The reef has more than 50 forms of coral and 500 species of tropical fish, and is the only living coral reef in the continental U.S.

2.   **Islamorada on Upper Matecumbe Key** is a popular fishing resort area, with the Theater of the Sea offering dolphin and sea lion shows plus a shark pool and aquarium; Lignumvitae Key State Botanical Site displaying rare lignum vitae trees, an extremely dense wood that can outlast steel; and Indian Key, a formerly settled key where John James Audubon visited in 1832. The latter two are uninhabited islands which can be toured with park rangers, but you have to get there by local boat service. Robbie's, ☎ *(305) 664-9814*, charges $20 for adults, $15 for kids, and Papa Joe's Marina, ☎ *(305) 664-5005*, charges $24 for adults, $14 for kids. Boat departures are timed to coincide with tour times.

3.   **Grassy Key** is the location of the Dolphin Research Center, where visitors can call on the first day of each month for a reservation to swim with dolphins later that same month. The swim also requires a hefty contribution to the center, but you can visit and look at the dolphins for a more modest fee sans appointment. ☎ *(305) 289-1121* for reservations.

4.   **Harry Harris County Park** in Key Largo at MM 92 is a wide expanse of sandy beach with palm trees and picnic tables facing the Atlantic. If you have your pet along, he'll have to stay in the RV.

5.   **Crocodile Lake National Wildlife Refuge** boasts the largest collection of crocodiles in the United States, up to 500. Located on Key Largo, the refuge represents a recent victory of environmentalists over real estate developers. (See "Miracle of the Keys.")

6.   Ever want to spend the night underwater? Then make a reservation at **Jules' Undersea Lodge**, the world's first underwater hotel, with two bedrooms below the surface and a price of around $200 a night per person. Beginning divers and snorkelers are

welcome, they say. ☎ *(305) 451-2353* for information. No alcohol is permitted unless you're on your honeymoon, in which case champagne is permissible. What we wonder is, how can they tell if you're really on your honeymoon?

7.   **Biscayne National Underwater Park** can be visited aboard one of two shallow-draft, glass-bottomed Reef Rovers that set out from the park's Convoy Point headquarters daily and skim lightly over the reefs. Afternoon snorkel and scuba trips with rental equipment available last four hours, departing at 1:30, while morning reef sightseeing tours start at 10 a.m. Reservations required; ☎ *(305) 247-2400*. Headquarters are located nine miles east of Homestead on SW 328th Street. Parts of the park were closed from Hurricane Andrew damage when we were last there, so call ahead.

8.   Check out the **July Underwater Music Festival** at Big Pine Key, when divers listen to an underwater symphony at Looe Key National Marine Sanctuary. For details, call ☎ *(800) USA-ESCA*.

9.   **Bahia Honda State Park** on Bahia Honda Key has one of the best sandy beaches in the Keys, with the luxury of wading out into the water on sand instead of—ouch— coral.

10. **Dog Beach**, near Louie's Backyard, is the only beach in Key West where owner and dog can swim together, while the so-called nude canals in an abandoned real estate development on Sugarloaf Key's Sugarloaf Boulevard are where clothing-optional sunbathers gather to catch some rays between dips.

INSIDER TIP:

The pieces of coral and the tacky coral souvenirs you'll see for sale in the Keys come from the Philippines. The taking of any Florida coral is illegal and snorkelers and divers who harm it or the other protected marine species are subject to fines and punishment.

KEY LARGO

Key Largo, the classic 1948 Humphrey Bogart-Lauren Bacall film, was shot almost entirely on a Hollywood soundstage, but that didn't stop the town of Rock Harbor from taking the name Key Largo after clearing it with the U.S. Postal Service in 1952, then building a cottage industry around the film's stars, none of whom were in town during the filming. The boat used in *The African Queen*, for instance, is proudly on display at the Holiday Inn Key Largo, and, according to local tourist handouts, is "a nostalgic addition to Key Largo's unique old film atmosphere."

The only location in town, ironically, where some second unit footage for *Key Largo* was actually shot is the funky Caribbean Club Bar at MM 104.

The old Tavernier Hotel in the downtown district claims to be the first hotel in the Keys, and managed to survive the great, unnamed, Labor Day hurricane of 1935. Back then, weathermen didn't do cute stand-ups in front of cameras, so tropical storms didn't need names.

Old hands say the upper Keys have the best fishing, especially around Marathon and Islamorada, the latter usually billed as Sportfishing Capital of the World, but visitors with visions of Hemingway dancing in their heads keep driving south to Key West before booking a boat.

Bonefish and permit are in shallow waters of mangrove islets on the Gulf of Mexico side (but not as easy to catch as they look), while marlin and sailfish are deep-water dwellers that require a captain and crew to take you out into the Atlantic.

Near John Pennekamp Coral Reef State Park is the Caribbean Shipwreck Museum and Research Institute, with exhibits of sunken treasure and rare maritime artifacts. It was for sale last time we were there but still open.

INSIDER TIP:

Privately-owned RV parks in the Keys, particularly those that are so-called condo parks, meaning they sell memberships or time-share spaces, can be very pricey, especially at high season. Expect to be charged $30 or more for an overnight hookup. Even the state parks are expensive compared to their peers in other states. They make half their sites available for advance booking, but only within 60 days of your anticipated arrival. For first-come, first-served sites in the state parks, go in the morning and get your name on a waiting list if the park is full and come back in midafternoon to see if you've scored a space.

EIGHT CAMPGROUND OASES

1. **Bahia Honda State Park** at MM 37 has a 48-site campground with water and electrical hookups, flush toilets and showers, some shade, sanitary dump, fishing, swimming, boating, marina. The beach is good, there are wading birds and a small nature trail. No pets. For advance reservations ☎ *(305) 872-2353.*

2. **Long Key State Park** at MM 67 has 60 sites with water and electrical hookups, most of them shaded. Flush toilets, showers, ocean front, fishing, boat rentals. There's a well-labeled nature walk and some good birdwatching on the flats. No pets. ☎ *(305) 664-4815* for advance bookings.

3. At Cudjoe Key, MM 23, a gigantic condo RV park called **Venture Out Inc.** makes 75 of its 659 sites available for those of us just passing through. While it's plush and posh, with heated pool and spa, ocean fishing, boat ramp and so on, the rates from $25 to $50 a night and the no-pets rule may cause some to keep moving. ☎ *(305) 745-1333.*

4. **Long Pine Key campground** in Everglades National Park 10 miles south of the junction of US 1 and route 9336, has 108 paved sites with no hookups, no reservations. Some are shaded. The park has toilets, a sanitary dump and bass fishing on Long Pine Key Lake. Wooden overlooks and boardwalks in the park allow good bird-watching.

5. **John Pennekamp Coral Reef State Park** at MM 102 has 47 gravel sites with water and electrical hookups, shade, flush toilets, showers, sanitary dump, swimming, fishing and boat rentals, plus park-run diving and snorkeling lessons and excursions. The reef lies several miles offshore, so you can just jump out of the RV and dive in. No pets. ☎ *(305) 451-1202* for campsite reservations, ☎ *(305) 451-1621* for dive information.

6. **Sugarloaf Key KOA** is a private RV park located north of Key West at MM 20 with 200 sites, half of them grass and half gravel. Full hookups in most, some shaded, cable TV, flush toilets, showers, laundry, groceries, fishing and swimming pool. Pricey at $30 to $55, they do allow pets and take reservations at ☎ *(305) 745-3549.*

7. **Fiesta Key KOA Resort** at Long Key has 288 sites with full or partial hookups, flush toilets, showers, sanitary dump, laundry, groceries, heated pool and spa, boat rental, adult recreation room, boat ramp, dock and rental. Pets are permitted, but rates are high—$45 to $60 a night. ☎ *(305) 664-4922.*

8. If camping in downtown Key West appeals to you, **Jabour's Trailer Court** at *223 Elizabeth Street* has 74 sites with full hookups and cable TV. Don't expect spacious or woodsy spots surrounded by nature, but at least you'll be able to leave the rig hooked up and walk wherever you want to go. Flush toilets, showers, sanitary dump, from $30 to $48 a night. ☎ *(305) 294-5723* for reservations.

INSIDER TIP:

Many Florida recreation areas and state parks, as well as some private RV parks, have a "no pets" rule. Be sure to check before checking in if you're traveling with furry friends.

PART ONE: CAYO HUESO BECOMES KEY WEST

Old houses of Key West

The eight-square-mile coral island used to be called Cayo Hueso (which means "bone key") from piles of human bones found by early visitors. No one is quite sure where the bones came from, but they were already in place when the first non-Indians, a bunch of bloodthirsty buccaneers, hit town. Ponce de Leon had probably discovered the Keys in 1513 as he worked his way north looking for the Fountain of Youth, which he found in St. Augustine.

In 1815, Cayo Hueso belonged Juan Pablo Salas of St. Augustine under a Spanish land grant, but when Florida became part of the United States in 1821, he sold it to John Simonton, an American businessman, for $2000. Simonton called in the U.S. Navy's Anti-Pirate Squadron, drove out the pirates and put the place under military control. From that day forward until 1974, there was always a navy base on Key West.

By the 1830s, the island, now anglicized into Key West, was inhabited primarily by "wreckers" who made their livelihood from what was euphemistically known in the early 1800s as the "wrecking trade," salvaging sunken ships for a good living, even perhaps, as some historians suggest, luring those same ships to wreck onto the shoals and then salvaging them. In a good season, there would be more than a ship a week run aground. The best wreckers, it's said, lived aboard their ships so they could get to a wreck even more quickly.

Most were Cockneys coming from the Bahamas, along with Loyalists to the British Crown after the Americans won the Revolutionary War, plus a polyglot assortment of Cubans, seafarers from New England, and later, emigrés from the Civil War.

But both the buccaneers and the wreckers missed the greatest haul of loot ever recovered by American salvage hunters, Mel Fisher's treasure trove from the sunken Spanish galleons *Atocha* and *Santa Margarita*, millions of dollars worth of gold bars, silver coins and emeralds. The ships sank off Key West in 1622 on their way back to Spain, laden with the riches of the New World. Some key pieces of the indescribably valuable find are on display in Fisher's museum at Whitehead and Greene Streets. (On our first visit there a decade ago, Fisher's mother sold us the tickets and showed us around with visible maternal pride.)

At the turn of this century, the city, already the richest settlement in Florida, was the cigar-producing capital of the world, with many of the 6000 cigar makers being Cubans who flocked here to find work.

The wrecking industry bottomed out in 1921—"The Navy put channel markers and buoys to warn the ships about the reef," locals said—and the cigar industry burned out when investors in Ybor City, near Tampa, lured the cigar manufacturers away with promises of fewer labor problems.

By the late 1920s, Key West had become a backwater and one of the poorest places in the United States. In 1934, with 80 percent of the population unemployed, the desperate city declared bankruptcy, and the federal government sent in a New Deal administrator called Julius Stone who decided to turn the island into a tropical tourist paradise. He put people to painting and cleaning up the town and the beaches, training young women to be hotel

maids, even suggesting that all the local men wear shorts to appear picturesque.

The plan was a huge success in the winter of 1934-35, but the Labor Day
hurricane of 1935 swept away the railway tracks and with them all the hopes
and dreams.

FIVE THINGS TO DO IN KEY WEST
FOR $5 OR LESS

1. Heft a solid gold bar and see silver bars, emeralds and golden chalices from 17th
    century Spanish galleons discovered by treasure hunter Mel Fisher at the Mel Fisher
    Maritime Heritage Society Museum, open daily year-round, *200 Greene Street.*

2. The old Turtle Kraals (a South African term for corrals) that once processed turtle
    steaks and canned turtle soup, now home of the Florida Marine Conservancy. Sick
    and injured sea turtles and birds are tended here, and there's a touch tank for kids.
    Free. Open daily from 11 a.m. to 1 a.m. Land's End Village at Land's End Marina.
    The Half-Shell Raw Bar is here, too, if it's time for lunch or a snack.

3. Wrecker's Museum, also called the Oldest House, where a sea captain and his nine
    daughters once lived, displays memorabilia of the wrecking business in an 1829 pine
    house. There's also an elaborately furnished period doll house. Open daily year-
    round, *322 Duval Street.*

4. A free guided tour of the Key West Hand Print Fabrics and Fashions company takes
    you backstage in a former 19th century tobacco warehouse to watch hand-printed
    fabrics being designed and sewn into tropical sportswear, fabric toys, bedding,
    placemats and napkins. Open daily year-round, *201 Simonton Street.*

5. Key West Lighthouse Museum, a 1987 award-winning restoration of an 1847 light-
    house with a spiral staircase inside leading up to a spectacular panoramic view of the
    island. Exhibits tell the history of the town and the Keys. Open daily except Christ-
    mas Day, *938 Whitehead Street.*

PART TWO: A BIRD IN THE BUSH

Writers and artists have always been fascinated with Key West. One of the
first artistic visitors was John James Audubon, who arrived in 1832 aboard
the cutter *Marion*. A crack shot, the Haitian-born painter, naturalist and
egoist had worked his way through the American south as a tutor and dancing master, often biting the hand that fed him. His modus operandi was to
kill as many birds from a species as he could because he enjoyed shooting,
then mount one or two of them and arrange them in a habitat, often tree
branches. While Audubon usually drew the birds himself, a young assis-
tant—one or another always traveled with him—filled in the backgrounds.
In Key West, Audubon produced two bird drawings, one of them a white-
crowned pigeon perched on a branch of an orange-blossomed Geiger tree.

This type of tree was introduced from the West Indies by a Captain John
Geiger, who also built the house now called the Audubon house, although
Audubon's connection with it is tenuous. However, there is a Geiger tree in
the yard of the Whitehead Street property. The tree, by the way, was not
named for the captain, and the house in its present incarnation was not at
this location in 1832. However, this island has a long tradition of inhabitants
moving buildings from one spot to another.

THREE KEY WEST SIGHTS FROM $5–$10

1. The Little White House was where Harry and Bess Truman vacationed in winter eleven times during his presidency, beginning in 1946. Recently restored to the 1940s period with original furniture, the museum offers a guided tour and video. Open daily. *111 Front Street.*

2. The Ernest Hemingway Home and Museum, where the author lived with his second wife Pauline from 1931 to 1940, is a National Historic Landmark. Self-guided or escorted tours are available through the house and the gardens, where a number of feral six-toed cats wander at will. Open daily. *907 Whitehead Street.*

3. At the Key West Aquarium you can hand-feed sharks, pet a barracuda or reach into a touch tank to feel sea creatures. The ticket is good for several days if you want to return. Open daily. *1 Whitehead Street.*

"AND THEN I WROTE..."

Key West claims eight Pulitzer Prize winners among its residents, and, according to a knowledgeable local, more than 100 published authors live there at present.

Writer John dos Passos passed through here in the 1920s, looked around and recommended it to fellow writer Ernest Hemingway, who arrived in 1928, finished off *A Farewell to Arms* in a rented house on Summer Street in 1929, then bought a fine house on Whitehead Street in 1931.

To Have and Have Not is what Hemingway called his Key West novel, published in 1937. One of the have-nots was Harry Morgan, a local fishing charter-boat operator reduced to rumrunning and smuggling Chinese immigrants into the United States. The author, however, was clearly one of the "haves" with a wealthy wife, a limestone mansion, the first swimming pool in Key West and a 40-foot boat named *Pilar.*

Somewhere in the mid-1930s, while still married to his second wife, Hemingway spotted journalist Martha Gelhorn sitting on a barstool at Sloppy Joe's. She would become his third wife in a short and tumultuous marriage after he divorced Pauline in 1940 and left Key West for good.

"You'll like Key West," Papa is reported to have written to a friend two decades later. "It's the St.-Tropez of the poor."

THREE GOOD WAYS TO GET AROUND KEY WEST

1. Rent a bicycle or moped from one of the shops along Truman Avenue, especially if you're traveling in a motorhome without a tow vehicle. That way you can leave the rig plugged in.

2. Hop aboard an Old Town Trolley or Conch Tour Train (the tickets are sold in Mallory Square or aboard the vehicles). These open-air trams zigzag back and forth across town for 90 minutes while a friendly, folksy driver fills you in with yarns, anecdotes and an over-generous collection of corny jokes.

3. Hail a pedicab and let a well-tanned and shapely young thing pedal you around. Coconut Cabs is one company name.

PART THREE: THE FURTHER ADVENTURES OF KEY WEIRD

A sidewalk chalk drawing of one of Key West's most famous citizens

Key West may sometimes be referred to as "Key Weird" by its detractors, but it's certainly a town that knows how to party.

For Hemingway Days in July, people dress as Hemingway characters, compete in contests for Hemingway look-alikes and write-alikes, and do a lot of drinking.

April's Conch Republic Days celebrate the time not long ago (April, 1982) when the Border Patrol put up road blocks on route 1 to look for drugs and illegal aliens. Tourists took one look and turned back, and the town's income fell off considerably. So, perhaps remembering when they declared bankruptcy back in 1934, Key West proclaimed itself the Conch Republic and seceded from the United States, then applied for foreign aid. This week-long celebration usually involves silliness such as a bed race and a lot of drinking.

Tennessee Williams' birthday, March 25, is often an occasion for celebrating, as is the weekly "Doris Day Night" at a local gay bar, and, of course, every day at sunset, when there's a lot of drinking.

We're fond of the laundromat at the corner of Margaret and Truman Streets in Key West, named, logically enough, the Margaret-Truman Drop-off Launderette.

The big brick building down by the dock, so a Conch Tour guide told us, was designed in 1890 as a government office building, and the engineer had almost completed it when he died. A second engineer was sent in from up north and made them start all over again, digging a huge basement for the oil-fired heating equipment, adding chimneys and making the roofs steep enough "so the snow could slide off."

Designer-icon Calvin Klein is said to have paid a million dollars for a house locals call the Bird Cage or Octagon House at *712 Eaton Street*, only one of a group of turn-of-the-century Bahamian-style wooden mansions on that street. Ship's carpenters were often the builders, and salvaged wood from wrecked ships was sometimes worked into the structures.

A restaurant called Pigeonhouse Patio recalls the original use of its building, to raise homing pigeons that could be sent out with boats so if the crew got into trouble at sea, the captain could release the bird and help could be sent.

The city's sizeable gay population has done more than anyone in restoring the old Conch houses, setting up a flourishing bed-and-breakfast community and generally glamourizing the mainstream in this laid-back, live-and-let-live community.

But some of the high hilarity of the 1980s has softened somewhat in the 1990s, in some cases to the detriment of the lounge scene. The outrageous La Te Da (local nickname of the La Terraza de Marti) and its Sunday afternoon tea dances have toned down the campiness, with no more owner-and-dog look-alike contests like the one described by Joy Williams in her excellent guidebook *The Florida Keys*—"The Look-Alike trophy went to Frank Cicalese and his Chihuahua Sam. They appeared as identical, perfectly pink Easter bunnies in identical bunny suits, slippers and hats carrying matching Easter Baskets. Both wore sunglasses."

INSIDER TIP:

Cruise ships that call at Key West, an increasingly popular port, are encouraged to sail away at least 45 minutes before sunset so their bulky lines don't block the view from Mallory Pier.

MIRACLE OF THE KEYS

Where Card Sound Road runs into route 905 at North Key Largo, you'll find the Crocodile Lake National Wildlife Refuge, some 12,000 acres of hammock and mangrove wetlands that is home to six endangered species, including the alligator, the wood rat and the cotton mouse.

It could also be called the modern-day miracle of the Keys when it replaced a proposed 2800-unit "faux Mediterranean" housing development called Port Bougainville, which would have featured man-made lakes and canals and drive-in boat garages. Despite a series of articles in the *Miami Herald* showing a pattern of political chicanery and conflicts of interest by Monroe County officials, the project continued to plow ahead.

The proposed site was atop the most fragile ecosystem in south Florida, and the resulting "big pollution dump," as ardent environmentalist Captain Ed Davidson called it, would have ruined the living coral reefs in Everglades National Park, John Pennekamp Coral Reef State Park and Biscayne National Underwater Park (See "10 Watery Wonders" earlier in this chapter.)

It would be nice to say the miracle happened solely because of the relentless battles of Captain Davidson, who operates the sightseeing boats at Biscayne National Underwater Park. But even his determined fight, which included a lawsuit he filed as president of the Florida Keys Audubon Society under the Endangered Species Act, only caused nuisance and delays. The project buckled under its own weight, due partly to the delays, and the developers went bankrupt. The property was ultimately purchased by the state of Florida, the Nature Conservancy and the U.S. Fish and Wildlife Service.

Seaplanes are a common form of transportation in the Florida Keys.

10 SPECIAL SPLURGES

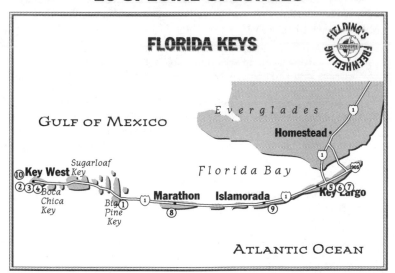

1. Book a day or two at the most laid-back and romantic, not to mention the most expensive, resort in the Keys, **Little Palm Island**, reached by launch from Little Torch Key at MM 28.5 by guests whose reservations are in the computer. Snorkeling, bonefishing, sunset sailing and fine dining are some of the popular activities. At

night you snuggle down in South Pacific-style ersatz grass huts that miraculously conceal a Jacuzzi tub, minibar and queen-sized bed. Non-resident guests may reserve for lunch or dinner. ☎ *(800) 3-GET-LOST.*

2.   In Key West's varied dining scene, most visitors regard **Louie's Backyard** as the obligatory dinner out. But we like lunch better, sitting at outdoor tables with a grand view of sailboats gliding past. A warm fried-chicken salad (spears of chicken atop greens) is a house special, and fresh grilled fish are accompanied by Cuban black beans, fried plantains and lime wedges. Reserve well ahead at this popular spot, ☎ *(305) 294-1061.* Musician Jimmy Buffet used to eat here when he lived in the big white house next door.

3.   Shell out for a lazy open-air tour of Key West aboard the colorful **Conch Train** or the **Old Town Trolley,** leaving from Mallory Square with 90 minutes of corny, good-natured jokes aimed at the over-50 cruise ship daytrippers and good views of 60 or so must-see spots around town.

4.   Fly high in the sky with **Vintage Air Tours** and their "Champagne Aerial Sunset Adventures" out of Key West International Airport ($41 per person). The vintage DC-3s (owned by Virgin Atlantic wunderkind Richard Branson) show off the world-class sunset from the air while passengers sip some bubbly. It goes up, up and away Wednesdays, Fridays, Saturdays and Sundays, $41 a person. ☎ *(305) 292-1323.*

5.   **The Amoray Diver**, a motorized catamaran from Key Largo's Amoray Dive Resort, can take 49 snorkelers or 34 scuba divers out to the Key Largo National Marine Sanctuary for some coral reef viewing.

6.   **Snuba Tours**, a combination of diving and snorkeling in which the air source is in a surface raft and the diver goes only 20 feet down, offers underwater sightseeing at John Pennecamp Coral Reef State Park and Key Largo National Marine Sanctuary. No dive certification is necessary. Tours ($35 to $70) are 45 minutes to a half-day. Call them in Key Largo at ☎ *(305) 451-6391.*

7.   Head out into international waters for a little gaming aboard the 150-passenger casino boat ***Pair-a-Dice*** from Key Largo's Holiday Harbor Marina. Four-hour mid-day sailings are from 11 a.m. to 3 p.m. for early birds; night owls can book a 6:30 p.m. to 11 p.m. cruise. The midday sailings are $12 a head plus a $12 port tax and include lunch, while evening cruises go for $20 a person plus $12 port tax and include dinner. Both feature live entertainment in addition to the ship's slot machines and blackjack, craps and poker tables. In deference to the boat's 92-foot length there are also miniroulette wheels and minibaccarat tables. For information, ☎ *(800) 843-5397.*

8.   Take a night off from the RV to sleep in a lighthouse or aboard a houseboat (the kids will love it) at **Faro Blanco Marine Resort** in Marathon, built in the 1940s. Call ☎ *(800) 759-3276* for information.

9.   Drop by **Cheeca Lodge** in Islamorada if you want to splurge on a politically correct seafood meal. The ever-eco-aware lodge took all conch dishes off its menu a couple of years ago because taking the mollusks in U.S. waters is illegal; therefore all conch is imported from the Bahamas and is "neither indigenous nor fresh," says Chef Dawn Seiber, a native of the Keys. She serves Jamaican seafood soup instead of conch chowder and buys much of her fish and shellfish from seafood farms. Polish off a piece of passionfruit pie for dessert. Call for a reservation at ☎ *(800) 327-2888.*

Fort Jefferson from the air

10. Take a **seaplane down to Fort Jefferson**, in the Dry Tortugas 68 miles west of Key West, to see the remains of the 19th century brick fort that was the Civil War prison for Dr. Samuel Mudd, who reset John Wilkes Booth's leg, broken on his jump to the stage of Fords Theater after he assassinated Abraham Lincoln. Mudd was accused of conspiring in the crime, although it is generally believed he was innocent of any knowledge of it. He was released in 1867 after a heroic stint taking care of 270 men who came down with yellow fever in an epidemic at the isolated fort. While the visit itself is free, getting there costs around $125 a person for a half-day trip. Call Key West Seaplane Service, ☎ *(305) 294-6978.* You can look down into the clear water from the plane and see numerous shipwrecks below, as well as swimming sharks and rays. The fort itself is as eerie and haunted a place as you'll ever see under a hard blue sky and dazzling sunlight.

INSIDER TIP:

The pretty little manchineel tree growing on the beach with its green and yellow leaves makes an inviting canopy in a rain shower. But watch out–it literally drips a burning, acid-like poison from its leaves as the rain runs down them. Never touch its tiny apple-like fruit, its thick, milky sap, or its smooth gray trunk. Everything about it is poisonous.

WILDLIFE WATCH

There are several wildlife refuges in the Keys, each named for the species that inhabits it. The new Crocodile Lake National Wildlife Refuge on North Key Largo has the single largest population of alligators in the U.S., for example, with as many as 500 in residence. Alligators are the most obvious reptiles, and the one a casual visitor is most likely to see, if you are patient enough to watch a floating log in a murky pond to see if that bump on it has an eyeball.

Less frequently seen are the state's numerous nonpoisonous snakes, and the three poisonous ones. Most deadly is the dainty, pretty orange-and-black-banded coral snake, but as an old swamper told us once, "He's gonna have to chew on you a long time before you die." Keep your eye out for cottonmouth moccasins sunning on a stretch of boardwalk in a swampy area, or diamondback rattlesnakes in a palmetto patch or hammock.

The shyest of Florida's indigenous fauna is the manatee, a one-ton, plant-eating sea mammal that is also called sea cow. Legend has it early sailors thought these were mermaids, but anybody who made a mistake like that must have been away from women a long, long time. The biggest threat to the dwindling manatee population is the south Florida boater with his whirring propellers that tear into the mammal's tender flesh.

The reclusive and extraordinarily beautiful roseate spoonbill, although rarely seen, nests in spring. They were once virtually extinct because feather collectors killed them and sold their wings for hats and fans, not realizing the brilliant orange and rose feathers gradually fade when the bird dies. Neither did Audubon, apparently, who depicted the bird's foliage as pink. He commented that they were hard to kill and their flesh was oily and bad-tasting.

You'll have easier sightings of osprey, especially in spring, who usually nest atop utility poles (their nests are big and klutzy-looking), and white egrets, who stalk haughtily in marshes and ponds. We spotted several from the wooden walkways in Everglades National Park. Check in at the Royal Palm Visitor Center; a campground without hookups is nearby. A number of walking trails, most of them over boardwalk, take you into the swamp.

At Big Pine Key, delicate little 30-inch Key deer, like miniature white-tailed deer, roam in the National Key Deer Refuge; go early in the morning or just before dusk for the best chance of sighting them. There are only about 300 left.

Also on this key is the Great White Heron National Wildlife Refuge. These big, graceful birds are among the most beautiful of all sea birds. Freshwater ponds on the key have led some geologists to suggest it may once have been part of the Appalachian Mountain range.

As for wasting away in Margaritaville, it's easy enough to do at singer Jimmy Buffet's popular eatery and nightspot, where you'll hear you-know-what played frequently if not incessantly. If you want something more down to earth, check out the Caribbean Club in Key Largo, the only local location that was actually shot for the eponymous movie. But don't expect yuppies and Bogart/Bacall types; it's more of a redneck-and-biker bar.

Kokomo in Islamorada is a South Pacific tiki hut where lithe people in bathing suits dance on the sand between rum drinks.

Hemingway's favorite bar in Key West, as everybody knows, was called Sloppy Joe's, and you can't miss a large Duval Street bar with neon signs screaming the name. When Hemingway drank there, however, Sloppy Joe's was down the street at the present site of Captain Tony's Saloon, which used to be owned by Tony Tarracino, a former and erstwhile Key West mayoral candidate who is still sometimes re-elected. Late one night back in 1937, Sloppy Joe Russell and his barflies moved the bar furniture from the old building over to the new building to protest a $1 raise in the rent on the former.

10 OFF-THE-WALL ATTRACTIONS

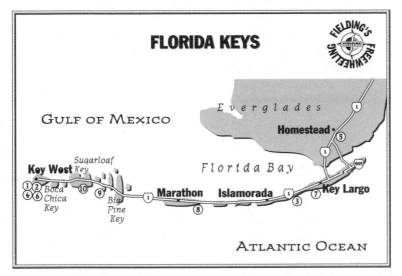

1. Sunset at Key West's Mallory Square is a nightly happening in the sixties sense, with wandering fire eaters, jugglers, mimes, contortionists, t-shirt sellers, fortune-tellers and a bicycling woman selling brownies with the call, "Here come the fudge!"

Mallory Square is where the world meets to see spectacular sunsets.

2. At the Key West Cemetery, seek out especially the stones of B.P. Roberts, 1929-1979, engraved "I Told You I Was Sick" (at the end of Seventh Street); another that says, "A Devoted Fan of Singer Julio Iglesias"; the grave of Joseph "Sloppy Joe" Russell, Hemingway's favorite bartender, who died on a 1941 fishing trip with the author; and the famous "bound woman" on the grave of Archibald John Sheldon Yates (at the intersection of Angela and Grinnel). Most are stone vaults raised above the impenetrable coral base and the high water table.

3. If you like to hang out in crowds with people who swap fishing stories and drink a lot of beer, Holiday Isle at MM 84 on appropriately named Windley Key is mobbed on winter weekends. If you don't, consider yourself warned.

4. The longest street in the world, Key West conchs claim, is Duval, because it stretches from the Gulf of Mexico to the Atlantic Ocean, a distance of about a mile-and-a-half. Late at night the pub-lined street is also the setting for "the Duval crawl."

5. Coral Castle in Homestead, on your way to the Keys, is a living testimony to "the magic and power of love." It seems a heartsick Latvian named Ed Leedskalnin was jilted by the 16-year-old girl he loved and so made his way to south Florida, where he spent the next 25 years carving 1100 tons of coral into pieces of furniture and other unwieldy artifacts, including a table shaped like the state of Florida, all in memory of her. What he did for love, or rather how he did it, is still a mystery, since he weighed only 97 pounds and did not use any heavy machinery to move the blocks of coral. (One lunatic-fringe tome suggests he had the help of aliens from flying saucers.) When the neighbors came around to look, he stopped working until they left. He died of starvation, it's said, in 1951, with thousands of dollars hidden around the coral house. There's a Psychic Fair held on the grounds on the fourth Saturday of every month.

6. Take in some table-rapping or a message from your late great-aunt Tess in Key West's new Spirit Theatre. A 19th-century parlor at *802 White Street* is the location for Victorian-era "spirit seances." Attendance is limited to 15, at least from the world of the living, and one or more seances is scheduled each evening. Call Joseph Baer at ☎ *(305) 296-0442* for details.

7. The funky Caribbean Club at Key Largo's MM 104 is strict about an "Absolutely No Dogs Allowed" rule since the day a patron had brought in his prize pit bull, along with her litter of puppies, to show them off in the bar. While he drank, the dogs went for a swim, and one frightened puppy climbed on his mother's back and wouldn't let go, causing the bitch to drown. The patron, unable to revive his valuable pit bull, kicked the guilty puppy to death in a rage. The club owner decided to 86 all dogs from that day to this.

8. Flipper's grave (yes, that Flipper, whose real name was Mitzi) and a 30-foot high monument to a mother and baby dolphin is at MM 59. The Dolphin Research Center (see "10 Watery Wonders") is also here on Grassy Key.

9. Fat Albert the spying balloon bobs around 2000 feet above Cudjoe Key (when he isn't blown off his tether) watching for drug dealers in small planes and boats heading across the Florida straits. His avoirdupois is made up of millions of bucks of electronic surveillance gear.

10. The Perky Bat Tower on Sugarloaf Key is not about pert nocturnal flying mammals but rather an earnest effort to lure same to devour the mosquitoes that were the scourge of the area. Built in 1929 by an eager real estate promoter named R. C. Perky, the tower was supposed to bring in bats so Perky's resort would be bug-free. Perky, his casino, cabins and fishing resort are long-gone, but the bat tower still stands. And the mosquitoes are still flying.

STRETCHING OUT YOUR VACATION

If you wanted to hang around Key West for the season—and a lot of people do—you could spend some time creatively by signing up for adult courses in Spanish, birdwatching or swamp ecology at the Florida Keys Community

College. Or take lessons in quilting, watercolors, or puppet theater, or learn pruning and transplanting at the garden club.

Or you could extend your RV trip into a full Florida tour, spending the winter covering the state (although you should bear in mind that from Orlando north it can be chilly in midwinter).

HITTING THE HIGHLIGHTS

For most freewheelers, it's an easy matter to drive all the way down from Miami to Key West and back in one day, but that would defeat the best reasons for coming—a little sightseeing, a little fishing, a little beach camping, and fresh seafood (maybe some you caught yourself) for dinner.

Allow a half-day for snorkeling at one of the national or state parks. Take a detour into Everglades National Park via route 9336 from Homestead and walk the boardwalk trails with binoculars to catch sight of herons, egrets, white ibis, alligators. Bicycle around Key West for a day and catch the highlights.

Who knows, you still might have time left over to take the kids to Disney World on the way back home.

INSIDER TIP:

Key limes, which in this country grow only in the Florida Keys, are not green but yellow fruits the size of a golf ball, with green speckles. Ergo, the filling in a genuine Key lime pie is also yellow, not green. The first Key lime pie is thought to have been whipped up in the kitchen of the Curry Mansion in Key West, now a popular Caroline Street bed-and-breakfast.

10 GREAT TAKEOUT (OR EAT-IN) TREATS

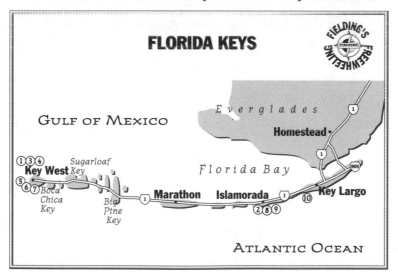

1. The **cheeseburgers** at Jimmy Buffet's Margaritaville restaurant in Key West are almost as famous as the song of the same name; most customers order Margaritas as well.

2. The **Key lime pie** at Manny and Isa's Kitchen in Islamorada can be purchased by the slice or the pie to eat in or take out. They grow the Key limes out back. If it's mealtime, sample their **Cuban black bean soup or conch fritters** too.

3. Tidbit tips: Try the deep-fried, **cheese-stuffed jalapeño peppers** at Kelly's Caribbean Bar, Grill and Brewery on Whitehead and Caroline, just off Duval, then the **fresh coconut ice cream** from Flamingo Crossing, both in Key West.

4. The Half-Shell Raw Bar on Margaret Street is a longtime local favorite with paper plates, plastic forks and a big turnover of tables around mealtime. They sell **shrimp** from the local fleet, as well as **clams and oysters** on the half-shell and a tasty conch chowder. The cracked conch—breaded and fried **conch steak**—is yummy.

5. The *Garrison Bite*, a houseboat on the Garrison Bight Marina in Key West, has good **conch fritters** and optimum sunset-viewing.

6. The 5 Brothers Grocery in Key West at the corner of Southard and Grinnell for **Cuban sandwiches** to take out or hot, **deep-fried cornmeal bollitos**. For good **fried fish sandwiches**, a Key West tradition, try Danny's Fish Market at *627 Duval Street*.

7. Key West street vendors proffer **conch fritters, Cuban coffee, hot dogs, piña coladas and dolphin sandwiches** (no, not Flipper, but the fish Hawaiians call mahi mahi).

8. Years ago, the Green Turtle Inn at Islamorada was the first (and last) place we ever knowingly ate **alligator**, and, yes, it does taste sort of like chicken. These days they serve farm-raised **turtle steaks and chowders**, as well as their own canned **conch chowder**, politically correct turtle soup—they use North Florida river turtles—and Key lime pie filling to go if you want to stock up the RV. It's old-fashioned, good-natured, eclectic and eccentric, as well as usually crowded, with only a faint whiff of tourist trap. At MM 81.

9. Craig's Restaurant promises "the world's best fish sandwiches" if you want a quick and casual lunch. At MM 90.5.

10. Try The Hideout at MM 103 for a **fish and grits** breakfast with biscuits on the side, served all morning long and into the early afternoon.

ON THE CHEAP: TRIMMING COSTS ON THE ROAD

The most expensive item for freewheeling RVers in the Florida Keys is a hookup site at a private campground, so if money is tight, head instead for the state parks and Everglades National Park for an overnight or two, easiest to occupy if you arrive early in the day on a weekday when public schools are in session.

Restaurant portions are very generous all over south Florida, so if you're not starving, plan to split some servings, especially the main dish. Pick up a walk-around lunch or snack from the Cuban sandwich or conch-fritter vendors.

While Key West has a number of entertaining options, we find some of the attractions overpriced. The Hemingway House is almost as interesting from the outside as it is inside, and considerably cheaper. Unless you're a real Hemingway fan or a six-toed cat freak, we suggest you stop, take a picture, then walk on by.

The Conch Train and Trolley tours are cute, ideal for day trippers that come off the cruise ships, but you can cover the same territory by bicycle (rentals are easy to find if you're not carrying your own on the RV) or even on foot with some free walking tour brochures from the tourist information office in Mallory Square. Since the open-air trolleys use amplified narration, you could tag along behind one on your bike and hear the same information the cruisers pay $15 for.

We've detailed some under-$5 attractions in Key West. See "Five Things To Do in Key West for $5 Or Less."

FYI

Florida Keys information—☎ *(800) FLA-KEYS* in U.S., *(800) GO-TO-KEYS* in Canada

Florida State Parks—For a free state parks guidebook, ☎ *(904) 488-9872*

Florida Campground Association—☎ *(904) 656-8878*

Florida Attractions Association—☎ *(904) 222-2885*

Fishing information—☎ *(904) 488-1690*

Saltwater fishing—☎ *(904) 488-7326*

Watersports: Diving—☎ *(904) 222-6000*

Canoeing—☎ *(813) 494-1215*

Boat regulations—☎ *(904) 488-1195*

Historical sites—☎ *(904) 487-2333*

Florida Black Heritage Trail booklet—☎ *(904) 487-2333*

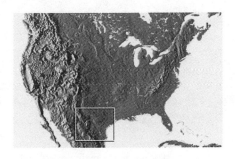

ALONG THE RIO GRANDE

The Rio Grande in Big Bend National Park

> *"The sun has riz, the sun has set,*
> *And here we is, in Texas yet!"*

19th century doggerel

Once inhabited by giant flying reptiles with 50-foot wingspans, Texas has more miles of inland lake and stream water than Minnesota, a million official road signs and markers on its highways, and, as its tourism publications frequently point out, a ranch, a military base and two counties bigger than certain New England states.

The bottom half of Texas is where rock'n roll got sent out all over the universe by Wolfman Jack in the 1950s, broadcasting from a Del Rio radio station's 500,000-watt "pirate" transmitter located across the river in Mexico. The Del Rio station was built in the 1930s by "Doctor" John R. Brinkley to promote his famous goat gland surgery to restore virility.

It's where Pancho Villa and Zsa Zsa Gabor once slept (but not at the same time) in El Paso's Paso del Norte Hotel, where nachos were invented by Ignacio "Nacho" Anaya at the Victory Club restaurant in Piedras Negras and fajitas were first served at Ninfa's restaurant in Houston on July 13, 1973.

John Dillinger and his gang vacationed in the sleepy little west Texas town of Balmorhea in 1934, pretending to be "Oklahoma oil men." Locals were mystified by their pastimes, things like jumping on and off the running boards of moving cars, shooting at tin cans tossed in the air and lobbing an occasional hand grenade. Only after the well-publicized gunning down of Public Enemy Number One outside a Chicago movie house a few months later did the good citizens of Balmorhea realize who their big-spending visitors really were.

Southwest Texas is where camels were trained for combat, where Mexican revolutionary Antonio Zapata was beheaded, and where queenmakers Rex Holt and Richard Guy of GuyRex Associates in El Paso became famous for grooming a string of beauty-contest winners.

General Black Jack Pershing and his troops gathered in El Paso by the Rio Grande to march on Pancho Villa but after 11 months of searching, never managed to find him, overlooking in their haste, perhaps, the Paso del Norte Hotel.

Typical roadside trading post in the southwest

FREEWHEELING ALONG THE RIO GRANDE

The road that follows the Rio Grande twists and turns 940 miles from the Gulf of Mexico to El Paso, laying out the border between Texas and Mexico.

It was all well and good to use the Rio Grande as the border, except that the river kept changing its course. A 600-acre piece of land called the Chamizal in El Paso/Juarez was wrangled over for a hundred years until President John F. Kennedy and Mexico's Adolfo Lopes Mateos worked out a compromise. And one mission church, Nuestra Señora del Socorro, was moved back and forth between Mexico and Texas by flooding a number of times without ever shifting from its foundations.

In west Texas, you can whiz through more territory in an hour in your RV than stagecoaches and wagon trains could make in three days. It's an easy and interesting journey, so long as you avoid the broiling hot days of summer.

Texas is one of those states that likes RVers a lot. Not only do many of their state parks offer hookups, but at the information centers when you drive across the border, you can usually find racks of free booklets with lists of RV campgrounds, state parks, sanitary dump station locations and places that sell LP gas. The state also puts out a wealth of other free printed materials available at all visitor information centers.

INSIDER TIP:

Particularly in west Texas, where stretches between gas stations may be long, top off your tank whenever convenient. Never let the needle drop below half.

When to go. Winter is best, mild and usually sunny days that cool down to crisp nights. Late fall and early spring are also comfortable. Summer is extremely hot, humid in the east and bone-dry in the west, except in the cooler upper reaches of Big Bend, where roads are not suitable for large RVs or trailers, and in the Davis Mountains, where big rigs are able to maneuver.

What to take. Camera and film, binoculars, strong sunblock and sun hat, insect repellent, stout high-topped hiking boots if you plan to hike the Big Bend and other desert terrain, and an antacid if you intend to follow the chili trail.

What to wear. Casual and comfortable clothing is correct all over Texas except in its biggest eastern-oriented cities, which this tour excludes. If you plan to dine out in one of the splurge restaurants (See "Five Special Splurges"), you might take along a slightly dressier outfit, but it's not essential.

TEXAS TALK

Down island—the roadless part of Padre Island, where two-wheel-drive vehicles, especially RVs, can't go, and if they do, no tow trucks will come to pull them out for less than $500 or so

Whoopers—short for whooping cranes, the endangered species that winters in Aransas National Wildlife Refuge

Winter Texans—RVers from colder climates, many of whom spend winter in the Lower Rio Grande Valley

Texas strawberries—pickled jalapeño peppers held by the stem and eaten whole in one bite

Blue norther—a fast-moving cold front in fall or winter that can cause temperatures to drop 50 degrees Fahrenheit in half an hour

Tinajas—rock cavities that trap rainwater, a good place to look for game after a rainstorm in Big Bend

Texas ironwood—the mesquite tree, its wood used for barbecuing and smoking meats or making furniture, its long bean pods used for animal feed, flour, beer or wine

Texas turkeys—armadillos, used for food during hard times like the Depression, also sometimes used in chili but not legally unless the animal has died from natural causes or been hit by a car

Dry whiskey—peyote cactus, also called mescal, which contains a variety of psychoactive alkaloids; grows wild in Big Bend and is illegal to harvest or possess

Maverick—an unbranded cow, named for Sam Maverick, who refused to brand his cattle so he could claim any unbranded animal on the range

Tejas—a group of Indian tribes Texas was named for, regarded as friendly by the Spanish invaders until the Spanish wore out their welcome

11 CAMPGROUND OASES

1. **Padre Island National Seashore's Malaquite Beach Campground**, with 42 paved, parallel parking or back-in sites along the beach, is three-quarters of a mile south of the ranger station. Picnic tables, toilets, cold showers, sanitary dump. No hookups, no reservations. Weekend ranger programs and ranger-led beach walks.

2. **South Padre Island's Isla Blanca Park**, operated by Cameron County, is located on a one-mile white sand beach on the Gulf of Mexico with 98 full hookup sites, flush toilets, showers, and laundry, as well as bike trails, a marina, water park, swimming

pool and grocery store. There are some 375 RV spaces at the park with sewer connections but without water and electricity.

3. **Brazos Island State Park**, self-contained camping only on a beautiful undeveloped beach without facilities or piped water. A small spit of land south of South Padre Island called Boca Chica, reached via route 4 from Brownsville.

4. **Bentsen-Rio Grande State Park**, on the river southwest of Mission down route 2062, is a great camping spot for birders because of the variety of birds that frequent the campground itself—the loudmouth chachalacas, gorgeous green jays, and black-bellied whistling ducks. Reservations can be made 90 days in advance ☎ *(210) 585-1107.* Bring your own firewood and insect repellent. There are 77 full hookup sites and a sanitary dump station, picnic tables and barbecue pits.

5. **Fort Clark Springs RV Park** is a private park near Bracketville's Alamo Village Movie Location and historic old Fort Clark cavalry post, with 56 full hookups, cable TV, flush toilets, showers, laundry. Just off US 90 at route 674.

6. At **Amistad National Recreation Area**, a sprawling 85-mile-long man-made lake jointly owned by the U.S. and Mexico, two park campgrounds have a total of 31 sites suitable for RVs with chemical toilets and cooking grills but no piped water or hookups. Year-round fishing, some shotgun and bow-and-arrow hunting are permitted, as well as scuba diving in the lake; best visibility is in winter and early spring.

7. **Seminole Canyon State Historic Park** is the home of ancient Indian pictographs and paintings on canyon walls. Those in Fate Bell Shelter are believed to have been painted 5000 years ago; visitors can only enter the area with a ranger. Guided tours are offered year-round Wednesdays through Sundays at 10 a.m. and 3 p.m. The hike is moderately strenuous. Some 23 campsites with water and electric hookups

and sanitary dumps on the premises are available, as well as hiking and mountain bike trails. Reservations are advised, especially during March through June. ☎ *(915) 292-4464* at least four weeks in advance. It's located near Comstock, 30 miles northwest of Del Rio on US 90.

8. **Rio Grande Village Campground** in Big Bend National Park is 20 miles southeast of the park's Panther Junction headquarters on the river. Adjacent to the 100 tree-shaded sites without hookups is a general store and a large parking lot that is called Rio Grande Village Trailer Park. Stay here if hookups are essential. Otherwise the campground is a much nicer place, with sites laid out in a circle like pioneer wagon trains. Hiking trails set out from here, and there are flush toilets, pay showers and a sanitary dump station.

9. **Lajitas on the Rio Grande RV Park**, part of the old western town complex that includes a resort and golf course, as well as a beer-drinking goat (see "10 Off-the-Wall Attractions"), has 77 full hookups, flush toilets, showers and laundry. ☎ *(915) 424-3471.*

10. **Davis Mountains State Park** on route 118 west of the town of Fort Davis has 27 full hookups, 47 with electricity and 88 with water. Spacious and well laid out, most are shaded by oak trees. Flush toilets, showers, sanitary dump station, playground. You may be visited in late afternoon by a family of mule deer or see a resident long-horn herd. When you camp here, imagine the families in covered wagons that used to stay here, an oasis in the middle of vast expanses of desert. The weather is comfortable for camping year-round. Reservations: ☎ *(915) 426-3337.* The Fort Davis National Historic Site nearby has been beautifully restored and offers a living history program in summer.

11. **Hueco Tanks State Historical Park**, 32 miles east of El Paso on road 2775 just north of US 62/180, has 17 campsites with water and electric hookups and a sanitary dump station on the premises. Flush toilets, showers, pond and playground. Advance reservations, ☎ *(915) 857-1135.* The huecos, or natural rock basins to trap water, have aided travelers in this arid terrain for centuries, and many, from prehistoric hunters and gatherers to'49ers on their way to the California Gold Rush, repaid the hospitality with primitive rock drawings and initials. Ruins from a stage stop from the old Butterfield Overland Mail stagecoach have also been moved here. Rock climbing is a major activity except during summer, when the rocks are too hot to handle.

INSIDER TIP:

Many Texas state park campgrounds have RV hookups and take advance reservations. Seniors, too, get free park entrance and a price break on camping if they apply for a special state park windshield sticker at any Texas state park.

THE COMANCHE MOON

Old-timers on both sides of the Rio Grande call the first full moon of autumn the Comanche moon, because that was when bands of Comanches would go out on raids into northern Mexico. They rode through Big Bend on what came to be called the Comanche War Trail, burning, pillaging, taking anything they could use or sell, including hostages. Thanks to the inadvertent gift of horses from the Spanish, they became perhaps the greatest horsemen the world will ever see.

The only way the U.S. Army could figure out how to get rid of the Comanches was to decimate the tribe's basic food supply, so they called in the buffalo hunters. One man could kill a thousand or more buffalo in three months. He was paid well for his skills.

SIX SPECIAL SIDE TRIPS

EAST TEXAS

1. **The King Ranch** in Kingsville, southwest of Corpus Christi, covers more than 825,000 acres and is three times bigger than the state of Rhode Island. It developed the Santa Gertrudis cattle breed. The Visitor Center here showcases a small museum and conducts bus tours around the ranch daily. Open between 10 a.m. and 3 p.m. Monday through Saturday, 1 to 5 p.m. on Sunday. ☎ *(512) 592 8055.*

2. See the rare whooping cranes at **Aransas Wildlife Refuge**. The flock which winters here has grown from only 18 in 1937, when the refuge was established, to some 140 today. The endangered five-foot-tall birds winter here. Local boats take you out from Rockport Harbor to see them, weather permitting, at around $25 a person. The season runs from late November through March. ☎ *(800) 782-BIRD, (800) 338-4551,* or *(800) 245-9324* for reservations for a boat tour.

3. The **Turtle Lady of South Padre Island**, Ila Loetscher, rescues and tends injured Ridley sea turtles in her home, which she has turned into a virtual turtle hospital. Visitors pay a modest donation to "Meet the Turtles" programs where she talks about and shows some of her turtles Tuesday and Saturday mornings at 9 a.m. in summer, 10 a.m. in winter. At *5805 Gulf Blvd.*

4.   Visit the no-bars **Gladys Porter Zoo** at *Ringgold and Sixth Streets in Brownsville*, where endangered species from all over the world make up the exotic population. Ranked as one of the top ten American zoos, it is open daily.

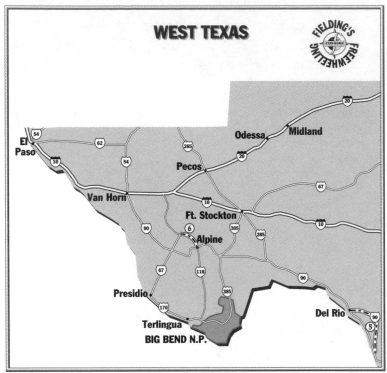

5.   Why fight traffic to get to San Antonio's Alamo when you could visit **John Wayne's Alamo**, the one built near Bracketville for his 1960 movie of the same name? The kids will like the imitation better, because there are daily shootouts staged during summer. The village has 28 buildings, including a John Wayne Museum. Parts of the TV miniseries *Lonesome Dove* were also shot here. You'll find it seven miles north of town on route 674. Open daily except Christmas week.

6.   Head'em off at the canyon like the cavalry tried with the Apaches. **Fort Davis National Historic Site** is an excellent recreation of a 19th century fort in a spectacular box canyon setting. It was home of the U.S. Ninth Cavalry "Buffalo Soldiers," African American troops nicknamed that by the Apaches for their courage and their dark curly hair. The fort presents a living history program in summer with costumed inhabitants, as well as Black History events in February. Most evocative of all if you're standing on the empty parade ground is the recording they play at regular intervals of bugle calls and the sound of calvary troops with jingling spurs and hoofbeats. Open daily, the fort has a museum and gift shop on the premises. In the Davis Mountains south of I-10 on route 17.

INSIDER TIP:

Avoid Padre Island, Corpus Christi and Port Aransas during "spring break" days in late March and early April unless you like to be inundated with rowdy crowds of party-hearty college students.

PADRE ISLAND NATIONAL SEASHORE

Tenacious wildflowers cling to the sand dunes, sea grasses blow in the gusty winds from the gulf, and collector-quality seashells sweep in with each tide— along with an unavoidable assortment of litter from Gulf of Mexico shipping.

In spite of, or perhaps because of, rumors of so many gold-laden Spanish ships running aground and sinking off Padre Island, the use of metal detectors or any other treasure-hunting devices is banned.

The only entrance to the paved road to the park is at North Padre Island outside Corpus Christi, and the paving ends in the parking lot of the Malaquite Visitor Center. The vast center of the island is accessible only to hikers and four-wheel drive vehicles. No driving or camping is permitted on the sand dunes or in the sea grass.

A standard automobile may be driven five miles past the end of the paved road in the park on the beach when conditions allow, but only four-wheel drive vehicles are permitted past the Milepost 5 sign.

RVers without a tow vehicle would be wise to leave the rig in the park parking lot and set out down the beach on foot. Stories abound of over-ambitious drivers miring down in the sand, and the park's newspaper cautions, "There are no services or means to contact anyone for help should you need it. The park service does not monitor CB radio, nor will it attempt to tow vehicles. Wreckers, when they can be induced to travel down island, cost hundreds of dollars."

Driving a vehicle of any sort is not permitted on the dunes, mud flats or grasslands.

The seashore has an ongoing program to protect endangered sea turtle species found in the Gulf of Mexico—the Kemp's Ridley, loggerhead, hawksbill, leatherback and green. If you see a sea turtle alive or dead along the beach, notify a park ranger of its location rather than approaching the turtle itself.

Bird-watching is exceptionally good here, with more than 350 species of seasonal and year-round residents.

For park information, call ☎ *(512) 949-8068.* Recorded messages about weather, tides, beach condition and fishing information can be gotten from ☎ *(512) 949-8175.*

South Padre Island, entered only from Port Isabel in the Brownsville area, has 34 miles of broad sandy beaches, the southernmost five miles adjacent to numerous low-and high-rise hotels, condominium towers and restaurants. The road, Park 100, is paved for 15 miles but the northern end has remained mostly undeveloped.

South Padre Island also has, according to local legend, some $62,000 worth of 19th-century gold coins and jewelry buried there by John Singer of the sewing machine family when the Civil War broke out. He and his wife, who lived in a driftwood house on the island about 25 miles north of the southern end, buried their valuables in the sand dunes, but when they came back after the war, the dunes had shifted and the gold was never found.

FIVE SPECIAL SPLURGES

WEST TEXAS

1. Allow some time and/or money for the little town of Marathon, gateway to Big
    Bend. The antique shops here have cornered the market on Georgia O'Keeffe-type
    cow skulls, and the vintage Gage Hotel from 1927 has been gentrified only to the
    extent it had to be, if you ignore the motel-like annex with pool next door. In early
    March the town hosts the Texas Cowboy Poetry Gathering. Marathon was named
    by a retired sea captain who said it reminded him of Marathon, Greece. (Funny, it
    doesn't remind us of Marathon, Greece.)

2. Check out the beautifully restored La Borde House in Rio Grande City, west of
    McAllen on US 83. Designed in France and built by a turn-of-the-century French
    merchant, the New Orleans-style mansion is now a sedate hotel and restaurant with
    a modern annex at the back. ☎ *(210) 487-5101* for reservations.

3. Drop into El Paso's elegant old Paso del Norte Hotel for a drink in the Dome Bar,
    the original lobby of the hotel, with its Tiffany stained-glass dome ceiling and mar-
    ble walls and floor. Who knows, you may glimpse Zsa Zsa Gabor.

4. Chow down on a steak at Cattleman's Steakhouse at Indian Cliffs Ranch, 33 miles
    southwest of El Paso to the I-10 Fabens exit, then north 5 miles on route 793.
    Open daily, the restaurant serves huge steaks that *People* magazine called the best
    in the country, plus side orders from ranch beans to homemade bread. ☎ *(915)*

544-3200 for a reservation. Open Monday through Saturday 4 to 9 p.m., Sundays noon to 9. Your dinner reservation also gives free admission to the ranch's western-style attractions, which kids particularly enjoy.

6. Grab yourself some cowboy garb, a Stetson, some hand-tooled boots or a saddle. (See "I See By Your Outfit That You Are A Cowboy.")

INSIDER TIP:

Each of Texas' 254 counties rules individually on alcohol sales, if, when, what and how. Liquor stores are closed on Sundays and holidays throughout the state.

"I SEE BY YOUR OUTFIT THAT YOU ARE A COWBOY..."

Saddles:

King Ranch Running W saddles from the ranch's own saddle shop at the Ragland Building, 6th and Kleberg, in Kingsville.

Saddle blankets:

El Paso Saddleblanket Trading Post has handwoven saddle blankets and rugs in traditional southwestern designs.

Boots:

El Paso—Justin Outlet, *7100 Gateway East, I-10 at Hawkins;* Tony Lama, *7156 Gateway East just off I-10;* Lucchese Factory Outlet, *6601 Montana;* Boot Trader Ltd., *10787 Gateway West* for ready-made boots.

Raymondville (on route 77 near Harlingen)—Armando's Boot Company for fine custom-made boots.

Wrangler Cowboy Cut jeans:

El Paso—Morris Saddlery, *10949 East Burt.*

Custom-crafted, working-cowboy leather accessories, and bandana, hat, belt, belt buckle:

Alpine—Big Bend Saddlery, north of town on US 67.

Spurs:

Sims Spurs, made in Bandera, west of San Antonio on route 16, makes the Rolex of the spur world.

INSIDER TIP:

When trying on a ready-made Western boot, be sure the heel slips a bit when you walk. When the sole gets more flexible, the slippage will stop. If it doesn't slip, it's too tight and will give you blisters. The instep should be snug, the boot shank long enough to cover your arch fully, and the ball of the foot should fit into the widest part of the boot, not sit forward or back of it.

THE TEXAS RIVIERA

The balmy Gulf coast likes to call itself "the Texas Riviera," but don't expect to find "Life-styles of the Rich and Famous." There's more Bubba-and-barbecue than Bardot-and-bouillabaisse.

Corpus Christi's Jean Lafite and his pirates hung around the area in the early 19th century, and General Zachary Taylor and his troops grouped here to invade Mexico in 1846. The oldest house, built in 1848, is called the Centennial house and has foundations made of shellcrete, a cement made from oyster shells. The city's sculptured 14-foot-high seawall was built after a 1919 hurricane by Gutzon Borglum, who went on to create Mt. Rushmore. The handsome wall is broken up with stairs leading down to the beach and opening up the view of the sea beyond.

Because of consistent moderate to high winds and expanses of open water, the Corpus Christi area has been named one of the world's 10 best windsurfing destinations. It's not a bad place to fly a kite, either. And Corpus Christi—locals call it Corpus—has become one of the top snowbird, or winter Texan, winter resorts.

If you take the free ferry over to Port Aransas on Mustang Island, watch for the bottle-nosed dolphins that usually swim along with the boat.

Brownsville was the site of the last shots fired in the Civil War, a full month after Lee surrendered to Grant at Appomattox. But then the city always had problems. It was taken over briefly in 1859 by Juan Cortina, either a Mexican bandit or a folk hero, depending on which side you were on, then occupied by the Confederates during the Civil War, after which it was taken by the Union, then the Confederates again. No wonder they hated to give it up.

INSIDER TIP:

Even if you decide to walk into a Mexican border town for a few hours, you'll still need to have proof of citizenship with you—a birth certificate, voter registration or passport. A driver's license is not considered adequate proof of citizenship.

TEN TERRIBLY TEXAS THINGS TO DO

1. **Go fishing**—dam fishing at Amistad Lake near Del Rio, salt water sport fishing at Corpus Christi, or join in the big daddy of them all, the Texas International Fishing Tournament, or TIFT, in Port Isabel in early August. For details, ☎ *(210) 943-8438.*

2. **River raft along the Rio Grande** on one-day trips into Santa Elena and Colorado Canyons in Big Bend National Park year-round when water flow permits. No previous river experience is necessary, but advance reservations are required. Contact **Far Flung Adventures in Terlingua,** ☎ *(915) 371-2489,* or **Big Bend River Tours in Lajitas,** ☎ *(915) 424-3219.*

3. **Pick up some fresh shrimp** in Aransas Pass, the shrimp capital of Texas. The seafood shacks around the Port Aransas ferry landing sometimes offer five pounds for $15 or $20. Another place to buy from the boats is Peoples Street T-Head at the marina in Corpus Christi. Also here: Landry's Seafood sells early-bird special shrimp and oysters with happy hour drinks starting at 4:30 p.m.

4. **Stare down a shark** at the new Texas State Aquarium in Corpus Christi, and see sting rays, barracuda, giant grouper and tropical fish swimming around an artificial reef created from an oil derrick. Open daily except Sunday mornings.

5. **Join a jalapeño-eating contest**—perhaps at the Brownsville-Matamoros Charro Days celebrations during Mardi Gras, when parades, carnivals and costume balls highlight the festivities, or hit the streets of Laredo, where the jalapeño-downing derby happens every February at George Washington's birthday party celebration. (Don't ask what chiles have to do with George's birthday; the town combined two

festivals into one.) The winner is crowned King Chile and may even get a spicy kiss from beauty queen Miss Jalapeño.

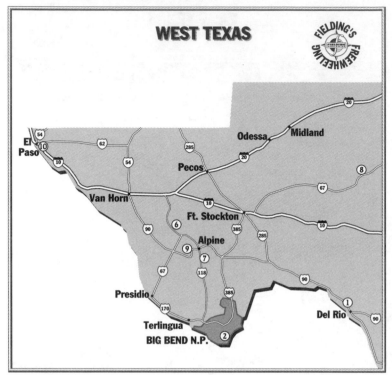

6. **See the stars at family "star parties"** on Tuesday and Saturday nights at Fort Davis's McDonald Observatory in the Davis Mountains. The entire family is welcome; no reservations required. Dress warmly and bring binoculars. Free tours are conducted daily at 2 p.m., and during summer months at 9:30 a.m. as well. Located on route 118 northwest of the town of Fort Davis. Call ☎ *(915) 426-3640* for information.

7. **Go prospecting** for red plume agate, precious opal and other minerals and gemstones at Woodward Ranch, 16 miles south of Alpine on route 118. They help you identify what you've got and charge per pound for the rocks you keep.

8. **Catch a game of cowboy polo**, sometimes featured at professional rodeos or at arenas in towns with National Cowboy Polo Association member teams. The season runs March through August, and players are required to wear jeans and western shirts and ride western saddle, never English. Headgear is optional; many play in cowboy hats. The cowboy polo field is smaller than in English polo, and the ball is made of rubber rather than wood. The audience is a bit rowdier too.

9. **Check out the rodeo classes** at Sul Ross State University in Alpine, considered the best school for "wannabe" professional saddle bronc riders, ropers, rodeo clowns, barrel racers and steer wrestlers. Call the school at ☎ *(915) 837-8059* for a visit and tour.

10. **Take the trolley to Mexico**. The El Paso-Juarez Trolley makes hourly trips in the daytime year-round from the Convention Center Plaza Terminal on Santa Fe Street; fare is around $8. Call for reservations, ☎ *(915) 544-0062*. In Juarez, the

trolley stops at Pueblito Mexicana, a shopping village for tourists; Sanborn's Department Store; Chihuahua Charlie's Bar & Grill; the colorful city market and other points of interest.

INSIDER TIP:

If you drive US 281 along the Rio Grande between Brownsville and Hidalgo, be extremely careful not to cross any bridges or you may find yourself in Mexico.

LOWER RIO GRANDE RIVER VALLEY

"Winter Texans" are RVers who are honorary citizens of Texas during the months when it gets cold in the north and midwest. So many visitors have flocked here lately that the Valley has had to add a new telephone area code.

At Los Ebaños near Mission, the last remaining hand-drawn ferry crosses the Rio Grande.

The town of Alice lights up for the entire month of December with more than 280,000 Christmas lights in a two-block area in the middle of town.

A rich river delta, the 100-mile strip along the river called "the Valley," has a 340-day growing season and a new crop to harvest every month. Citrus was planted more than a century ago, and the area's ruby red grapefruit is cherished by breakfast-eaters.

The town of McAllen, center of the winter Texan activity, was founded by a canny Scot who built a hotel here, then donated land for a railroad depot so the train would stop near his property.

Laredo is where Antonio Zapata, military leader of the self-proclaimed Republic of the Rio Grande, was captured and beheaded after 283 days of revolution against the government of Mexico's General Santa Anna. His head was displayed on a pole, which ended the dissension. Artifacts and history of that period are on display in the town's Museum of the Republic of Rio Grande.

INSIDER TIP:

If you want to venture into any of the Mexican border towns along the Rio Grande, park your RV on the U.S. side and walk across to go shopping or dining. This saves having to buy Mexican auto insurance.

10 OFF-THE-WALL ATTRACTIONS

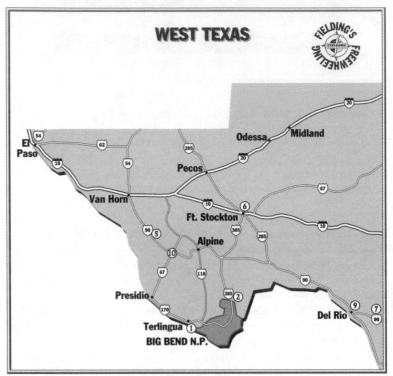

WEST TEXAS

1. Clay Henry Jr., **the beer-drinking goat** at Lajitas Trading Post in Lajitas, a funky combination of authentic old and ersatz new West Texas. The original goat, we are sure, has long since succumbed to cirrhosis of the liver, but judging from the dozing goats and empty beer cans we saw in the goat pen, he has worthy successors.

2. **Hallie's Hall of Fame Museum** near Boquillas is a tribute to 96-year-old Hallie Still-well, a genuine pioneer who arrived here at the age of 12, ran a ranch, taught school, carried a gun, and last time we passed through was still going strong. Call ahead to find out museum hours, ☎ *(915) 376-2244.*

3. **Replicas of the *Nina*, the *Pinta* and the *Santa Maria*** are moored in Corpus Christi, along with the authentic World War II aircraft carrier ***Lexington***, which is now a naval museum.

4. The **killer-bee crossing** in Hidalgo, on the border just west of Brownsville, commemorates the first crossing of the Africanized honeybees into the United States at this point in 1990. A frequently photographed $20,000, 20-foot fiberglass and steel model of the Africanized bee stands by a fire station on the town's Espersenza Avenue.

5. The town of **Valentine** gets very busy every February postmarking heart-shaped cards for romantics everywhere. You can drop off your cards anytime in person at the town's only post office, or mail them in before February 14 to Postmaster, Valentine, TX 79854.

6. The **world's largest roadrunner** is Paisano Pete in Fort Stockton, 11 feet tall and 22 feet long.

The world's largest roadrunner, Paisano Pete

7. **Crystal City** is the former home of the spinach capital of the U.S. (see "The Ozarks and Branson, Missouri, 10 Off-the-Wall Attractions" for the present capital). Don't tell any of the Texans they're passé; they still have their Popeye statue in place on the main street.

8. Laredo can claim not six but Seven Flags Over Texas, adding to the usual six—Spain, France, Mexico, the Republic of Texas, the Confederacy and the United States—its unique claim as the capital of the short-lived **Republic of the Rio Grande**. And Fredonia didn't start with the Marx Brothers in *Duck Soup;* the Republic of Fredonia was founded in east Texas by disgruntled Anglo settlers in the 1820s.

9. **Val Verde Winery** in Del Rio is the oldest licensed winery in Texas, founded by Italian immigrants, offering free tours and tastings. Their tawny port is a local favorite; they also produce a so-so Cabernet Sauvignon, a Johannisberg Riesling and a Rio Grande blush. Open Monday through Saturday, *100 Qualia Drive.*

10. The mysterious **"Marfa ghost lights"** have been seen almost nightly since the first reporting back in 1883. After it gets dark, drive west of town on route 90/87 for eight miles and you'll see the sign for the "official viewing area." Look southwest toward the mountains, and sooner or later you may or may not see a series of shimmering white balls of light in the distance. No one has ever been able to determine what causes them, but our favorite try was the expert who said they are flying bats with radioactive dust on their wings. Marfa is at the junction of US 67 and US 90, northwest of Big Bend.

INSIDER TIP:

We used to think tumbleweeds were quintessentially Texan. Turns out they're really Russian and were accidentally imported in 1873 when a few tumbleweed seeds arrived in a shipment of flax seed.

WILDLIFE WATCH

Birds are a primary reason to travel the Rio Grande Valley, especially in winter. The Santa Ana National Wildlife Refuge near the town of Alamo claims the national record for the most bird sightings in a single day, and famed naturalist Roger Tory Peterson ranks it in the top 12 birding areas in the U.S. To date, 390 species have been recorded on the 2088 acres. Between Thanksgiving and Easter, a tram travels through the refuge on Thursdays through Mondays, making birding easy. For the tram's schedule, ☎ *(210) 787-3079.*

Even endangered wild cats may be glimpsed by a diligent searcher in the Santa Ana National Wildlife Refuge. Four of the only five remaining wild cat species in the U.S. still live in the Valley—cougars, bobcats, ocelots and jaguarundi. Two other species, the jaguar and the margay cat, have disappeared during the last half-century.

Laguna Atascosa National Wildlife Refuge, east of Harlingen on the lagoon inside Padre Island, hosts as many as 394 bird species during the year, notably in fall and winter when Canada geese, snow geese and sandhill cranes can be seen, along with the great blue heron. On the mammal side, inhabitants include bats, armadillos, coyotes, foxes, mountain lions, ocelots, jaguarundis, bobcats, javalinas and white-tailed deer. Both driving and walking tours can be taken.

The rare and distinctive five-foot-tall whooping crane winters at Aransas National Wildlife Refuge north of Corpus Christi, but you may also see roseate spoonbills, ibis, egrets, herons, Canada geese and diving ducks. We came across dozens of alligators sunning themselves by the edges of the water. Indigenous armadillos and javalinas can also be seen there.

The whole Rio Grande River Valley is dotted with wildlife refuges that celebrate the unique bird, plant and animal life here. Bentsen-Rio Grande Valley State Park near Mission is a good place to see green jays, gold-fronted woodpeckers, white-winged doves, crested caracaras and the omnipresent chachalacas. At Audubon Sabal Palm Sanctuary south of Brownsville, you can walk through the last remaining grove of native Texas palm trees, Sabal texana. Take your binoculars (and some insect repellent) on the nature trail walk from the visitor center and maybe you'll glimpse a green jay, black-bellied whistling duck or hummingbirds.

Horse racing with pari-mutuel betting can be found at Sunland Park Race Track in El Paso, where the season runs from October through May, and Val Verde Downs in Del Rio, a nine-month season. In Nuevo Laredo, across the river from Laredo, off-track betting on live transmissions of horse and greyhound races is available at the Nuevo Laredo Turf Club, in walking distance of the international bridge.

If you prefer going to the dogs, Harlingen's Valley Greyhound Track seats 4000. Corpus Christi Greyhound Race Track usually includes discount tickets in a packet of coupons available at area visitor centers.

Bullfights are held seasonally across the river in the border towns of Mexico, particularly in Juarez, Piedras Negras and Reynosa.

As for nightlife, there's very little, unless you cross over the bridge into a Mexican city with a disco or nightclubs, such as Ciudad Acuña, across from Del Rio; Nuevo Laredo, across from Laredo; Ojinaga, across from Presidio; or Piedras Negras, across from Eagle Pass. The Cadillac Bar in Nuevo Laredo, famous (or notorious) since the 1920s, has changed its name to El Dorado but has kept pretty much the same restaurant menu. A Ramos gin fizz is the signature house tipple.

All along the Rio Grande, listen for the unique local music called variously *conjunto, norteño, tejano* or Tex-Mex, an odd mix of eastern European accordion, Mexican 12-string guitar, string bass and trap drums, with electric bass and guitar, keyboards and alto saxophone sometimes laid in. The sound is influenced by the polka, Mexican ballads, country/western and salsa. The border towns between Brownsville and Laredo are good places to hear it.

You'll find zydeco alive and well in Corpus Christi, where the Texas Jazz Festival takes place every year in early July. And the Tortuga Flats Oyster Bar in Port Aransas usually has some live rock 'n roll and rhythm and blues on weekends.

If all else fails, you could head for the goat compound in Lajitas and share a beer with Clay Henry Jr.

INSIDER TIP:

RVers headed for Big Bend National Park should fill up their gas tanks before leaving US 90 at Marathon or Marfa. There is a service station in the park but hours of operation are limited.

BIG BEND NATIONAL PARK

A huge but lightly visited park because of its relatively inaccessible location, Big Bend sprawls over 1250 miles of mountain, desert, river flood plains and narrow, rocky canyons bisected by a sometimes turbulent Rio Grande.

The local Indians say this is where the Great Spirit put all the leftover rocks after he created the earth. The Big Bend pterodactyl, with its 51-foot wing-span, the largest flying creature known, lived here 65 million years ago.

The scenery through Big Bend is wildly varied, from the vast Chihuahua desert to the rocky Chisos peaks and the river's flood-plain vegetation.

While the park is home to 1100 plant species, 75 mammal species, six amphibians and reptiles and 400 species of birds, you'll see mostly roadrunners and jackrabbits, creosote bush and ocotillo if you don't take a hike or spend some time searching them out. We photographed some exquisite beavertail cactus in vivid fuchsia bloom on a December visit. The dagger-tipped lechaguilla is a unique local plant you'll see frequently; it's a favored food for the javalina, or collared peccary, a wild pig found throughout the park. Endangered peregrine falcons are still found as well, protected during nesting season when rafting through the canyons is forbidden.

Watch out for scorpions and centipedes, both nocturnal, that might be waiting inside your shoes if you leave them outside overnight. Rattlesnakes and copperheads also inhabit the area, so wear high boots when hiking off the usual tourist trails. While mountain lions are rarely seen, there have been two attacks on people in recent years. If you encounter one, say park rangers, stay where you are, waving your arms, shouting and throwing rocks. Never run.

Teepees are roadside picnic spots in west Texas.

A breathtaking drive that should not be missed by travelers with smaller RVs is the route through the newly acquired Big Bend Ranch State Environmental Area along route 170 between Presidio and Study Butte. Some guidebooks discourage RVers from this route because of a one-mile-long 15 percent grade between Lajitas and Redford, although we had no problem driving it in our 27-foot motorhome. Roadside rests along the way sport individual teepee shelters housing picnic tables and grills.

Primitive hiking and backpacking, rafting and canoeing are available in the environmental area. For information on them, plus the occasional 10-hour bus tours offered through the park's outback, visit the Warnock Environmental Education Center in Lajitas.

There are two unusual industries that used to be in Big Bend—the second-largest cinnebar mine in the world, which produced liquid mercury until the veins ran out before World War II, and the unique candlelilla plant whose wax was used for candles, chewing gum and phonograph records until 1950. It's now illegal to gather it in the park.

INSIDER TIP:

While the Rio Grande Village Trailer Park in Big Bend has 25 paved, full hookup spaces that are booked on a first-come first-served basis inside the adjacent village store, it is basically a parking lot with electricity and plumbing. If you can go self-contained for a couple of days, consider staying instead at the nearby Rio Grande Village Campground (see "11 Campground Oases").

INSIDER TIP:

In Big Bend National Park, the seven-mile, dead-end Green Gulch Road to Chisos Basin is limited to RVs under 24 feet or 20-foot travel trailers pulled by trucks or autos. The same recommendation is made for the Ross Maxwell drive between the Sotol Overlook and Castolon. If you have questions about which area roads may be inaccessible for your RV, ask the rangers at the Panther Junction Visitor Center. A Road Guide booklet sold at the center is also helpful.

THE WILDS OF WEST TEXAS

"Not a stone, not a bit of rising ground, not a tree, not a shrub, nor anything to go by," Coronado is said to have sighed as he passed through west Texas en route to the seven cities of Cibolo, where he expected to find gold. He didn't realize what wonders he was missing en route.

One of our favorite west Texas towns is Marfa, site of the famous "Marfa ghost lights" (see "10 Off the Wall Attractions"). It was also the primary location for the 1956 blockbuster film *Giant*. The El Paisano Hotel, listed on the National Register of Historic Places, has a photo display in the lobby with photographs of stars James Dean, Elizabeth Taylor and Rock Hudson. The town was also the setting for the play and film, *Come Back to the Five and Dime Jimmy Dean, Jimmy Dean*, about the effect the filming of *Giant* had on the town. To complete the trio of trivia lore, Marfa also boasts the highest golf course in Texas, at a 4882-foot elevation.

Another of our favorites is Langtry, perhaps the most famous of all the windblown, tumbleweed-tossed, one-horse Texas towns. Here Judge Roy Bean ruled as "the law west of the Pecos" and indulged in his admiration of voluptuous British actress Lillie Langtry by naming his combination saloon and courtroom The Jersey Lilly (sic) and claiming he had also named the town for her. Railroad records of the time show it was actually named for a construction foreman named Langtry, so the wily Bean probably cashed in on the coincidence.

The interior of Judge Roy Bean's combination courtroom and bar in Langtry.

Although often invited to visit by the judge, who knew her only from photographs in the popular press, the actress never got to Langtry until a few months after the judge's death in 1904, when she was welcomed effusively by his son and other locals. A nicely-restored version of his Jersey Lilly saloon, where a defendant after a trial would be ordered to buy a round of drinks for the judge and jury, tells the whole story. Also here, a museum with dioramas and recorded tales of the judge, a visitor center and a short nature trail through a cactus garden with area trees and plants labeled.

There are two replicas of the Jersey Lilly in south Texas, one in the White-head Memorial Museum in Del Rio where the judge and his son are buried on the museum grounds, the other in Pecos in the West of the Pecos Museum.

Cary Grant slept in Van Horn, they say, at the old El Capitan Hotel, now the Van Horn State Bank. Shafter, a ghost of a town on US 67 between Presidio and Marfa, was once the silver mining capital of Texas.

Presidio's original town name was Nuevo Real Presidio de Nuestra Señora de Betlena y Santiago de Las Amarillas de La Junta de Los Rios Norte y Conchos. It is also known as "the hottest town in Texas" and "the onion capital of the world."

Camels were trained for combat at Fort Davis in the Davis Mountains after an idea introduced in the pre-Civil War days by Jefferson Davis, then Secretary of War, whom the fort was named for. The camels worked out much better than mules in the desert terrain, except for an unfortunate tendency for the males to bite each other in the legs if left untended. When the Civil War started, the fort was abandoned, then taken over by the Confederates briefly before it was burned by the Mescalero Apaches. Although the U.S. Army rebuilt the fort after the war, they never followed up on the combat camel idea because Davis, having served as president of the Confederacy during the war, was considered a traitor.

Fort Davis

FIVE WAYS TO ENTER TERLINGUA'S INTERNATIONAL CHILI COOK-OFF

1. Enter a sanctioned CASI (Chili Appreciation Society International) cook-off and win one of the top three prizes. ☎ *(713) 667-4652*, the *Goat Gap Gazette*, for a free list.

2. Accumulate 12 points at these cook-offs during the chili year (October 1 to September 30) for placing among the top 12 at each.

3. Show up in Terlingua on the first Sunday in November and see if one of the competing qualifying teams needs an extra helper at the CASI cook-off. Get CASI information from ☎ *(817) 365-2504*.

4. Cook your chili anyhow. While the judges will ignore you, you might get some attention from the chili-heads. Remember, no beans are allowed!

5. Look for the rival Terlingua cook-off, labeled the Original and held the same weekend behind Arturo White's store on highway 170 which claims to be the original version and has less rigid rules. ☎ *(903) 874-5601* for a nitty-gritty rundown.

In early February, Terlingua holds a Cookie Chill-Off—a competition for no-bake desserts—to raise funds for the Terlingua Foundation.

INSIDER TIP:

In Juarez, the sign "Ladies Bar" does not designate a drinking spot that welcomes female tourists; it is rather a spot where male tourists will find women who want to meet them.

EL PASO

Originally named El Paso del Norte by Juan de Oñate, the rich grandson-in-law of Cortés, the pass here was the main route between Mexico and the missions in San Antonio and east Texas.

The local Tigua Indians, many of them Christianized by the Spanish in the 17th century, settled at Ysleta when a mission was established there in 1680. Today the town, completely surrounded by El Paso, is the oldest continuously occupied settlement in Texas.

El Paso del Norte was eventually divided into the two border towns that are today called Juarez and El Paso.

You can get guided downtown walking tours from El Paso County Pioneer Association members by calling ☎ *(915) 566-8621*, or take your own following a free walking tour folder you can pick up at the information center at the freeway where you enter the state.

Together in one compact area you'll find the handsome 1910 Paso del Norte Hotel with its Tiffany stained-glass dome on Mills and El Paso; the Plaza Theater on West Mills Avenue, built in 1930, with a ceiling full of twinkling stars and a cloud machine; and the site of the old Acme Saloon on San Antonio, where outlaw John Wesley Hardin, considered the fastest gun in the west, was shot in the head in 1895 (some say the back of the head). Both Hardin and his killer, lawman John Selman, are buried in the city's Concordia Cemetery. Hardin's grave is in the Boot Hill section of the graveyard near the gate to the walled Chinese section. He claimed to have shot 40 men. A newspaper of the time reported, "except for being dead, Hardin looked remarkably well."

The city's wild and woolly gun-slinging era ran from around 1880 to 1916, with everyone from trigger-happy Texas Rangers to Mexican revolutionaries engaging in daily brawls and shootouts. Neither of its most famous marshals, Bat Masterson nor Wyatt Earp, were able to tame El Paso. One marshal, Dallas Stoudenmire, saw four men gunned down in five seconds (he himself killed three of them) only a block away from the spot where he would be shot dead a year later.

The San Jacinto Plaza in downtown El Paso was donated to the city in 1873 by a city parks commissioner who stocked a small pond in it with alligators; some of these reptiles continued to live there until the 1960s.

The El Paso Museum of History at 12901 Gateway West is a good place to get filled in on local history with exhibits and dioramas. The museum is located in an easily accessible area just off I-10 with a parking area big enough for RVs.

The distinctive architecture of the University of Texas at El Paso was inspired by a *National Geographic* magazine photograph of a Bhutan lamasery because the Himalayas in the background reminded the first dean's wife of El Paso's mountains.

Fort Bliss, we are reminded, is bigger than the state of Rhode Island. It has four different military-related museums, one about noncommissioned officers, another about the Third Cavalry, a third about air defense artillery, and the last a museum about the fort itself.

El Paso is also home to the Coors World Finals Rodeo in November, the top end-of-season international event with American, Mexican and Australian riders competing.

Western sunset with saguaro

STRETCHING OUT YOUR VACATION

If you want to spend the winter in the Rio Grande Valley, you'll be welcomed with open arms by the dozens of RV parks, some of them quite lavish, that dot the area between Brownsville and McAllen. The climate is semitropical, with a wide range of fresh fruits and vegetables locally grown, and prices are moderate based on the national average.

There's plenty to do, with golf courses, nearby beaches, extraordinary birdwatching, shopping in Mexican border towns, and organized activities in every community. Wanna dance? You can learn and practice tap, jazz dancing, square dancing, clog and line dancing. Some RV parks have their own dance halls and regular square or line dance programs.

Adult education classes are offered through colleges in Harlingen, McAllen and Brownsville in classes such as Spanish, art, music and local ecology.

Three months is the average winter Texan stay, and the RV parks will give discounted rates for long stays. The state parks in the area usually limit your stay to 14 consecutive days.

HITTING THE HIGHLIGHTS

Spend one night in the Corpus Christi area, visit Padre Island National Seashore but skip South Padre Island, and take the back road, route 281, through the Rio Grande Valley, allowing time to visit at least one bird sanctuary if you're there in winter.

If you have kids along, detour up to Bracketville for the Alamo Village theme park, then drive fairly briskly along the border, stopping in Langtry to see Judge Roy Bean's Jersey Lilly Saloon.

Spend as much time as you can spare in Big Bend and the Davis Mountains, then finish up with a day or two in El Paso.

15 TAKEOUT (OR EAT-IN) TREATS

1. The green chili at **El Paso's Tigua Indian Reservation** is fiery enough to sear and the red chili is only slightly less incendiary. "White-eyes don't know how to make chili," one of the Tigua told us once. The casual cafeteria is open at lunchtime, the prettier, more formal restaurant called Wyngs 'n Spirit in the evening, and both will dish up takeout portions if you carry your own dishes inside. Homemade bread baked in an outdoor adobe oven is sold in the cafe and gift shop area as well. Take Avenue of the Americas exit off I-10 south to Ysleta.

2. Try a shrimp and crawfish boil at **The Crazy Cajun** restaurant in Port Aransas on Mustang Island; take the free 24-hour ferry over from the end of highway 361 in Aransas Pass. A sort of southern clambake, the boil includes shrimp, crawfish, stone-crab claws, smoked sausage, potatoes and corn on the cob, served on butcher paper. The Crazy Cajun is on Alister Street Square. Closed Mondays.

3. In tiny Gregory, north of Corpus Christi on highway 35 just north of 181, **Mac's Pit Barbecue** serves old-fashioned Texas barbecue cooked over mesquite wood. Chomp down on beef brisket, beef finger ribs, pork spare ribs, ham, chicken or Polish sausage. Mac's been 30 years in business at his Rockport location at *815 Market* Street, open daily. The Gregory location is closed Sundays.

4. The ruby red grapefruit of the Lower Rio Grande Valley is justifiably famous. Hit the late January–early February **Citrus Fiesta** in Mission and buy a bagful, or find an orchard that lets you pick your own. Don't forget the mild Supersweet 1015 onions you can bite into like an apple. Both are on sale at **Bell's Farm to Market** in McAllen at *116 South Ware Road and Business 83.* ☎ *(800) 798-0424.*

5. In the streets of Laredo, feast on Cotulla pit-style barbecue, very like Mexico's **carne asada**, and all the side dishes at **Cotulla Style Pit Bar-B-Q**, *4502 McPherson*. There's a separate take-out area to the right of the restaurant. We noticed the locals all call their order in ahead of time on weekends, and it's ready to pick up when they get there, ☎ *(210) 724-5747*. Otherwise, lines can be long. You might also want to try two unique Laredo dishes, the mariachi, a fiery local version of a breakfast taco, and panchos, which are nachos with beef layered in alongside the cheese and jalapenos.

6. Some ice cream aficionados swear by Texas' Blue Bell brand, not distributed outside the state. *Time* magazine went on record not long ago saying it was the best in the U.S. The old-fashioned "**Little Creamery in Brenham**" (on route 290 about half-way between Austin and Houston) keeps its small-town image and its logo, a girl and a cow, but you can find the brand in seven Southwestern states. Top flavor is vanilla, but strawberry, rocky road, pistachio almond and chocolate chip also scoop up compliments. If you want to tour the plant, reserve ahead at ☎ *(800) 317-8135*. You get a free sample at the end of the tour.

7. The sloppy, gloppy barbecue at **Bud's Place** in Langtry comes topped with pickles and onions. Untouched by paint, the restaurant is on an unpaved side street called loop 25 with a couple of wagon wheels balanced against a wooden sidewalk.

8. **Dolphin Cove Oyster Bar**, South Padre Island, serves up fresh-shucked oysters and you-peel-'em shrimp from a little grass shack in Isla Blanca Park.

9. Lone Star folks say the best barbecue in South Texas is at **Joe Cotten's Barbecue**, in Robstown, eight miles southeast of Corpus Christi on 77. Closed Sundays. Pick it up to go at an off-hour, or prepare to stand in line at mealtimes.

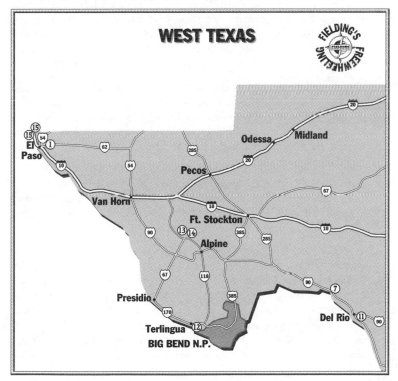

10. Winter Texans flock to **Maria's Better Mexican Food** in Brownsville at *1124 Central* for breakfast gorditas on thick homemade tortillas.

11. **Memo's** in Del Rio, run by the same family for more than 55 years, serves fajitas, enchiladas and chalupas on the banks of the San Felipe Creek at *804 East Losoya*.

The Starlight Theatre in Terlingua

12. Terlingua, famous for its annual World Championship Chili Cook-off in early November, also has the **Desert Deli & Diner**, a cafe that purveys another southwest classic, the Frito or taco pie, a paper plate layered with tortilla chips, heaped with thick chili con carne, then topped with more chips and grated cheese. It's messy and filling but surprisingly mild, considering the amount of incendiary ground red chiles used at the cook-off.

13. An authentic old-fashioned soda fountain with banana splits, malts, sodas, shakes and hand-mixed Cokes, plus a jukebox of 1950s hits, is waiting at **The Drugstore Restaurant** in Fort Davis. Also homemade chili with Mexican cornbread and fajita burritos. Friday and Saturday nights from March through August they serve a full steak dinner for under $10.

14. Across the street in Fort Davis, the doughty pink limestone **Hotel Limpia** features dishes you would have expected to find in 1912, the year it was built, including homemade buttermilk pies, chicken-fried steak, fried chicken and fresh catfish. They also serve the only alcohol in town, but you have to join a club to get it.

15. Two El Paso tortilla factories, one on each side of the city, make great stops to pick up fresh tortillas, gorditas, green or red enchiladas and other favorites to go. **The Tortilla Factory and Little Diner** is northwest of town, exit 6 off I-10 at *7209 Seventh Street in Canutillo*, open 11 a.m. to 6:30 p.m. daily except Wednesdays. **The Best Buy Tortilla Factory** is southeast of town, just off I-10 at *1110 Pendale Road*, open daily except Sundays from early morning until 5 p.m. weekdays, 2 p.m. Saturdays. To top them off, stop by the **El Paso Chili Company** at *100 Ruhlin Court in downtown El Paso* next to the river for terrific cactus salsa, chile con queso, chile beans or fajita marinade, all in jars to take away with you.

ON THE CHEAP: TRIMMING COSTS ON THE ROAD

Fortunately, this part of Texas is relatively inexpensive for the RV traveler, even if you eat out more often than in. Roadside produce stands year-round sell regional food products at low prices.

Winter Texans get rates by the month or season in most of the commercial RV parks in the Rio Grande Valley, lowering the per diem cost somewhat.

The state of Texas permits RVers who sleep inside their vehicles to park for rest periods of up to 24 hours at any of the more than 1000 highway roadside rest areas. Pitching a tent is forbidden, however. While we have some personal reservations about overnighting in a roadside rest area (see "Getting Ready to Hit the Road, Should You Sleep by the Side of the Road?"), many RVers don't worry about it. And you would be able to save a lot of campground fees.

INSIDER TIP:

Sign in on the King Ranch Visitor Center guest register and you too may get a Christmas card in the mail that reads, "The grass is short, the range is dry/ Good prospects ain't a half inch high/The cows ain't fat, this verse ain't clever/But Merry Christmas, same as ever."

FYI

General Texas travel—☎ *(800) 8888-TEX*

Texas Travel Information Centers—☎ *(800) 452-9292*—for free booklets on public and private RV parks and campgrounds

THE BLUE RIDGE PARKWAY AND SKYLINE DRIVE

At the Old-Time Fiddlers' Convention in Gala , VA, some RVing musicians get together.

Virginia is where eight U.S. presidents were born, 60 percent of the Civil War's battles were fought, where "Taps" was composed, *Dirty Dancing* was filmed and Chap-Stick invented. It's where George Marshall wrote his Plan, where Jerry Falwell launched the Moral Majority, and Walt Disney lost the Third Battle of Manassas.

Country singing legend Patsy Cline, who died in a plane crash at the age of 30, was born and buried in Winchester, the Statler Brothers were born and continue to live in Staunton, and Bela Bartok dropped by Hot Springs long enough to compose his *Piano Concerto No. 3.*

It's where John-Boy said goodnight to the rest of the Walton family, where Cyrus McCormick invented the first mechanical reaping machine, where a local doctor named Charles Kenneth Pepper gave his name to a soft drink, and where Rudolph Valentino's 1925 Rolls Royce came to rest in the Historic Car and Carriage Caravan at Luray Caverns.

Ronald Reagan filmed *Brother Rat* in the cadet barracks at Virginia Military Institute, the same school where Stonewall Jackson's horse Little Sorrel was stuffed for the VMI Museum. Despite being somewhat moth-eaten, Little Sorrel is their most popular exhibit. The horse fared better than the general, who was accidentally shot by his own troops at Chancellorsville in 1863 and died a week later after having his arm amputated. The raincoat he was wearing with the bullet hole in evidence is in the same museum. He himself is buried in two places, his arm in Wilderness Battlefield and the rest of him in Stonewall Jackson Memorial Cemetery in Lexington.

Germany's General Erwin Rommel, "the Desert Fox," came to VMI to study the military tactics of Stonewall Jackson, which he later used in his North Africa campaign against the Allies during World War II.

Western Virginia is where Henry Ford couldn't cash a check—he was on one of his famous camping trips with Thomas Edison and Harvey Firestone (see "The Tin Can Tourists")—where John D. Rockefeller used to throw dimes into the pool by the first tee at the Homestead's Cascades golf course to watch the caddies scramble for them, and multimillionaire treasure-hunter Mel Fisher came up from Key West to search for the mysterious Beale Treasure, now worth about $23 million (see "15 Off-the-Wall Attractions").

And it's where—we cannot tell a lie—a young George Washington carved his initials in one of the seven wonders of the natural world, Virginia's Natural Bridge.

In the Blue Ridge Mountains of North Carolina, Tom Dula (better known as Tom Dooley of "Hang down your head" ballad fame) was imprisoned in Wilkes County Jail in Wilkesboro after killing his sweetheart, and Frankie Silver, heroine of an even bigger ballad, became the first woman to be hanged in the state when she was tried and put to death in Morganton for murdering her two-timing lover Johnny, who "done her wrong."

Typical Blue Ridge farmhouses are restored along the Blue Ridge Parkway.

FREEWHEELING ALONG THE ROUTE

The combined mileage of the Blue Ridge Parkway and Skyline Drive is 575 miles, plus any side trips you'll want to add along the route.

If you're going from north to south, the drive begins at Front Royal, Virginia, and the two-lane road snakes its way 105 miles through Shenandoah National Park, then joins up with the Blue Ridge Parkway at Rockfish Gap near Waynesboro, Virginia. The mileposts are numbered from 0.6 at Front Royal's fee entrance station to 105 at Rockfish Gap and the entrance to the Blue Ridge Parkway, which starts again at milepost 0.

The maximum speed limit along the parkway is 45 miles an hour.

Hikers will find plenty of trails, from 10-minute leg-stretchers to much longer and more demanding walks along the way. In Shenandoah National Park, more than 500 miles of side trails set out from the ridge road.

One of the most famous walking trails in America, the Appalachian Trail, stretches from Maine to Georgia across the crest of the mountains. Some of the prettiest of the trail's 500 miles in Virginia are those in Shenandoah National Park between Front Royal and Rockfish Gap. The trail also parallels the Blue Ridge Parkway for 103 miles between Rockfish Gap and Mile 103.

Canoe trips along the Shenandoah River for novices or experienced canoeists can be booked with **Downriver Canoe Company** in Bentonville, Virginia, between early April and late October by calling ☎ *(703) 635-5526*. If you want to paddle your own canoe, they can provide a shuttle service for you. **Front Royal Canoe Company** in Front Royal, ☎ *(703) 635-5440*, can also take you canoeing along the Shenandoah between mid-March and mid-November. **Shenandoah River Outfitters** in Luray, ☎ *(703) 743-4159*, is open all year for rentals, overnight trips and all-you-can-eat steak dinners on the trail.

Horseback riding along mountain trails is particularly popular in the fall, and a good alternative to driving when traffic on the roadways may be bumper-to-bumper. Guided trail rides from **Luray's Skyland Lodge** in Shenandoah National Park leave several times a day; call them at ☎ *(703) 999-2210* for times and details. **Overnight Wilderness Camping** at ☎ *(703) 786-7329* in Locust Grove will take families out and provide horses, sleeping bags, a candlelight dinner, fishing gear or whatever you need.

Or you can spend the time doing nothing more urgent than watching a robin search for worms or marvel at the opening of a bud or the unfolding of a leaf.

INSIDER TIP:

Winter is often mild, but periods of fog or rain may make driving larger RVs along the ridge route difficult. In summer, unfortunately, increased pollution and haze along Skyline Drive have reduced visibility tremendously. You can check out the day's clarity with park rangers by calling ☎ (703) 999-3644 or ☎ (703) 999-2243.

When to go. Early spring through late fall is best. Dogwood and wildflowers begin to bloom in April. Peak time for the showiest bloom comes mid-May to mid-June for flame azalea and mountain laurel, with June the best month for the thickets of vivid purple Catawba rhododendron. Craggy Gardens around Mile 365 is a particularly good place to see the latter. Autumn foliage creates another peak season as the trees turn color and begin to drop their leaves. Expect sometimes long and slow-moving lines of traffic in spring blossom, late summer and autumn foliage seasons. Many of the facilities along the route are closed in winter.

What to take. Binoculars, cameras and film, hiking boots, sunscreen, mosquito repellent, detailed area maps and fishing tackle if you want to go trout fishing. Carry a sweater or jacket even in midsummer because evenings are cool.

What to wear. Casual but smart sportswear is best if you plan to visit resorts or restaurants, especially in fashionable northern Virginia. Along the Blue Ridge Parkway and in North Carolina, things are a bit more casual, so your usual RV garb will pass muster almost everywhere.

INSIDER TIP:

Because the two-lane roadways are heavily traveled, RVers should remember to pull out into the frequent overlooks and turnouts to let traffic behind them go past.

SOUTHERN ACCENTS: A GLOSSARY

Pop—a soft drink (See the following "Insider Tip")

Holler—a yell of communication between farms in the days before telephones; also, a valley

Put up—to can or preserve foods for winter

Moonshining—making illegal corn liquor in "dry" areas of the south; most rural areas have a few moonshiners, but you're not likely to encounter any unless you know the locals very well

Bald—a treeless area at about 4000 feet in elevation covered with shrubs or grass, perhaps part of earlier Indian agricultural clearings or the product of lightning fires

INSIDER TIP:

"The South is that part of America where no soft drink is ever called a soda."
Reynolds Price

EVERYTHING YOU EVER WANTED TO KNOW ABOUT COUNTRY HAM

Yankees may invest fortunes in mail order Smithfield hams, but the fine cured ham you'll encounter in restaurants and roadside stands throughout this drive is correctly called "country ham."

The Smithfield ham began in the 17th century when local farmers let their hogs run loose in the peanut fields after harvest to eat up the leftovers. They soon found they had an excellent-tasting ham with yellow fat which kept the meat from drying out, an export in great demand back in England. These hams are smoked and coated with black pepper. Only hams produced by peanut-fed hogs in the peanut belt and processed in Smithfield, a small town in Tidewater Virginia near Norfolk, can be called Smithfield hams.

Country ham, on the other hand, is a product of the Appalachians that can be either smoked or dry-cured without smoke. The fresh ham is rubbed down with a dry mix of salt, sugar and perhaps saltpeter, then covered for four to six weeks in a bed of salt. After this, it is washed and trimmed, then usually hung by the hock in a smokehouse where it sweats in hickory smoke through the summer. A total of nine to 12 months is the minimum curing period. Some processors skip the smoking stage, saying the smoke makes little flavor difference. And some processors label their hams "sugar cured," although the sugar has no part in the curing.

The finished ham is a salty, densely textured and intensely flavored meat that can be sliced raw and fried for breakfast or boiled whole and then baked. If you buy a country ham to take home, rest assured it will keep for a long time, up to a year, if stored in a cool, dark place. A cooked ham also keeps well under refrigeration, and a small bit of it sliced or diced can add flavor to any number of dishes.

To prepare a country ham, you need to soak it for 24 hours in a pot of cold water, then drain it, scrub off the spices and any mold from the surface, and put it in a fresh kettle of cold water to cover. Cook it at a simmer for 20 minutes per pound or until the flat bone at the butt end is loose enough to move back and forth, usually from four to five hours. Let it cool enough to handle, cut off the skin and excess fat but leave a half-inch layer of fat to cover. Remove the loose, flat bone. Put liquid in the pan (water, wine, ginger ale or sherry) to cover it up to one inch and bake in a slow oven for an hour, covered with foil. Then remove the foil, score the fat and cover it with any paste or glaze you wish. A mix of brown sugar, cornmeal and a little prepared or dry mustard is good. Return it to the oven for another half hour, basting frequently. Then let it cool and slice it in very, very thin slices to serve. It's delectable with hot biscuits.

The word "ham," to denote a bad actor, comes from "hamfatter," a word 19th-century audiences applied to second-rate actors such as minstrel show performers, who had to use ham fat to take off their makeup because they couldn't afford cold cream.

10 CAMPGROUND OASES

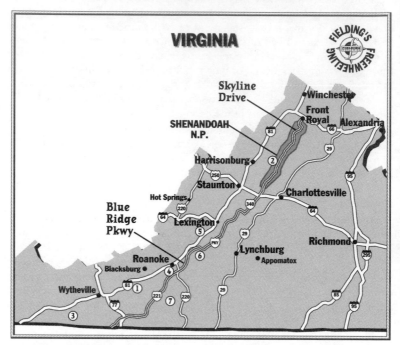

1. **Claytor Lake State Park** near Radford, VA, has 132 sites, 44 of them with water and 15-amp electric hookups. Bass fishing, swimming, fishing, boating and boat dock at the lake. Some shaded sites, some pull-throughs. Closed in winter. Located on state road 660 two miles off I-81 at exit 101. The historic Howe House in the park features exhibits about the life of the early settlers in this region.

2. **Shenandoah National Park** has four campgrounds—Mathews Arm at Mile 22, Big Meadows at Mile 51.3, Lewis Mountain at Mile 57.5 and Loft Mountain at Mile 80—all available for tents and RVs on a first-come, first-served basis. All have a 14-day limit, no pets are allowed and there are no RV hookups. Campgrounds are usually closed in winter. Call the park at ☎ *(703) 999-2266* for weather forecasts, campground reservations and other information. A number of privately-owned campgrounds are also adjacent to Skyline Drive at connecting highways.

3. **Beartree Campground** in Mt. Rogers National Recreation Area, tucked into the corner of southwestern Virginia where its border touches both North Carolina and Tennessee, has 91 gravel sites without hookups, closed in winter. Flush toilets and showers, sanitary dump station, trout fishing and swimming. Seven miles east of Damascus via US 58.

4. **Roanoke Mountain** near Vinton at Mile 120 has 105 campsites, some shaded, all paved, with flush toilets, piped water and sanitary dump station. No hookups, no reservations, 14-day camping limit. Towed vehicles are not permitted on the Roanoke Mountain scenic loop drive.

5. **Natural Bridge/Lexington KOA** is open all year off I-81, exit 180, with some full hookups and pull-throughs for most of its 87 sites. Flush toilets, showers, sanitary dump, laundry, groceries, LP gas. ☎ *(703) 291-2770.*

6.   **Peaks of Otter**, on the Blue Ridge Parkway at Milepost 86 near Bedford, VA, with 52 paved sites, some with shade, 25 pull-throughs, flush toilets, piped water, sanitary dump, no hookups. Each site has a table and fireplace. Closed November through April.

7.   **Fairy Stone State Park** near Bassett, VA, is named for the little brown, cross-shaped stones found in the area that legend says are the tears shed by elves and fairies when Christ was crucified. Don't worry if you can't find one on the ground; the gift shops in the area will be glad to sell you one. 51 sites with water and electrical hookups (20 amps), flush toilets, showers, sanitary dump station, bass fishing, swimming, boat ramp and rentals. Closed in fall and winter.

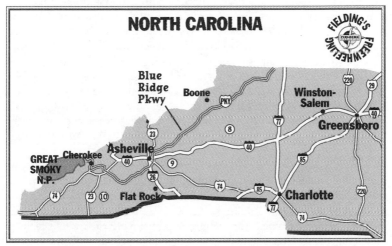

8.   **Doughton Park**, on the Blue Ridge Parkway near Mile 240, has 20 grass sites open May 1 to November 1. Flush toilets, sanitary dump, planned activities schedule. No hookups, no reservations. This is an especially good place to spot deer at dawn and dusk. Closed November through April.

9.   **Julian Price Memorial Park** on the parkway near Mile 297 has 68 paved sites, flush toilets, sanitary dump, fishing and boating. No hookups, no reservations. Most sites shaded, some pull-throughs, 14-day maximum stay. Open May to November.

10. **Mt. Pisgah**, on the Blue Ridge Parkway near Mile 408, has 70 paved campsites available with patios, some shade. Flush toilets, sanitary dump station, groceries. No hookups or reservations. Open May to November, 14 day camping limit.

THE SHENANDOAH VALLEY

Nobody knows for sure what Shenandoah means. It has been translated variously as "sprucy stream," "land of the big mountains," even "daughter of the stars." One etymologist says it is the Iroquois word for "deer," animals which are still plentiful in the valley.

The fragrance of apples perfumes the valley, from the pink-and-white blossoms in spring through the harvest of the fruit in autumn, and the sweetsour tang of apple cider in winter in the apple sheds.

History is deeply etched in the towns along the Shenandoah River, once America's western frontier. During the Civil War, the northern Virginia town of Winchester changed hands 72 times during the Civil War, 13 times in a single day.

Pick up a walking tour map at the city's welcome center and set out to see the modest log-and-limestone cabin on Braddock Street, now a museum, that was George Washington's office during the French and Indian War. A brick house down the street was Stonewall Jackson's headquarters during the Civil War. Don't be startled to see a picture of TV star Mary Tyler Moore at the headquarters; her great-grandfather owned the house at the time and invited the general to use it.

Virginia's Museum of American Frontier Culture in Staunton is a recently recreated village of cottages and barns and small farms that show both the farmsteads the settlers left in the Old World, and the way they reinterpreted them in the New World. (See "Where History Comes Alive.")

Thomas Jefferson is still very much alive in the countryside around Charlottesville, where people speak often of "Mr. Jefferson" as they would any respected neighbor and friend. Monticello, the dream home he designed and built himself, is magnificent but not overwhelming because it is built on a human scale. The moose and deer antlers on display in the entry hall were brought back to Jefferson by Meriwether Lewis and William Clark from their explorations in the west.

Jefferson was always generous and hospitable to guests, spending freely to entertain them although he died with debts of $100,000, the equivalent of a million today.

Dinner began at 4 p.m. and often continued until dark, with the fine wines the president had shipped from France accompanying the fresh vegetables from his gardens. Dishes were prepared by one of Jefferson's servants, who had trained in Paris.

Jefferson, who tried to establish a vineyard at Monticello, would be pleased to note that today the Charlottesville area is the wine capital of Virginia, with 10 local wineries producing table vintages. Oakencraft Vineyard and Winery, Simeon Vineyards, Montdomaine Cellars and Totier Creek Vineyard usually offer tours and tastings except in winter. Get a free wine country guide from the **Virginia Wine Marketing Program**, *VDACS, Division of Marketing, PO Box 1163, Richmond, VA 23209*, ☎ *(804) 786-0481.*

10 TERRIFIC SPOTS WHERE HISTORY COMES ALIVE

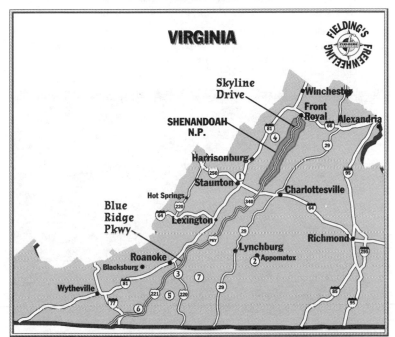

1. **Museum of American Frontier Culture** in Staunton, VA, shows us where many of our 18th and 19th century settlers came from—neat, small farms in England, Northern Ireland and the German Rhineland—and a typical Shenandoah Valley farm that reflects the influence of all three. Costumed interpreters carry out daily and seasonal tasks from plowing to planting, spinning to gardening. From I-81 take exit 222, then follow the signs on 250 west. It's open daily.

2. **Appomattox Court House National Historic Park**, 20 miles east of Lynchburg via route 460 to route 24, has recreated the entire village at the time of Lee's surrender to Grant here. Living history exhibits in summer animate Meeks Store, Woodson Law Office and Clover Hill Tavern, and there's a museum as well. The park is open daily except major holidays February through November.

3. **Explore**, a new living history museum near Roanoke, VA, interprets the pre-Civil War period with its Blue Ridge Settlement depicting life on the Virginia frontier in the early 1800s. Historic buildings have been reassembled on site, including the Hofauger farmstead where costumed interpreters cook at the hearth, weave, spin, garden and tend livestock. Gardens are planted in heirloom seeds, orchards grow traditional varieties of fruit and farm animals represent now-rare breeds that were typical of the time. Open Saturdays, Sundays and Mondays between April and the end of October. A gift shop on site sells candle holders made by the local blacksmith and other crafts from the project. From the Parkway's Milepost 115 follow the signage to *3900 Rutrough Road, in a residential area.* ☎ *(703) 427-3107.*

4. Every May 15 a **recreation of the 1864 Battle of New Market** takes place, recalling when 247 young cadets, the entire student body of Virginia Military Institute, fought alongside veteran Confederate soldiers against the Union Army. Ten cadets died, including a descendent of Thomas Jefferson, and 47 others lay wounded. The

Hall of Valor in the New Market Battlefield Park poignantly commemorates the battle. For a schedule of other Civil War battle reenacts around the country, write to **Camp Chase Gazette**, *PO Box 707, Marietta, OH 45750.*

5. **The Blue Ridge Farm Museum** in tiny Ferrum, VA, displays an 1800 German-American farm and the daily life of settlers who came here, with heirloom vegetables, vintage livestock breeds and costumed interpreters. It's open weekends only between mid-May and mid-August but closed Sunday mornings.

Mabry Mill on the Blue Ridge Parkway

6. **Mabry Mill** at Mile 176 of the Blue Ridge Parkway is animated with working craftsmen and musicians during the peak summer and fall season. Besides the water-powered gristmill and a shop selling its stone-ground flours and meal, there's also a coffee shop serving pancakes and country ham all day long.

7. At **Booker T. Washington National Monument**, where the great educator and inventor was born in 1856, 19th century farming methods are demonstrated, and the house where Washington, his mother and two other children slept on a bare dirt

floor, has been reconstructed. It's located 20 miles southeast of Roanoke via routes 116 south, then 122 north, near Smith Mountain Lake. Open daily.

8. **The Mast General Store** near Boone, NC, is a living example of a 19th century country store with its pot-bellied stove and old advertising posters. With merchandise "from cradles to caskets" and the family's 1812 log cabin and 1885 farmhouse (now an inn) nearby, it makes a good one-stop example of a mountain farm complex. It's also great fun just to browse through the stacked and packed shelves of this rambling store built in 1883, now listed on the National Registry of Historic Places. In Valle Crucis, seven miles south of Boone on route 194.

9. **The Museum of Appalachia** in Norris, TN, is a bit off the basic driving route, but for anyone going or coming from the midwest or west, it could be on the way. Located 16 miles north of Knoxville at exit 122 from I-75, this living village is open daily year-round, and preserves the life-style of the southern Appalachians as its costumed interpreters split shingles, plow the fields, play fiddles and cook meals in dirt-floored cabins. A museum displays 250,000 regional artifacts, including a Roy Acuff fiddle and Sergeant Alvin York's World War I leather Army jacket.

10. **Oconaluftee Indian Village** in Cherokee, NC, is a recreated Cherokee village from 225 years ago, before many of the tribe were taken to Oklahoma on a forced relocation still remembered as the Trail of Tears. One-fourth of them died along the thousand-mile journey. Descendents of the 1200 tribal members who escaped and fled into the nearby Great Smoky Mountains in 1838 make up an 8000-member reservation here today. Costumed animators produce pottery, weave baskets, sew beadwork and build canoes in traditional fashion. The nearby Museum of the Cherokee Indian on route 441 in town is a remarkable exhibit of Cherokee history. The museum is open daily year-round except for major holidays; the village is open mid-May to late October.

> ### INSIDER TIP:
> *Some small southern towns are notorious speed traps, fattening city coffers by ticketing unwary drivers. Locals warned us about Boones Mill, VA, on route 220, but not West Jefferson, NC, along route 221, where we were ticketed and had to go directly over to the county court to pay your fine at night, because of an out-of-state license plate. (See "Nuts and Bolts, Speeders Beware.")*

THE BLUE RIDGE PARKWAY

Construction began in 1935, and the final leg of the 469-mile road was finally completed in 1987 with the spectacularly engineered Linn Cove Viaduct, which seems to float lightly around venerable Grandfather Mountain as if suspended in midair.

Skyline Drive and the Blue Ridge Parkway were among President Franklin D. Roosevelt's make-work projects for the CCC (Civilian Conservation Corps) during the 1930s Depression. The intention was to provide drivers with a variety of untrammeled rural scenes, with the road following the landscape for optimum scenery rather than speed, which is limited to 45 miles per hour. The park itself averages about 1000 feet wide, including the roadbed.

Split-rail fences, small log cabins, water-operated mills, barns and farm fields may be glimpsed along the roadsides, as well as brilliant pink and lavender stands of wild rhododendron and vivid orange splashes of flame aza-leas in late spring and early summer. Arched stone bridges ornament the roads that cross over or under the parkway.

Nine visitor centers and 11 campgrounds, none with hookups but all acces-sible to any but the largest RV, are along the route. It passes through four national forests and the Cherokee Indian Reservation at its southern end, where it connects with Newfound Gap Road and the Great Smoky Moun-tains National Park.

The Appalachian Mountains were once the western frontier of America, and the isolated homesteads that remain—such as the Puckett Cabin at Mile 189, where "Aunt Orlean" Puckett gave birth to 24 children, none of whom lived past infancy; and the Brinegar Cabin at Mile 238, where weavers show how mountain women made their own fabrics—give a clearer picture than any history book of the hard and often lonely life of of these fiercely inde-pendent people.

Our own favorite stop along the parkway is Mabry Mill, where you may wander into an impromptu dulcimer concert or hear an old mountaineer telling tall tales to a group of wide-eyed children. Someone's usually weaving split-willow baskets or whittling or blacksmithing. And the miller is almost always there, turning out white stone-ground cornmeal for sale by the bag. You can sample cornmeal and buckwheat pancakes at the little restaurant next door, along with slabs of country ham and hot homemade biscuits.

Animal life along the parkway is fairly sparse, except around campgrounds and at road crossings in early morning and late afternoon. White-tailed deer, opossums, raccoons and skunks are the most common, along with chip-munks, squirrels and woodchucks, also called groundhogs.

LITERARY LIGHTS

1. Poet and Lincoln biographer Carl Sandburg, whose name is linked forever with Chicago, spent the last 22 years of his life on his farm at Flat Rock, near Henderson-ville, NC. Now a National Historic Site, the Connemara farm is where the two-time Pulitzer Prize winner wrote a novel, poems, a screenplay (*The Greatest Story Ever Told*), and his autobiography, in between playing his guitar and singing folk songs; his wife Paula Steichen, sister of photographer Edward Steichen, raised prize goats. There's still a herd of them around. The farm is on Little River Road off route 25, three miles south of Hendersonville.

2. Old Kentucky Home, the boardinghouse at *48 Spruce Street in Asheville* where author Thomas Wolfe spent his childhood and which he immortalized as Dixieland in his autobiographical novel *Look Homeward, Angel*, is today the Thomas Wolfe Memorial State Historic Site. It's fascinating for both its insight into the author's early life and its evocative picture of middle-class life in a southern town in 1916 or so. Although Wolfe never had his own bedroom when growing up (his mother moved the kids around to accommodate her boarders), one bedroom now contains the furniture from his last New York apartment. It's open daily except Sunday mornings for a modest entrance fee. The angel of the book title, a funeral monu-ment sold by Wolfe's father, can be seen in Hendersonville's Oakdale Cemetery ornamenting the grave of Margaret E. Johnson.

ASHEVILLE

Thomas Wolfe's house in Asheville

The pretty mountain city of Asheville will be forever mingled with the memory of native son Thomas Wolfe for many readers. His thinly-fictionalized story of "Altamont" and Eliza Gant's "Dixieland" boardinghouse in his epic first novel, *Look Homeward, Angel* apparently embarrassed everyone in town, including his mother, the model for the boardinghouse keeper. His books were banned by the local public library until 1935, when F. Scott Fitzgerald, shocked that the local author was not represented, bought two copies of *Look Homeward, Angel* and donated them to the library.

Later, after Wolfe's death (he died before his 38th birthday), all was forgiven, and Old Kentucky Home, that boardinghouse at 48 Spruce Street, is today the Thomas Wolfe Memorial State Historic Site.

In sharp contrast to the Wolfes' worn furniture is the splendor of Biltmore House, a 250-room French Renaissance mansion built in the 1890s at the edge of Asheville by George Washington Vanderbilt, grandson of the fabulously wealthy Commodore Vanderbilt. Today Biltmore is open daily for fairly pricey house tours, as well as rose garden tours and wine-tasting from the Vanderbilt vineyard. If the mansion looks familiar, you're remembering it as the location for the Peter Sellers film *Being There*, a classic forerunner to *Forrest Gump*, as well as the home of Macaulay Culkin's *Richie Rich*.

Another Blue Ridge author, Greensboro-born short story writer O. Henry, is also buried in Asheville's Riverside Cemetery not far from Thomas Wolfe.

A lot of wealthy Americans liked the city's cool summer climate and clear mountain air enough to set up seasonal residence, including Henry Ford, Thomas Edison, John D. Rockefeller, Grover Cleveland and Theodore Roosevelt.

Besides its evocative turn-of-the-century resort buildings, Asheville also is a treasure trove of art deco architecture, with a city hall and First Baptist Church from the late 1920s, as well as the handsome S&W Cafeteria on Patton Avenue.

10 SPECIAL SPLURGES

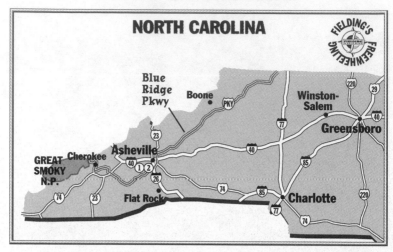

1.   Plan a meal or even an overnight in Asheville's splendidly baronial **Grove Park Inn**, built in 1913 by a patent-medicine tycoon from Tennessee. Author F. Scott Fitzgerald frequently stayed here when visiting his wife Zelda, who spent the latter part of her life in a local mental hospital. He usually stayed in room 441, which is still decorated as it was during his visits. Do check out those elevators by the huge, walk-in stone fireplaces; they actually run up the chimney shafts.

2.   Go shopping for authentic mountain handicrafts at the **Folk Art Center of the Southern Highland Handicraft** Guild on the North Carolina end of the parkway at Mile 385. With an RV, you can probably find space to stow some split-willow baskets, a handmade broomcorn broom, finely polished wooden toys or even a hand-stitched heirloom quilt.

3.   Don your smartest outfits and hit **The Homestead** resort at mealtime (call ahead for reservations, ☎ *800-336-5771*) for a sumptuous lunch or dinner in the grand old American resort tradition. Teatime with violins is also a classic pleasure here in this red brick, Colonial-style building dating from 1892. A hotel has been on the site for nearly 230 years because of the healing springs on the premises. At one time, the waters promised to cure such exotic maladies as gum-boot poisoning, clergyman's throat and a surfeit of freckles. There's a lot large enough for RV parking halfway down the hill to the hotel, but the doorman may eye your rig nervously if you drive right down to the porte-cochere. It's in Hot Springs, VA, on US 220 near the West Virginia border.

4.   Splurge on a superlative meal at the esteemed **Inn at Little Washington** in Washington, VA, at Middle and Main Streets. A seven-course fixed-price dinner is served nightly during June and October, nightly except Tuesdays the rest of the year. Call ahead at ☎ *(703) 675-3800* for reservations, which are essential.

5.   Go antique-hunting in the 100-shop **Strasburg Emporium** in the northern Virginia town of Strasburg; at the **Lexington Historical Shop** in Lexington, specializing in original Confederate-related materials from belts and buttons to letters and autographs; or the **Verona Flea Market**, open Thursdays through Sundays in the tiny town of Verona on US 11 off I-81, exit 227, near Staunton.

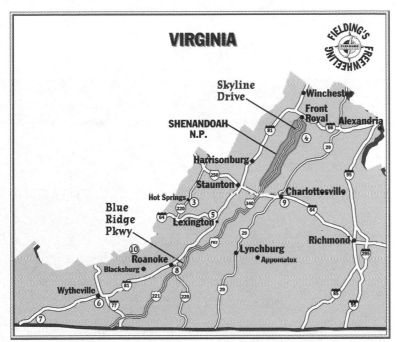

6. Hit the hiking trail near Wytheville, VA, with some humming llamas from **Virginia Highland Llamas**, ☎ *(703) 688-4464*, for an all day picnic hike on the Big Walker Mountain section of the Appalachian trail. You walk while the llamas carry lunch, each humming a different tone. Why do they hum? "Because they don't know the words," says their owner.

7. Cash in a chicken or ham for some theater tickets at Virginia's state theater, the classic **Barter Theater in Abingdon**, which started during the Depression when area farmers paid for their tickets with produce. (Only kidding; these days you have to pay with cash or credit card.) This is where Gregory Peck, Patricia Neal, Hume Cronyn and George C. Scott worked early in their careers. The theater once paid royalties to famous Irish playwright George Bernard Shaw by sending the noted vegetarian a country ham, which he returned with a note requesting spinach instead.

8. If you're in the Roanoke area and looking for some trendy vegetarian dishes, or even a steak, along with a glass of wine, try **Buck Mountain Grille**, open daily except Mondays for all three meals. It's at Blue Ridge Parkway exit 121 on route 220 south; ☎ *(703) 776-1830* for reservations.

9. Take a hot-air balloon ride over some of the Shenandoah Valley's outstanding landmarks from the lavish grounds of the **Boar's Head Inn** in Charlottesville, ☎ *(800) 296-2181*. It's also a top-seeded tennis resort, ranking among *Tennis Magazine's* top fifty, and scene of a predictable Merrie Olde England Christmas banquet starring a you-know-what on a silver platter.

10. Find a secluded mountain lodge that takes you back 30 years. At least that's what the producers of the film *Dirty Dancing* thought when they used **Mountain Lake Hotel** to stand in for an upstate New York resort in the sixties. To find it, leave I-81 at exit 118 and follow route 460 west, bypassing Blacksburg, to road 700, then

drive seven miles farther up a winding road to Mountain Lake. Call them at
☎ *(800) 346-3334.*

WILDLIFE WATCH

*Black bears are sometimes seen in the Great Smoky Mountains; this one lives in
a zoo at Grandfather Mountain.*

The Blue Ridge Mountains are the stomping ground for all manner of
birds and mammals, from plentiful whitetail deer and black bears, on display
at the privately-owned Grandfather Mountain Park, to wild turkeys, which
we've glimpsed several times from the roadway. Seldom seen but indisput-
ably present are bobcats, sometimes glimpsed at night. Most commonly
sighted along the roadways are woodchucks (groundhogs), chipmunks and
squirrels in the daytime, skunks, raccoons, opossums and foxes at night.
More than 100 bird species may be seen during spring migrations.

Some 300 or more wild ponies wander in Grayson Highlands State Park,
off US 58 near the point where Virginia, North Carolina and Tennessee
meet, a few of them rounded up each fall to be auctioned off during the last
week of September in the park.

As for nightlife, things are better than they used to be. We remember visiting in North Carolina a few years ago when someone suggested going out
for a drink. "Where's the nearest bar?" we asked. "Washington, D.C.," our
host answered dryly.

The best places to look for life after dark are college towns like Charlottesville, Virginia, where Miller's offers live jazz on weekends. Max and next-
door Trax provide live country music on weekends. Groucho's in Roanoke's
City Market with a comedy club and some dance nights wows the locals, and
country-western line dancers gravitate to The Top Rail or Billy's Barn.
Frankly, we prefer Cockram's General Store in Floyd and its free-for-all Friday night clog-dancing wingdings.

10 BLUE RIDGE THINGS TO DO

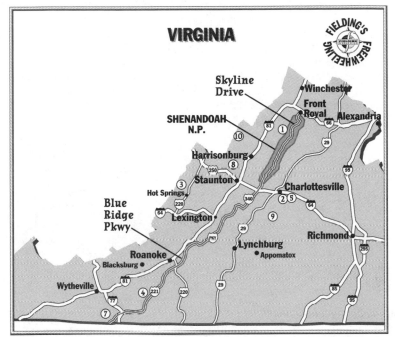

1. Head down into Luray Caverns, biggest of a number of cave complexes that lie like honeycombs beneath the Shenandoah Valley. It's big enough for claustrophobes to go inside to see and hear the world's only "stalacpipe" organ in which rubber-tipped hammers tap tuned stalactites to make music. (How do you tune a stalactite? By grinding it down slightly.) Trivia-lovers will like discovering the petrified fried eggs on one canyon wall, and the blind albino shrimp that live in the underground river. But check out the times for the frequent carillon concerts at the entrance. You don't want to be standing too near.

2. Visit Thomas Jefferson's vegetable gardens at Monticello, a re-creation of his original plantings in the late 18th century, painstakingly documented by him in 1807. Some rare and exotic vegetables no longer produced anywhere else share space with familiar favorites such as asparagus and artichokes, as well as 15 different varieties of English peas. Jefferson's the gardener who introduced eggplant to the United States.

3. Check out the mansion in rural Bath County, VA, where the romantic, Civil War-era film *Sommersby*, starring Jodie Foster and Richard Gere, was shot. Take US 39 west from Warm Springs about four miles, then turn right on route 261 for one mile, then left on Hidden Valley Road to the historic Warwickton Mansion, built in 1860. The filmmakers added slave quarters, a barn, a blacksmith shop, church, medical offices, a bank and general store along the banks of the Jackson River for the filming. The house is sometimes open for tours on weekends.

4. Check out far-out Floyd, VA, six miles off the Blue Ridge Parkway near Mile 165, where a New Age/neo-hippie handicrafts gallery called New Mountain Mercantile co-exists with a 75-year-old general store named Cockram's that holds free hoe-downs every Friday night. Just down the road a piece is Poor Farmers Market, a produce stand and deli with down-home, fried apple pies on the menu. Next door to

Cockram's is Country Records, featuring the biggest collection of bluegrass music in the world, they say. Finally, just when you think you're getting a fix on Floyd, you run into Chateau Morrisette Winery with its jazz concerts, wine tastings and French restaurant.

5.   Lunch at Charlottesville's historic Michie (pronounced Mickey) Tavern on traditional southern dishes from fried chicken and biscuits to black-eyed peas, stewed tomatoes and cornbread. This and more is served daily year-round for well under $10. Located on route 53 southeast of the city.

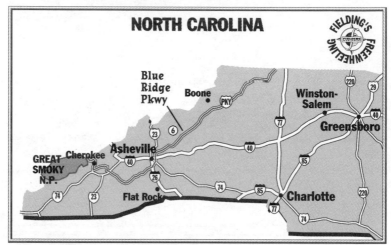

6.   Attend the annual Singing on the Mountain at NC's Grandfather Mountain beside the Blue Ridge Parkway. Gospel music fills the air on the fourth Sunday in June, a tradition now going into its 62nd year. Turn off at Linville and Mile 305.

Musicians at the Old-Time Fiddlers' Convention in Gala , VA

7.   Head for the Old-Time Fiddlers' Convention in Galax, VA, just off the Blue Ridge Parkway via route 97 west. It happens for several days during the second week in August, and draws musicians who play as much for their own pleasure and each other as for the audience of thousands who congregate to this 60-year-old tradition.

Many of the musicians arrive and stay in their own RVs, so other RVers should feel right at home here.

8. The annual Natural Chimneys Jousting Contest is the oldest continuously operated sporting event in the country, set against a backdrop of castle-like rock towers. The tournament, scheduled in mid-June, has been going on since 1821 at this site near Mount Solon, southwest of Harrisonburg on route 607. Natural Chimneys Regional Park with 120 RV hookup sites is nearby. ☎ *(703) 350-2510* for jousting information.

9. Run over and say "hidy" to John-Boy and his family at The Waltons Mountain Museum in Schuyler, VA, on route 617. The museum commemorates the home town of Earl Hamner Jr., creator of the popular TV series, and includes video interviews and episodes from the show, as well as re-creations of the Hollywood sets for the series. (The "real" Waltons Mountain can be found at Frazier Park near Gorman in southern California, where location filming for the series often took place; one of this book's authors appeared occasionally on the show.) The museum is open daily from early March until the end of November except for major holidays.

10. Enroll at Bear Mountain Outdoor School in Hightown, VA, to learn to build log cabins, cultivate mushrooms, keep bees, or spin and dye your own fabrics with natural products. Call ☎ *(703) 468-2700* for more about the unusual, hands-on workshops in mountain crafts and culture. The Campbell Folk School in Brasstown, NC, near Franklin on route 64, also offers courses in mountain crafts from a weekend to a semester in length. They teach woodworking, basketry, enameling, knife-making, quilting, spinning, blacksmithing, music and dance.

INSIDER TIP:

Southern states have local liquor-control laws governed by the city, county or community. If you are accustomed to having wine with dinner, it's a good idea to inquire about the restaurant's policy before you go.

GREAT SMOKY MOUNTAINS NATIONAL PARK

The entrance to Dollywood in Pigeon Forge, TN

The most-visited national park in the system, Great Smoky Mountains gets some eight million people a year passing through its rather garish portals, the commercial strip in Cherokee on the east side with its "Indian chiefs" standing by Plains Indian teepees, holding tom toms and wearing feathered war bonnets Cherokees never used, and gaudy Gatlinburg, which has turned shopping, sleeping and eating into big business.

The only place tackier than either is nearby Pigeon Forge with its flashy Dollywood theme park and bumper-to-bumper traffic inching its way past wall-to-wall motels and fast-food joints. Country singer/movie star Dolly Parton, keeping abreast of the trend, has turned this formerly bucolic, pottery-making village near her birthplace into a tawdry tourist town gripped with gridlock. If we didn't know better, we'd think she built it to get even with some brats who snubbed her in grammar school.

But you can get away if you try. Pay heed to any of the "Quiet Walkways" signs within the park to take an easy and enchanting streamside or woodland stroll. Exploring the side roads leads to special pleasures. A detour to Clingmans Dome winds past the Indian Gap Trailhead with its ruts well worn from the countless horse-drawn vehicles that labored along this former toll road in the 19th century. Hiking trails, except in the most popular months of June, July and October, are often uncrowded, since many of the visitors are making a beeline for Gatlinburg or Pigeon Forge.

Bear sightings are still fairly common in the park, with some 850 of the furry fellows in residence. Both peregrine falcons and river otters have also been seen there lately.

15 OFF-THE-WALL ATTRACTIONS

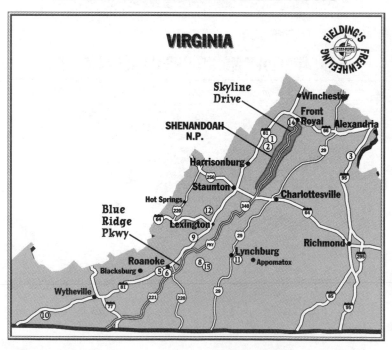

1. Tuttle & Spice Museum, four miles north of New Market off I-81 at the Shenandoah Caverns exit, houses spice boxes and tobacco boxes, corsets and cruets, as well as a reproduction of a small town main street, circa 1900. Everything jammed into the museum's nine period replica shops is a museum item not for sale, but a large gift shop on the premises takes care of any acquisitive stirrings you may feel. The museum is free and open daily.

2. Bedrooms of America Museum and Pottery, at the traffic light on Congress Street (aka US 11) in New Market, is a period house crammed full of antiques, collectibles and junk, including 11 bedrooms, each filled with vintage furniture and furbelows depicting a different specific period between 1650 and 1930.

3. The Dog Mart in Fredericksburg, VA, has been held annually in early October since 1698. A dog auction, contests for ugliest, best-dressed and funniest dogs, a dog parade, and foxhorn-blowing, turkey-calling and hog-calling contests fill the day.

4. More mysterious ghost lights (see "Along the Rio Grande, 10 Off-the-Wall Attractions") called the Brown Mountain Lights can sometimes be seen near Morganton, NC, the area Indians first noted them. In the 1950s, locals attributed the phenomenon to UFOs. A good spotting place is from Beacon Heights off the Blue Ridge Parkway near Grandfather Mountain, and the best time is a clear fall night.

5. In Roanoke, VA, a truly dedicated couple named Epperly have built a Miniature Graceland in their front yard on Riverland Boulevard in tribute to Elvis. It includes an Elvis doll singing Elvis songs to a throng of Barbies, replicas of Graceland, his birthplace in Tupelo and some of the theaters he performed in. Elvis fans are invited to visit; Kim Epperly is also editor of an Elvis newsletter.

6. Also in Roanoke, the world's largest, man-made, illuminated star, 88 1/2-feet high, shines nightly until midnight from a mountain above town. Like a fluorescent tube, the 44-year-old monument usually glows in a ghostly blue-white and hums to itself, but turns red, white and blue on patriotic holidays or whenever there's a traffic fatality in the area.

7. In Saluda, NC, the annual Coon-Dog Barking contest salutes the lyrical voices of packs of local hounds who are paraded around town on floats the first Saturday after July 4. Each float has a tree and in the top of each tree is a very nervous raccoon. Dogs clustered around the trunk of each tree have one minute to make a howling impression on the judges. Saluda is southeast of Hendersonville on US 176.

8. Fantasyland Hobby Horse Farm in Bedford, VA, breeds the world's tiniest horses, as well as miniature donkeys, sheep, mules, pigs, bulls and goats. For two decades the owners have been selectively downsizing Arabians, Clydesdales, Appaloosas and Pintos until they stand no taller than a tot. There's an admission fee; the farm is located three miles from town off route 746.

9. The haunted caves of Natural Bridge Caverns have a moaning female ghost somewhere inside the limestone formations who pipes up periodically, scaring guides and tourists alike. The sound has been going on for more than a century at the caverns, located on US 11 near the Natural Bridge. If that ghost disappoints you, there's a wax museum on the premises as well.

10. In southwestern Virginia, a ramp is not a freeway entrance but a particularly strong-smelling wild onion. At the annual Mount Rogers Ramp Festival the third weekend in May you get the chance to sample ramps cooked with bear meat, trout, in soups and salads. It's held on Whitetop Mountain in the Mount Rogers National Recreation Area, with bluegrass music, a crafts fair and quilting display as well.

11. The Pest House Medical Museum and Confederate Cemetery, an irresistible name, attracts the morbid and medical-minded to Lynchburg's Old City Cemetery at 4th and Taylor Streets. In the 19th century, patients ill with smallpox or measles were quarantined in the Pest House, then when they almost inevitably died, were buried in the cemetery next door. The museum shows curiosities such as an 1860s hypodermic needle and an early chloroform mask.

12. Want to check out a real, working outhouse? Maury River Mercantile in Rockbridge Baths, VA, on Byway 39 offers you a chance, as well as the unique opportunity to cross the river on a swinging bridge. The century-old store sells local crafts plus traditional general-store stock.

13. Blowing Rock, NC, is where a strong updraft at a rock ledge hanging over the Johns River Gorge usually returns items tossed over the edge. An old Indian legend says a maiden prayed to the God of the Winds for return of her warrior, who had fallen over; the wind came up and blew him back. About 50 miles south, as the crow flies, Dr. Elisha Mitchell, a college professor making measurements on a mountain later named for him, had no such luck. He fell to his death over a ledge by a waterfall in 1857.

14. In Front Royal, a pretty teen-aged girl named Belle Boyd doubled as a Confederate spy, and her cottage at *101 Chester Street* is now a museum. She gathered information on a Union Army plan by eavesdropping, then hopped on a horse and rode 15 miles in the middle of the night to take the information to Stonewall Jackson and the Confederates so they defeated the Yankees at the Battle of Front Royal in 1862.

15. The mysterious Beale Treasure is based on three pages of cryptically coded information in a strongbox left for safekeeping with a Lynchburg hotel owner in 1822. Only one of the pages has been decoded; it claims there are 2,981 pounds of gold and 5,092 pounds of silver buried in the Bedford, VA, area, worth approximately $23 million today. A group of 100 computer experts are presently working to unravel the multiple substitution ciphers. Key West treasure hunter Mel Fisher has also taken a crack at it without any luck.

STRETCHING OUT YOUR VACATION

If you're a craftsman or collector of antiques, you could happily and perhaps profitably spend a season or two ensconced in the Appalachians, where people are friendly and prices are modest. There are crafts courses open to the public (see "Ten Blue Ridge Things to Do") and countless antique shops and rural flea markets. One of the biggest and most famous is the Hillsville Flea Market every Labor Day weekend with more than 2,000 vendors on hand. It's about eight miles north of the Blue Ridge Parkway, near Mile 200, via old route 52 or I-77.

If you're a Civil War buff, Virginia will be endlessly fascinating, since 60 percent of all the war's battles were fought there and battlefields and museums take the subject seriously. Even the mighty Walt Disney Company got rebuffed when they wanted to create a historical theme park adjacent to the Manassas battlefield.

HITTING THE HIGHLIGHTS

If you diligently drive the route from the Washington, D.C., area to the Great Smoky Mountains, you could spend less than a week covering it by cutting down on the side trips.

While the ridge routes along Skyline Drive and the Blue Ridge Parkway are beautiful drives, do plan to drop down into parallel routes through country towns and farm communities from time to time to get a better sense of the people who live there.

Plan ahead selectively to cover some but not all the many battlefields, living history exhibits and historical homes throughout the Appalachians.

15 TAKEOUT (OR EAT-IN) TREATS

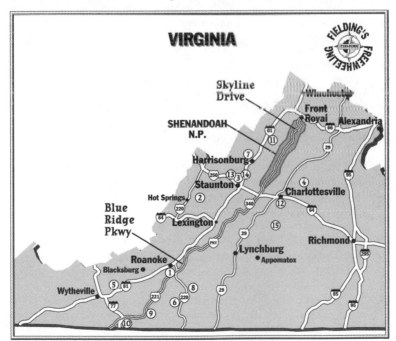

1. **Hot dogs from the Roanoke Weiner Stand** at *25 Campbell Avenue in Roanoke, VA,* have been a local favorite since 1916, when they cost a nickel. Today at under $1, they still represent a great lunchtime bargain.

2. Golf nuts have to try a **Samburger from Sam Snead Tavern** in Hot Springs, VA, not far from the famous Cascades course where Snead was pro for so many years.

3. An authentic Victorian-era ice cream parlor dishes up sodas and sundaes in the restored **C&O railway station** in Staunton, VA. For more railway comestibles, try the crab croquettes at Charlottesville's C&O Restaurant across from the train station.

4. For old-fashioned **fried chicken**, visit the **Toliver House Restaurant** in the little town of Gordonsville, VA, at the junction of US 15, 33 and state road 231 northeast of Charlottesville.

5. Order some **pinto beans and cornbread** to go from **Daynell's Delight** in Pulaski, VA, by the courthouse, and grab a couple of Otis Spunkmeyer cookies for dessert.

6. In Rocky Mount, VA, **Olde Virginia Barbecue** on Meadowview Street dishes up **chicken and ribs** slathered with their own secret sauce (you can buy a bottle of it to take with you). And don't skip the coleslaw, even if you think you don't like coleslaw. You'll like this version.

7. **Hudyard's Country Kitchen**, run by a former Mennonite missionary, is set inside the Dayton, VA, Farmer's Market south of Harrisonburg on route 42. The moderately priced buffet of home cooking includes ham, chicken, beef and vegetables. You may see horse-drawn buggies tied up outside, traditional transportation for the Old Order Mennonites who live in the area.

8. Farther south near Waynesboro, the **Cheese Shop** on route 608 sells fresh **Mennonite cheeses**, while **Kinsinger's Kountry Kitchen** on route 651 just off 608 sells **Mennonite baked goods**, including hummingbird cake and cheese herb bread. The German Baptists, another self-reliant sect similar to Mennonites, sell **sticky buns** and other baked goods plus main dishes at **Boone's Country Store** in Burnt Chimney, a small town very near the Booker T. Washington National Monument.

9. At **Mabry Mill**, Mile 176 on the Blue Ridge Parkway, **corn and buckwheat pancakes** made from grains stone-ground by the mill, along with country ham and biscuits, are available all day long. You can also buy the pancake mix and cornmeal to take home. The restaurant is open from late April through October between 8 a.m. and 6 p.m.

10. **Orchard Gap Deli** in Fancy Gap, VA, just off the parkway between mileposts 193 and 194, sells big **sandwiches to go**, homemade sourdough and raisin bread and Moravian sugar cakes, as well as domestic and imported cheeses, beer and wine, an instant picnic.

11. We've always been fond of **peanut soup** and the non-fancy **Southern Kitchen** on US 11 in New Market is famous for it, along with Lloyd's fried chicken.

12. The **Hardware Store Restaurant** at East Main and Water Streets in Charlottesville makes great **gourmet sandwiches** to go amid the authentic furnishings of a turn-of-the-century hardware store. Park your RV on the Water Street side.

13. **Rowe's Family Restaurant** on route 250 in Staunton is a longtime sanctuary for real **Virginia home cooking**—and coincidentally where the Statler Brothers often eat. Fried chicken, real mashed potatoes, hot biscuits and hot homemade rolls, and for dessert, traditional banana pudding. Exit 222 off I-81.

14. If you're driving along I-81 and want breakfast or a snack, pop off onto route 11 via exit 227 into tiny Verona, VA, for a **ham bun**. While everybody else serves ham biscuits, **Brooks Restaurant** serves its fried country ham in a large buttered yeast bun, more manageable to handle on the road.

15. **The Pig 'N Steak** is one of Virginia's top barbecue places, but also where the fictional Jason Walton from the TV series used to play the piano at the "Dew Drop Inn." **Hickory pit smoked ribs** are the draw here. Closed Mondays, the restaurant is

on Valley Street in Scottsville, south of Charlottesville at the intersection of routes 6 and 20.

ON THE CHEAP: TRIMMING COSTS ON THE ROAD

Shop at local fruit stands for fresh produce; you'll find fresh-from-the farm seasonal fruits and vegetables at much less than supermarkets charge.

Steer clear of commercial theme parks and heavily touted roadside attractions such as Natural Bridge and Luray Caverns. Besides admission fees, they also are surrounded by other attractions that seem particularly alluring to children. Instead, take a free hike to a nearby waterfall or scenic overlook.

You'll save money too, if you can stay self-contained with overnight stops rather than hooking up at a private campground adjacent to the Parkway. By driving every day, you'll keep the battery charged and can top off water storage and empty holding tanks in many of the public campgrounds.

Fresh fruits and vegetables for sale along the roadsides in Virginia

FYI

For a packet of **Virginia information**, call ☎ *(800) VISIT-VA.* They deliver it more promptly than any other state in our experience.

For **Shenandoah National Park information**, write *Route 4, Box 348, Luray, VA 22835* or ☎ *(703) 999-2266,* or *999-2229.*

For information about the **Blue Ridge Parkway**, write *200 BB&T Building, One Pack Square, Asheville, NC 28801,* ☎ *(704) 259-0701.*

To get more information about **private campgrounds**, contact **Virginia Campground Association**, *9415 Hull Street Road, Suite B, Richmond, VA 23236,* ☎ *(804) 276-8614.*

For details about state parks, write **Virginia State Parks Department of Conservation and Recreation**, *203 Governor Street, Suite 302, Richmond, VA 23219,* ☎ *(804) 786-1712.*

SOUTHERN UTAH'S NATIONAL PARKS COUNTRY

Countryside around Zion National Park

"This is the most beautiful place on earth."

Edward Abbey, Desert Solitaire
The book's opening sentence

"This is the place!"

Brigham Young, 1847
On first seeing Salt Lake Valley

The southern half of Utah contains an unprecedented five national parks, four national monuments, three national forests, a national recreational area with the second largest reservoir in North America, and 22 million acres of public land—43 percent of the state—administered by the Bureau of Land Management.

Southern Utah is where Butch Cassidy and Etta Place rode a bicycle in *Butch Cassidy and the Sundance Kid,* where Thelma and Louise drove off the cliff into the canyon, and where Max von Sydow delivered the Sermon on the Mount in *The Greatest Story Ever Told.*

It's where the California gull is the state bird, where the world's most famous automobile commercial was filmed and where Brigham Young took his 27th wife.

This is the place dinosaurs roamed 500 million years ago, the Anasazi or Ancient Ones planted corn two thousand years ago, and Chinese miners at Silver Reef put food on family graves a century ago (giving local Paiutes a taste for Chinese cuisine).

France's Madam Curie used radioactive ore from Moab to develop radium in 1896; by 1952, uranium prospectors came from everywhere to really dig it.

Utah has the highest literacy rate, largest average household size, second highest birth rate and second lowest death rate in the fifty states. The average citizen lives to be 75.76 years old, and the average age is 25.7. More than 70 percent of the state's population are members of the Church of Jesus Christ of Latter-Day Saints, also known as Mormons.

When to go. Any time of year, some part of Utah is in its prime. Skiers flock to "the greatest snow on earth," Utah's champagne powder, in winter. Most of its dozen major ski areas are clustered to the east of Salt Lake City, outside our adventure area, but Brian Head ski resort, nearly 10,000 feet with a long snow season, is 12 miles off I-15 at Parowan, near Cedar City. St. George in the southwest's Dixie area is mild in winter. Fall and spring are the ideal times for RVers to visit southern Utah's national parks; summer is hot in the lower elevations, cooler at Brian Head, Cedar Breaks and Bryce Canyon. All the national parks, however, are jam-packed in summer.

What to take. Sunblock, a sun hat, good walking or hiking shoes, an adequate supply of favorite spirits, a camera and at least twice as much film as you'd expect to use (it's that photogenic!)

What to wear. Take layered clothing for all of Utah's parks. In late fall and winter, you'll want heavy parkas and boots or shoes with snow-safe treads. We encountered considerable snow in mid-October at Bryce Canyon and Cedar Breaks, while Zion, Canyonlands, Arches and Capitol Reef still had sunny, shirt-sleeve weather. In summer's heat, natural fibers help absorb perspiration.

UTAH TALKIN': A GLOSSARY

Hoodoo—an eroded pillar of sandstone topped with a hard rock cap and sculpted into eerie shapes

Wash—the dry bed of a sometimes stream; never camp in these areas and avoid them during rainstorms

Butte—an isolated hill or mountain rising suddenly out of flat land

Mesa—a flat-topped, steep-walled land area; a table mountain

Petroglyphs—carvings incised on rock surfaces

Pictographs—pictures drawn on rock surfaces

Slickrock—a smooth, slippery rock formation burnished by "desert varnish"

Desert varnish—a dark, glossy finish on rock created by heat-loving bacteria that draw iron and manganese from airborne dust

Natural bridges—water-cut (including snow melting and refreezing) rock formations in the bottoms of canyons

Natural arches—water-cut rock formations that stand on the skyline

LDS—Church of Jesus Christ of Latter-day Saints, also called Saints or Mormons

Gentile—in LDS usage, any non-Mormon

FREEWHEELING THROUGH UTAH'S NATIONAL PARK COUNTRY

Henry Mountains along the Bicentennial Highway

Early on an October morning, the snowcapped Henry Mountains glisten against a blue sky. Down every wash a stalwart line of cottonwoods has turned a glowing gold. Flocks of tiny Berwick's wrens, exuberant after the rain, flutter up past our windshield and across the Bicentennial Highway. Water shines from holes and grooves in slickrock, and snow dusts the red mesas and buttes and throws twisted black junipers into sharp relief. As we begin to climb toward Natural Bridges National Monument, the whole desert forest of piñon pines and sagebrush is covered with puffy white clumps of snow. Everything is indescribably, breathtakingly beautiful.

The state tourism people have divided southern Utah into four different areas—Color Country in the south central and southwest, including Zion and Bryce Canyons National Parks; Canyonlands to the southeast, including Canyonlands and Arches National Parks; Panoramaland in the west central region, including Capitol Reef National Park; and Castle Country in the east central sector, the terrain where Butch Cassidy used to ride. You'll need to remember the divisions when using the otherwise excellent state travel guides.

Because so much of the state is public lands, it makes an ideal getaway for RVers, especially those who enjoy self-contained camping in parklands and the wilderness.

Driving through Utah, we always try to imagine the pioneers and early Mormon settlers moving slowly through the incredibly eerie terrain with plenty of time on their hands and a little creative daydreaming. It's the only way some of the geological landmarks could have been named. We stare in vain at spots like Capitol Dome or Great White Throne and wonder who on earth could have thought that particular rock really looks like a dome or a throne.

GOING FOR THE LONG HAUL

We ran across quite a few people in southern Utah who came out on a vacation and never went home, so consider yourself warned. One could certainly spend a long, happy season RVing, hiking and biking in and around the public lands with an occasional hop into town to restock the larder, fill up with gas, top off the water and dump the holding tanks.

Two weeks in each park or national monument, taking into consideration the 14-day camping limit, would give plenty of time to explore each, and a week or two on a houseboat in Lake Powell would provide pure pleasure. Add another two weeks at particularly scenic BLM areas such as the Colorado River outside Moab and you'll find an entire season filled with appealing things to do.

The temporary employment scene in Moab is usually active, so full-timers can find seasonal shops looking for clerks and restaurants hiring waiters.

HITTING THE HIGHLIGHTS

Zion National Park, Kolob Canyons area

The roads are generally very good in Utah, so you'll be able to move along as briskly as necessary except when the first snow begins to fall in late October or early November. The highlights could be covered in as little as seven days, but you'd have very little time to hike and explore.

Zion and Bryce Canyon National Parks require a minimum of a full day each, with two days in each allowing time to hike a bit as well.

RVers who choose not to take the tunnel route from Zion to Bryce can return to I-15, make the short detour into Kolob Canyons from the interstate, then exit at Cedar City to drive through Cedar Breaks and along route 143 past Panguitch Lake, a very scenic route, before turning south on US 89 to connect with route 12 to Bryce.

While geology buffs will enjoy the dead-end scenic drive that delves more deeply into Capitol Reef National Park, travelers pressed for time can skip it. But everyone should take the time to drive into the orchards and campground area at Fruita, as well as making roadside stops along the way for the old schoolhouse and the cliff petroglyphs.

If time permits, swing south from the junction at Hanksville to drive Bicentennial Highway, including a good look at Glen Canyon National Recreation Area at Hites Crossing and a visit to Natural Bridges National Monument. Otherwise, head north to I-70 and take US 191 south at exit 180 to drop down in Moab, Arches and Canyonlands.

Allow a full day each for Arches, The Needles and Islands in the Sky, adding to the latter a side detour into Dead Horse Point State Park.

Lake Powell at Hites Crossing

FIVE SITES WITH DÉJÀ VU
ALL OVER AGAIN

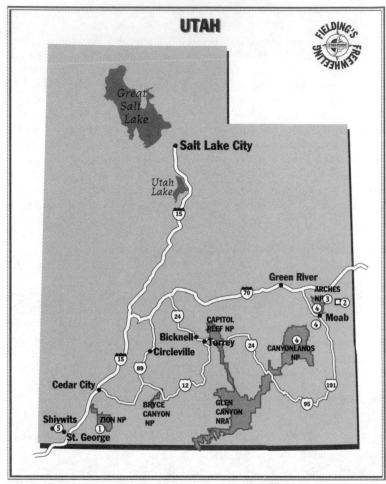

1.   Grafton, a picturesque ghost town set against the towering rock walls of Zion
     National Park, is where Paul Newman and Katherine Ross rode a bicycle to the
     music of "Raindrops Keep Fallin' on My Head" in the film *Butch Cassidy and the
     Sundance Kid*. Turn south on Bridge Road in Rockville, near the entrance to Zion
     National Park on route 9, cross an old iron bridge and follow a four-mile dirt road
     to the old cemetery and town. Larger motorhomes and trailers might find it a tight
     squeeze in some spots. The road, also called the Smithsonian Butte Scenic Backway,
     terminates in Hildale.

2.   Outside Moab at a pair of 1500-foot looming spires called Fisher Towers, history's
     most famous TV car commercials were shot, with a Chevrolet lowered by helicopter
     sitting all alone atop a tall, narrow pinnacle rising high into the air, surrounded only
     by desert and craggy red rocks in all directions. The first commercial was such a big
     hit in 1964, a second one was shot in 1974 to wow a new buying generation. The
     towers are on Scenic Route 128 east from Moab at mile 21, with a road sign iden-
     tifying them. A hiking trail to the towers and a picnic table are also at the site.

3. All the book covers and posters you've ever seen about Utah leap to life at Delicate Arch in Arches National Park. Early cowboys called the much-photographed 45-foot-high red sandstone arch "The Schoolmarm's Drawers," but to us it most closely resembles the bottom half of a bow-legged cowboy wearing chaps. The hike, the park's most popular walk, is a strenuous 480-foot ascent over a huge rock mountain similar to Australia's Ayers Rock and seemed much longer than the three-mile roundtrip the park literature claims, especially on the uphill part. Once there, many visitors sit and stare in awe at the arch (trying, perhaps, to catch their breaths) while photographers clamber over precarious rocks for an ever-better angle. Late afternoon is best for the golden light against the stone. The walk sets out from the Wolfe Ranch parking lot off the park's main road.

4. Pick up a free Moab Movie Locations sheet in the Moab Visitor Center, and you can head for all your favorite movie locations in the area. A fan of Indiana Jones? See places from his childhood *(Indiana Jones and the Temple of Doom)* at Double Arches in Arches National Park. Check out Canyonlands' Island the Sky, where Max von Sydow as Christ delivered the Sermon on the Mount in *The Greatest Story Ever Told* and Thelma and Louise drove off the cliff 2000 years later.

5. Northwest of St. George, Snow Canyon State Park (see "10 Campground Oases") is where Robert Redford as *The Electric Horseman* freed his stallion at the end of the 1979 film set in Las Vegas, directed by Redford's chum Sidney Pollack and costarring Jane Fonda and Willie Nelson.

THE MORMONS

In the spring of 1830, a devout young man named Joseph Smith published the *Book of Mormon* and founded the Church of Jesus Christ of Latter-day Saints, a charismatic religion claiming to be a restoration of the original church, in Fayette, New York. Among its tenets were polygamy and an active program of proselytism, neither of which found favor in the neighborhood.

Chased from New York to Ohio and Missouri, they settled in Nauvoo, Missouri, where they developed a city of 20,000. But the new neighbors were no more hospitable than the old ones, burning and killing until Smith decided in 1844 it was time to move again. In the meantime, however, he declared himself a candidate for president of the United States and said if elected, he would not move west.

When members of the church smashed a printing press they believed was publishing libel against them, Smith and his brother were jailed, then taken from prison by a mob which killed them both.

The man who succeeded Smith as church leader was Brigham Young. At the end of 1845, when the state of Illinois repealed the city charter for Nauvoo, he organized an advance party to go west looking for a new settlement. Beginning in early 1846, church members loaded their goods onto covered wagons, hitched up their horses and led them down to ferries on the Mississippi River. The great Mormon exodus had begun.

That year they got as far as Iowa, and the next year Brigham Young and his company of pioneers entered the Salt Lake Valley on July 24, 1847. The migration continued, with thousands of the devout literally walking and pulling their possessions in hand carts, until by 1900 the Mormons had established 500 settlements in and around Utah, many of them in arid, inhospitable desert.

Certainly the most dramatic moment was at Hole-in-the-Rock in 1879, when 230 Mormons blasted a hole through a 50-foot cliff at Glen Canyon and lowered their 80 wagons by chains and ropes to the river 1800 feet below, where homemade rafts waited. They went on to found the town of Bluff, which today claims a population of 250, or 20 more than its founding fathers. Today boaters and four-wheel-drive travelers can see the spot where the hole was blasted in the rock.

The Mormon cause was severely set back in 1857 when some xenophobic members, fearful of federal interference and anxious to keep out both miners and eager new settlers, triggered the infamous Mountain Meadows Massacre, where Mormon militia members and local Indians together slaughtered 120 of the 137-member Fancher wagon train party bound for California. The only survivors were 17 children under the age of seven. Ironically, the Fancher party had taken the southern route despite warnings of possible friction in Utah, because all had heard the terrible stories of the Donner Party tragedy crossing a northern route a decade earlier. A marker off route 18 near the town of Central in southwestern Utah identifies the massacre site.

It took almost fifty years and the church's outlawing of polygamy before Utah achieved statehood in 1896.

INSIDER TIP: HOW TO READ UTAH STREET PLATS

Brigham Young directed Utah's early Mormons to lay out street plats like a giant checkerboard, with streets running true north and south and true east and west from a central meridian point. If an address is 500 South 700 East, for instance, you drive five blocks south from the center and then seven blocks east. Blocks are laid out in increments of 100. Whether you're in Salt Lake City or Moab, the plan holds true.

Kolob Reservoir Road in Zion National Park

INSIDER TIP:

RVs entering Zion National Park are subject to parking and tunnel restrictions that do not cause any major inconveniences but must be adhered to. A fee of $10 is required for any RV wider than 7'10" (including side mirrors) or taller than 11'4" to drive through the 1.1 mile tunnel on the Zion-Mt. Carmel road. This is because the vehicle has to proceed through the middle of the tunnel without oncoming traffic, which is controlled by park rangers posted at either end. The tunnel is open to RVs between 8 a.m. and 8 p.m. March through October; to pass through any other time, ☎ (801) 772-3256 to make advance arrangements.

IT IS NOT ESSENTIAL TO GO THROUGH THE TUNNEL IF YOU DON'T WISH TO; SIMPLY ARRIVE AND LEAVE THE PARK BY THE SPRINGDALE GATE.

ZION NATIONAL PARK

Scenery along Kolob Reservoir Road in Zion National Park

The national park, which began its official life as Mukuntuweap National Monument in 1909, dates from 1917 with the name Zion, given to it by Mormon settlers in the area who did not like the Paiute name. Its early description as an "extraordinary example of canyon erosion" fails to do justice to the rich palette of colors in the canyon that range from creamy white to burnished copper and dark rose.

Dramatic, beautiful and accessible, Zion is Utah's most-visited national park with more than two million tourists a year. Some 900 species of wildflowers bloom here; to find out which flowers are blooming where in the park, call the wildflower hotline at ☎ *(801) 581-5322* between April and September.

There are four driving entrances into Zion, only two of which connect—the route 9 south entrance at Springdale and the east entrance on Zion-Mt. Carmel Highway. The 25-mile, dead-end drive along Kolob Terrace Road from the town of Virgin to the Kolob Reservoir winds in and out of the park's western boundaries through varying terrain, and the not-to-be-missed Kolob Canyons Road enters the northernmost part of the park from I-15 south of Cedar City. For more about both, see "10 Scenic Side Trips."

Despite its hot summers, Zion's mild spring, autumn and winter weather makes the park a year-round destination for RVers. There may be some snow in winter but the roads are plowed and the Watchman campground is open.

The seven-mile drive through Zion Canyon is the park's top drive, even though it is frequently clogged with slow-moving traffic. Do park your RV when you find a turnout with enough space so you can look up to the mountains' majesty above you. You can turn around at the Temple of Sinawava parking lot at the road's end, although you will not be permitted to park there.

A propane-fueled shuttle-bus system to ferry visitors through the canyon instead of permitting private vehicles to enter is in the planning stages, although it would not likely be implemented before 1999.

Among the park's most popular hiking trails are several that are short and/or easy. Weeping Rocks is a fairly steep quarter-mile climb leading to an enormous rocky ledge covered with mosses and plants with a constant stream of "tears" dripping from it. It's also a cool place to visit on a hot summer day.

The two-mile Emerald Pools trail loop is not too demanding if you go uphill via the right-hand trail after crossing the footbridge by the parking lot, climb to the Middle Pool and then take the other trail, somewhat rougher and steeper, back downhill.

The Lower Emerald Pool trail and the Gateway to the Narrows trail at the Temple of Sinawava are wheelchair-accessible if a companion is along to help with the rough spots along the cement paving. The latter is a fairly level, two-mile loop that goes through the hanging gardens area, bright with wildflowers in spring and early summer.

Dedicated hikers like to strike out along the ten-mile West Rim trail between the canyon and Lava Point, but those starting from the canyon are cautioned not to try to make it uphill to Lava Point on a one-day hike. The Zion Narrows trail, which splashes through the icy waters of the Virgin River at some points, requires a free hiking permit for the two-day, 32-mile round trip. Fall is best, when water levels in the river are lowest; take a dry change of clothing along in a sealed plastic bag.

Bicyclists are limited to paved roads in the park, and are not permitted to ride through the Mt. Carmel tunnel. Rangers will transport your bicycle through the tunnel free of charge, however.

Photographers should try to drive through the canyon in early morning and again in late afternoon to take advantage of the dramatic light that models the contours of the rocks.

10 CAMPGROUND OASES

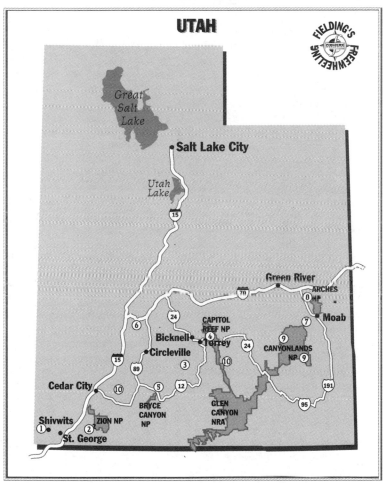

1. **Snow Canyon State Park**, near St. George in Utah's Dixie district, has 14 sites with water and electrical hookups and picnic shelters that are lined up in a row, plus 22 non-hookup sites that are more spacious and tree-shaded. The park has flush toilets, showers, sanitary dump station and hiking trails through spectacular scenery. It's open all year and the weather is mild; the canyon was named for a pioneer family's surname, not the falling white stuff. Take exit 6 (Bluff Street) from I-15 and drive northwest of St. George on route 18 ten miles, then two miles on route 300. The

three-quarter-mile hike to Johnson's Arch is the park's most popular, although some visitors take flashlights and explore the lava caves near the north end of the park. Reservations: ☎ *(800) 322-3770.*

2. The two campgrounds in **Zion National Park** suitable for RVs can be found just beyond the park's Springdale entrance, Watchman Campground with Loops A, B and C (270 sites), and adjacent South Campground (140 sites). The sites, without hookups, are generally widely spaced with some shade trees. All have metal picnic tables and cooking grills; some of the nicest are along the Virgin River at the edge of Loop A. Campgrounds have flush toilets but no showers, and a 14-day limit on a first-come first-served basis. Many sites are handicap-accessible. All spaces fill before noon in summer. A sanitary dump station is located at the entrance to Watchman.

3. **Calf Creek Recreation Area** near Escalante lies in a river bottom canyon surrounded by red cliff walls with 11 well-spaced sites, some shaded by aspen trees. Trout fishing is nearby. There are no hookups, a 14-day limit and toilets. A five-mile trail leads to lovely Calf Creek Falls. This Bureau of Land Management park, closed mid-November to mid-March, is 15 miles northeast of Escalante off route 12.

4. **Capitol Reef National Park's** only campground is among the orchards in an old Mormon farm settlement called Fruita, where campers may pick ripe fruit from the trees, weigh it and deposit a modest price per pound in an honor cash box. The 71 sites are mostly level, grassy and tree-shaded with gorgeous red rock cliffs on all sides and grazing mule deer at dawn and dusk. It's open all year. The last of the community's residents moved away in 1960, and now the park maintains the village as a restored historic site. There are no hookups, no reservations, 14-day limit, flush toilets, sanitary dump station. One wheelchair accessible campsite in Loop B is held until 6 p.m. nightly.

5. **Bryce Canyon National Park** has two campgrounds, both near the entrance. North Campground offers 105 sites and Sunset has 111, none with hookups. A sanitary dump station (fee), showers (fee) at Sunset, and flush toilets are available. Picnic tables, fireplaces and piped water are supplied. Bring your own firewood. There's a 14-day camping limit. Reservations are not taken but to check ahead if there's space for the night, call the visitor center at ☎ *(801) 834-5322.*

6. **Fremont Indian State Park** near Richfield is a former Fishlake National Forest campground called Castle Rock, a couple of miles off I-70 near the junction of I-15. It was shifted over to state park status to supplement the park, where part of a large Fremont River Indian village has been excavated. The little-known Fremont River Indians, who preceded the Anasazi, vanished before the first Spanish arrived. We found the campground quiet and uncrowded (we shared its 20-odd sites with one other RV one moonlit October night). The camping fee also includes admission to the museum. Sites are well spaced out, many shaded by aspens, all with tables; there are flush toilets but no hookups or dump station.

7. **Dead Horse Canyon State Park** makes an excellent alternative to Arches or Canyonlands when they are full, which is most of the time. The camping fee at Kayenta Campground is $7, and advance reservations can be made for an additional $5 surcharge (☎ *800-322-3770*). There are 21 campsites with covered cooking/eating areas and windbreaks, metal picnic tables and concrete pads for RVs. A sanitary dump station is available but no hookups. A family of mule deer are often seen grazing in the area. The campground is closed in winter. The park is located off route 313 northwest of Moab.

8. **Devil's Garden Campground** in Arches National Park is situated amid red rocks and green pines near the end of an 18-mile road, with 53 first-come first-served sites.

We would suggest that if campground space is still available when you enter the park, no matter what the time of day, that you drive straight to the campground, pick out a spot and register, then go back out to do your sightseeing. The fee is $7 a night, and sites include tables and grills, with flush toilets and piped water. While all the pads are paved, RVs owners will need to check the level, since many of them are uneven. There is no camping fee when the water is turned off, usually from the end of October until mid-March.

9.   **Squaw Flat** in the Needles section of Canyonlands has 26 well-separated sites, many snuggled into rock-surrounded coves with trees, and most but not all adequate for larger RVs. Each site has fire grates and table, and there are pit toilets and water available by the bucketful from a water wagon. If you need to top off your RV tank, follow signage to a water hose connection on Cave Spring Road near Wooden Shoe Arch. The only campground in the Island in the Sky area of Canyonlands accessible to most RVs is Willow Flat, down a rough washboard dirt road with 12 primitive sites for smaller RVs only (under 25 feet). Unfortunately, gnats are a problem much of the summer. There are pit toilets and fire grates but no water at Willow Flat.

10.   At Cedar Breaks National Monument, **Point Supreme Campground** one mile north of the visitor center offers 30 sites suitable for RVs, with picnic tables, piped water and flush toilets. Because the elevation is above 10,000 feet, the campground is open June through September only. No reservations are taken, there are no hook-ups and a fee is charged.

> ### INSIDER TIP:
>
> *It was 4 p.m. The Canyonlands park ranger, standing by a sign saying "Campground Full," suggested we might drive around anyhow and check for space. We discovered a couple packing up to check out and nabbed the last free space in the park. Moral: Don't give up without a try.*

> ### INSIDER TIP:
>
> *RV restrictions abound in Bryce Canyon National Park, but should not inhibit freewheelers from sampling some of the park's best and most distinctive scenery. Vehicles towing trailers are not permitted beyond Sunset Point turnoff, but after a winter snowfall, the road is usually closed off at this point anyhow. Travel trailers may be left in designated parking areas at the visitor center or Sunset Campground. RVs longer than 25 feet are not allowed at Bryce Point or Paria Point at any time due to extremely limited turn-around space.*

BRYCE CANYON NATIONAL PARK

Bryce Canyon, "a hell of a place to lose a cow," in the words of one early rancher, is a collection of needle-like red limestone hoodoos (see "Utah Talkin': A Glossary"), jewel-like eroded spires seen at their best in early morning or late-day light or, best of all, after a snowfall when puffs of white snow dust the bright red rocks.

The local Paiute thought they were men turned into stone by an angry god.

Winter can be a rewarding time to visit if you enjoy cross-country skiing or snowshoeing; the park lends snowshoes to visitors free of charge at the Visitor Center if you leave a credit card or driver's license for deposit.

Snow in Bryce Canyon

Mule deer are plentiful and easily spotted, especially in winter. Elk are also present but more rarely seen. With 172 species of birds identified in the park, you'll have a good chance of spotting something; a checklist is available at the visitor center.

A number of hiking trails, a total of 61 miles, wend their way down into the canyons among the hoodoos. The most popular half-day trek is a combination of the Queens Garden and Navajo Loop trails, a three-mile roundtrip jaunt through the most dramatic part of the ampitheater. Just remember that every trail that goes down in the early part of the hike when you're fresh and eager comes back up later when you may be tired; don't overestimate your ability.

Bristlecone Loop trail from Rainbow Point takes a one-and one-half mile circuit through a pine forest. If a level walk sounds ideal, the Rim trail follows an 11-mile route with smooth paved walking areas accessible for wheelchairs between Sunrise and Sunset Points. Naturalists offer morning walks daily in summer, as well as moonlight hikes on the three evenings a month preceding a full moon.

The reconstructed Bryce Canyon Lodge, a National Historic Landmark, echoes some of the 1920s feeling of the original. Ruby's Inn, just outside the park, dates from 1919 but has suffered so many fires over the years that it has lost its period look. There is a private campground at Ruby's Inn with hookups, closed in winter.

The most direct connection to Bryce Canyon is from Zion National Park north on US 89, then east on route 12, one argument in favor of paying the $10 RV tunnel fee on the Zion-Mt. Carmel Road (see "Insider Tip" page 366). Otherwise, you can access US 89 from the west via routes 14 or 20 from I-15, or from the north via I-70. Red Canyon on route 12 is a particularly scenic approach with rock tunnels and bridges framing the road ahead.

INSIDER TIP:

Be careful to allow a day or two to acclimatize to the area's elevation—in Bryce, 6500 to 9100 feet—before setting out on a major hike. And if a lightning storm comes up, stay away from the canyon rims, particularly the iron railings.

10 MACHO THINGS TO DO IN SOUTHERN UTAH

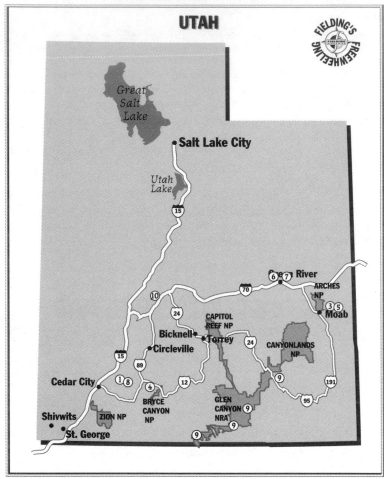

1. **Mountain biking** at Brian Head offers 12 different routes rated "easy" to "advanced." Because the area is at 10,000 feet, it's cool enough in summer to enjoy biking but usually snow-covered from November through May. Expect a rich variety of flora and fauna in the four life-zones: Alpine, subalpine, Canadian and transitional. You can get essential detailed maps locally. Four bike-rental shops are in the tiny town of Brian Head, reached via route 143 from exit 78 on I-15. Local shuttle services or chairlifts can ferry you to the top of the hill and you can ride down. The nearest camping is in Cedar Breaks (see "Ten Campground Oases").

2. One-day expeditions that combine **whitewater river rafting and four-wheel-drive land tours** are offered by Navtec Expeditions of Moab, ☎ *(800) 833-1278*. A morning sportsboat ride goes along the Colorado River gorge just underneath Dead Horse Point State Park (see "Ten Scenic Side Trips"), stopping to see dinosaur tracks, petrified wood and Indian rock art. A buffet picnic lunch is served, then a transfer to 4 x 4s for a tour up Long Canyon and Gemini Bridges. Cost is around $75 for adults, $58 for kids up to 17.

3. **Trail rides** from Pack Creek Ranch near Moab can be as short as an hour or two or as long as a three-night pack trip into the back country. Morning and evening rides into Courthouse Wash in Arches National Park are also available in summer for $20 an hour, $35 for two hours. Call the ranch at ☎ *(801) 259-5505*. Meals and cabin or bunkhouse lodging are also available at the ranch, but reservations need to be made well ahead of time.

4. Bryce Canyon in winter offers extraordinary views of bright red Navajo sandstone sprinkled with snow and sparkling in the sunlight against a clear blue sky. **Cross country skiing or snowshoeing** are two excellent ways to see it. Self-contained RVs can stay in the park's North Campground near the visitor center during winter, although water is cut off and the sanitary dump closed down. There are no hookups. The 11-mile Rim Trail with its level terrain and sensational views down into the canyon is a good place to start. Snowshoer-wannabes can borrow a pair free from the rangers at the visitor center, leaving a credit card or driver's license as a deposit, and set off in the snow.

5. **Mountain biking** in Moab, North American capital of the sport, can start on the 10-mile Slickrock Trail, tackled by 100,000 eager sprocketheads a year. Beginners are advised to start with Gemini Bridges or Hurrah Pass, each 14 miles long. In town three bike shops, each with its obligatory espresso machine, rents or sells anything you may need from maps to machines.

6. A **one-day river run** through Gray Canyon on the Green River is a quick, easy option for beginners from Moki Mac River Expeditions in Salt Lake City. They'll pick you up at your campground in the Green River area off I-70 and take you through six or so splashy rapids and some rugged scenery on an oar-powered expedition that costs $45 for adults, $35 for children. Call them at ☎ *(800) 284-7280* for information and reservations.

7. Want to **paddle your own canoe?** Experienced river runners can get a permit from the Bureau of Land Management for an 84-mile run along the Green River between Sand Wash and the town of Green River. Rapids in Desolation and Gray Canyon are generally rated Class II and III; life jackets are required, as are reservations. Contact the BLM at the Price Area Office, *900 North 700 East, Price, Utah 84501,* ☎ *(801) 637-4591*.

8. **Snowmobile tours** set out from Brian Head during ski season on one-and-a-half-hour, half-day or custom tours priced from $40. Kids 10 and under travel free. Cedar Breaks National Monument, gorgeous against a bright blue sky when decorated with winter snow, is nearby. Call Crystal Mountain Recreation at ☎ *(801) 677-2FUN* for details.

9. Explore ancient Anasazi caves, photograph remote Rainbow Bridge, swim and picnic at a deserted beach, and all from the comfort of home. **Houseboating on Lake Powell**, second largest manmade lake in North America, is something akin to having your RV walk on water. Three sizes, 36', 44' and 50', are available for rent year-round from four perimeter marinas in Glen Canyon National Recreation Area—Bullfrog, Hite Marina, Wahweap and Halls Crossing. Between October and May, houseboats can be reserved for trips as short as one or two days. The rest of the year, minimum rental requirements are longer. Call ARA Leisure Services, ☎ *(800) 528-6154*, for reservations, well ahead of time in summer.

10. **Off-road or all-terrain vehicles**, including four-wheelers, dune buggies, dirt bikes and ATVs, have access to 60,000 acres of Little Sahara Recreation Area, including the 200-mile Paiute ATV Trail over three mountain ranges. The trail can be entered near the junction of I-15 and I-70 between Fillmore and Beaver and also from Rich-

field on I-70. For more information, contact Utah Tourism's Panoramaland division in Richfield, ☎ *(800) 748-4361.*

INSIDER TIP:

The direst thing you can do in southern Utah is to walk, bike, drive on or otherwise break the cryptobiotic crust, a fragile and ancient covering that looks dark brown and crumbly and nurtures virtually all desert life, both flora and fauna. One careless step can destroy crust that will take 50 to 100 years to recover. Always stay on the trail or roadway. As locals say, Tiptoe through the crypto.

CEDAR BREAKS NATIONAL MONUMENT AND CEDAR CITY

Snowy overlook at Cedar Breaks National Monument

The name comes from early settlers in the region, who called any terrain too steep for wagon travel "breaks" or "badlands." The same folks thought the junipers and ancient bristlecone pine trees growing on the rim of the redrock ampitheater were cedars.

Similar to Bryce Canyon but even more vivid in color, Cedar Breaks is less visited than the former, despite its convenient location only 23 miles from I-15 via route 14.

A huge rock ampitheater with trails leading 3400 feet down into the gorge, it offers a special challenge to hikers in good shape. Two special two-mile walks for those already acclimated to the elevation are the Alpine Pond Trail, a fairly easy jaunt to a pond and forest glade, and the Spectra Point Trail, a good place to see bristlecone pines. There are also ranger-led nature walks, geology talks and campfire programs in summer.

Although roads are closed by snow in winter, visitors can come into the park by cross-country skis or snowmobiling, entering via Brian Head ski resort. A campground inside the monument is open June through September only.

The Utah Shakespearean Festival in nearby Cedar City, going strong for 33 years, presents three classic plays in repertory every summer in the outdoor Shakespearean theater, as well as three contemporary plays in a smaller indoor theater. The season runs from early July through September, and playgoers come early to enjoy the evening's Greenshow of jugglers, puppeteers and vendors dressed in Elizabethan costume. They can also dine at a lively Renaissance Feaste. Call ☎ *(801) 586-7878* for reservations, tickets or more information about the festival.

INSIDER TIP:

Bring along tapes or CDs, because on the car radio in Utah you can only get three sounds day or night—the Mormon Tabernacle Choir, country music and Rush Limbaugh.

ABOUT EDWARD ABBEY

". . you can't see anything from a car; you've got to get out of the goddamned contraption and walk, better yet crawl, on hands and knees, over the sandstone and through the thornbush and cactus. When traces of blood begin to mark your trail, you'll see something, maybe. Probably not."

From the introduction to *Desert Solitaire*

You won't travel far in southeastern Utah without running across the ghost of the late Edward Abbey, a tough-minded, combative, outdoor writer and environmentalist who spent several seasons as a park ranger in Arches.

He was best-known for comments like these we quote. Nevertheless, he wasn't above poking fun at himself as he railed against over-use of his beloved Utah desert. On an early trip into The Maze, the most remote part of Canyonlands, he and a friend stopped to look at an almost-new hiker register.

"'Keep the tourists out,' some tourist from Salt Lake City has written. As fellow tourists we heartily agree.'"

Later, still at The Maze, he writes, "For God's sake leave this country alone—Abbey," to which his friend adds, "For Abbey's sake leave this country alone—God."

Pick up a copy of his book at any of the park visitor centers. It makes a good companion on the journey.

10 SCENIC SIDE TRIPS

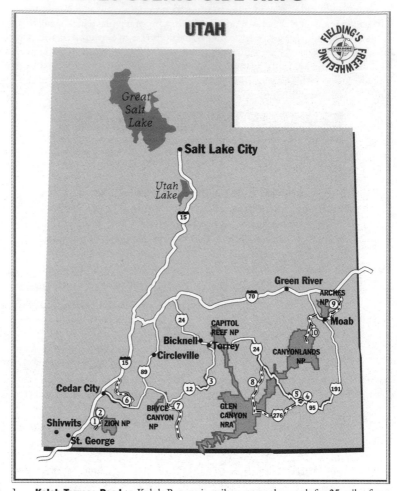

1.   **Kolob Terrace Road** to Kolob Reservoir strikes out to the north for 25 miles from
     the town of Virgin (like the river) on route 9 west of Zion NP. From farms with lush
     green grass and trees it climbs up through ranchland terrain set amid rich red rocks,
     then into groves of aspen and oaks and finally into the secluded high country. If the
     dirt road to Lava Rock looks clear, take the short detour out to an overlook down
     into Zion Canyon. The lightly-traveled Kolob Terrace Road, paved for most of its
     length, is not recommended for long travel trailers and RVs over 32 feet because
     there are few pullouts and no good turn-arounds along the way. Allow one-and-a-
     half to two hours for the round trip.

2.   **Kolob Canyons**, the northern end of Zion National Park, is only five minutes away
     from I-15 at exit 42, and cannot be reached by vehicle from the rest of the park. The
     stunningly beautiful five-mile drive winds its way between the red Navajo sandstone
     Finger Canyons to a forested overlook among groves of piñon pine and aspen. Sev-
     eral hiking trails set out from the overlook area, including a moderately strenuous
     five-mile trek along Taylor Creek and a strenuous 14-mile hike to Kolob Arch,
     believed to be the world's largest freestanding arch.

3. **Scenic Byway route 12** between Escalante and Boulder climbs a narrow hogback
    ridge near Calf Creek Recreation Area amid breathtaking views and sheer dropoffs
    on both sides of the road. The Civilian Conservation Corps built the road here in
    the early 1940s; until then, the mail was delivered by muleback into Boulder.
    Mountain bikers and four-wheel drive vehicles can take the original Hell's Back-
    bone dirt road into Dixie National Forest and Box Death Hollow Road, scourge of
    the mule-riding mailmen. Petrified Forest State Park at Escalante displays colorful
    specimens of petrified wood, while Anasazi Village State Park at Boulder exhibits a
    reconstructed pueblo where you can try your hand at grinding corn the Indian way.
    The former also has a campground, but a more attractive spot to overnight, if
    there's space, is Calf Creek Recreation Area (see "Ten Campground Oases"). The
    32-mile road between Boulder and Grover, the last of it not paved until 1985,
    passes through elegant groves of aspen, past several forest service campgrounds and
    over a 9600-foot pass.

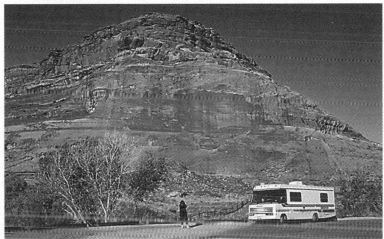

A stop along the Bicentennial Highway at Hog Springs

4. **Bicentennial Highway**, so-named because it was built in 1976, opens up one of the
    most sensational stretches of countryside in the entire west. From Hanksville south
    on 95 to Blanding in the Four Corners country, the terrain unfolds with one spec-
    tacular vista after another. The Henry Mountains, snow-capped and framed with
    red rock buttes and golden fields of hay, stand out against a vast blue sky. Washes
    are delineated with narrow stripes of cottonwood, leaves bright green in summer
    and gold in autumn. After a rain, birds flock to the water shining from holes and
    grooves in the rock. At Hites Crossing on Lake Powell, a delicate arched bridge
    crosses the Colorado River while all around the nooks and crannies of the lake
    houseboats bob at anchor.

5. **Natural Bridges National Monument** contains three natural bridges easily seen from
    roadside viewpoints for freewheelers in a hurry, or accessible by hiking trails for trav-
    elers who want to explore. A small visitor center details the differences between nat-
    ural bridges and arches, in case you were wondering. The campground here, while
    dotted with trees and very attractive, is too small for any RVs over 21 feet long.
    Don't even attempt to drive a big rig into it.

6. **The 50-mile loop** around Brian Head and Cedar Breaks National Monument is
    beautiful any time of year, but especially in winter when snow sets off the bright red
    rock formations of the huge natural ampitheater. Many photographers feel it's even

more dramatic than Bryce Canyon. The roads are usually clear into Brian Head but may sometimes be closed in winter into Cedar Breaks. Exit 78 at Parowan from I-15 leads to route 143 and Brian Head; from there, take route 148 through Cedar Breaks and route 14 back downhill into Cedar City.

7.   The aptly-named **Kodachrome Basin State Park**, seven miles off highway 12 at Cannonville, makes a short but dramatic detour by paved road into still more stunning rock formations. Hiking trails and horseback riding are available, as well as a campground with 24 concrete pad sites, tables, grills, piped water, flush toilets and showers. You'll find a sanitary dump station and camper supply store but no hookups. The National Geographic Society, by the way, is the group that named this colorful basin.

8.   **The Bullfrog Basin loop**, some 75 miles long, ventures more deeply into Glen Canyon National Recreation Area than route 95. Take the route 276 cutoff north of Hite Crossing and rejoin route 95 just before Natural Bridges National Monument. The Bullfrog Marina provides rentals for power and houseboats, as well as an 86-unit campground and some beach area for swimmers. To complete the loop, you'll have to take the toll ferry called the John Atlantic Burr that goes to Halls Crossing; it can handle all sizes of RVs. You could also take a houseboat out for a few days, towing a small power boat behind, and explore Anasazi caves, discover remote rock arches and go hiking.

9.   North of Moab, **route 128**, also called the Riverway, strikes east along the Colorado River for 45 miles, following a winding scenic drive into Negro Bill Canyon, named for William Granstaff, a mixed-race prospector who ventured through in 1877, some said selling whiskey to the Indians. Along the route you can go camping, river running by raft, kayak or canoe, mountain biking, hiking or riding off-road vehicles on designated trails. Big Bend Recreation Site offers attractive non-hookup campsites by the river big enough for RVs and with tables and grills, a good alternative when Arches is full. The Bureau of Land Management suggests wearing a life jacket when swimming or boating in the river.

10. **Dead Horse Point State Park** literally takes your breath away as you peer over the edge of a sheer 2000-foot cliff into the double gooseneck loops of the muddy Colorado River cutting its way through red earth and green vegetation. Because of exposed cliff edges and a paucity of railings, we heard a young local guide caution his group of chattering Japanese schoolgirls to "Be careful." They chorused back cheerfully in unison, "Be care..full." Wild mustangs were herded and broken here in the old days because a simple brush fence could close the narrow neck to the point. After taking the best of the horses, cowboys would leave the fence open to let the "broomtails" (culls) from the herd pick their way back to the open range. Unfortunately, one group of broomtails got confused and wandered in circles until they died of thirst, ironically while looking down at the waters of the Colorado far below. (For more about Dead Horse Point, see "Ten Campground Oases.")

WILDLIFE WATCH

Mule deer are almost everywhere in southern Utah, especially in Bryce Canyon, Capitol Reef around the Fruita campground, Dead Horse Point State Park and Natural Bridges National Monument.

Unexpected glimpses of Shiras moose, as well as elk and Great Basin mule deer, are possible in the Hogan Pass area along route 72 between I-70 at Fremont and the town of Loa 32 miles to the south, with the best possibility between the pass and Loa.

Buffalo have been re-established in the Henry Mountains around Hanks-ville.

We saw lots of inquisitive Utah prairie dogs, a threatened species of this ubiquitous western rodent, popping up from holes beside the road on route 211 into The Needles area of Canyonlands.

Along the Colorado river, keep a lookout for river otter, beaver and birds. Bald eagles winter in the area around Fremont Indian State Park, and Canyonlands offers glimpses of soaring peregrine falcons and other birds of prey.

Nightlife as the rest of the world knows it is scarce in southern Utah. In Moab, you can go bowling (only until 11 p.m.) or boutique-beer tasting, dance to live country music on weekends at the Sportsman's Lounge at *1991 South Highway 191*, or belt out karaoke (singing along on mike with lyrics and backup music supplied electronically) every Friday night at the Branding Iron Restaurant and Lounge.

Down in St. George, the new outdoor musical drama *Utah* is open summer nights between June and September, with a cast of 80, along with lightning bolts, floods and waterfalls, burning cities, Indian raids, galloping horses, coyotes that howl on cue, and a full-fledged fireworks display. ☎ *(800) SHOW-UTAH* for reservations; adult tickets are $14.50 to $26.50, kids under 12, $9 to $16. An optional western Dutch-oven dinner is served at $7.95 for adults, $5.95 for children, but must be reserved at the same time tickets are booked. The theater is located 10 miles from St. George at Tuacahn, off route 300 near Snow Canyon State Park. (See "Ten Campground Oases," for more about Snow Canyon.)

INSIDER TIP: UTAH'S MYSTERIOUS LIQUOR LAWS

Utah's liquor laws allow purchases of wine and spirits by the bottle in state liquor stores in many areas except on Sundays and holidays. Beer with 3.2 percent alcohol can be purchased in grocery and convenience stores seven days a week. Licensed restaurants may serve alcohol by the drink, but neither drinks nor a wine list can be offered by the server; the patron must request them. In some areas alcohol by the drink can only be served if patrons "join" a private club by paying a small fee. Lounges and taverns serve only beer. "Brown-bagging," bringing your own alcohol for consumption in a location, is no longer permitted.

CAPITOL REEF NATIONAL PARK

Little-known and little-visited Capitol Reef lies about halfway between Bryce Canyon and Canyonlands on route 24. The park is notable primarily for its unique Waterpocket Fold, a 100-mile wrinkle in the earth's crust formed by enormous pressures deep inside the earth that caused ancient rock beds to buckle. After a rain, pockets in the fold hold water and serve as residence and nursery for the unique spadefoot toad, which lays eggs in the water as soon as it rains so they can hatch into tadpoles, perhaps even make it to adulthood, before the puddles dry up.

Early settlers thought a white sandstone formation in the park resembled the Capitol Dome in Washington and that the Waterpocket Fold looked like a coral reef (although few of them had ever seen either). Ergo, the park is named Capitol Reef.

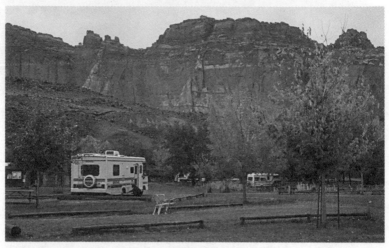

Fruta Campground in Capitol Reef National Park

A 10-mile, one-way, scenic drive is accessible to small to medium-sized RVs; pick up a self-guiding trail map at the beginning of the drive to follow the different layers of rock that tilted, folded and eroded to create today's dramatic formations. While we confess to a certain shortsightedness in recognizing every Egyptian Temple, Golden Throne, Castle and Chimney dotted on the map, we admire the general structure of them. Let's face it, the old-timers had more leisure to sit and contemplate what they resembled than we do.

Fifteen hiking trails from a tenth of a mile to four-and-a-half miles are designated as very easy, easy, moderate and strenuous. A trail to Hickman Bridge, a natural bridge, is one mile each way and termed moderate, while a strenuous climb to Cassidy Arch is one-and-three-quarter miles each way. Petroglyphs on the canyon walls on the main drive near the Visitor Center are only a few short steps from the turnout.

In 1900, eight to 10 Mormon families lived here, planting orchards, operating a blacksmith shop, teaching in a one-room log schoolhouse. The park campgrounds are built in and around the orchards, which are open for visitors to pick their own fruit, then pay by weight at a scale and honor cashbox. Browsing mule deer are common in the campgrounds, especially at dawn and dusk.

Butch Cassidy and his gang used to hang out in the neighborhood. Cassidy Arch, on the Grand Wash road off the Scenic Drive, was named for the famous outlaw.

Even more fascinating is the Behunin Cabin, a tiny one-room rock cabin where an early Mormon settler raised 10 children. The historical plaque beside it says they ate their meals outdoors, which is only logical, since it would be hard for all of them to be inside at the same time. What we can't imagine is where they all slept.

INSIDER TIP:

Always take drinking water with you, especially in summer, when hiking or exploring in Capitol Reef National Park. There's no reliable source of water outside the Fruita settlement near the Visitor Center.

CANYONLANDS NATIONAL PARK

The pristine serenity of Canyonlands has been protected for more than a century, largely because early white settlers deemed the land totally worthless. The Anasazi had lived and farmed the region until 1200, when they mysteriously left, perhaps because of drought, tribal warfare or the arrival of hostile strangers.

What makes the land so fascinating is that it is still evolving on a natural clock where one tick may take an eon.

Canyonlands National Park is divided into three separate areas, each self-contained and reached only by exiting one area of the park and re-entering elsewhere. The Maze, a dense, impenetrable mass of convoluted rock described as "a 30-square-mile puzzle in sandstone," lies southwest of the confluence of the Green and Colorado Rivers. The Needles is southeast of it, and Island in the Sky is north of it. A trail leads to the confluence from the road's end at Big Spring Canyon Overlook in The Needles.

Only experienced hikers with good topographic maps and compasses should venture into The Maze, the most remote and forbidding part of Canyonlands, a dense and complex system of chasms and ravines and dead-end routes. Two roads suitable only for four-wheel drive vehicles enter it from the west, but only after a very long and rough journey from route 24 near Goblin Valley State Park.

Spired sandstone walls, some as high as 400 feet, characterize The Needles in the southern part of Canyonlands, 75 miles from Moab, 49 miles from Monticello, and 31 miles off US 191 via route 211. Less-visited than its northern counterpart, The Needles has a particularly scenic drive outside park perimeters as an introduction.

Island in the Sky, the mesa that comprises much of the northern part of Canyonlands, is outlined in a V-shape as the Colorado and the Green Rivers meet at the park's bellybutton. This area is reached by route 313 off US 191 north of Moab.

Views are memorable, especially in early morning or late afternoon when the landscape is gilded with red and gold. Upheaval Dome, a short walk from the parking lot at the end of the road at Holman Spring Canyon Overlook, may have been formed when struck by a meteorite; at least it's the explanation we prefer of the two possibilities offered by the information sign at the overlook. The other, much less sexy reason is underground salt buildup that eroded until a crater appeared.

Here at the edge of Canyonlands' Island in the Sky, not in what most viewers assumed was Grand Canyon, is where Thelma and Louise drove their Thunderbird convertible off the cliff in the film of the same name.

Both bobcats and mountain lions are occasionally seen in the park, as well as mountain sheep in the White Rim area.

Four-wheel drive vehicles and backpackers can get much more deeply into the park than RVs and family cars, and there are primitive campsites spotted at intervals along the routes. Throughout Canyonlands, campers are expected to carry their own water and firewood. The only water supply in the park is at the Squaw Flat campground in The Needles, and it is not operative in winter.

10 OFF-THE-WALL ATTRACTIONS

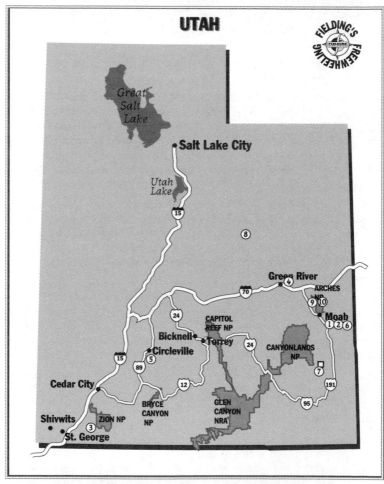

1.   **The Hollywood Stuntman's Hall of Fame** in a former LDS church in Moab at 111 East 100 North Street (see "How to Read Utah Street Plats") has dioramas showing how some stunts are performed, as well as costumes, stuntman equipment and special effects props. Stuntmen from the area sometimes stage live demonstrations, and a screening room runs action films shot nearby. Artifacts from area-location films as recent as *City Slickers II* and *Geronimo* are on display. The museum's Hall of Fame has movie star footprints in cement blocks.

2. **Hole 'N' the Rock** in Moab (not to be confused with the place the Mormons crossed Glen Canyon) is a 5000-square-foot, drilled-out cavern that was home for Albert and Gladys Christensen beginning in 1952. It has 14 rooms, a 65-foot chimney, a built-in deep fryer and a bathtub carved from a rock. During the 12 years Albert spent creating it, he also had time to paint a Sermon on the Mount and carve the head of Franklin D. Roosevelt in the rock above the house. After Albert died in 1957, Gladys continued to run their cafe and gift shop until her death in 1974. Now their family operates it as a museum and memorial, and the gift shop sells souvenirs.

3. It's hard to believe, but near the entrance to Zion National Park is a new **IMAX big-screen theater** purporting to show "the Zion you came to see...the *real* Zion." Since we didn't succumb to the come-on and pay $6.50 a ticket for a 37-minute film, we are not sure what it shows that we missed by driving into the park itself. If your curiosity causes you to stop by when leaving the park by the Springdale exit, the theater promises to refund your park admission if you buy a movie ticket.

4. **The John Wesley Powell River History Museum** on Main Street in Green River has to be the only museum in America dedicated to river-rapids runners, with some 15 Hall of Fame members to date. (We didn't notice Meryl Streep among them). Admission is free but donations are appreciated. The handsome new museum commemorates Powell, the one-armed Civil War veteran who first mapped the Grand Canyon and navigated the Colorado River seated in a chair lashed atop a pine rowboat.

5. **Circleville**, on US 89 about 25 miles south of I-70, was the boyhood home of Butch Cassidy, and where he came on his return from Bolivia (if, indeed, he ever went there), to meet with his mother for the last time in 1925. The family shared a blueberry pie, said Butch's sister, Lula Parker Betenson, who wrote a book about her famous brother. The outlaw's real name was Robert LeRoy Parker. Their two-room log cabin is said to still be standing, but we didn't find it.

6. **Charlie Steen's dream house**, now the Mi Vida Restaurant, sits perched atop the tallest hill in Moab, north of town on route 191. (Locals opine the view considerably surpasses the food, mostly steaks, pasta and seafood.) Charlie was, you may remember, the Texan who became an overnight millionaire in the uranium market during the Cold War days of the 1950s. He struck paydirt in 1952, and the rush of miners that followed quadrupled the population of Moab. His mine, also named Mi Vida, brought him $60 million in a few short years. The house became a restaurant in 1974 when Charlie ran into bad tax and mining luck.

7. **Newspaper Rock State Historical Monument**, 12 miles off US 191 via route 211 east, is an Indian-era billboard made up of petroglyphs (carvings incised on rock surfaces). Most of the drawings date back 1000 years, attributed to prehistoric Indians, early Utes, white pioneer settlers and, unfortunately, a few contemporary vandals. An attractive, ten-site primitive campground is here among the aspens with two spaces for RVs up to 40 feet, along with grills and picnic tables but no water or hookups.

8. **Price City Cemetery** is the final resting place for a body shot by a proud posse in 1898, identified as Butch Cassidy, and laid out with great fanfare before burial. One of the many visitors couldn't stop laughing when viewing the corpse. Later, when a Wyoming lawman made a positive identification of the body as another outlaw, people realized the amused stranger had been Cassidy himself. The whole story is carved on the stranger's tombstone. Price is at the junction of US 6 and US 191 in the center of the state.

Indian petroglyphs at Newspaper Rock State Park

9. **The Sauropod Track Site**, eight miles south of I-15 on US 191 and north of the Arches National Park entrance, then two miles down a dirt road, is where four dinosaurs tramped through a damp river channel some 150 million years ago, leaving only footprints (but probably not taking pictures). Discovered in 1989, the brontosaurus prints are two feet wide, and one of the carnivores leaves evidence of having a limp. Don't attempt the trip in an RV during or after a rain or you may be a sightseeing attraction for some 21st century tourists.

10. **Wolfe Ranch** in Arches National Park is the weathered wood cabin built by Civil War veteran John Wesley Wolfe, who came here with his oldest son Fred searching for a place to raise cattle. His wife and three younger children remained in Etna, Ohio. Eventually, in 1906, his daughter Flora, with her husband and two children, came to stay, and talked her father into gentrifying the ranch. For her sake, he built a new cabin with a wood floor, ordered a 100-piece set of blue china dishes from the Sears Roebuck catalogue because she disliked tin plates, and bought her a camera and developing kit, with which she made one of the earliest known photographs of Delicate Arch.

MOAB

Suddenly this faded, uranium-prospecting town best known as a Western-movie location area has become the mountain bike capital of the world, attracting as many European yuppies as American outdoorsmen to its gentrified streets. The Moab Slickrock Bicycle Trail follows a 10-mile loop through orange Navajo sandstone for experienced bikers with only a little time to spare, but the big deal is the 128-mile Kokpelli's Mountain Biking Trail, still under construction, between Moab and Grand Junction, Colorado. Each October the town celebrates the Fat Tire Festival for mountain bikers.

An itemized list of things to do in the Moab area detailed in the town's visitor guide includes aerial tours, backpacking, campouts and cookouts, dirt-biking, hiking, horse and llama pack rides, hot-air balloon rides, helicopter rides, boating, cross-country skiing, four-wheel drive and all-terrain tours, golf, hunting, fishing, motorcycling, mountain biking, picnicking, photography, river running, rock climbing, rock hounding, rock-art hunting, shopping, sightseeing, skateboarding, swimming, snowmobiling, tennis, touring movie locations, wildlife watching and windsurfing.

Later, the writer added others—watching the local sound-and-light show called "Canyonlands by Night," taking a jet-boat cruise, kayaking, canoeing, hang-gliding, bird-watching, star-gazing and painting.

We were intrigued during our most recent visit at the large numbers of young Germans, and noted two restaurants serving "authentic" German food, the Grand Old Ranch House and the Sundowner.

The uranium miners wouldn't recognize the town with its trendy business names, everything from Poison Spider Bikes with its espresso bar to Honest Ozzie's (a pun on Anasazi, get it?), probably the only restaurant in Utah recommended in a French truck-drivers guide. A boutique brewery with a dozen flavors on tap is next door to an art gallery promising "an eclectic mix of fun, folk art and funk." Also in town is Utah's only winery, turning out a vintage Chardonnay. Can Brie and sun-dried tomatoes be far behind?

10 TAKEOUT (OR EAT-IN) TREATS

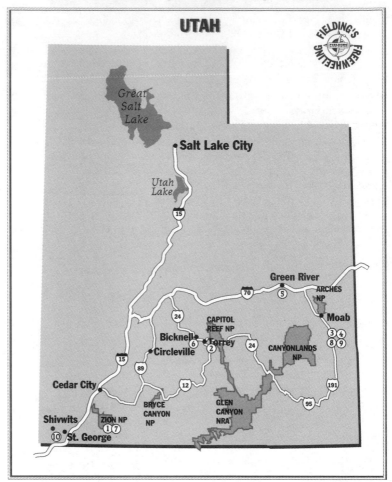

1. **Bumbleberry pie** is the house specialty at the Bumbleberry Inn in Springdale, gateway town to Zion National Park. While the house hands out a whimsical description of its fruit—"burple and binkel berries that grow on giggle bushes"—it's a black-red berry like loganberry or boysenberry in a cornstarch-thickened sauce and fairly thick crust. A wedge to go costs a pricey $2.95.

2. Capitol Reef Inn and Cafe in Torrey, just west of Capitol Reef National Park, may or may not be the only restaurant in southern Utah serving **fresh vegetables**, but it's the best bet in the area for vegetarians as well as carnivores. The former can feast on 10-vegetable salad and stir-fry vegetables atop steamed brown rice, while the latter can tuck into fresh local rainbow trout, grilled ribeye steak or char-broiled lemon hickory chicken. Beer and wine are available. Breakfast-eaters get hearty omelets with optional bacon or smoked trout, or an order of French toast or pancakes. It's a good idea to call ahead, ☎ *(801) 425-3271.*

3. Fat City Smokehouse, *36 South 100 West in Moab*, not only dishes up **pit-style barbecue ribs** in what was once a turn-of-the-century dance hall, but also turns out fine **vegetarian sandwiches** from grilled eggplant, zucchini, onions and green pep-

pers with fresh tomato pesto. Prices are modest, and you can save time by calling ahead on orders to go, ☎ *(801) 259-4302.*

4. Green River is famous for its **melons**, which reach their peak in late summer and early fall. We tried Dunham's on the east end of town and found their honeydew, Crenshaw and cantaloupe were all delicious. They grow watermelons too.

5. Bicknell is the southern Utah capital for offbeat food, with the town's Sunglow Motel and Cafe serving up **pickle pie and pinto bean pie**, and the nearby Aquarius Motel and Cafe promising "unusual menus."

6. The **Virgin Burgers** from Electric Jim's Cafe in Springdale by the entrance to Zion National Park are world-famous, the cafe claims, probably because the park attracts people from all over the world, some of whom undoubtedly get hungry after a hike. Jim's also claims the best shakes in the west. Utah is heaven for a milkshake freak.

7. Moab's Eddie McStiff's Brew Pub offers several unique **boutique brews**, including a jalapeño beer, a spruce beer with the foresty tang of spruce needles and bark, light blueberry and raspberry wheat beers, cream ale, amber ale, chestnut brown beer and full-bodied stout. You'll find it at *57 Main Street*, and all food and beer is available to go.

8. "Fresh **roadkill of the day**" is the special at JR's in Moab, *1075 South Highway 191*, serving sheepherder spuds and omelets at breakfast, which is dished up any time after 6 a.m. It's just what you need before a long day of driving.

9. Arches Vineyards in Moab is Utah's only **winery**, located at *2182 South Highway 191*, a convenient stop to wash down your roadkill from JR's. Tasting daily from 11 a.m. for their red and white table and dessert wines, but never on Sundays.

10. In St. George, Dick's Cafe, at *114 East St. George Blvd.*, serves huge **T-bone steaks** amid a heap of western kitsch amassed by owner Dick Hammer during his days as a champion rodeo rider and movie stuntman.

ARCHES NATIONAL PARK

Campground in Arches National Park

Arches National Park boasts the world's largest concentration of natural stone arches, perhaps as many as 2000 by the most recent tally. To qualify as an arch, the formation has to pass light through an opening at least three feet wide.

Some are visible from the paved roadway, others reached by short or medium hikes from one-tenth of a mile to seven miles long. Daily ranger-guided hikes are also available; check schedules at the visitor center. The Fiery Furnace, for instance, in a labyrinth of red sandstone cliffs and narrow passageways, can only be visited with a ranger; hikes are scheduled twice a day in season and must be reserved in person ahead of time at the visitor center.

See "Five Sites with Déjà Vu All Over Again" for the park's most popular long hike, a half-day trip to Delicate Arch.

Rock climbers also love the Arches for its cliffs, walls, towers and cracks in the rock, coupled with incredible views. Modern techniques in rock climbing often avoid the old system of pounding pitons into the rock, then ascending by nylon ladders. Today the goal is to do "free" climbing, either "face climbing," in which the climber grasps or steps on natural holds in the rock, or "crack climbing," by wedging part of the body into cracks in the rocks. Women can often outdo men in their dexterity in rock climbing.

If you're hiking or camping here, be sure your gas tank is adequately full, and take along your own water, food and firewood, since nothing is available in the park.

ON THE CHEAP: TRIMMING COSTS ON THE ROAD

As a state, Utah is much less expensive than many, although sparsely-settled southern Utah does not offer frequent or varied shopping opportunities. Keep your larder well stocked and your gas and water tanks topped off when venturing into less-traveled territory.

With so much of southern Utah's most scenic terrain under Bureau of Land Management administration, RVers will find some no-fee undeveloped campsites where camping is permitted under the following conditions: camping in one site is limited to 14 days; campers must pack out all trash; campfires may not be left unattended; and camping is not permitted within 300 feet of springs or ponds so that water is accessible to wildlife. Self-contained RVs will meet with BLM's regulations so long as dumping of gray or black water takes place only in designated sanitary dump stations and never on the ground.

FYI

Utah Travel Council, ☎ *(800) 200-1160*

Arches National Park, ☎ *(801) 259-8161*

Bryce Canyon National Park, ☎ *(801) 834-5322*

Canyonlands National Park, ☎ *(801) 259-7164*

Capitol Reef National Park, ☎ *(801) 425-3791*

Cedar Breaks National Monument, ☎ *(801) 586-9451*

Dead Horse Point State Park, ☎ *(801) 259-6511*

Glen Canyon National Recreation Area, ☎ *(602)645-2471*

Natural Bridges National Monument, ☎ *(801) 259-5174*

Zion National Park, ☎ *(801) 772-3256*

PUBLICATIONS FOR CAMPERS & RV OWNERS

Camperways • Woodall Publishing Co. • 28167 North Keith Drive • Lake Forest, IL 60045 • (monthly) $15/year • ☎ (708) 362-6700

Camping and RV Magazine • P.O. Box 458 • Washburn, WI • (monthly) $17.95/year • ☎ (715) 373-5556

Camp-orama • Woodall Publishing Co. • 28167 North Keith Drive • Lake Forest, IL 60045 • (monthly) $15/year • ☎ (708) 362-6700

Chevy Outdoors • P.O. Box 2063 • Warren, MI 48090-2063 • (quarterly) $8/4 issues • (1 year) • ☎ (810) 575-9100

Disabled Outdoors • 2052 W. 23rd Street • Chicago, IL 60608 • (4 issues) $10/year • ☎ (708) 358-4160

Family Motor Coaching • 8291 Clough Pike • Cincinnati, OH 45244 • (monthly) $24/year • ☎ (513) 474-3622 • (800) 543-3622

4 Wheel and Off Road • Petersen Publishing Co. • 6420 Wilshire Blvd. • Los Angeles, CA 90048 • (monthly) $19.95/year • ☎ (310) 854-2222

Highways • TL Enterprises , Inc.• 3601 Calle Tecate • Camarillo, CA 93012 • (11 issues) $6/year • ☎ (805) 389-0300

Midwest Outdoors • 111 Shore Drive • Burr Ridge, IL 60521-5885 • (monthly) $11.95 • ☎ (708) 887-7722

MotorHome • TL Enterprises, Inc. • 3601 Calle Tecate • Camarillo, CA 93012 • (monthly) $26/year • ☎ (805) 389-0300

Northeast Outdoors • 70 Edwin Ave. • Box 2180 • Waterbury, CT 06722 • (monthly) $8/year • ☎ (203) 755-0158

RV Times • Royal Productions, Inc. • P.O. Box 6294 • Richmond, VA 23230 • (11 issues) $15/year • ☎ (804) 288-5653

RV West • 4125 Mohr Avenue, Suite E • Pleasanton, CA 945466 • (monthly) $12.99/year • ☎ (510) 426-3200

Southern RV • Woodall Publishing Co. • 28167 North Keith Drive • Lake Forest, IL 60045 • (monthly) $15/year • ☎ (708) 362-6700

The Recreation Advisor • Recreation World Services, Inc. • P.O. Box 520 • Gonzalez, FL 32560-0520 • (10 issues) $15/year • ☎ (904) 477-7992

Trailer Life • TL Enterprises, Inc. • 3601 Calle Tecate • Camarillo, CA 93012 • (monthly) $22/year • ☎ (805) 389-0300

Trails-A-Way • Woodall Publishing Co. • 28167 North Keith Drive • Lake Forest, IL 60045 • (monthly) $15/year • ☎ (708) 362-6700

Western RV News • 56405 Cascade View Lane • Warren, OR 97053-9736 • (monthly) $8/year • ☎ (503) 222-1255

Workamper News • 201 Hiram Road • Heber Springs, AR 72543 • (6 issues) $23/year • ☎ (501) 362-2637

NATIONAL CAMPING CLUBS

Canadian Family Camping Federation • P.O. Box 397 • Rexdale, Ontario, Canada M9W 1 R3

Escapees Club, Inc. • c/o Kay Peterson • 100 Rainbow Drive • Livingston, TX 77351 • ☎ (409) 327-8873 • *Escapees Magazine*

Family Motor Coach Association (Motorhome owners only) • c/o Ginny Bauman • 8291 Cough Pike • Cincinnati, OH 45244 • ☎ (513) 474-3622 or (800) 543-622 • *Family Motor Coaching*

The Good Sam Club • c/o Susan Bray • P.O. Box 6060 • Camarillo, CA 93011 • ☎ (805) 389-0300 • *Highways*

Loners on Wheels • P.O. Box 1355 • Poplar Bluff, MO 63902 • FAX: (314) 686-9342

Family Campers and RVers • c/o Fran Opela • 4804 Transit Road, Bldg. 2 • Depew, NY 14043 • ☎ (716) 668-6242 • *Camping Today*

RVing WOMEN • 201 E. Southern Avenue • Apache Junction, AZ 85219 • ☎ (602) 983-4678

Smart • Special Military Active Retired Travel Club Inc. • 600 University Office Blvd., Ste 1A • Pensacola, FL 32504 • ☎ (904) 478-1986

The International Family Recreation Association • P.O. Box 520 •Gonzalez, FL 32560-0520 • ☎ (904) 477-7992 • *The Recreation Advisor*

The National RV Owners Club • P.O. Drawer 17148 • Pensacola, FL 32522-7148 • ☎ (904) 477-7992 • *The Recreation Advisor*

Wandering Individuals Network (WIN) • P.O. Box 2010, Dept B • Sparks, NV 89432-2010 • ☎ (800) 445-1732

BRAND NAME CLUBS
(LIMITED TO OWNERS OF PARTICULAR BRANDS
OF RECREATIONAL VEHICLES.)

Alpenlite Travel Club • Bob & Claudia Smith, Executive Directors • P.O. Box 918 • Clackamas, OR 97015 • ☎ (503) 698-4461 • *The Traveling Echo*

American Clipper Owners Club • c/o R.M. Cornwell, D.D.S. • 514 Washington Blvd. • Marina Del Rey, CA 90292 • ☎ (310) 823-8945 (O) or (310) 823-6433 (H)

Avion Travelcade Club • c/o Peggy Baker • 101 E. Sioux Road, #1078 • Pharr, TX 78577-1719 • ☎ (210) 787-0445

Barth Ranger Club • c/o Lee Merriman • State Road 15, S. • P.O. Box 768 • Milford, IN 46542 • ☎ (219) 658-9401

Beaver Ambassador Club • c/o Frank Ballantyne • 20545 Murry Road • Bend, OR • ☎ (503) 389-1144

Bounders United Inc. • c/o Rod Swartwood • 4533 Catalina Drive • San Jose, CA 95129-3359 • ☎ (408) 441-1423 • *Bounders Sounder*

Carriage Travel Club, Inc. • Dick & Lillian Hillyer, Executive Directors • P.O. Box 246 • Millersburg, IN 46543-0246 • ☎ (219) 642-3622 • *The Campin Nooz*

Cortez National Motorhome Club • c/o Tony & Jan Noto • 11022 E. Daines Drive • Temple City, CA 91780 • ☎ (818) 444-6030

Country Coach International • c/o Jack & Jan Gossett or Karen Smith • P.O. Box 207 • Junction City, OR 97448 • ☎ (503) 998-3712

El Dorado Caravan Club • c/o Francis Byrne • 15012 Johansson Avenue • Hudson, FL 34667 • ☎ (813) 868-6700

Firan Owners Association • c/o Karen Wilson • P.O. Box 482 • 58277 S.R. 19 South • Elkhart, IN 46515 • ☎ (219) 293-6581 • *The Crow's Nest*

Fireball Caravaner • c/o Patton McNaughton • 302 W. Walnut Avenue • El Segundo, CA 90245 • ☎ (310) 322-7085

Georgie Boy Owners Club • c/o Syd & Pauline Collins • P.O. Box 44209 • Cincinnati, OH 46030 • ☎ (219) 258-0591

Foretravel Motorcade Club • c/o Gordon Wagner • 1221 N.W. Stallings Drive • Nacogdoches, TX 75961 • ☎ (409) 564-8367 • *Motorcader*

Gulf Streamers International RV Club • c/o Diana Lynch • P.O./ Box 1005 • Nappanee, IN 46550-0905 • ☎ (219) 773-7761

Hitch Hiker of America International (NuWa) • c/o Bob & Vera Van Sickle • 1700 Claybank Road • Logan, OH 43138 • ☎ (219) 258-0591

Holiday Rambler RV Club • c/o Wayne Dahl • East 600 Wabash Street • P.O. Box 587 • Wakarusa, IN 46573 • ☎ (219) 862-7330 • *Holiday Ramblings*

International Coachmen Caravan Club • c/o George Jordan • P.O. Box 30, Hwy. 13 N. • Middlebury, IN 46540 • ☎ (219) 825-8245 • *Coachmen Capers*

International Skamper Camper Club • c/o Lewis & Ethel Baughman • P.O. Box 338 • Bristol, IN 46507 • ☎ (219) 848-7411

Jayco Jafari • c/o Ray & Donna Horning • 1660 Nash • White Cloud, MN 49349 • ☎ (219) 258-0591

Lazy Daze Caravan Club • c/o Don Nelson • 4303 E. Mission Blvd. • Pomona, CA 91766 • ☎ (909) 627-1219

National Collins RV Club • c/o Gene Bunnel • 2206 Kimberly Drive • Klamath Falls, OR 97603 • ☎ (503) 884-2749 • *Collins RV Club Chronicle*

Newmar Kountry Klub • Dave & Pam Wilson • P.O. Box 30 • Nappanee, IN 46550-0030 • ☎ (219) 773-7791

Serro Scotty Club • c/o Gary Pirschl • 450 Arona Road • Irwin, PA 15642-9512 • ☎ (412) 863-3407

SOI Club • c/o Scott Brady • 3550 Foothill Boulevard • Glendale, CA 91214 • ☎ (818) 249-4175 • *The SOI Club*

Starcraft Camper Club • c/o Ron & Bev Covert • 4159 Woodington Drive • Mississuaga, Ontario • Canada L4Z 1K2 • ☎ (905) 275-4848

Wally Byam Caravan Club International (Airstream) • c/o David Reed • 803 E. Pike Street • Jackson Center, OH 45334 • ☎ (513) 596-5211

Wings RV Club (Shasta) • c/o Hank Daniels • 14489 U.S. 20 • P.O. Box 631 • Middlebury, IN 46540 • ☎ (219) 825-8555

Winnebago Itasca-Travelers • c/o Mike Anderson • P.O. Box 268 • Forest City, IA 50436 • ☎ (515) 582-6874 • *The WIT Club News*

RV RALLY AND CARAVAN OPERATORS

Adventure World R.V. Tours • The Seachest • Broad Park, Oreston Plymouth PL9 7QF • United Kingdom

Creative World Rallies and Caravans • 4005 Toulouse Street • New Orleans, LA 70119 • ☎ (504) 486-7259 or (800) 732-8337

Wagontrain Tours Inc. • 520 Hartford Turnpike • Vernon, CT 06066 • ☎ (800) 875-7978

Woodall's World of Travel • 306 Maplewood Drive • P.O. Box 247 • Greenville, MI 48838 • ☎ (616) a754-2251 or (800) 346-7572

INDEX

Y

Z

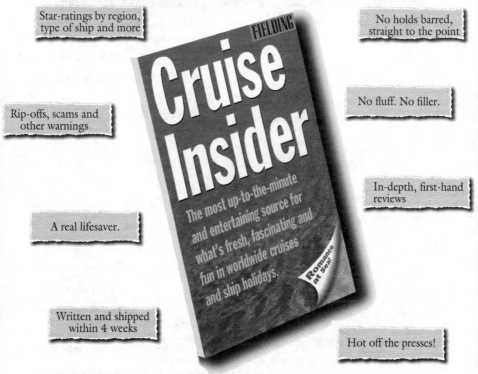

Order Your Fielding Travel Guides Today

BOOKS	$ EA.
Amazon	$16.95
Australia	$12.95
Bahamas	$12.95
Belgium	$16.95
Bermuda	$12.95
Borneo	$16.95
Brazil	$16.95
Britain	$16.95
Budget Europe	$16.95
Caribbean	$18.95
Europe	$16.95
Far East	$16.95
Freewheelin' USA	$19.95
Hawaii	$15.95
Holland	$15.95
Italy	$16.95
Kenya's Best Hotels, Lodges & Homestays	$16.95
London Agenda	$12.95
Los Angeles Agenda	$12.95
Malaysia and Singapore	$16.95
Mexico	$16.95
New York Agenda	$12.95
New Zealand	$12.95
Paris Agenda	$12.95
Portugal	$16.95
Scandinavia	$16.95
Seychelles	$12.95
Southeast Asia	$18.95
Southern Vietnam on Two Wheels	$16.95
Spain	$16.95
The World's Great Voyages	$16.95
The World's Most Dangerous Places	$19.95
The World's Most Romantic Places	$16.95
Vacation Places Rated	$19.95
Vietnam	$16.95
Worldwide Cruises	$17.95

To order by phone call toll-free 1-800-FW-2-GUIDE

(VISA, MasterCard and American Express accepted.)

To order by mail send your check or money order,
including $2.00 per book for shipping and handling (sorry, no COD's) to:
Fielding Worldwide, Inc. 308 S. Catalina Avenue, Redondo Beach, CA 90277 U.S.A.

**Get 10% off your order by saying "Fielding Discount"
or send in this page with your order**

Favorite People, Places & Experiences

ADDRESS:	NOTES:

Name

Address

Telephone

Name

Address

Telephone

Name

Address

Telephone

Name

Address

Telephone

Name

Address

Telephone

Name

Address

Telephone

Name

Address

Telephone

Favorite People, Places & Experiences

Name

Address

Telephone

Name

Address

Telephone

Name

Address

Telephone

Name

Address

Telephone

Name

Address

Telephone

Name

Address

Telephone

Name

Address

Telephone

Order Your Fielding Travel Guides Today

BOOKS	$ EA.
Amazon	$16.95
Australia	$12.95
Bahamas	$12.95
Belgium	$16.95
Bermuda	$12.95
Borneo	$16.95
Brazil	$16.95
Britain	$16.95
Budget Europe	$16.95
Caribbean	$18.95
Europe	$16.95
Far East	$16.95
Freewheelin' USA	$19.95
Hawaii	$15.95
Holland	$15.95
Italy	$16.95
Kenya's Best Hotels, Lodges & Homestays	$16.95
London Agenda	$12.95
Los Angeles Agenda	$12.95
Malaysia and Singapore	$16.95
Mexico	$16.95
New York Agenda	$12.95
New Zealand	$12.95
Paris Agenda	$12.95
Portugal	$16.95
Scandinavia	$16.95
Seychelles	$12.95
Southeast Asia	$18.95
Southern Vietnam on Two Wheels	$16.95
Spain	$16.95
The World's Great Voyages	$16.95
The World's Most Dangerous Places	$19.95
The World's Most Romantic Places	$16.95
Vacation Places Rated	$19.95
Vietnam	$16.95
Worldwide Cruises	$17.95

To order by phone call toll-free 1-800-FW-2-GUIDE

(VISA, MasterCard and American Express accepted.)

To order by mail send your check or money order,
including $2.00 per book for shipping and handling (sorry, no COD's) to:
Fielding Worldwide, Inc. 308 S. Catalina Avenue, Redondo Beach, CA 90277 U.S.A.

**Get 10% off your order by saying "Fielding Discount"
or send in this page with your order**

Favorite People, Places & Experiences

Name

Address

Telephone

Name

Address

Telephone

Name

Address

Telephone

Name

Address

Telephone

Name

Address

Telephone

Name

Address

Telephone

Name

Address

Telephone